P · O · C · K · E · T · S

SCIENCE
ENCY
C L O
PEDIA

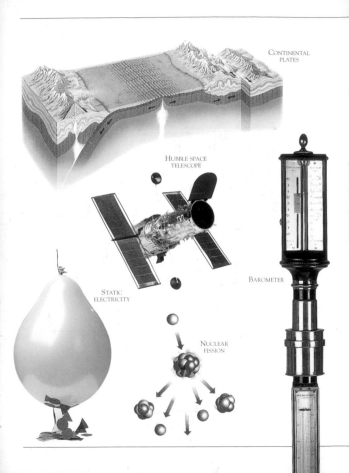

CONTINENTAL PLATES

HUBBLE SPACE TELESCOPE

BAROMETER

STATIC ELECTRICITY

NUCLEAR FISSION

P · O · C · K · E · T · S

SCIENCE ENCYCLOPEDIA

SEAHORSES

CARBON
ATOM

MANNED
MANOEUVRING
UNIT

DORLING KINDERSLEY
London • New York • Sydney • Moscow

A DORLING KINDERSLEY BOOK

Writers and consultants: David Burnie, Jack Challoner,
Philip Eden, Dr William A. Gutch,
Cally Hall, Jeffery Kaufmann,
Scarlett O'Hara, Steve Setford,
Carole Stott, Clint Twist,
Dr Warren Yasso

Produced for Dorling Kindersley by
PAGE*One*, Cairn House, Elgiva Lane, Chesham,
Buckinghamshire, HP5 2JD

Published in Great Britain by
Dorling Kindersley Ltd., 9 Henrietta Street,
London WC2E 8PS

2 4 6 8 10 9 7 5 3 1

Copyright © 1998 Dorling Kindersley Ltd., London

The material in this book originally appeared in the following
DK Pocket titles: *Earth Facts, Essential Facts, Nature Facts,
Science Facts, Space Facts, Weather Facts.*

Visit us on the World Wide Web at
http://www.dk.com

A CIP catalogue record for this book is available
from the British Library.

ISBN 0-7513-5641-7

Colour reproduction by Colourscan, Singapore
Printed and bound in Italy by L.E.G.O.

CONTENTS

COMPOUND
MICROSCOPE

EMERALD

INSIDE A
VOLCANO

MILKY WAY

PIONEER 10
SPACE PROBE

SUN
STRUCTURE

FOX CUB

HOW TO USE THIS BOOK

These pages show you how to use the *DK Pockets Science Encyclopedia*. The book is divided into four sections that provide information about chemical and physical science, the Earth around us, the universe, and plant and animal life. At the back of the book, conversion tables are followed by a comprehensive index.

HEADING AND INTRODUCTION
Every spread has a subject heading. This is followed by the introduction, which outlines the subject and gives a clear idea of what these pages are about.

CHARTS
Many pages contain charts. These supply facts and figures. The chart below compares the density of materials.

Chart

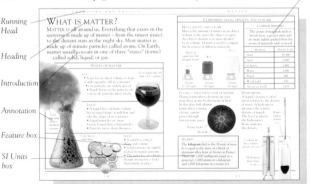

Running Head

Heading

Introduction

Annotation

Feature box

SI Units box

FEATURE BOXES
The feature boxes that appear on some pages contain detailed information and illustrations to explain a topic that is related to the main subject of the page.

SI UNITS BOXES
On some spreads SI units boxes explain a measurement relevant to the subject. SI units are an international set of standard units of measurement.

DATA BOX
Some pages have data boxes, which contain detailed numerical information. This box gives data about the Sun.

LABELS
For clarity, some pictures have labels. These give extra information about the picture, or provide clearer identification.

RUNNING HEADS
Across the top of the pages there are running heads. The lefthand page gives the section, the righthand the subject.

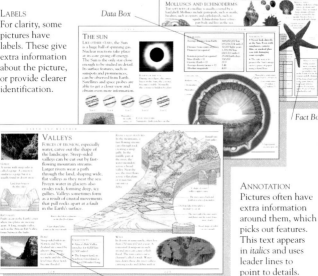

Data Box

Fact Box

Caption

ANNOTATION
Pictures often have extra information around them, which picks out features. This text appears in *italics* and uses leader lines to point to details.

FACT BOXES
Many pages have fact boxes. The information in these is related to the main topic on the page.

CAPTIONS
Each illustration in the book is accompanied by a detailed, explanatory caption.

INDEX
There is an index at the back of the book that alphabetically lists every subject. By referring to the index, information on particular topics can be found quickly.

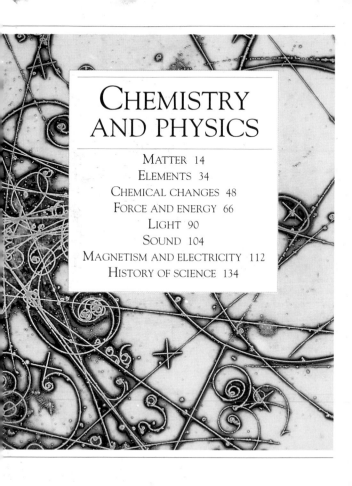

CHEMISTRY
AND PHYSICS

WHAT IS MATTER?

MATTER IS all around us. Everything that exists in the universe is made up of matter – from the tiniest insect, to the distant stars in the night sky. Most matter is made up of minute particles called atoms. On Earth, matter usually occurs in one of three "states" (forms) called solid, liquid, or gas.

STATES OF MATTER

GAS
• A gas has no fixed volume or shape: it will expand to fill its container.
• Gas particles are widely spaced.
• Bonds between the particles are very weak: particles move freely.

Every liquid takes the shape of its container

LIQUID
• A liquid has a definite volume but no fixed shape: it will flow and take the shape of its container.
• Liquid particles are more loosely bound than solid particles.
• Particles move short distances.

Gas dispersing from a chemical reaction

Coins have a rigid shape

SOLID
• A solid has a fixed shape and volume.
• Solid particles are tightly packed in regular patterns.
• The particles can vibrate, though strong forces hold them firmly in place.

COMPARING MASS, DENSITY, AND VOLUME

MASS, DENSITY, AND VOLUME

Mass is the amount of matter in an object. Volume is the space the object occupies. An object's density is its mass divided by its volume. Density is used to compare the heaviness of different materials.

Blocks of equal mass but unequal density

BALSA

WAX

LEAD

Density 11,300 kg/m³

Density 900 kg/m³

Density 200 kg/m³

COMMON DENSITIES

The atoms of materials such as metals have a greater mass and are more tightly packed than the atoms of materials such as wood.

MATERIAL	DENSITY KG/M³
Gold	19,300
Steel	7,900
Concrete	2,400
Water	1,000
Petrol	800
Wood (oak)	650
Air (at sea level)	1.025

PLASMA – THE FOURTH STATE OF MATTER

Plasma forms when electrons are torn from their atoms by electricity or heat. In this glass ball, plasma forms when a strong electric current passes through low-pressure gases.

Plasma streaks

Electrode

HYDROMETERS

A liquid's density is often given relative to the density of water. A hydrometer measures the relative density of liquids. The level at which the hydrometer floats indicates the density.

Water's relative density is 1

Cooking oil has a relative density of 0.91

Hydrometer floats lower in oil

SI UNITS

The **kilogram** (kg) is the SI unit of mass. It is equal to the mass of a block of platinum alloy kept at Sèvres in France. There are 1,000 milligrams (mg) in a gram (g), 1,000 grams in a kilogram, and 1,000 kilograms in a tonne (t).

Changing state

The state of a substance is determined by its temperature. When heated, solids change to liquids, and liquids to gases because their particles vibrate faster, weakening the bonds that hold the particles together. When cooled, gases change to liquids (condense), and liquids to solids. Their particles slow down and the bonds between them strengthen.

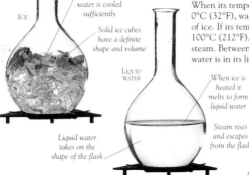

ICE

Ice forms when water is cooled sufficiently

Solid ice cubes have a definite shape and volume

LIQUID WATER

When ice is heated it melts to form liquid water

Liquid water takes on the shape of the flask

Steam rises and escapes from the flask

STEAM

THE THREE STATES OF WATER
When its temperature falls below 0°C (32°F), water takes the form of ice. If its temperature rises above 100°C (212°F), water turns to steam. Between these temperatures water is in its liquid state.

Bubbles of steam form when the liquid is heated to boiling point

Safety valve lets out excess steam

PRESSURE COOKING
The increased pressure inside a pressure cooker raises the boiling point of water because the water molecules need more heat energy to escape as a gas. The higher temperature cooks the food more quickly.

GAS CHANGES

- A gas condenses to a liquid.
- Condensation takes place at or below the boiling point.
- Sublimation occurs when a gas, such as carbon dioxide, changes to a solid without first forming a liquid.

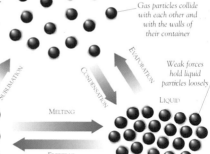

GAS

Gas particles collide with each other and with the walls of their container

Solid particles are fixed rigidly in position

SUBLIMATION

CONDENSATION

EVAPORATION

Weak forces hold liquid particles loosely

LIQUID

MELTING

SOLID

FREEZING

SOLID CHANGES

- Above a temperature called the melting point, most solids become liquids.
- Many solids can change directly into a gas (sublime), without becoming a liquid first.

LIQUID CHANGES

- A liquid evaporates to form a gas. Above a temperature called its boiling point, all of the liquid becomes a gas.
- A liquid freezes to a solid below a temperature called its freezing point.

Over centuries, ancient glassware starts to flow

GLASS

A "supercooled" liquid such as glass can cool below its freezing point without solidifying. Glass is rigid, but its particles are arranged more randomly than those of a solid.

MELTING/FREEZING POINTS	
SUBSTANCE	MELTING POINT
Alcohol (ethanol)	−169°C (−272°F)
Water	0°C (32°F)
Wax	57°C (135°F)
PVC	197°C (387°F)
Nylon	212°C (414°F)
Salt (sodium chloride)	801°C (1,474°F)
Gold	1,064°C (1,947°F)
Steel (stainless)	1,527°C (2,781°F)
Diamond	3,550°C (6,422°F)

KINETIC THEORY

ACCORDING TO KINETIC THEORY, particles of matter
are constantly in motion. The energy of the "kinetic"
(moving) particles determines the temperature and
behaviour of matter. The "gas laws" use kinetic theory
to explain how gases behave.

Air

Partition

Bromine
and air

Partition
removed

Diffusion
of bromine
gas in air

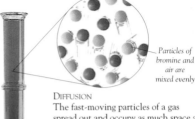

Particles of
bromine and
air are
mixed evenly

DIFFUSION
The fast-moving particles of a gas
spread out and occupy as much space as
possible. This is why two gases quickly
intermingle (diffuse) when they meet.
Solids and liquids form solutions by
diffusion, although they diffuse more
slowly than gases.

Pollen suspended
in water

MOVING MATTER FACTS

• Austrian physicist
Ludwig Boltzmann
developed kinetic
theory in the 1860s.

• Scottish botanist
Robert Brown observed
Brownian motion in
1827. (Albert Einstein
explained it in 1905.)

BROWNIAN MOTION
Seen under a microscope,
pollen grains in water
bounce about randomly.
This phenomenon is
called Brownian motion.
It is caused by tiny,
unseen water molecules
that bombard the
pollen grains.

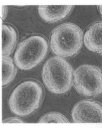

CHARLES' LAW IN ACTION

1 COOLING GAS
When a gas-filled balloon is placed in liquid nitrogen at –196°C (–321°F), the gas inside cools down.

Balloon collapses

2 SHRINKING VOLUME
Gas molecules slow down as the gas cools. The molecules collide less with the balloon walls, so the balloon shrinks.

Liquid nitrogen

Balloon expands

3 REFLATION
Removing the balloon from the liquid nitrogen lets the gas warm in the air. The gas molecules speed up and the balloon expands again.

EXPANSION RATES OF SELECTED MATERIALS

Heating a solid gives its atoms more kinetic energy. The atoms vibrate faster and take up more space, causing the solid to expand.

SUBSTANCE	EXPANSION OF HEATED 1 M BAR AT 100°C (212°F)
Invar (steel/nickel alloy)	0.1 mm
Pyrex	0.3 mm
Platinum alloy	0.9 mm
Steel	1.1 mm
Aluminium	2.6 mm

GAS LAWS

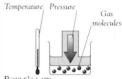

Temperature *Pressure* *Gas molecules*

BOYLE'S LAW
At constant temperature (T), the volume of a gas (V) is inversely proportional to the pressure (P) (the gas contracts if the pressure rises): $PV=$constant.

PRESSURE LAW
At constant volume, the pressure of a gas is proportional to the temperature (increasing the temperature raises the gas's pressure): $P/T=$constant.

CHARLES' LAW
At constant pressure, the volume of a gas is proportional to the temperature (the gas expands if the temperature rises): $V/T=$constant.

DESCRIBING MATTER

A MATERIAL CAN be described by its physical properties as well as by its chemical make-up. Colour, shape, texture, and smell are the simplest properties. Others include hardness, solubility, and viscosity, and the way a material behaves when forces act on it.

HONEYCOMB

VISCOSITY
A viscous liquid such as honey does not flow easily because of friction between its molecules. Free-flowing liquids such as water have a low viscosity.

The viscous honey spreads out very slowly

MOHS' SCALE OF HARDNESS		
HARDNESS	MINERAL	SCRATCHED BY
10	Diamond	Diamond only
9	Corundum	Silicon carbide
8	Topaz	Tungsten carbide
7	Quartz	Hard steel file
6	Feldspar	Sand
5	Apatite	Nickel
4	Fluorite	Glass
3	Calcite	Iron nail
2	Gypsum	Fingernail
1	Talc	Tin

HARDNESS
The ability to resist scratching is called hardness. It is measured on Mohs' scale, which compares the hardness of ten minerals. A material will scratch any other with a lower Mohs' rating.

DUCTILITY AND MALLEABILITY
Ductile solids such as copper can be stretched out into a wire. Malleable solids can be shaped while cold by hammering or rolling. Gold is the most malleable metal.

COPPER WIRE

ELASTICITY

RUBBER ATOMS	STRETCHED RUBBER	FURTHER STRETCHING

Strip is 15 cm long when no force acts upon it

1 kg mass stretches rubber to 17 cm

2 kg mass stretches rubber to 19 cm

1 ELASTICITY
Elastic solids such as this rubber strip get larger (extend) when stretched, get smaller when squeezed, and return to their normal size and shape when no force acts upon them.

2 STRETCHING
When a 1 kg mass is hung from the strip, the force of tension stretches the strip by 2 cm. The rubber atoms move apart as the bonds between them extend under tension.

3 DOUBLE STRETCHING
Doubling the force of tension will also double the stretching, so when a 2 kg mass is hung from the strip, the rubber stretches by 4 cm.

BRITTLENESS
Brittle materials break suddenly when stretched or squeezed, and shatter if given a sharp knock. But even fragile materials such as glass and pottery have some elasticity before they break.

Glass shatters into tiny pieces

A wine glass breaks easily if dropped on the floor

SOLUBILITY IN WATER
The following masses of each substance dissolve in 100 g of water at 25°C (77°F):

- Alcohol (ethanol): almost limitless
- Sugar: 211 g
- Salt: 36 g
- Carbon dioxide: 0.14 g
- Oxygen: 0.004 g
- Sand: insoluble

ATOMS

MATTER IS MADE UP of tiny particles called atoms.
Since most atoms are very stable structures, they
form the building blocks for everything in the
universe. There are just over a hundred types of
atom, which are themselves made up of even smaller
"subatomic" particles.

Electron shell

Orbiting electron

CROSS-SECTION
OF CARBON ATOM

Nucleus

ATOMIC STRUCTURE
The centre, or nucleus, of an atom
contains protons (which have a
positive charge) and neutrons
(which have no charge). Negatively
charged particles called electrons
orbit the nucleus in layers, or "shells".

CARBON–12 ATOM

Proton

NUCLEON NUMBER
The total number of protons and
neutrons in the nucleus is the atom's
nucleon number. The most common
form of carbon has 6 protons and
6 neutrons, so it is called carbon–12.

*Nucleus contains
6 protons and
6 neutrons*

Neutron

CARBON–14 ATOM

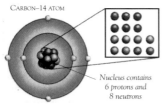

*Nucleus contains
6 protons and
8 neutrons*

ISOTOPES
All atoms of the same element contain
the same number of protons, but some
forms of the element may have different
numbers of neutrons. These are isotopes.
The isotope carbon–14 has two more
neutrons than the isotope carbon–12.

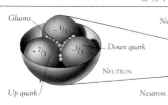

Gluons
−1/3
Nucleus
Electron
+2/3 −1/3 — Down quark
NEUTRON
Up quark
Neutron

QUARKS
Neutrons and protons contain smaller particles called quarks, stuck together by tiny particles called gluons. "Down" quarks have one-third of a negative charge, and "up" quarks two-thirds of a positive charge.

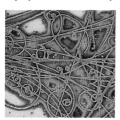

PARTICLE COLLISIONS
Scientists discover new particles by smashing together subatomic particles at high speed. The collision briefly creates new particles, whose movements are recorded by computers.

DESCRIBING ATOMS

• The **relative atomic mass (RAM)** of an element compares the average mass of its atoms to the mass of a carbon–12 atom.

• An element's **atomic number** tells you the number of protons in the nuclei of its atoms.

RELATIVE ATOMIC MASS (RAM)		
ELEMENT	SYMBOL	RAM
Hydrogen	H	1
Carbon	C	12
Sodium	Na	23
Iron	Fe	55.9
Bromine	Br	79.9
Tungsten	W	183.9
Mercury	Hg	200.6

ATOM FACTS

• Protons and neutrons are 1,836 times heavier than electrons.

• Scientists have discovered more than 200 different subatomic particles.

• Specks of dust contain a million million atoms.

RADIOACTIVITY

THE NUCLEI OF some atoms are radioactive. This means they are unstable and will decay (break up) over time. Most elements have unstable forms called radioisotopes. As they decay, they give out three types of radiation: alpha, beta, and gamma rays. Radiation can be very dangerous.

Alpha particle

Beta particle

Gamma ray

Paper blocks alpha particles

Aluminium blocks beta particles

Lead blocks gamma rays

RADIATION
Alpha rays are streams of positively charged particles made up of two neutrons and two protons. Beta rays are streams of electrons. Gamma rays, the most penetrating type of radiation, are electromagnetic waves.

SI UNITS:
The **becquerel** (Bq) is the unit of radioactivity. The radioactivity of a substance measured in becquerels is the number of its nuclei that decay each second.

Geiger counter

Dial shows amount of radioactivity

GEIGER COUNTER
When a radioactive particle enters a Geiger counter, it causes a brief pulse of electric current to flow. The radioactivity of a sample is calculated by the number of these pulses.

DECAY SERIES
As the nucleus of a radioisotope decays, the number of particles it holds falls, and it becomes a different element. The process continues until it becomes a stable nucleus. Such a sequence is called a decay series.

KEY TO DECAY SERIES
1. Alpha decay of uranium–238
2. Two stages of beta decay
3. Five stages of alpha decay
4. Beta decay of lead–214
5. Alpha decay of polonium–214
6. Three stages of beta decay
7. Alpha decay of polonium–210
8. The element lead–206 forms

RADIOACTIVE HALF-LIVES
The time taken for half of the nuclei in a radioactive substance to decay is called the substance's half-life. Over each half-life period, radioactivity falls first to a half, then to a quarter, and so on. The half-life of each radioisotope is different.

HALF-LIVES OF RADIOISOTOPES		
ISOTOPE	HALF-LIFE	TYPE OF DECAY
Uranium–238	4,500 million years	Alpha
Carbon–14	5,570 years	Beta
Cobalt–60	5.3 years	Gamma
Radon–222	4 days	Beta
Unnilquadium–105	32 seconds	Gamma

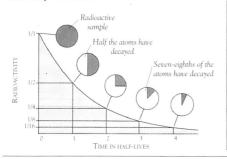

Radioactive sample

Half the atoms have decayed

Seven-eighths of the atoms have decayed

RADIOACTIVITY

TIME IN HALF-LIVES

RADIOACTIVITY FACTS

• Though radiation can be dangerous, it has many uses in medicine, including sterilizing equipment and killing cancer cells.

• Radioactivity was discovered by the French physicist Antoine Henri Becquerel in 1896.

BONDS AND MOLECULES

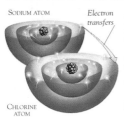

SODIUM ATOM

Electron transfers

CHLORINE ATOM

ATOMS MAY STICK together to form molecules by a process called "bonding". The bonds between atoms are electrical forces made by the movement of electrons. They form when atoms try to gain a full outer shell of electrons.

POSITIVELY CHARGED SODIUM ION

Both ions now have eight electrons in outer shell

Ionic bond

IONIC BONDS
In ionic bonding, electrons transfer between atoms, leaving the atoms as charged particles called ions. The atom losing the electron becomes a positive ion, or cation, and the atom gaining the electron becomes a negative ion, or anion. The force of attraction between the opposite charges forms a strong ionic bond.

NEGATIVELY CHARGED CHLORIDE ION

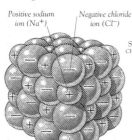

Positive sodium ion (Na^+)

Negative chloride ion (Cl^-)

SODIUM CHLORIDE

GIANT IONIC STRUCTURE
A crystal of salt (sodium chloride) contains sodium and chloride ions arranged in a regular network that extends throughout the crystal. This network is called a giant ionic lattice.

COVENANT BONDS

COVALENT BONDS

In covalent bonding, atoms share electrons. Two atoms each "donate" an electron, and the electrons form a pair that orbits both nuclei, holding the atoms together as a molecule. In a double bond, each atom donates two electrons.

Hydrogen atom

Shared electrons form single bond

Nitrogen atom

Nitrogen bonds with three hydrogen atoms

AMMONIA MOLECULE (NH₃)

Electrons move freely between atoms

Metal filament

METALLIC BONDS

Electrons in the outer shell of metal atoms are loosely attached. These free-moving electrons form a common pool that bonds the atoms firmly together. They also make metals good conductors of heat and electricity.

LIGHT BULB

MOLECULE FACTS

• In 1811, the Italian Amedeo Avogadro was the first to distinguish molecules from atoms.

• At normal pressure and temperature, one litre of any gas contains 25,000 million million million molecules.

PARTICLES AND THEIR STRUCTURE FORMS

STRUCTURE	COMPOSITION	TYPE OF SUBSTANCE	EXAMPLES
Metallic	Atoms	Metals	Sodium, iron, copper
Ionic	Ions	Compound of a metal with a non-metal	Sodium chloride (salt), calcium hydroxide (lime)
Simple molecular	Small molecules	Non-metal, or a non-metal compound	Iodine, sulphur, water, carbon dioxide
Giant molecular	Large molecules	Non-metal, or a non-metal compound	Diamond, graphite, polythene, sand

CRYSTALS

MOST SOLIDS have a crystalline structure, in which particles link up in regular, repeating patterns. There are seven basic crystal shapes, or crystal systems. All have straight edges, symmetrical corners, and smooth faces. Well-formed crystals are often prized for their beauty.

CRYSTAL FORMATION
• Crystals may form as a molten solid cools, or as a liquid evaporates from a solution.
• Atoms, ions, or molecules link up to form a framework called a lattice.
• The smallest complete piece of a lattice is a basic arrangement of particles called a unit cell.
• The lattice is made up of identical unit cells repeated many times over.

Sulphur forms both orthorhombic and monoclinic crystals

SULPHUR CRYSTALS

CRYSTAL FACTS
• Photographic film records images using special light-sensitive crystals of silver salts.

• Crystals of pure silicon are used in electronics. They are created artificially because they do not occur naturally.

• Diamonds are crystals of pure carbon.

This calculator displays figures using an LCD

LIQUID CRYSTALS
A liquid crystal can flow, but its particles line up in regular patterns. Heat or electricity can alter the pattern of the particles, and change the passage of light through the crystal. This process forms letters or numbers on a liquid-crystal display (LCD).

CRYSTAL SYSTEMS

Crystal systems are based on the lengths of any three edges in the unit cell that meet at a corner, and the angles at which they meet.

CUBIC CRYSTALS OF GALENA (IRON ORE)

CUBIC SYSTEM
Every angle is 90°. All three edges are equal in length.

TETRAGONAL SYSTEM
Every angle is 90°. Two of the three edges are equal in length.

ORTHORHOMBIC SYSTEM
Every angle is 90°. None of the three edges are of equal length.

MONOCLINIC SYSTEM
Two of the three edges meet at 90°. None are equal in length.

HEXAGONAL SYSTEM
Edges form angles of 90° and 120°. Two are of equal length.

TRIGONAL SYSTEM
None of the three edges meet at 90°. All are of equal length.

TRICLINIC SYSTEM
None of the edges meet at 90°. None are equal in length.

PIEZOELECTRIC CRYSTALS

Some crystals produce an electric current when squeezed or made to vibrate. When an electric current is applied to them, they vibrate at a precise frequency. They are used in electronic devices and clocks.

Current from battery makes quartz crystal vibrate

Vibrating crystal controls watch hands

WATER OF CRYSTALLIZATION

Some crystals are "hydrates", meaning that they have water molecules trapped inside them. Heating blue copper sulphate crystals drives off this "water of crystallization", leaving white "anhydrous" crystals behind.

Adding water turns the white crystals blue again

MIXTURES AND COMPOUNDS

IN THE NATURAL WORLD, few elements exist alone.
Most substances are made up of two or more elements,
either mingled loosely as mixtures
or, after chemical reactions,
combined strongly as compounds.
The main types of mixtures
are solutions and colloids.

*Potassium
permanganate
forms a
solution in
water*

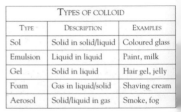

*Water molecule
attracts positively
charged
potassium ion*

SOLUTIONS
A solution is a mixture of one
substance (the solute) dissolved
in another (the solvent). Many
compounds break down in water
into charged particles (ions) that
form weak bonds with water molecules.

COLLOIDS
In a colloid, tiny particles of
matter are dispersed evenly
throughout a solid,
liquid, or gas.
Hair gel is a
colloid of
solid fat
particles
that are
suspended
in water.

HAIR
GEL

TYPES OF COLLOID		
TYPE	DESCRIPTION	EXAMPLES
Sol	Solid in solid/liquid	Coloured glass
Emulsion	Liquid in liquid	Paint, milk
Gel	Solid in liquid	Hair gel, jelly
Foam	Gas in liquid/solid	Shaving cream
Aerosol	Solid/liquid in gas	Smoke, fog

COMPARING MIXTURES AND COMPOUNDS

- A loose combination of sulphur and iron filings is a mixture. Heating the mixture causes a chemical reaction and forms a compound.
- The mixture separates easily with a magnet; the compound requires a chemical reaction.

Iron filings are attracted to a magnet

COMPOUND OF IRON SULPHIDE

Magnet does not attract new compound

MIXTURE OF IRON FILINGS AND SULPHUR

DIFFERENT COMPOUNDS

Copper and oxygen can form two different compounds. Copper(I) oxide contains twice as many copper atoms as oxygen atoms. Copper(II) oxide contains equal numbers of oxygen and copper atoms.

COPPER(I) OXIDE (Cu_2O)

COPPER(II) OXIDE (CuO)

PROPERTIES OF COMPOUNDS

DANGEROUS ELEMENTS

Compounds often have different properties from those of the elements they contain. Common salt contains sodium, a dangerously reactive metal, and chlorine, a poisonous gas.

CHLORINE

SODIUM

SODIUM CHLORIDE OR COMMON SALT

VITAL COMPOUND

In a chemical reaction, sodium and chlorine combine to form white crystals of salt – the compound sodium chloride. The sodium and chlorine lose their dangerous properties. The resulting compound is not only safe and edible, but also a vital part of our diet.

Separating mixtures

Scientists need to separate mixtures in order to investigate their components. Decanting involves pouring a liquid off from a solid sediment or a denser liquid. Centrifuging separates dense components from less dense ones by spinning them round. Other separation methods include distillation, evaporation, filtration, and desiccation.

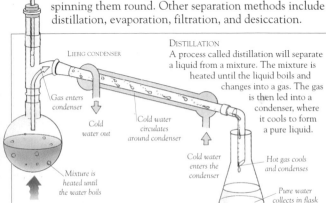

DISTILLATION

A process called distillation will separate a liquid from a mixture. The mixture is heated until the liquid boils and changes into a gas. The gas is then led into a condenser, where it cools to form a pure liquid.

LIEBIG CONDENSER

Gas enters condenser

Cold water out

Cold water circulates around condenser

Cold water enters the condenser

Mixture is heated until the water boils

Hot gas cools and condenses

Pure water collects in flask

FRACTIONAL DISTILLATION

This process is used to separate a mixture of liquids with different boiling points. To extract gases from air for industrial use, the air must be cooled first and liquefied. As the air warms, liquid gases boil off at different temperatures.

Air

Oxygen boils at −183°C (−297°F)

Argon boils at −186°C (−303°F)

Liquid air −200°C (−328°F)

Nitrogen boils at −196°C (−321°F)

EVAPORATION

Heat can drive off a liquid from a mixture by making it evaporate. In tropical climates, evaporation is often used to obtain salt (sodium chloride) from sea water. Shallow salt pans, dug out on the coast, flood with sea water. The water evaporates in the sun, leaving salt crystals.

Filter paper holds back sulphur particles

FILTRATION

It is possible to separate large solid particles from a liquid mixture using a filter. A filter is a porous barrier that allows the liquid (the filtrate) to pass through, but holds back the solid particles (the residue).

Mixture of powdered sulphur and copper sulphate solution

Copper sulphate solution passes through filter paper

Airtight glass lid

Prism of rock salt to be kept dry

Silica gel desiccant absorbs moisture

DESICCATION

A desiccator removes water from a solid mixture. It is a sealed glass dish containing a moisture-absorbing substance called a desiccant. Rock salt is stored in a desiccator to keep it dry for laboratory use.

WHAT ARE ELEMENTS?

AN ELEMENT IS a substance made of only one type of atom. Of the 109 known elements, 89 occur naturally on Earth. The rest are made artificially. A few "unreactive" elements, such as gold, occur in their pure state; most form compounds with other elements.

VEINS OF PURE GOLD IN QUARTZ

ALLOTROPES OF CARBON

ALLOTROPES
Allotropes are different physical forms of the same element. The different arrangement of their atoms gives them different appearances and properties.

Diamond

Graphite

GRAPHITE
The atoms form huge sheets. Only weak bonds link the sheets together. Graphite is soft because the sheets can slide over each other easily.

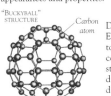

"BUCKYBALL" STRUCTURE

Carbon atom

DIAMOND
Each atom links strongly to four others in a rigid, compact framework that stretches throughout the diamond. This makes the diamond extremely hard.

BUCKMINSTERFULLERENE
The molecules of this newly discovered carbon allotrope have 60 atoms linked in a sphere. It is called a "buckyball".

Carbon atom

MOLECULAR STRUCTURE OF A DIAMOND

Carbon atom

MOLECULAR STRUCTURE OF GRAPHITE

COMPOSITION OF THE EARTH'S CRUST

The bulk of the Earth's crust is oxygen and silicon, mostly combined in rocks or sand (silicon oxide). Clays are made of silicon and oxygen combined with the third most common element – aluminium.

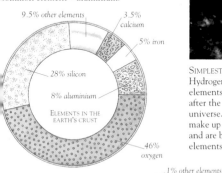

9.5% other elements

3.5% calcium

5% iron

28% silicon

8% aluminium

ELEMENTS IN THE EARTH'S CRUST

46% oxygen

SIMPLEST AND MOST ABUNDANT

Hydrogen and helium, the simplest elements, were the first to form after the Big Bang created the universe. Hydrogen and helium make up 97% of the mass of stars, and are by far the most abundant elements in the universe.

BODY ELEMENTS

The tissues of your body are made up of hydrogen, oxygen, carbon, and nitrogen, while bones contain calcium. Together, these five elements account for 98% of your body mass. Elements such as copper, iron, and zinc occur only in tiny amounts, but these "trace" elements are vital for good health.

Over 50% of your body mass is water

1% other elements

1% phosphorus

2% calcium

3% nitrogen

10% hydrogen

18% carbon

65% oxygen

ELEMENT FACTS

• Ancient Greek philosophers believed there were just four elements: earth, fire, air, and water.

• Astatine is the rarest element on Earth; the rarest metal is rhodium.

• Technetium was the first element to be made artificially.

• Earth's atmosphere is 78% nitrogen.

PERIODIC TABLE

CERTAIN ELEMENTS share similar chemical properties and atomic structures. These similarities become clear when all the known elements are set out in a chart called the periodic table. This chart arranges elements into "groups" (columns) and "periods" (rows).

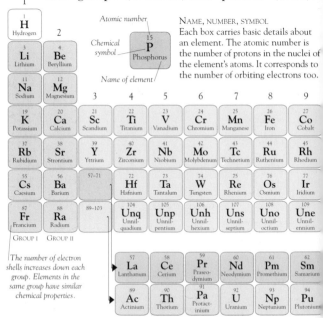

NAME, NUMBER, SYMBOL
Each box carries basic details about an element. The atomic number is the number of protons in the nuclei of the element's atoms. It corresponds to the number of orbiting electrons too.

Atomic number

Chemical symbol

Name of element

GROUP I   GROUP II

The number of electron shells increases down each group. Elements in the same group have similar chemical properties.

TYPES OF ELEMENT KEY

ALKALI METALS

ALKALINE-EARTH METALS

TRANSITION METALS

LANTHANIDES

ACTINIDES

POOR METALS

SEMIMETALS

NON-METALS

NOBLE GASES

GROUPS AND PERIODS

Each period starts on the left with a highly reactive alkali metal with an outer shell of one electron. It ends on the right with a stable noble gas in group 18 (0) with eight electrons in its outer shell. Elements in the same group have the same number of electrons in their outer shells.

As the atomic number increases by one along each period, the chemical properties of the element gradually change

18

			13	14	15	16	17	2 **He** Helium
			5 **B** Boron	6 **C** Carbon	7 **N** Nitrogen	8 **O** Oxygen	9 **F** Fluorine	10 **Ne** Neon
10	11	12	13 **Al** Aluminium	14 **Si** Silicon	15 **P** Phosphorus	16 **S** Sulphur	17 **Cl** Chlorine	18 **Ar** Argon
28 **Ni** Nickel	29 **Cu** Copper	30 **Zn** Zinc	31 **Ga** Gallium	32 **Ge** Germanium	33 **As** Arsenic	34 **Se** Selenium	35 **Br** Bromine	36 **Kr** Krypton
46 **Pd** Palladium	47 **Ag** Silver	48 **Cd** Cadmium	49 **In** Indium	50 **Sn** Tin	51 **Sb** Antimony	52 **Te** Tellurium	53 **I** Iodine	54 **Xe** Xenon
78 **Pt** Platinum	79 **Au** Gold	80 **Hg** Mercury	81 **Tl** Thallium	82 **Pb** Lead	83 **Bi** Bismuth	84 **Po** Polonium	85 **At** Astatine	86 **Rn** Radon

GROUP III GROUP IV GROUP V GROUP VI GROUP VII GROUP 0

Setting the lanthanides and actinides apart from the main table, makes its shape easier to understand

Two alternative number systems are used to group the elements

63 **Eu** Europium	64 **Gd** Gadolinium	65 **Tb** Terbium	66 **Dy** Dysprosium	67 **Ho** Holmium	68 **Er** Erbium	69 **Tm** Thulium	70 **Yb** Ytterbium	71 **Lu** Lutetium
95 **Am** Americium	96 **Cm** Curium	97 **Bk** Berkelium	98 **Cf** Californium	99 **Es** Einsteinium	100 **Fm** Fermium	101 **Md** Mendelevium	102 **No** Nobelium	103 **Lr** Lawrencium

Elementary data

Chlorine

Most of the known elements were first identified by scientists during the 18th and 19th centuries, but a few have been known since ancient times. Some can only be produced artifically in a laboratory. Of the 109 elements, all are solids at room temperature, except eleven gases, and mercury and bromine, which are liquids.

Sodium

Potassium

ANCIENT ELEMENTS	
Elements	Known since
Carbon	prehistoric times
Sulphur	prehistoric times
Gold	prehistoric times
Lead	prehistoric times
Copper	c.8000 BC
Silver	c.4000 BC
Iron	c.4000 BC
Tin	c.3500 BC
Mercury	c.1600 BC
Antimony	c.1000 BC

ELEMENTS PRODUCED ARTIFICIALLY		
Element	Year first made	Maker
Technetium	1937	C. Perrier (France) & E. Segré (Italy/USA)
Astatine	1940	D.R. Corson (USA)
Neptunium	1940	E.M. McMillan & P.H. Abelson (USA)
Plutonium	1944	G. Seaborg (USA)
Americium	1944	G. Seaborg (USA)
Curium	1944	G. Seaborg (USA)
Promethium	1947	J.A. Marinsky (USA)
Berkelium	1949	S.G. Thompson (USA)
Californium	1950	S.G. Thompson and others (USA)
Einsteinium	1952	A. Ghiorso (USA)
Fermium	1952	A. Ghiorso (USA)
Mendelevium	1955	A. Ghiorso (USA)
Nobelium	1958	A. Ghiorso (USA)
Lawrencium	1961	A. Ghiorso (USA)
Unnilquadium	1964	G. Flerov (USSR)
Unnilpentium	1967	A. Ghiorso (USA)
Unnilhexium	1974	A. Ghiorso (USA); G. Flerov (USSR)
Unnilseptium	1976	G. Munzenburg (Germany)
Unnilennium	1982	P. Armbruster (Germany)
Unniloctium	1984	P. Armbruster (Germany)

BOILING POINTS

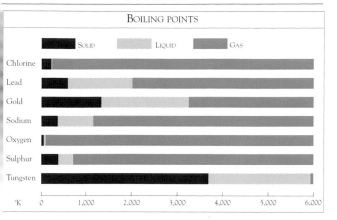

| ■ SOLID | ▨ LIQUID | ▥ GAS |

Chlorine
Lead
Gold
Sodium
Oxygen
Sulphur
Tungsten

°K 0   1,000   2,000   3,000   4,000   5,000   6,000

NAMING ELEMENTS

The names of many elements are derived from Greek words. They give clues about the elements' properties.

ELEMENT/SYMBOL	GREEK WORD	MEANING
Argon (Ar)	Argos	Inactive
Astatine (At)	Astatos	Unstable
Barium (Ba)	Barys	Heavy
Bromine (Br)	Bromos	Stench
Chlorine (Cl)	Chloros	Pale green
Dysprosium (Dy)	Dysprositos	Hard to get
Hydrogen (H)	Hydro genes	Water forming
Mercury (Hg)	Hydragyrum	Liquid silver
Phosphorus (P)	Phosphoros	Bringer of light
Technetium (Tc)	Tekhnetos	Artificial

MORE ELEMENT FACTS

• Helium has the lowest boiling point: –268.93°C (–453.07°F).

• Fluorine gas is the most reactive of all elements.

• At room temperature, osmium is the densest element and lithium the least dense metal. Radon is the densest gas and hydrogen the least dense.

SULPHUR

METALS

MOST ELEMENTS are metals. Many are found in the Earth's crust, combined with other elements as deposit called ores. Metals in their pure form are either not ver strong or they rust and tarnish easily. Most of the "metals" we use today are alloys. Alloys are solid mixtures of different metals. They provide hard, strong, long-lasting materials.

COMMON PROPERTIES OF METALS
- Metals have high melting and boiling points.
- They conduct heat and electricity well.
- Metals have a high density, and are malleable (can be beaten) and ductile (can be drawn out into wire).
- Most metals react with air to form oxides, and with acids to release hydrogen.
- Metals form positive ions.

Blacksmith hammers hot iron into shape

ALLOYS

ALLOYS
A metal may be mixed with other metals or non-metals to produce an alloy with more useful properties than the metal alone. The new substance alters the atomic structure of the metal so that the metal's atoms do not move. A tough alloy results.

Added atoms

Bronze spearhead

ALLOY STRUCTURE

COMPOSITION OF COMMON ALLOYS

ALLOY	TYPICAL COMPOSITION	PROPERTIES
Cast iron	Iron 97%, carbon 3%	Hard but brittle
Duralumin	Aluminium 96%, copper 4%	Strong and light
Pewter	Tin 73%, lead 27%	Fairly soft
Brass	Copper 70%, zinc 30%	Easy to shape
Solder	Tin 50%, lead 50%	Low melting point
Stainless steel	Iron 70%, chromium 20%, nickel 9.5%, carbon 0.5%	Hard and does not rust
Bronze	Copper 70%, tin 30%	Resists corrosion and wear

POOR METALS

A "tin" can may be made of steel coated with tin

Tankard made of pewter, a tin-lead alloy

The poor metals are aluminium, gallium, indium, thallium, tin, lead, bismuth, and polonium. They are softer and weaker than other metals, and melt more easily. Despite their name, they are very useful, especially in making alloys.

SEMIMETALS

Boron, silicon, germanium, arsenic, antimony, selenium, and tellurium are called semimetals because they have some of the properties of metals and some of non-metals. Silicon and germanium are used to make electronic components because they are "semiconductors", that is, they will conduct electricity but only under certain conditions.

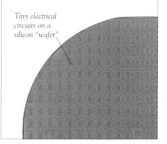

Tiny electrical circuits on a silicon "wafer"

Transition metals

In the middle of the periodic table lies the group of typical metals called the transition metals. They are less reactive than the

alkali metals and alkaline-earth metals, and have higher melting and boiling points. Some transition metals, such as copper and nickel, are magnetic.

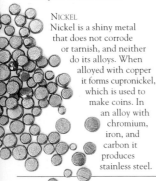

ZINC
A bluish-grey metal, zinc often provides the casing for batteries. Its main use is as a protective coating that prevents iron or steel from rusting. With copper, it forms the alloy brass. Zinc oxides are used to make rubber and plastic compounds more stable.

NICKEL
Nickel is a shiny metal that does not corrode or tarnish, and neither do its alloys. When alloyed with copper it forms cupronickel, which is used to make coins. In an alloy with chromium, iron, and carbon it produces stainless steel.

SILVER
Apart from jewellery, silver is used mainly in the photographic industry. Black-and-white photographic film is coated with a compound of silver, and either iodine, chlorine, or bromine. The compound is sensitive to light.

Developing the film turns the light-affected areas into pure silver – the dark areas on the negative

IRON
Iron is the most important and cheapest of all the metals we use. However, when exposed to air it oxidizes – that is, it reacts with oxygen in the air to form rust (iron oxide). This problem can be overcome by turning iron into steel.

PLATINUM
Rare and attractive platinum is used in jewellery. It never corrodes or wears away naturally. Platinum's main industrial use is as a catalyst. It is also used in electronic circuits.

MAGNETIC METALS
Iron, cobalt, and nickel are the only transition metals that can be made into strong magnets. The magnetism of an electromagnet can be switched on and off using an electric current.

INNER TRANSITION METALS

• The inner transition series consists of the lanthanide and actinide series.

• They are named after the first elements in their series: lanthanum and actinium.

• The lanthanides are so similar that chemists find it difficult to tell them apart.

• All the actinides are radioactive.

URANIUM
Uranium is a radioactive, silvery metal from the actinide series. It is extracted from the ores pitchblende and carnotite. Nuclear reactors use the isotope uranium–235 as a fuel.

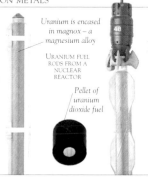

Uranium is encased in magnox – a magnesium alloy

URANIUM FUEL RODS FROM A NUCLEAR REACTOR

Pellet of uranium dioxide fuel

Other metals

At the beginning of the periodic table are two groups of highly reactive metals: the alkali metals and the alkaline-earth metals. Our bodies need small amounts of some of these – potassium, sodium, magnesium, and calcium – to stay healthy. Francium and radium are radioactive metals.

DANGEROUS METALS

The alkali metals are very reactive. Potassium reacts violently with water, skidding across its surface and creating bubbles of hydrogen gas, which burn with a blue-pink flame. Caesium and rubidium will explode if they touch water.

Potassium reacts violently with water

PROPERTIES OF ALKALI METALS

• The alkali metals are: lithium, francium, potassium, rubidium, sodium, and caesium.

• They form Group 1(I) of the periodic table.

• They are soft enough to cut with a knife.

• They are stored under oil to stop them from reacting with oxygen in the air.

• Their oxides and hydroxides dissolve in water to give strongly alkaline solutions.

• They form ions with a single charge.

• Alkali metals react with some non-metals to form white, soluble, crystalline salts.

• They have low melting points, low boiling points, and low densities compared with other metals.

POTASSIUM FERTILIZER

Plants take in potassium from the so because it is crucial for their healthy growth. Intensive farming depletes the soil, so farmers must replenish it by adding fertilizers that contain potassium and other nutrients.

SODIUM

Sodium, a silvery, soft alkali metal, tarnishes on exposure to the air. An atom of sodium has 11 electrons, but only one in its outer shell, which makes it very reactive. It is extracted from common salt by electrolysis.

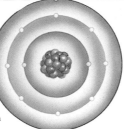

ATOMIC STRUCTURE OF SODIUM

PROPERTIES OF ALKALINE-EARTH METALS

• The alkaline-earth metals are: beryllium, magnesium, calcium, strontium, barium, and radium.

• They form Group 2 (II) of the periodic table.

• They react with water to form alkaline solutions. Their compounds are widely found in nature.

• Alkaline-earth metals are reactive, though less so than the alkali metals.

MAGNESIUM

A magnesium atom has 12 electrons, but only two in its outer shell. This makes it reactive, but less so than sodium. Magnesium, a light, alkaline-earth metal, is used in alloys with aluminium and zinc.

ATOMIC STRUCTURE OF MAGNESIUM

CALCIUM

Calcium is one of the Earth's most abundant metals. There are vast deposits in the form of limestone (also called calcium carbonate). Calcium is also present in bones, teeth, and the shells of molluscs and other sea creatures. The average human contains 1 kg (2.2 lb) of calcium.

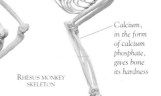

RHESUS MONKEY SKELETON

Calcium, in the form of calcium phosphate, gives bone its hardness

NON-METALS

THE NON-METALS are phosphorus, sulphur, hydrogen, carbon, nitrogen, oxygen, the halogens, and the noble gases. Although they form a small part of the periodic table, they are vital to life on Earth. The non-metals include elements that are gases at room temperature (20°C, 68°F) such as hydrogen and oxygen. Solid non-metals include sulphur and phosphorus.

HYDROGEN
Hydrogen is at the top of the periodic table because it has the simplest atom, with just one proton orbited by a single electron. It is a colourless, odourless, tasteless, non-toxic gas, and is the least dense of all the elements.

Electron

Proton

HALOGENS

• The halogens are fluorine, chlorine, bromine, iodine, and astatine.
• They form group 17 (VII) of the periodic table.
• They are all poisonous and have a strong smell.
• Halogens form molecules of two atoms (Cl_2, Br_2, I_2, etc.).
• They react with metals to form salts (such as NaCl, LiF).
• Halogen ions have a single negative charge (F⁻, Cl⁻, Br⁻, I⁻, At⁻).

NATURAL HALOGENS
The most widespread natural compound containing fluorine is the mineral fluorite (calcium fluoride). Iodine is found in sea water and was once extracted from certain types of seaweed.

Pink fluorite crystal

Laminaria seaweed contains iodine

NOBLE GASES

- The noble gases are helium, neon, argon, krypton, xenon, and radon.
- They form group 18 (0) of the periodic table.
- The noble gases have very low melting and boiling points.
- They all have a full outer shell of electrons, making them extremely unreactive.
- Noble gases exist as single atoms (He, Ne, Ar, Kr, Xe, Rn).

SAFE GAS
Helium is a light noble gas that is used in balloons and airships. It is very safe to use because it is so unreactive that it cannot catch fire. It is extracted from natural gas wells.

ATOMIC STRUCTURE OF NEON

Helium-filled balloons

SWALLOWTAIL BUTTERFLY

CARBON
All life on earth is based on the element carbon because carbon compounds are vital to the functioning of living cells. Carbon circulates through air, oceans, rocks, and living things in a "carbon cycle".

COMPOSITION OF AIR
Many of the non-metallic elements are present in the air that we breathe.

ELEMENT	PERCENTAGE OF AIR
Nitrogen (N_2)	78%
Oxygen (O_2)	21%
Argon (Ar)	0.93%
Carbon dioxide (CO_2)	0.03%
Neon (Ne)	0.0018%
Helium (He)	0.0005%
Krypton (Kr)	0.00001%
Other gases	0.03769%

CHEMICAL REACTIONS

WHEN A CHEMICAL reaction occurs, new substances (called products) form from the substances taking part in the reaction (called reactants). The atoms of the reactants rearrange themselves to form the products.

As log gives off heat, the surrounding air becomes hotter

EXOTHERMIC REACTIONS
Burning is an exothermic reaction – more heat is given out during the reaction than is taken in. Oxidation occurs when a substance combines with oxygen. When a log burns, it combines with oxygen and gives out heat. Reduction occurs when a substance loses oxygen.

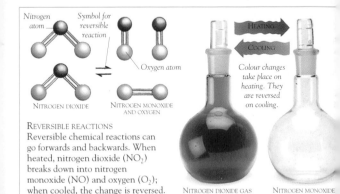

Nitrogen atom

Symbol for reversible reaction

Oxygen atom

NITROGEN DIOXIDE

NITROGEN MONOXIDE AND OXYGEN

HEATING

COOLING

Colour changes take place on heating. They are reversed on cooling.

REVERSIBLE REACTIONS
Reversible chemical reactions can go forwards and backwards. When heated, nitrogen dioxide (NO_2) breaks down into nitrogen monoxide (NO) and oxygen (O_2); when cooled, the change is reversed.

NITROGEN DIOXIDE GAS

NITROGEN MONOXIDE AND OXYGEN GAS

MAKING AND BREAKING BONDS

Heat is absorbed during cooking

1 DURING A CHEMICAL REACTION
Energy is taken in when chemical bonds are broken, and it is released when new bonds are formed. When methane (CH_4) burns, it reacts with oxygen (O_2) in the air.

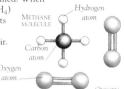

METHANE MOLECULE

Hydrogen atom

Carbon atom

Oxygen atom

OXYGEN MOLECULES

ENDOTHERMIC REACTIONS
Some reactions take in more heat energy than they give out. These reactions are called "endothermic". When a reaction takes place during cooking, it is endothermic.

Bonds between atoms break

Bonds will rejoin to form carbon dioxide and water

2 BROKEN BONDS
During the reaction, all the bonds between the atoms are broken. New bonds form as the atoms join up in different combinations.

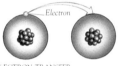

Electron

ELECTRON TRANSFER
During the oxidation process, atoms lose electrons and are "oxidized". During reduction, atoms gain electrons and are "reduced".

ACTIVATION ENERGY
Most reactions need some energy to get them started. This energy is called activation energy. Striking a match gives it the energy to ignite.

CARBON DIOXIDE MOLECULE

WATER MOLECULES

3 NEW BONDS FORM
The reaction produces carbon dioxide (CO_2) and water (H_2O). The new bonds have less stored energy than the original ones, so the reaction gives out energy as heat.

Chemicals in match head contain energy

Describing reactions

Each element has a chemical symbol to identify it, and each compound a chemical formula. The formula indicates how the elements in the compound are combined. A chemical equation shows which substances react together during a chemical reaction and the products that result

Lead nitrate solution

Potassium iodide solution

Solid yellow precipitate of lead iodide forms

CHEMICAL EQUATIONS ALWAYS BALANCE

No atoms are lost during a chemical reaction, so its chemical equation must balance, with equal numbers of atoms of each element on either side. Here, lead nitrate solution reacts with potassium iodide solution. The chemical equation for this reaction is shown below.

$$2KI + Pb(NO_3)_2 \longrightarrow PbI_2 + 2KNO_3$$

| *Potassium iodide* | + | *Lead nitrate* | $\longrightarrow$ | *Lead iodide* | + | *Potassium nitrate* |

Sodium is high in the activity series, and reacts violently with air

REACTION FACTS

• No mass is lost during any chemical reaction – this was first noted by French chemist Antoine Lavoisier in 1774.

• Caesium is the most reactive metal element.

• The present system of using letters to represent elements was devised in 1811.

THE ACTIVITY SERIES

The activity series compares the reactivity of different metals – that is, how readily they form compounds with other substances. Elements at the top of the series are highly reactive. Those at the bottom are very unreactive. Highly reactive metals cannot be found uncombined in nature.

Potassium
Sodium
Calcium
Magnesium
Aluminium
Zinc
Iron
Lead
Copper
Mercury
Silver
Platinum
Gold

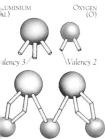

ALUMINIUM
(AL)

OXYGEN
(O)

Valency 3

Valency 2

ALUMINIUM OXIDE (AL₂O₃)

*Two aluminium atoms bond
with three oxygen atoms*

SI UNITS

The **mole** (mol) is a
measure of the number
of atoms, molecules, or
ions in any substance.

• 1 mole contains 6 x
10^{23} particles. This
number is called
Avogadro's constant,
after Italian scientist
Amedeo Avogadro.

• Although the
number of particles
in one mole of any
element is the same,
their masses vary due to
different-sized nuclei.
A mole of copper has
a mass of 64 g, a mole
of aluminium 27 g.

VALENCY

An atom's valency shows the number of
chemical bonds it can form. It is the number
of electrons the atom gains, loses, or shares
when it makes bonds. When a compound
has formed, the total valencies of the
different atoms involved will be the same.

DISPLACEMENT

A metal will displace (put
out of place) a less reactive
metal from a solution.
Here, atoms from a "tree"
of copper wire displace
silver atoms from a clear
solution of silver nitrate.
The copper turns the
solution blue, while the
displaced silver forms
crystals on the wire.

*Copper
crystals
grow on the
copper wire*

Copper wire

$$Cu + 2AgNO_3 \longrightarrow Cu(NO_3)_2 + 2Ag$$

Copper + Silver nitrate ⟶ Copper nitrate + Silver

*Blue copper
nitrate solution
forms*

SUFFIXES AND PREFIXES		
SUFFIX	DESCRIPTION	EXAMPLE
-ide	Contains just the two elements in the name	Iron sulphide (FeS)
-ite	Contains oxygen as well as the other elements in the name	Iron sulphite ($FeSO_3$)
-ate	Contains more oxygen than -ites	Iron sulphate ($FeSO_4$)
PREFIX	EXAMPLE	ATOMS IN PREFIX
Mono-	Carbon monoxide (CO)	1
Di-	Nitrogen dioxide (NO_2)	2
Tri-	Boron trichloride (BCl_3)	3

Controlling reactions

Chemists speed up reactions by making the reacting particles collide with each other more often or with greater energy. Substances called catalysts speed up reactions by helping substances react together. They remain unchanged by the chemical reaction.

Rate of reaction is slower with a weak dye solution

Strong dye solution reacts faster with material

CONCENTRATION

Increasing the concentration of a reactant speeds up a reaction. Dyeing a material is faster with a concentrated dye – there are more dye molecules to collide with the material.

SURFACE AREA

The surface area of a solid object is the size of its outer surface. Increasing the surface area of a reacting substance speeds up a chemical reaction. This is why chips fry faster than the potato from which they are made. The chips' greater surface area reacts with the hot cooking oil.

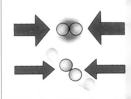

COLLISION THEORY

When particles collide, they usual bounce harmlessly off each other. But if the particles collide with enough force or energy, the bonds holding them together break, and a chemical reaction takes place.

CATALYSTS IN INDUSTRY		
PROCESS	REACTANTS	CATALYST
Manufacture of ammonia	Hydrogen and nitrogen	Iron and iron(III) oxide
Manufacture of nitric acid	Ammonia and oxygen	Platinum
Manufacture of sulphuric acid	Sulphur dioxide and oxygen	Vanadium(V) oxide
Manufacture of margarine	Vegetable oil and hydrogen	Nickel or platinum
Manufacture of methanol	Methane and oxygen	Chromium(III) oxide or zinc oxide

Sugar lump dropped in fizzy drink

SUGAR AS A CATALYST
Sugar makes a fizzy drink fizz harder. It acts as a catalyst for the dissolved carbon dioxide gas to come out of the solution.

CATALYTIC CONVERTER
A car's catalytic converter provides a large surface area for chemical reactions to take place. Harmful gases formed when fuel burns are forced into close contact with catalysts in the converter. The substances react together to produce less harmful gases. The catalysts are unchanged by the reaction.

CATALYTIC CONVERTER

Polluting gases enter converter

Honeycomb structure gives large surface area

Coating of catalysts rhodium and platinum

Gas bubbles make dough expand

NATURAL CATALYSTS
Yeast is a fungus containing enzymes, which are biological catalysts. The enzymes in yeast make starches and sugars break down more rapidly into carbon dioxide gas and ethanol. In bread making, yeast helps the dough to rise.

Dough is left in warm place

Yeast mixture

MORE REACTION FACTS
• Raising temperature or pressure increases the rate of reaction.
• The human body contains over 1,000 different enzymes.
• Biodegradable plastics decompose faster in strong sunlight.

ACIDS AND ACIDITY

STRONG ACIDS are corrosive and burn clothes or skin. However, acids are found in fruit, ants, rain, and even our stomachs. Some acids dissolve metals. The strength of an acid is measured on the pH scale.

CORROSIVE WARNING SYMBOL FOR STRONG ACIDS

Hydrochloric acid poured over metal

Acid reacts furiously with metal chippings, releasing hydrogen gas

Zinc chippings

REACTION OF ACID ON METAL
Hydrochloric acid poured onto zinc chippings causes a fizzing as the hydrogen (present in all acids) is released. The zinc replaces the hydrogen in the solution to form zinc chloride.

Water molecule (H_2O)

Hydrogen ion (H^+) splits from water molecule

Hydroxide ion (OH^-)

ACIDS IN WATER
Water (H_2O) can split into (OH^-) hydroxide and (H^+) hydrogen ions. Acidic compounds add more H^+ ions when they dissolve. A solution's pH is a measure of its H^+ ion concentration

COMMON ACIDS				
ACID	FORMULA	STRENGTH	pH	OCCURRENCE
Hydrochloric	HCl	Strong	1	Human digestive system
Sulphuric	H_2SO_4	Strong	1–2	Car batteries
Nitric	HNO_3	Strong	1	Industrial processes
Acetic	CH_3COOH	Weak	3–4	Vinegar
Citric	$C_6H_8O_7$	Weak	3	Citrus fruit
Formic	HCOOH	Weak	4.5	Ant bites, nettle stings
Carbonic	H_2CO_3	Weak	4–5	Rainwater, fizzy drinks

UNIVERSAL INDICATOR COLOUR/pH CHART OF ACIDS

1	2	3	4	5	6	7
DIGESTIVE JUICES	CAR BATTERY ACID	LEMON JUICE	VINEGAR	ACID RAIN	TAP WATER	PURE WATER

MEASURING ACIDITY

The pH scale measures acidity (and alkalinity). On the pH scale, 1 is highly acidic, 7 neutral, and 14 highly alkaline. Acidity is measured with indicator papers or solutions, which change colour in acids or alkalis, or with pH meters, which record the concentration of hydrogen ions.

Hydrochloric acid

Indicator paper shows pH of 1

ACID RAIN

Rainwater naturally contains weak carbonic acid, but pollution is now adding sulphuric acid and nitric acid to it. This creates a strong cocktail of acids that can kill trees and aquatic life, and erode statues and buildings.

USES OF SULPHURIC ACID

Sulphuric acid is widely used in industry because it reacts readily with other compounds. It is produced in large quantities after a reaction between sulphur and oxygen.

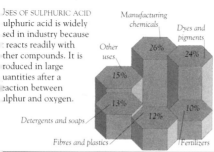

Manufacturing chemicals 26%

Dyes and pigments 24%

Other uses 15%

Detergents and soaps 13%

Fibres and plastics 12%

Fertilizers 10%

ACID FACTS

• pH or "potential of hydrogen", indicates the number of hydrogen ions a substance forms.

• The word "acid" comes from the Latin word for "sour".

• "Heartburn" is caused by excess hydrochloric acid in the stomach.

Alkalis, bases, and salts

Bases are compounds that cancel out, or neutralize, acidity. When a base reacts with an acid, a substance called a salt is created. Water (H_2O) is also produced. Pure water is neutral: it is neither acidic nor alkaline. Alkalis are bases that are soluble in water.

BEE

Painful stings contain acids or alkalis

BEE STINGS AND WASP STINGS
A bee sting is acidic and can be neutralized by a weak alkali such as soap or bicarbonate of soda. Wasp stings are alkaline, so they can be neutralized by a weak acid such as vinegar.

AMMONIA
Fertilizers containing nitrogen are made from the alkali ammonia (NH_3). Ammonia is produced by the Haber process, which causes nitrogen and hydrogen to react together.

WASP

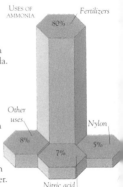

USES OF AMMONIA

Fertilizers 80%

Other uses 8%

Nitric acid 7%

Nylon 5%

COMMON BASES				
BASE	FORMULA	STRENGTH	pH	OCCURRENCE
Sodium hydroxide	NaOH	Strong	14	Soap manufacture
Calcium hydroxide	$Ca(OH)_2$	Strong	12	Neutralizing soil acidity
Ammonium hydroxide solution	NH_4OH	Weak	10–11	Household cleaning fluids
Milk of magnesia	$Mg(OH)_2$	Weak	10	Neutralizing stomach acid
Sodium hydrogencarbonate	$NaHCO_3$	Weak	8–9	Bicarbonate of soda
Blood		Weak	7.4	Human body

UNIVERSAL INDICATOR COLOUR/PH CHART OF BASES

7	8	9	10	11	12	13	14
PURE WATER	SOAP	BICARBONATE OF SODA	DISINFECTANT	HOUSEHOLD CLEANER	CALCIUM HYDROXIDE	OVEN CLEANER	SODIUM HYDROXIDE

THE pH OF BASES

The pH scale for bases ranges from neutral pure water (pH 7) to strong alkalis such as sodium hydroxide (pH 14). Soaps are made by making weak organic acids react with a strong base. This makes soaps mildy alkaline, with a pH of 8–9.

Universal indicator paper dipped in calcium hydroxide shows pH of 12

ADD SULPHURIC ACID

ADD HYDROCHLORIC ACID

ADD CARBONIC ACID

COPPER SHAVINGS

COPPER SULPHATE

COPPER CHLORIDE

COPPER CARBONATE

MAKING SALTS

A salt is a compound of a metal and non-metal joined by ionic bonds. A salt forms when an acid reacts with a base or a metal. Like other metals, copper forms a variety of salts. Making it react with different acids produces very different salts.

CORROSIVE ALKALI WARNING

Alkalis are chemically opposite to acids. They dissolve in water to form negatively charged hydroxide ions (OH^-), making them as corrosive as acids.

BASE AND SALT FACTS

• In 1908, a German chemist named Fritz Haber devised the manufacturing process for ammonia.

• Alkalis, like acids, are good conductors of electricity. This is because they break up in water to form ions.

CHEMISTRY OF CARBON

THERE ARE MORE than ten million known carbon compounds. All living things contain some compound of carbon. The study of substances containing carbon is known as organic chemistry.

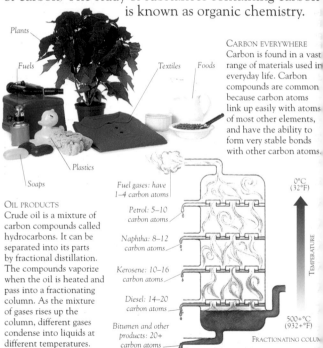

Plants

Fuels

Textiles Foods

Plastics

Soaps

CARBON EVERYWHERE
Carbon is found in a vast range of materials used in everyday life. Carbon compounds are common because carbon atoms link up easily with atoms of most other elements, and have the ability to form very stable bonds with other carbon atoms.

OIL PRODUCTS
Crude oil is a mixture of carbon compounds called hydrocarbons. It can be separated into its parts by fractional distillation. The compounds vaporize when the oil is heated and pass into a fractionating column. As the mixture of gases rises up the column, different gases condense into liquids at different temperatures.

Fuel gases: have 1–4 carbon atoms

Petrol: 5–10 carbon atoms

Naphtha: 8–12 carbon atoms

Kerosene: 10–16 carbon atoms

Diesel: 14–20 carbon atoms

Bitumen and other products: 20+ carbon atoms

0°C (32°F)

TEMPERATURE

500+°C (932+°F)

FRACTIONATING COLUMN

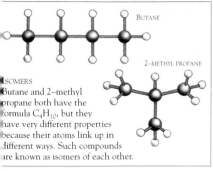

BUTANE

2–METHYL PROPANE

ISOMERS
Butane and 2–methyl propane both have the formula C_4H_{10}, but they have very different properties because their atoms link up in different ways. Such compounds are known as isomers of each other.

AROMATIC COMPOUND
Benzene is a strong-smelling liquid obtained from coal. The molecular structure of benzene – a ring of six carbon atoms – is the basis of many useful "aromatic" compounds.

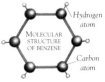

Hydrogen atom

MOLECULAR STRUCTURE OF BENZENE

Carbon atom

ORGANIC TERMS

TERM	MEANING	EXAMPLE
Hydrocarbon	Organic compound of hydrogen and carbon atoms only	Methane (CH_4)
Aromatic	Organic compound with a ring of carbon atoms	Benzene (C_6H_6)
Aliphatic	Organic compound with a chain of carbon atoms	Ethane (C_2H_6)
Alkane	Aliphatic hydrocarbon with single bonds between its carbon atoms	Octane (C_8H_{18})
Alkene	Aliphatic hydrocarbon with a double bond between two of its carbon atoms	Ethene (C_2H_4)
Alkyne	Aliphatic hydrocarbon with a triple bond between two of its carbon atoms	Ethyne (C_2H_2)
Alkyl group	Alkane that has lost one hydrogen atom	Methyl (CH_3-) forms from methane Ethyl (C_2H_5-) forms from ethane
Aryl group	Aromatic compound that has lost one hydrogen atom	Phenyl (C_6H_5-) forms from benzene
Alcohol	Organic compound with a hydroxyl ($-OH$) group	Ethanol (C_2H_5OH) – ethyl plus a hydroxyl group
Carbohydrate	Organic compound with hydrogen and oxygen atoms in the ratio of 2 to 1	Glucose ($C_6H_{12}O_6$)

POLYMERS

POLYMERS ARE giant
molecules made up of
winding chains of thousands
of smaller molecules called
"monomers". Fats, starches, and
proteins are natural polymers, while
plastics and many artificial fibres are
made from synthetic polymers.

INFLATABLE
PVC (POLYVINYL
CHLORIDE) SNAKE

*PVC is a
"thermoplastic" –
it melts very easily*

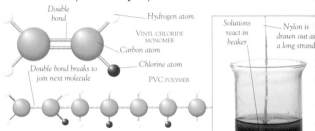

*Double
bond*

Hydrogen atom

VINYL CHLORIDE
MONOMER

Carbon atom

*Double bond breaks to
join next molecule*

Chlorine atom

PVC POLYMER

*Solutions
react in
beaker*

Nylon is
drawn out as
a long strand

MONOMERS AND POLYMERS
Vinyl chloride monomers are chemical compounds
of single molecules. They link up end-to-end to form
a long PVC polymer. The double bond in the vinyl
chloride monomer breaks: one bond links to the chain
and the other is able to bond with the next monomer.

MAKING NYLON POLYMERS
Hexanedioic acid and
1,6-diaminohexane react
together to produce nylon.
Their monomers join
up to form long nylon
polymers, which can be
drawn out like thread.

*Rug made from
woollen thread*

NATURAL POLYMERS
Wool and other natural fibres
are made of strong, flexible,
protein polymers. The
fibres are spun
into thread.

TYPES OF POLYMER

Polymer	Produced from	Uses
Polythene (polyethylene)	Ethene	Plastic bags, bottles, food wrappings, insulation
Polystyrene	Styrene (phenylethene)	Plastic toys, packaging, insulation, bowls, ceiling tiles
Polyvinyl chloride (PVC)	Vinyl chloride	Guttering and pipes, electrical insulation, waterproof clothing
Acrylic	Derivatives of acrylic acid	Synthetic fibres for clothing, paints
Nylon	Hexanedioic acid and 1,6-diaminohexane	Synthetic fibres for clothing, carpets, plastic ropes, engineering parts
Polyester	Organic acids and alcohols	Fibreglass, synthetic fibres for clothing, boat sails, photographic film
Polymethyl methacrylate (Perspex)	Methyl methacrylate	Glass substitute
Polyurethane	Urethane resins	Packaging foam, adhesives, paints, varnishes
Polytetrafluoroethene (PTFE)	Tetrafluoroethene	Non-stick coating for cooking utensils, artificial body parts, machine bearings
Kevlar	Phenylenediamine, terephthalyl chloride	Bullet-proof vests and other high-strength materials

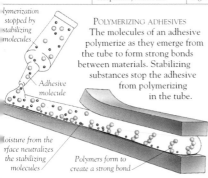

Polymerization stopped by stabilizing molecules

Adhesive molecule

Moisture from the surface neutralizes the stabilizing molecules

Polymers form to create a strong bond

POLYMERIZING ADHESIVES
The molecules of an adhesive polymerize as they emerge from the tube to form strong bonds between materials. Stabilizing substances stop the adhesive from polymerizing in the tube.

POLYMER FACTS

• In 1862, English chemist Alexander Parkes made Parkesine, the first plastic.

• Kevlar fibres are stronger than steel, but much lighter.

• There are two types of plastic: thermosets (which do not melt), and thermoplastics (which melt easily).

ELECTROCHEMISTRY

USING ELECTRICITY to break down a substance is called electrolysis. It happens when metal or carbon rods (called electrodes) pass an electric current through a dissolved or molten compound containing ions (called an electrolyte).

Chlorine gas collects in test tube

Electrolyte of copper(II) chloride solution loses its colour

Copper forms at cathode as copper ions gain electrons and become atoms

Chloride ions lose electrons at anode and become atoms of chlorine

ELECTROLYSIS OF COPPER(II) CHLORIDE
Electrolysing a solution of copper(II) chloride ($CuCl_2$) makes copper ions (Cu^{2+}) move to the negatively charged electrode (cathode) where they become copper atoms. Chloride ions (Cl^-) are attracted to the positively charged electrode (anode) where they become chlorine atoms.

ELECTROPLATING
Using electricity to coat an object with metal is called electroplating. Here, a nickel spoon is plated with silver. Silver ions (Ag^+) in the solution move to the nickel cathode, where they gain electrons and form a deposit of silver. They are replaced by atoms from the silver anode that give up electrons and go into the solution as ions.

BARE NICKEL

SILVER-PLATED

Spoon turns in electrolyte of silver nitrate solution

Silver dissolves during electrolysis

FARADAY CONSTANT

The electricity needed to produce 1 mole of an element by electrolysis is always a multiple of 96,500 coulombs. This figure is the Faraday constant (F). The multiple depends on the charge carried by the element's ions.

For example:
• 96,500 (1 x F) coulombs produce 1 mole of iodine (I-).
• 193,000 (2 x F) coulombs produce 1 mole of copper (Cu^{2+}).

1 MOLE OF COPPER
MASS OF 64 GRAMS

1 MOLE
OF IODINE
MASS OF
127 GRAMS

ELECTROLYSIS FACTS

• In 1807, English chemist Humphry Davy discovered the element potassium by electrolysing molten potash (potassium carbonate).

• Electrorefining – using electrolysis to rid a metal of its impurities – can produce copper that is 99.99% pure.

GALVANIZING

A steel car body may be galvanized – that is, given a coating of zinc to guard against rust. The body is electrified and dipped in a bath of an electrolyte containing zinc. The body forms the cathode, so it attracts the zinc ions (Zn^{2+}) in the electrolyte.

MAKING ELECTRICITY

Chemical reactions can produce an electric current. In this cell, a reaction tears ions (Zn^{2+}) from the zinc plate, leaving it negatively charged. The copper plate loses electrons and becomes positively charged. A current flows as electrons move through the wire to the copper plate.

Electrons flow towards the copper anode

As the zinc electrode dissolves, electrons flow out of the cell and through the wire

Electrolyte of dilute sulphuric acid solution

Bulb lit by flow of electrons

CHEMICAL ANALYSIS

CHEMISTS USE various techniques to analyse and identify substances. Qualitative analysis reveals which elements or compounds a substance contains; quantitative analysis shows how much of each element or compound is present.

TITRATION

A sample solution is made to react with a chemical whose concentration is known. When all the solution has reacted, a colour change occurs. Measuring the amount of the chemical used up reveals the concentration of the sample.

Dyes travel up paper at different speeds

Blotting paper

The colour of the test solution changes as the pink chemical drops into the flask

PAPER CHROMATOGRAPHY

The ingredients in a dissolved mixture can be revealed by using absorbent paper. The paper takes up different substances at different rates. Black ink, for example, reveals a mixture of dyes.

Black ink

FLAME TESTS

Metallic elements can be identified by flame tests. A small amount of a metal salt is placed on the end of a platinum wire and heated in a flame. The metal burns and gives the flame a particular colour. Fireworks use metal compounds to produce coloured sparks.

Sodium burns with an orange flame

| FLAME TEST FOR IDENTIFYING METAL | |
METAL	FLAME COLOUR
Barium	Brown-green
Calcium	Orange-red
Copper	Green-blue
Lithium	Red
Potassium	Lilac
Sodium	Orange

SPECTROSCOPY

SPECTROSCOPY
A heated substance gives out light, which a spectroscope separates into an "emission spectrum" of coloured bands on a dark background. Different elements produce different emission spectra.

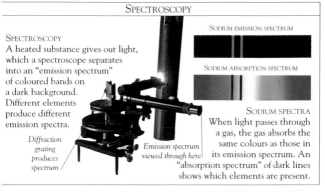

SODIUM EMISSION SPECTRUM

SODIUM ABSORPTION SPECTRUM

Diffraction grating produces spectrum

Emission spectrum viewed through here

SODIUM SPECTRA
When light passes through a gas, the gas absorbs the same colours as those in its emission spectrum. An "absorption spectrum" of dark lines shows which elements are present.

MASS SPECTROSCOPY
Ions of a substance accelerate along a tube. Ions with a particular charge and mass are deflected by a magnetic field so that they strike a detector at the other end of the tube. One by one different ions are detected, producing a mass spectrum.

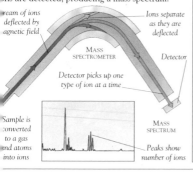

Stream of ions deflected by magnetic field

Ions separate as they are deflected

MASS
SPECTROMETER

Detector picks up one type of ion at a time

Detector

Sample is converted to a gas and atoms into ions

MASS
SPECTRUM

Peaks show number of ions

DNA PROFILING
Fragments of the genetic material from skin, blood, or hair roots are analysed using a technique known as electrophoresis. The result is a unique DNA profile that can be used to help identify individual people or animals.

FORCES AT WORK

WHAT MAKES a magnet attract iron filings or an arrow fly towards a target? The answer is force. You cannot see a force, though you feel its effects. Forces push, pull, stretch, or turn an object. Forces are measured in newtons (N).

First component acts along top half of bowstring

Arrow is thrust forwards by resultant force

Second componen acts on bottom ha of bowstring

COMBINING FORCES

When more than one force acts on an object, the forces (or "components") combine to produce a single force (the "resultant") that acts in one direction only. The force of an arrow fired from a bow is the resultant of component forces acting along the bowstring.

FORCE FACTS

• A jet engine produces a force of at least 200,000 newtons (N).

• Car brakes exert force of up to 5,000 N.

• It takes a force of 5 N to switch on a light.

• To squash an egg requires a force of 50 N.

TORQUE OR TURNING FORCE

Torque is the force that makes an object rotate. It helps a spanner turn a nut. Applying the force far from the nut increases the turning effect. The size of the torque is found by multiplying the force by its distance from the nut.

Extendable spanner

A long hand makes turnin the nut easi

BALANCED FORCES

If the forces acting on an object are balanced, the object is said to be in equilibrium. It will either stay at rest, or continue moving at the same speed and in the same direction. These magnets exert exactly equal and opposite forces on the line of ball bearings.

Attraction from north pole of magnet

Equal and opposite component forces mean that the resultant force is zero, so ball bearings remain stationary

Attraction from south pole of magnet

TYPES OF FORCE

- Tension stretches objects.
- Compression squeezes objects.
- Torsion twists objects.
- Shear forces tear objects.
- Centripetal force keeps objects moving in a circle.
- Friction opposes motion.
- Upthrust acts on objects immersed in fluids.

FORCES ON IMMERSED OBJECTS

UPTHRUST IN WATER

Fluids (liquids and gases) exert pressure on immersed objects, producing an upward resultant force called "upthrust". The upthrust equals the weight of the fluid displaced (pushed aside) by the object. In this experiment, the upthrust of the water on the 1 kg mass is 1.2 N.

Newton meter reads 8.8 N

Water level rises as object is immersed

Peach displaces water equal to its own weight

Displaced water fills pan

Newton balance

1 kg mass

Water weighs 1.2 N

FLOATING

If the upthrust on an immersed object is greater than, or equal to, its weight, the object floats. If the upthrust is less than its weight, the object sinks.

The force of gravity

Gravity keeps our feet firmly on the ground. It is a force of attraction between all bodies of matter. All objects experience and exert a certain amount of gravity, depending on their mass. Most people are aware that the Earth's gravity acts on us; few people realize that we pull on the Earth with the same gravitational force.

This apple weighs about 1 N

Mass is the same but weight is different

ON THE MOON

ON EARTH

WEIGHT AND MASS
Weight is the force exerted on an object by gravity. An object's mass is the same on the Moon as it is on Earth, but it weighs less, because the Moon's surface gravity is weaker.

MEASURING FORCE
Gravity pulling on an object creates a force called weight. This force is measured in newtons. A simple instrument that measures force is the newton meter. (A spring balance works in the same way.)

NEWTON'S LAW OF GRAVITATION

According to Newton's law, to find the force of gravity between two objects, you multiply their masses and divide the result by the square of the distance between them. For example, if the Moon was only half as far from Earth, gravity between the two bodies would be four times as strong. If the Moon had twice its mass, the force of gravity between the Moon and Earth would be twice as great.

EARTH

MOON

Force of gravity = 1

Mass = 1

Force of gravity = 2

Mass = 2

Force of gravity = 4

Mass = 1

Moon half as far

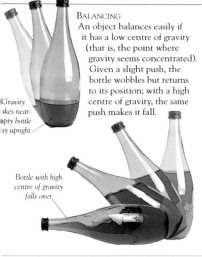

BALANCING

An object balances easily if it has a low centre of gravity (that is, the point where gravity seems concentrated). Given a slight push, the bottle wobbles but returns to its position; with a high centre of gravity, the same push makes it fall.

Gravity makes nearly empty bottle stay upright

Bottle with high centre of gravity falls over

GRAVITY FACTS

• The pull of gravity between the Earth, Moon, and Sun causes the oceans' tides.

• Earth's surface gravity is six times stronger than the Moon's surface gravity.

SI UNITS

The **newton** (N) is the SI unit of force: 1 newton of force causes a mass of 1 kilogram to move with an acceleration of 1 metre per second per second.

EINSTEIN'S GENERAL THEORY OF RELATIVITY

Albert Einstein (1879–1955), the German–American physicist, suggested that gravity is a property of space rather than a force of attraction between bodies of matter. He argued that bodies of matter make space curve, causing other bodies to "fall" towards them, and even bend light as it passes around them.

Passing comet

Sun

Space is distorted by Sun's mass like a rubber sheet holding a heavy object

Gravity bends path of comet

MOTION

FROM TINY PARTICLES to the huge planets, the whole universe is in motion. All objects tend to resist effort to change their state of motion, whether they are actually moving or at rest. This is called inertia. On Earth, the force of friction causes moving objects to stop, but in space, objects can continue moving foreve

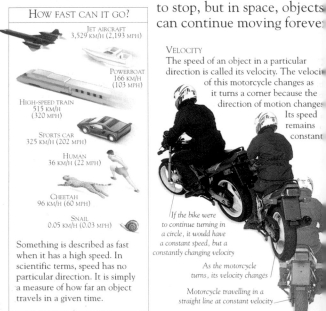

HOW FAST CAN IT GO?

JET AIRCRAFT
3,529 KM/H (2,193 MPH)

POWERBOAT
166 KM/H
(103 MPH)

HIGH-SPEED TRAIN
515 KM/H
(320 MPH)

SPORTS CAR
325 KM/H (202 MPH)

HUMAN
36 KM/H (22 MPH)

CHEETAH
96 KM/H (60 MPH)

SNAIL
0.05 KM/H (0.03 MPH)

Something is described as fast when it has a high speed. In scientific terms, speed has no particular direction. It is simply a measure of how far an object travels in a given time.

VELOCITY
The speed of an object in a particular direction is called its velocity. The veloci of this motorcycle changes as it turns a corner because the direction of motion changes Its speed remains constant

If the bike were to continue turning in a circle, it would have a constant speed, but a constantly changing velocity

As the motorcycle turns, its velocity changes

Motorcycle travelling in a straight line at constant velocity

MOTION FACTS
• The Earth travels through space at 107,000 km/h (66,500 mph).

• Earth's gravity accelerates all falling objects at 9.8 m (32.1 ft) per second per second.

ACCELERATION
An object accelerates as its speed increases. Sprinters accelerate most as they pull out of the starting blocks. They decelerate as they cross the finishing line, and their speed decreases.

OVERCOMING INERTIA AND FRICTION

OVERCOMING INERTIA
Pushing the pedals of a bicycle is harder at first, because you need to overcome both your own inertia and that of the bicycle. Once underway, inertia helps to keep you moving.

OVERCOMING FRICTION
Friction tries to oppose motion. It occurs where surfaces or materials rub together. Unless you keep pedalling, friction will bring your bicycle to a halt. Friction also helps the wheels to grip the road.

Friction helps hands grip handlebars

Brakes use friction to stop

Friction with air slows bicycle and rider

Friction slows pedals and gears

Friction helps tyres grip road

Friction helps feet grip pedals

More motion

Not all motion is "linear" (in a straight line). An object may "oscillate" (move back and forth about a fixed point). It may also have circular motion, caused by "centripetal force", which keeps it moving in a circle. Moving objects have "momentum", which is velocity multiplied by mass.

Ball gains momentum when struck by cue

CONSERVATION OF MOMENTUM

When two objects collide, momentum is transferred between them. If a moving snooker ball strikes a stationary one, the first ball transfers some of its momentum to the second ball, which is set in motion. The total momentum of the two balls is the same as it was before the collision.

White ball strikes red ball, transferring momentum

NEWTON'S LAWS OF MOTION

• **First law**
An object will remain at rest or continue travelling at a uniform velocity unless a force acts on it.

• **Second law**
The acceleration of an object is equal to the force acting on it, divided by the object's mass.

• **Third law**
When one object applies a force on another, the second object exerts an equal and opposite force on the first.

Red ball gains momentum, and moves away

Weight is displaced to left

Weight swings towards equilibrium point

OSCILLATING PENDULUM
In an oscillation, such as a pendulum swing, an object is displaced and then pulled back to its equilibrium position (where no resultant force acts on it) by a force (gravity in the case of the pendulum).

Equilibrium point

Momentum takes weight past equilibr

Athlete pulls on hammer, producing centripetal force

Hammer flies off when released

Centripetal force pulls hammer inwards

Hammer's direction changes constantly

Hammer's inertia pulls it outwards

CIRCULAR MOTION
A whirling object, such as an athletics hammer, tries to fly off in a straight line, but centripetal force pulls the object towards the centre of the circle. This force constantly changes the direction of the object, keeping it moving in a circle.

SPINNING OBJECTS
A spinning object such as a gyroscope has "angular momentum", which gives it stability and makes it resist the force of gravity that tries to topple it. As gravity tries to pull the gyroscope over, its axis moves at right angles to the force of gravity, tracing a small circle.

MORE MOTION FACTS
• A navigational gyrocompass contains a gyroscope that keeps pointing north once it is set in motion.

• A satellite is kept in a circular orbit by the pull of Earth's gravity, which acts as a centripetal force.

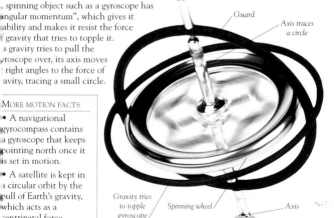

Guard

Axis traces a circle

Gravity tries to topple gyroscope

Spinning wheel

Axis

GYROSCOPE

PRESSURE

THE AIR AROUND us presses on us. At the same time, we push on the ground under our feet. Swimmers can feel the surrounding water press on their bodies. This is called pressure. Pressure measures how "concentrated" a force is when it presses on a particular area.

PINPOINT PRESSURE
It is much easier to push a drawing pin into a wall than a thick nail. This is because the drawing pin concentrates all the force exerted by your thumb onto a very small area.

Thumb presses on pin

2-kg (20-N) block exerts pressure of 80 Pa

Base covers 0.25 m² (25 squares)

MEASURING PRESSURE
It is possible to calculate the amount of pressure exerted by dividing the force applied by the area over which it acts. Increasing the area of the surface or reducing the force acting upon it reduces the pressure. Reducing the area or increasing the force acting upon it increases the pressure.

Base covers 0.50 m² (50 squares)

Base covers 0.25 m² (25 squares)

2-kg (20-N) block exerts pressure of 40 Pa

1-kg (10-N) block exerts pressure of 40 Pa

Grid has squares of area 0.01 m²

HOW AN AIRCRAFT FLIES

The curved upper surface of an aircraft's wing makes the air above it travel faster than the air under it. The faster the air moves, the lower its pressure. The difference in pressure creates "lift", a force which pushes the aircraft off the ground.

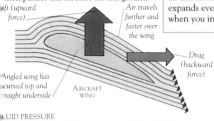

Lift (upward force)

Air travels further and faster over the wing

Drag (backward force)

Angled wing has curved top and straight underside

AIRCRAFT WING

PASCAL'S LAW

Pascal's Law of Fluid Pressures (or Pascal's Principle) states that the pressure is transmitted equally through a fluid (a liquid or a gas) in all directions. This is why a balloon expands evenly in all directions when you inflate it with air.

SI UNITS

The **pascal** (Pa) is the SI unit of pressure: 1 pascal is equal to a force of 1 newton applied to an area of 1 square metre (1 N/m^2).

FLUID PRESSURE

The pressure of a fluid increases with depth. This is why pressures in the deepest oceans are greater than they are just below the surface. Below, holes at different depths allow coloured water out at different pressures.

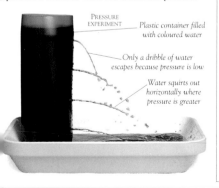

PRESSURE EXPERIMENT

Plastic container filled with coloured water

Only a dribble of water escapes because pressure is low

Water squirts out horizontally where pressure is greater

PRESSURE FACTS

• The pressure at the bottom of the deepest ocean is 1.1 x 10^8 Pa.

• Standard atmospheric pressure at sea level is 101,325 Pa.

• Sharper knives cut better than blunt ones because their blades exert more pressure.

• Snowshoes help you walk on snow, spreading the weight and reducing the pressure underfoot.

SIMPLE MACHINES

MACHINES CAN CHANGE the direction or
size of a force. For example, an axe is a
machine called a wedge that splits a log
easily. The effort used to wield the axe is
sent a long way into the log, pushing it
apart a short distance with a greater force.

*Axe
blade is
a wedge*

AXE SPLITTING
A LOG

Turning effort

SCREW
Turning the head of the screw
moves the whole screw forwards
with a greater force than is
used to turn it.

*Total length
of screw
thread*

*Effort applied
to rim is
magnified
by axle*

WHEEL AND AXLE
Applying a small
effort to the rim
of the wheel makes
the axle turn with
a greater force. A large effort at
the axle means that the rim turns
with less force, but travels further.

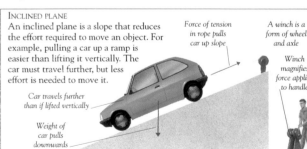

INCLINED PLANE
An inclined plane is a slope that reduces
the effort required to move an object. For
example, pulling a car up a ramp is
easier than lifting it vertically. The
car must travel further, but less
effort is needed to move it.

*Force of tension
in rope pulls
car up slope*

*A winch is a
form of wheel
and axle*

*Winch
magnifies
force applied
to handle*

*Car travels further
than if lifted vertically*

*Weight of
car pulls
downwards*

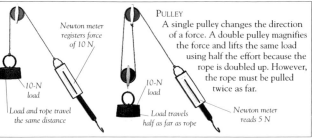

PULLEY

A single pulley changes the direction of a force. A double pulley magnifies the force and lifts the same load using half the effort because the rope is doubled up. However, the rope must be pulled twice as far.

Newton meter registers force of 10 N

10-N load

Load and rope travel the same distance

10-N load

Load travels half as far as rope

Newton meter reads 5 N

SIMPLE LEVER

A lever is a bar that exerts a force by turning on a pivot, or "fulcrum". A small effort moved through a greater distance at one end moves a larger load through a shorter distance at the other end.

Small force is applied

Direction of movement

Large load is moved

Lever magnifies force

Fulcrum

MACHINE EQUATIONS

A machine's force ratio shows how effective the machine is as a force magnifier. The velocity ratio shows how effective the machine is as a distance magnifier.

$$\text{Force ratio} = \frac{\text{load}}{\text{effort}}$$

$$\text{Velocity ratio} = \frac{\text{distance moved by effort}}{\text{distance moved by load}}$$

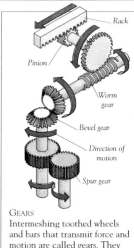

Rack

Pinion

Worm gear

Bevel gear

Direction of motion

Spur gear

GEARS

Intermeshing toothed wheels and bars that transmit force and motion are called gears. They can alter the force's size, and the motion's speed and direction.

ENERGY

EVERYTHING WE DO is fuelled by energy.
Our energy comes from food, which
contains chemical energy stored in
chemical compounds. Light, sound,
heat, and electricity are forms of energy.
Movement energy is called kinetic energy.

If the kitt
falls, it w
have kine
energy

Box has kinetic
energy when opened

POTENTIAL ENERGY

An object gains
potential energy if
it is squeezed or
stretched; the energy
is stored until the
object is released.
The coiled spring
of a jack-in-the-
box has potential
energy. When the
box is opened and
the jack leaps out, the
energy becomes kinetic energy.

GRAVITATIONAL POTENTI

A raised object has
gravitational potential
energy – the potential to
fall back to Earth. If the
kitten loses its grip, this
energy converts to kinet
energy as the kitten
tumbles to the ground.

ENERGY FACTS

• There are about
1,000 million million
joules of heat and
potential energy in
a thunderstorm.

• A teenage girl needs
about 10,000 kJ of
energy each day.

CHEMICAL ENERGY

When we digest
food, chemical
compounds in the
food are broken down and
energy is released for our
bodies to use. Different
foods contain different
amounts of energy. This
chocolate has as much
energy as all these tomatoes.

24 g (0.8 oz) of
milk chocolate

1 kg (2.2
of tomato

ENERGY USE	
TIVITY BY 70-KG PERSON	ENERGY USED IN JOULES PER SECOND (J/s)
eeping	60
tting reading	120
aying the piano	160
alking slowly	250
unning or swimming	800
alking up stairs	800

SI UNITS

The **joule** (J) is the SI unit of energy and work: 1 joule of energy is used when a force of 1 newton moves through a distance of 1 metre. A kilojoule (kJ) is 1,000 J.

The **hertz** (Hz) is the SI unit of wave frequency: 1 hertz is one complete wave, or vibration, per second. A kilohertz (kHz) is 1,000 Hz.

WAVE ENERGY

TYPES OF WAVES

Energy often travels as moving vibrations called waves. Light and other forms f electromagnetic radiation ravel as transverse waves: the ibration is at right angles to he wave's direction. Sound vaves travel as longitudinal vaves: the vibration is in the ame direction as the wave.

TRANSVERSE WAVE

Direction of motion⟶ Amplitude

Peak

Wavelength

Trough

LONGITUDINAL WAVE Wavelength

Direction of motion⟶

IN STEP

Peaks meet peaks

Larger wave results

OUT OF STEP Peaks meet troughs

Waves cancel each other out

INTERFERENCE

When waves meet, they "interfere" with each other. If two waves are in step, their peaks coincide and they combine to form a bigger wave (constructive interference). If the waves are out of step, the troughs cancel out the peaks and there is no resulting wave (destructive interference).

Work, power, efficiency

Work is done when a force moves something.
Work cannot be done without energy. Energy
provides the ability to do work. When work is
done, energy converts from one form to another.
The rate at which work is done, or energy changed
from one form to another, is called power.

Bar carries two
sets of 200-N
weights

Weights are
raised about
1.5 m (4.9 ft)

Total weight
is 400 N

WEIGHTLIFTER
RAISING
WEIGHTS

Raised weights
have gravitational
potential energy

Weightlifter raises
weights in two seconds

WORK AND POW
When this man ra
a heavy weight, the power
lifting the weight is calcula
by multiplying the weight
the height to which it is rais
and dividing the result by
time taken to lift it. So if he
400 newtons by 1.5 metres
two seconds, the power is 300

SI UNITS

The **watt** (W) is the SI
unit of power: 1 W is
the conversion of 1
joule of energy from
one form to another in
1 second. A kilowatt
(kW) is 1,000 watts,
and a megawatt (MW)
is 1,000,000 W.

The **kilowatt-hour**
(kWh) measures
electrical energy use:
1 kWh is energy used
when a 1-kW appliance
runs for 1 hour.

WORK FACTS

• The efficiency of
a 100-watt light bulb
is 15%, because 85
joules in every 100
are lost as heat.

• The first internal
combustion engine wa
built by Étienne Lenoi
a Belgian engineer.

ENERGY CONVERSION

Machines are really "energy converters": they change energy from one form to another to do work. A car is powered by an internal combustion engine, which burns petrol or diesel fuel. The chemical energy in the fuel is converted to the kinetic energy of moving pistons, which make the car move.

INTERNAL COMBUSTION ENGINE

Fuel-air mixture sucked in

Explosion forces piston down

Chemical energy in fuel changes to kinetic energy of moving piston

Piston rises, expelling waste gases, and process starts again

EFFICIENCY

Efficiency tells you how good a machine is as an energy converter. It compares the energy you put into a machine to the energy you get out of it.

MACHINE		ENERGY OUTPUT (% OF INPUT)
Car petrol engine		15%
Rocket		about 15%
Steam train		15%
Jet engine		20%
Diesel train		35%
Electric train		35%
Coal-fired power station		35%
Wind farm		about 40%
Magnetic levitation train		about 60%
Hydroelectric plant		80%
Bicycle		90%

LAW OF CONSERVATION OF ENERGY

Energy can neither be created nor destroyed. The Law of Conservation of Energy states that energy can be converted into different forms, but the total amount of energy always stays the same. This law applies even to nuclear reactions, such as those that occur at the core of the Sun.

ENERGY EQUATIONS

Work (joules) = force (newtons) x distance moved (metres)

$$\text{Power (watts)} = \frac{\text{work done (joules)}}{\text{time taken (seconds)}}$$

$$\text{Efficiency (\%)} = \frac{\text{energy (or power) in}}{\text{energy (or power) out}} \times 100$$

HEAT AND TEMPERATURE

THE MORE ENERGY an object's particles have, the hotter the object is. Heat is the total kinetic energy of an object's moving particles. Temperature is a measure of the average kinetic energy of the particles.

Height of liquid shows temperature

Liquid-crystal display

Heat-sensitive resistor in tip

Meter records temperature of filament

THERMOMETERS
Everyday thermometers measure temperature on the Celsius and Fahrenheit scales. Liquid thermometers use a column of mercury or alcohol that expands as the temperature rises. An electronic thermometer measures temperature with a tiny, heat-sensitive resistor.

PYROMETER
A pyrometer measures high temperatures. When pointed at a hot, glowing object, an electric current heats a filament until the colour matches that of the object. Measuring the electric current reveals the temperature.

Light from glowing object

Electric filament is heated until its colour matches light from hot object

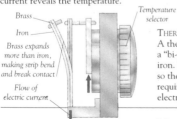

Brass

Iron

Brass expands more than iron, making strip bend and break contact

Flow of electric current

Temperature selector

THERMOSTAT
A thermostat regulates temperature using a "bi-metallic strip" made of brass and iron. The metals expand at different rates so the strip bends as it heats up. At the required temperature, the strip breaks an electrical contact and turns off a heater.

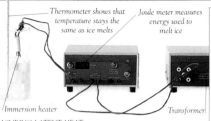

Thermometer shows that temperature stays the same as ice melts

Joule meter measures energy used to melt ice

Immersion heater

Transformer

MEASURING LATENT HEAT

This experiment measures the heat needed to melt ice. As a substance changes state, for example, from solid to liquid, it takes in or gives out heat without changing its temperature. This hidden heat is called "latent" heat.

SI UNITS

The **kelvin** (K) is the SI unit of temperature. There are no minus values on the kelvin scale. This is because 0 K is "absolute zero" – the lowest possible temperature, at which the motion of all particles would cease. Absolute zero has never been attained.

RANGE OF TEMPERATURES

TEMPERATURE	EXAMPLE
14 million K (14 million °C; 25 million °F)	Sun's core
30,000 K (29,727°C; 53,540°F)	Lightning bolts
5,800 K (5,527°C; 9,980°F)	Surface of the Sun
4,000 K (3,727°C; 6,740°F)	Core of the Earth
523 K (250°C; 482°F)	Burning point of wood
373 K (100°C; 212°F)	Boiling point of water
331 K (58°C; 136°F)	Highest recorded air temperature on Earth
310 K (37°C; 98.6°F)	Normal human body temperature
273 K (0°C; 32°F)	Freezing point of water
184 K (−89°C; −128°F)	Lowest recorded air temperature on Earth
43 K (−230°C; −382°F)	Surface temperature of Pluto (most distant planet)
0 K (−273.15°C; −459.67°F)	Absolute zero

SPECIFIC HEAT CAPACITIES

Specific heat capacity (symbol c) is the amount of heat energy needed to raise the temperature of 1 kilogram of a substance by 1 kelvin (or 1°C).

SUBSTANCE	SPECIFIC HEAT CAPACITY (J/kg/K)
Water	4,200
Alcohol	2,400
Ice	2,100
Nylon	1,700
Marble	880
Concrete	800
Glass	630
Steel	450
Copper	380
Lead	130

Heat transfer

Heat energy always passes from hot
objects or materials to cooler ones. Heat
travels through solids by a process called
conduction, and through fluids (liquids
and gases) by convection. Matter can
also lose or gain heat energy by radiation.

Swirling colour trails show how heat spreads through liquid

Hot, coloured water floats to the top of the jar

Bottle contains hot, coloured water

CONVECTION IN WATER

The hot, coloured water is less dense
than the cold water surrounding it. The
hot water floats to the surface and loses
heat to the air. As it cools it sinks once
more. This circulation, or "convection
current", spreads heat through the liquid.

Thermometer reads 18.7°C   *Metal block at room temperature*

MEASURING HEAT RADIATION

At room temperature, all objects emit infrared
radiation: hotter objects emit more radiation
than cooler ones. The lamp in the picture
emits a lot of radiation, which travels through
the air and heats the metal block below.

Desk lamp

Radiation from lamp absorbed by particles in metal block

Heat from feet conducts into ston[e] leaving feet feeling c[old]

CONDUCTION

When one part of a
substance is heated, its
particles vibrate faster.
They "conduct" (pass
on their heat energy)
as they knock against
neighbouring particles.

Thermometer reads 31°C

CELSIUS & FAHRENHEIT

Temperatures are usually given in degrees Celsius (°C) or Fahrenheit (°F). The Celsius scale is based on the freezing point of water (0°C/32°F) and the boiling point of water (100°C/212°F). The kelvin scale is used in scientific work.

THERMAL CONDUCTIVITY

Thermal conductivity tells you the rate of transfer of heat. Here, the temperature of a material is raised through 1 m by 1 K (or 1°C).

SUBSTANCE	CONDUCTIVITY (W/m/K)	
Copper	385	Good conductor
Gold	296	
Iron	72	
Glass	1	
Brick	0.6	
Water	0.6	
Nylon	0.25	
Wood (oak)	0.15	Bad conductor
Concrete	0.1	
Wool	0.040	
Air	0.025	

INSULATORS

Materials that are poor conductors of heat are called insulators. They include plastics, wood, cork, fibreglass, and air. Architects and builders use insulators in houses and offices to reduce the loss of heat through walls, roofs, ceilings, windows, and floors. A good insulating material is said to have a very low "U-value".

Cavity wall filled with polystyrene foam

Fibreglass insulation between ceiling beams

Air trapped between panes of a double-glazed window

Thick carpet on floor

U–VALUES (FOR HEAT CONDUCTION)

U-value (W/m²/K) is a measure of the rate of heat flow in watts (W) per square metre (m²) of a material so that its temperature increases 1 K (or 1°C).

MATERIAL	U–VALUE (W/m²/K)
Roof with no insulation	2.2
Insulated roof	0.3
Single brick wall	3.6
Double brick wall, air cavity between	1.7
Double brick wall filled with foam	0.5
Single-glazed window	5.6
Double-glazed window with air gap	2.7
Floor without carpets	1
Floor with carpets	0.3

ENERGY SOURCES

MOST OF THE WORLD'S electricity is generated by burning fossil fuels. But there are limited supplies of these fuel and they are only replaced over many millions of years. In the future, we will have to rely on renewable sources, such as wind and solar power, and hydroelectricity.

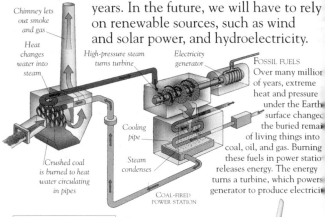

Chimney lets out smoke and gas

Heat changes water into steam

High-pressure steam turns turbine

Electricity generator

Cooling pipe

Steam condenses

Crushed coal is burned to heat water circulating in pipes

COAL-FIRED POWER STATION

FOSSIL FUELS
Over many million of years, extreme heat and pressure under the Earth surface changed the buried remain of living things into coal, oil, and gas. Burning these fuels in power station releases energy. The energy turns a turbine, which powers generator to produce electrici

ENERGY SOURCE FACTS

• Hydroelectricity supplies about 3% of the world's energy needs.

• One gram of coal contains about 25 kJ of energy, and one gram of oil about 45 kJ.

• Most people in the world still use firewood.

WIND POWER
A wind turbine is a tall tower with large rotating blades that harness the wind's kinetic energy to produce electricity. A "wind farm" is a large group of wind turbines.

Blades can be up to 20 m (65 ft) long

As the blades turn in the wind, they power an electricity generator

Lightning conductor

To

HYDROELECTRIC POWER

Hydroelectricity is an efficient, pollution-free energy source. A hydroelectric power station is situated below a dam at the head of a reservoir. Water rushing down from above turns the power station's turbines at great speed. The turbines are connected to generators that produce electricity.

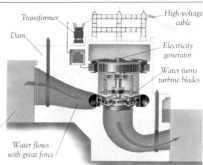

Transformer

High-voltage cable

Dam

Electricity generator

Water turns turbine blades

Water builds up behind dam at end of reservoir

Water flows with great force

SOLAR POWER

Solar cells transform the energy of sunlight into electricity. To generate useful amounts of electricity, solar power stations use hundreds of large mirrored panels that concentrate sunlight onto large solar cells.

ENERGY SOURCES THROUGH TIME

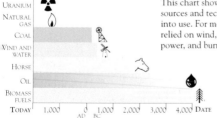

FUELS

URANIUM

NATURAL GAS

COAL

WIND AND WATER

HORSE

OIL

BIOMASS FUELS

TODAY   1,000   0   1,000   2,000   3,000   4,000   DATE
                 AD BC

This chart shows when different energy sources and technologies first came into use. For most of history, people relied on wind, water, and muscle power, and burned biomass fuels (such as wood). Today, non-renewable energy sources, such as coal and oil, are much more commonly used.

Nuclear energy

Atoms are tiny storehouses of energy. This energy comes from strong forces that hold the particles in the centre, or nucleus, of an atom. Tremendous "nuclear" energy can be released when the nucleus of an atom splits (fission), or when two nuclei fuse together (fusion). Nuclear reactors harness this energy to produce electricity.

INTERNATIONAL
WARNING SYMBOL
FOR RADIOACTIVIT

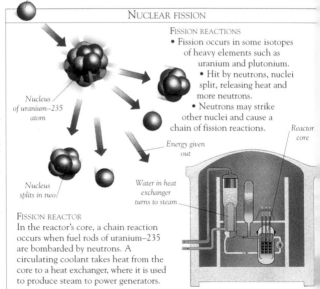

Neutron

NUCLEAR FISSION

FISSION REACTIONS
• Fission occurs in some isotopes of heavy elements such as uranium and plutonium.
• Hit by neutrons, nuclei split, releasing heat and more neutrons.
• Neutrons may strike other nuclei and cause a chain of fission reactions.

Nucleus of uranium–235 atom

Nucleus splits in two

Energy given out

Water in heat exchanger turns to steam

Reactor core

FISSION REACTOR
In the reactor's core, a chain reaction occurs when fuel rods of uranium–235 are bombarded by neutrons. A circulating coolant takes heat from the core to a heat exchanger, where it is used to produce steam to power generators.

NUCLEAR FUSION

FUSION REACTIONS

• Fusion occurs only with isotopes of light elements such as hydrogen.

• At high temperatures, fast-moving hydrogen nuclei smash into each other.

• A helium nucleus forms, and heat and neutrons are released.

Hydrogen nucleus with one neutron (deuterium)

Hydrogen nucleus with two neutrons (tritium)

Helium nucleus forms

Nuclei collide and fuse together

Energy given out

Neutron expelled

Powerful electromagnets

Plasma circulates in the torus

FUSION REACTOR

A practical fusion reactor has not yet been built. Experimental "tokamak" reactors contain a circular tube or "torus". Fusion occurs in the tube when hydrogen plasma is heated to very high temperatures. Powerful electromagnets confine the plasma.

NUCLEAR WEAPONS

The violent power of nuclear weapons comes from a fission or fusion reaction. The nuclear reaction in the bomb changes a tiny amount of mass into a vast amount of destructive energy.

Mushroom-shaped cloud of smoke and flames

NUCLEAR FACTS

• The first nuclear reactor was built by the physicist Enrico Fermi in the USA in 1942.

• Nuclear fusion occurs in the heart of the Sun and other stars.

• The USA has the most nuclear reactors (109) in the world.

ELECTROMAGNETIC RADIATION

LIGHT IS ONE of several types of wave energy called electromagnetic radiation. This radiation also includes radio waves, microwaves, infrared rays, ultraviolet rays, X-rays, and gamma rays. Together, they form the electromagnetic spectrum.

ELECTROMAGNETIC RADIATION AS WAVES AND PARTICLES

Electric field
Wavelength
Direction of travel
Magnetic field

RED LIGHT PHOTON
Longer wavelength, less energy

BLUE LIGHT PHOTON
Shorter wavelength, more energy

WAVES
Electromagnetic radiation travels as waves of oscillating (fluctuating) electric and magnetic fields. These are at right angles to each other and to the direction of travel.

PARTICLES
Electromagnetic radiation also travels as a stream of particles called photons – tiny "energy packets" given off when charged particles lose energy.

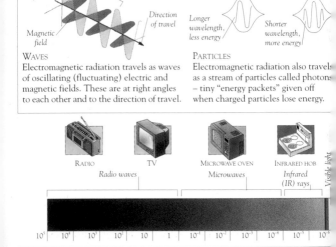

RADIO

TV

MICROWAVE OVEN

INFRARED HOB

Radio waves

Microwaves

Infrared (IR) rays

Visible light

| 10^5 | 10^4 | 10^3 | 10^2 | 10 | 1 | 10^{-1} | 10^{-2} | 10^{-3} | 10^{-4} | 10^{-5} | 10^{-6} |

TABLE OF USEFUL X-RAYS	
WAVELENGTH (M) OF X-RAYS	USES AND APPLICATIONS
3 x 10⁻¹³	Killing deep cancer tumours
3 x 10⁻¹²	Inspecting welded joints in steel pipes
1.8 x 10⁻¹¹	Diagnostic chest X-rays
6 x 10⁻⁹	Treatment of skin diseases

COMMON PROPERTIES OF ELECTROMAGNETIC WAVES

All types of electromagnetic radiation:
• Transfer energy from place to place
• Can be emitted and absorbed by matter
• Do not need a material medium to travel through
• Travel at 3 x 10⁸ m/s in a vacuum
• Are transverse waves
• Can be polarized
• Can produce interference effects
• Can be reflected and refracted
• Can be diffracted
• Carry no electric charge.

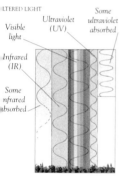

FILTERED LIGHT

Visible light
Ultraviolet (UV)
Some ultraviolet absorbed
Infrared (IR)
Some infrared absorbed

FILTERED LIGHT
Electromagnetic radiation reaches us from the Sun, stars, and galaxies. The Earth's atmosphere absorbs most types of electromagnetic radiation, but allows radio waves and light to pass through. Some wavelengths of IR and UV are filtered out before reaching the ground.

UV SUNBED — Ultraviolet (UV) rays
X-RAY MACHINE — X-rays
NUCLEAR EXPLOSION — Gamma rays

ELECTROMAGNETIC SPECTRUM

Waves at this end of the spectrum have more energy

WAVELENGTH (IN METRES)

10⁻⁹ 10⁻¹⁰ 10⁻¹¹ 10⁻¹² 10⁻¹³ 10⁻¹⁴ 10⁻¹⁵ 10⁻¹⁶ 10⁻¹⁷

LIGHT SOURCES

LIGHT IS A FORM of energy. It is produced
by two processes – incandescence
and luminescence. Incandescence
is the emission of light by hot
objects. Luminescence is
the emission of light
without using heat.

*Electron gives out photon as
it falls back to its original orbit*

LIGHT FROM THE SUN

Most of the light that reaches
us from space comes from the
Sun. Light is produced in the
Sun by incandescence. The light
travels through space at 300,000 km
per second (186,000 miles per second).

PHOTONS

If an atom gains energy, electrons
orbiting the nucleus jump to higher
orbits, or "energy levels". When the
electrons return to their original
orbits, they release photons of light
or other electromagnetic radiation.

LUMINESCENCE	
TYPE	EXAMPLE
Triboluminescence Light released by friction	When some crystals, such as sugar, are suddenly crushed, the friction makes them briefly emit light.
Bioluminescence The emission of light without heat by living organisms	Creatures such as fireflies have chemicals in their bodies that combine to release light energy.
Phosphorescence The gradual emission of stored energy as light	Glow-in-the-dark paints absorb light energy and release it slowly. The light energy is especially noticeable in the dark.
Fluorescence The rapid re-emission of light energy	Fluorescent dyes often contain fluorescent chemicals that briefly absorb ultraviolet light and then emit it as visible light.

Glowing
filament

Unreactive
gas

Bulb screws
into electrical
socket

INCANDESCENCE

An incandescent bulb
contains a thin filament of
tungsten wire. An electric
current heats the filament
so that it glows white and
gives off light. The bulb is
filled with an unreactive
gas such as argon to stop
the filament burning up,
as it would do in air.

LIGHT SOURCE FACTS

• Fireflies produce
light to attract mates.

• Prehistoric peoples
used stone lamps that
burned animal fat.

• Laser stands for
"Light Amplification
by Stimulated Emission
of Radiation".

light reflects up
and down tube

Beam leaves through
partly silvered mirror

Power supply − +

Photons
of light

LASER LIGHT

A laser produces pure
light of intense heat and
energy. Light from a
coiled tube "excites"
atoms in a central tube
of "lasing medium". The
light that these "excited"
atoms produce is reflected
between the tube's
mirrored ends, escaping
as an intense laser beam.

SI UNITS

• The **candela** (cd) is the SI unit
of brightness (luminous intensity).
A light source of 1 candela
is approximately equal to the
brightness of a burning candle.

• The **lux** (lx) is the SI unit of
illumination. A 1-candela light
source gives an illumination of 1 lux
to a surface of 1 m² (10.8 sq ft)
at a distance of 1 m (3.28 ft).

DISCHARGE TUBE

A discharge tube is a
gas-filled tube fitted
with two electrodes.
When a powerful
electric current flows
between the electrodes,
the vapour gives out,
or "discharges", light.
Most street lamps
use sodium vapour
discharge tubes.

Sodium
vapour
in discharge
tube glows
with yellow-
orange light

Electrode

SODIUM
VAPOUR
LAMP

LIGHT AND MATTER

A MATERIAL appears shiny, dull, or clear depending
on whether it reflects, absorbs, or
transmits light rays. Light may
bend as it passes through
materials, creating optical
illusions such as mirages.

Transparent
(clear)

Translucent
(milky)

Opaque
(dull)

Reflective
(shiny)

LIGHT PASSING THROUGH MATTER
Light passes through transparent materials.
Opaque materials block light. Translucent
materials let light through, but scatter it. Light
rays bounce off the surface of reflective materials.

REFRACTIVE INDEX

When a light ray passes through a
material, its speed changes. If it enters
the material at an angle, the difference
in speed "refracts", or bends, the light
ray. The refractive index shows
how much a material reflects light:

Refractive = Speed of light in vacuum
index   Speed of light in material

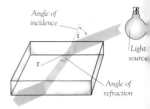

Angle of
incidence

i

Light
source

r

Angle of
refraction

MATERIAL	REFRACTIVE INDEX	SPEED OF LIGHT (KM/S)
Air	1.00	300,000 (186,000 miles)
Water	1.33	225,000 (140,000 miles)
Perspex	1.40	210,000 (130,000 miles)
Glass (variable)	1.60	185,000 (115,000 miles)
Diamond	2.40	125,000 (78,000 miles)

The refractive index can
also be calculated from
the angles in the diagram,
using an equation known
as Snell's Law:

Refractive = Sin i
index   Sin r

INTERNAL REFLECTION OF LIGHT

If a light ray enters a material at a shallow enough angle (called the "critical angle"), it is refracted so much that it does not emerge from the material, but is reflected inside it.

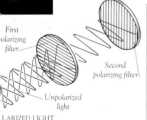

Rays hit sides at shallow angle

No light escapes as ray is reflected

Ray hits end of bar at steep angle

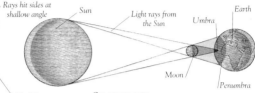

Sun

Rays travel in straight lines in cool air

Light rays from the Sun

Earth

Umbra

Moon

Penumbra

SOLAR ECLIPSE

During a solar eclipse, the Moon, because it is opaque, casts a shadow over the Earth. No rays reach the shadow's centre (umbra); some rays reach its outer area (penumbra).

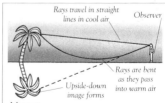

Rays travel in straight lines in cool air

Observer

Rays are bent as they pass into warm air

Upside-down image forms

First polarizing filter

Second polarizing filter

Unpolarized light

POLARIZED LIGHT

Light rays vibrate in many different planes. A polarizing filter only allows light vibrating in one plane to pass. A second filter can be used to block out the remaining light. Sunglasses may use polarizing filters to cut out glare.

MIRAGE

Light is refracted as it passes through layers of air at different temperatures. Light rays travelling from the palm tree to the ground are bent upwards by the warm air so that it seems to an observer that the tree has a watery reflection.

LENSES AND MIRRORS

LENSES ARE CURVED transparent materials that make light rays converge (come together) or diverge (spread out). Mirrors are shiny materials that reflect light. Curved mirrors can also make light rays converge or diverge.

Magnified image

Magnifying glass

MAGNIFYING WITH A LARGE CONVEX LENS

MAKING LARGER

This stamp looks much bigger when an outwardly curving convex lens is held above it. The lens bends light rays from the stamp inwards before they reach your eyes. Your brain assumes that the rays have travelled in a straight line, as if they were coming from a much larger stamp. The more curved a lens, the more it magnifies an object.

MAKING SMALLER

An inwardly curving concave lens gives a reduced image of the squares. It makes light rays from the squares spread, but your brain assumes they have travelled in a straight line, as if they were coming from much smaller squares.

CONVEX AND CONCAVE LENSES

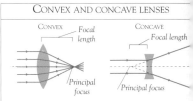

CONVEX — Focal length

CONCAVE — Focal length

Principal focus

Principal focus

A convex lens converges parallel light rays at the principal focus. The distance from here to the centre of the lens is the focal length. A concave le[ns] spreads out light rays so that they appear to come from a principal focus behind the lens. The focal length is the distance from here to the lens' centr[e]

VIRTUAL IMAGE

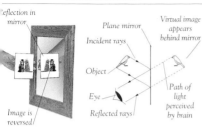

Reflection in mirror

Image is reversed

Plane mirror

Incident rays

Object

Eye

Reflected rays

Virtual image appears behind mirror

Path of light perceived by brain

When you see an object in a mirror, light rays from the object reflect from the mirror's surface into your eyes. Your brain assumes that the rays have reached your eyes by travelling in a straight line, so you see a "virtual" image that appears to be behind the mirror.

LAW OF REFLECTION

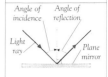

Angle of incidence

Angle of reflection

Light ray

Plane mirror

According to the Law of Reflection, the angle at which a light ray is reflected from a surface (the angle of reflection) is equal to the angle at which the light ray strikes the surface (the angle of incidence).

REAL IMAGES

Convex lenses and concave mirrors can focus light to form an inverted "real" image on a surface. In a movie projector, light shines through an inverted film. This is so that the image projected onto the screen appears the right way up.

CONVEX AND CONCAVE MIRRORS

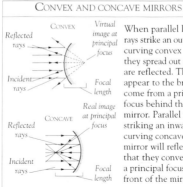

CONVEX

Reflected rays

Incident rays

Virtual image at principal focus

Focal length

CONCAVE

Reflected rays

Incident rays

Real image at principal focus

Focal length

When parallel light rays strike an outwardly curving convex mirror, they spread out as they are reflected. The rays appear to the brain to come from a principal focus behind the mirror. Parallel rays striking an inwardly curving concave mirror will reflect so that they converge at a principal focus in front of the mirror.

VISIBLE SPECTRUM

LIGHT IS WAVES of electromagnetic radiation. "White" light" is a mixture of many different colours of light, each with its own frequency and wavelength. These colours make up the visible spectrum. Our eyes and brains detect colours by recognizing the different wavelengths of visible light.

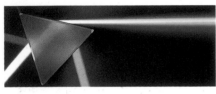

SPLITTING LIGHT

A beam of white light is refracted (bent) as it enters and leaves a prism. The prism refracts different wavelengths of light by different amounts, splitting the beam of white light into the visible spectrum.

LIGHT, COLOUR, AND HEAT

The atoms of a hot object give out infrared radiation and some red light. As the object gets hotter, its atoms give out shorter and shorter wavelengths and it appears orange and then yellow. Very hot objects give out the whole spectrum and appear white.

Atoms emit light at red end of spectrum

Hotter atoms emit orange light

Heated further, atoms emit yellow light

The hottest atoms now emit white light

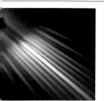

FFRACTION COLOURS

ll forms of wave energy
ffract", or spread out,
en they pass through
os or around objects.
diffraction grating is
glass slide engraved
th narrow slits. Light
ys diffract as they pass
rough the slits, and
terference between
e bent rays produces
eaks of different colours.

SKY COLOUR

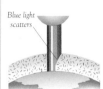

Blue light
scatters

Sunlight passes
through
atmosphere

BLUE SKIES
The Sun gives off
pure white light which
is scattered by air
molecules as it enters
the Earth's atmosphere.
Blue light is scattered
more than other
colours, making the
sky appear blue.

RED SKIES
When the setting Sun
is low in the sky, light
from the blue end of the
spectrum is scattered.
The Sun appears orange-
red because colours from
this end of the spectrum
pass through to our eyes
but blue colours are lost.

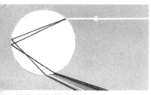

MARY RAINBOW

rainbow is visible during heavy rain,
en the Sun is behind you. As rays of
light pass through raindrops in the
the raindrops act like tiny prisms.
e white light is split into a spectrum
ide the raindrops and reflected back
an arc of colours.

COLOUR WAVELENGTHS AND FREQUENCIES

The wavelengths and frequencies of
the different colours vary according to
the energy they carry. For example, red
light has less energy than violet light.

COLOUR	WAVELENGTH (M)	FREQUENCY (Hz)
Violet	$3.9–4.5 \times 10^{-7}$	$6.7–7.7 \times 10^{14}$
Blue	$4.5–4.9 \times 10^{-7}$	$6.1–6.7 \times 10^{14}$
Green	$4.9–5.8 \times 10^{-7}$	$5.3–6.1 \times 10^{14}$
Yellow	$5.8–6.0 \times 10^{-7}$	$5.1–5.3 \times 10^{14}$
Orange	$6.0–6.2 \times 10^{-7}$	$4.8–5.1 \times 10^{14}$
Red	$6.2–7.7 \times 10^{-7}$	$3.9–4.8 \times 10^{14}$

Mixing colour

Paints, dyes, inks, and coloured objects get their particular colour because they absorb some light wavelengths but reflect others. This is called the subtractive process. In the additive process, colours are created by mixing different-coloured light. Each process has three pure "primary" colours, which cannot be produced by mixing other colours.

RED LIGHT

Red and blue give magenta

Red, blue, and green give white

THE ADDITIVE PROCESS

Red, green, and blue are the primary additive colours. Mixing the three together gives white light. When two primary colours are mixed, the eye sees a mixture of colours that the brain interprets as a single colour, called a secondary colour. In the additive process, the secondary colours are yellow, cyan, and magenta.

GREEN LIGHT

BLUE LIGHT

Red and green give yellow

Blue and green give cyan

In white light, shoes reflect only red light and absorb all the other colours

WHITE LIGHT

In blue light, red pigment absorbs blue light and shoes look nearly black

BLUE LIGHT

COLOUR FILTERS

A colour filter will absorb some colours but let others pass through. Placing a blue filter over a spotlight gives blue light. The filter absorbs the green and red parts of the spectrum and allows only blue light to pass. These shoes look very different in blue light.

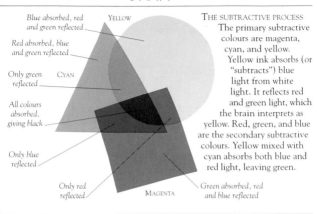

THE SUBTRACTIVE PROCESS
The primary subtractive colours are magenta, cyan, and yellow.
Yellow ink absorbs (or "subtracts") blue light from white light. It reflects red and green light, which the brain interprets as yellow. Red, green, and blue are the secondary subtractive colours. Yellow mixed with cyan absorbs both blue and red light, leaving green.

Diagram labels:
- Blue absorbed, red and green reflected — YELLOW
- Red absorbed, blue and green reflected — CYAN
- Only green reflected
- All colours absorbed, giving black
- Only blue reflected
- Only red reflected — MAGENTA
- Green absorbed, red and blue reflected

FOUR-COLOUR PRINTING

YELLOW   MAGENTA   CYAN   BLACK

- Black is treated as separate colour
- Overprinted inks give full-colour image
- PRINTED IMAGE

FOUR-COLOUR PRINTING
Colour printing reproduces an image in yellow, magenta, and cyan. When printed over each other, these three colours make all the colours in the original image. The image is overprinted in black to make the outlines look sharper. A separate printing plate is needed for each colour.

OPTICAL INSTRUMENTS

TELESCOPES BRING distant stars into view, while microscopes enable us to examine minute objects in great detail. Optical instruments use lenses and mirrors to reveal a world that would be quite impossible to see with the naked eye alone.

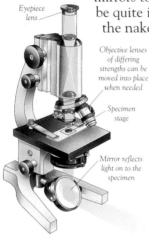

Eyepiece lens

Objective lenses of differing strengths can be moved into place when needed

Specimen stage

Mirror reflects light on to the specimen

COMPOUND MICROSCOPE

A compound microscope has more than one lens. First, it magnifies an object with a powerful "objective" lens. Then, the magnified image is enlarged by the eyepiece lens, which acts as a simple magnifying glass. The microscope may be fitted with extra lenses to give greater clarity.

TYPES OF TELESCOPE

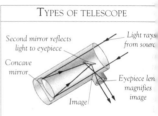

Second mirror reflects light to eyepiece

Light rays from source

Concave mirror

Eyepiece lens magnifies image

Image

REFLECTING TELESCOPES

A reflecting telescope forms an image using a large concave mirror that gathers and concentrates light rays.

Eyepiece lens magnifies image

Light rays from source

Image

Objective lens gathers light

REFRACTING TELESCOPES

A refracting telescope uses a convex lens to refract light and form an upside-down image of a distant object.

BINOCULARS

A pair of binoculars consists of two compact refracting telescopes joined together. Each telescope contains two prisms. The prisms reflect light rays from a distant object to form an image that can be focused with an eyepiece lens.

adjustable epiece lens

Prisms lengthen distance travelled by light rays

Prisms "fold up" the light, king binoculars very compact

Viewfinder

Prism reflects light

Light enters lens

KON

LR CAMERA

an SLR (single-lens reflex) mera, light enters the camera rough the main lens. A mirror flects the light up through a prism d out of the viewfinder. Pressing e shutter release button raises the irror, so that light strikes the film the back of the camera.

Mirror Film

NDOSCOPE

octors look inside the body using a long be called an endoscope. One end of the be is fed into the body. Optical fibres in the be carry light to and from the area being amined, which is seen with an eyepiece lens.

octor sees mage in piece lens

Light is internally reflected in the optical fibres

Light enters body through optical fibres

MAGNIFICATION

A telescope with a magnification of 100x forms an image that is 100 times larger than the object appears without the telescope. Magnification equals the focal length of the objective lens divided by the focal length of the eyepiece.

SOUND WAVES

SOUND WAVES ARE the vibrations that occur in a material as a sound passes through it. When we listen to someone speak, our ears detect sound waves in the air around us caused by the person's vibrating vocal chords. Sound waves can travel through solids, liquids and gases, but not through a vacuum, because there are no particles of matter to transmit the vibrations.

COMPOSITION OF SOUND WAVES

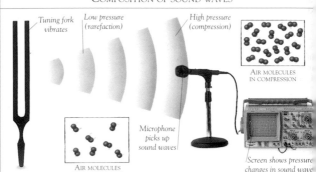

Tuning fork vibrates

Low pressure (rarefaction)

High pressure (compression)

AIR MOLECULES IN COMPRESSION

Microphone picks up sound waves

AIR MOLECULES IN RAREFACTION

Screen shows pressure changes in sound wave

COMPRESSIONS
A vibrating tuning fork causes pressure variations in the surrounding air. As the prongs move outwards, they squeeze the air, creating a high-pressure area called a compression.

RAREFACTIONS
As the prongs move inwards the air expands, creating a low-pressure area called a rarefaction. These rarefactions and compressions travel through air as sound waves.

Echoes bounce back from wall

Clapping sets off sound waves

MAKING ECHOES

...ounds bounce off hard surfaces and return ...their source as echoes. Most sounds we ...ar are a combination of the original sound ...d echoes bouncing off nearby objects.

THE SPEED OF SOUND

...ound travels at different speeds through ...fferent materials. Sound also travels faster ...t higher temperatures. Unless stated, all ...igures are for substances at 20°C (68°F).

Substance	Speed m/sec	Speed ft/sec
...ubber	54	177
...arbon dioxide	260	853
...ir at 0°C	331	1,086
...ir at 20°C	343	1,125
...ir at 100°C	390	1,280
...ork	500	1,640
...ater at 0°C	1,284	4,213
...ydrogen	1,286	4,219
...ater at 20°C	1,483	4,865
...ood (oak)	3,850	12,631
...eel	5,060	16,601

HOW SONAR WORKS

A ship's sonar system emits ultrasound waves, which have a frequency above 20,000 Hz. The sound waves bounce off underwater objects. The time between sending the wave and receiving its echo reveals the depth of the object.

Ultrasound pulse reflected by wreck

Sound waves pile up when a jet travels at speed of sound

Shock wave released as jet breaks sound barrier

SONIC BOOM

When an aircraft breaks the sound barrier, sound waves build up in front of the aircraft. The sound forms as a massive shock wave. It is heard on the ground as a "sonic boom".

Measuring sound

The loudness of a sound depends on changes in pressure. The greater the pressure changes between the highest and lowest point of the sound wave, the louder the sound. The loudness of a sound is measured in decibels. The pitch of a sound describes how high or low a sound is. It depends on the frequency (vibrations per second) of the sound waves. The frequency of waves, including sound, light and radio waves, is measured in hertz (Hz).

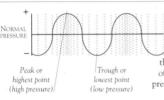

NORMAL
PRESSURE

Peak or
highest point
(high pressure)

Trough or
lowest point
(low pressure)

PLOTTING SOUND WAVES
The shape of a sound wave plotted on a graph is called a waveform. The peaks and troughs of the waveform correspond to the regions of high pressure (compressions) and low pressure (rarefactions) in the sound wave.

SOFT SOUNDS
The waveform produced by a quiet sound shows little difference between the low- and high-pressure regions.

LOUD SOUNDS
As a sound gets louder, the difference between the low- and the high-pressure regions becomes much greater.

LOW-PITCHED SOUNDS
The waveform of a low-pitched sound shows few waves per second, because it has a low frequency.

HIGH-PITCHED SOUNDS
As the pitch of a sound increases, its frequency rises and the waveform shows more waves per second.

EXAMPLES ON THE DECIBEL SCALE

LOUDNESS IN DECIBELS (dB)	AMPLITUDE IN PASCALS (Pa)	POWER (INTENSITY) IN WATTS PER SQUARE METRE (W/m²)	SOUND
140	300	100	Permanent ear damage; rocket taking off 100 m (328 ft) away
120	30	1	Pain threshold; jet aircraft taking off 100 m (328 ft) away
100	3	10^{-2}	Rock concert
80	0.3	10^{-4}	Door slamming in room; busy traffic in street
60	0.03	10^{-6}	Normal conversation
30	0.0009	10^{-9}	People whispering 1 m (3.28 ft) away
10	0.00009	10^{-11}	Falling leaves 1 m (3.28 ft) away
0	0.00002	10^{-12}	Threshold of human hearing; sound just audible

ANIMAL SOUNDS

Most animals hear more frequencies of sound than they can produce. Compared with many animals, the range of sounds produced by humans is very limited. Sound below the range of human hearing is called infrasound.

BAT MAKES
10,000–120,000 Hz
HEARS
1,000–120,000 Hz

DOG MAKES
450–1,080 Hz
HEARS
15–50,000 Hz

HUMAN MAKES
85–1,100 Hz
HEARS
20–20,000 Hz

GRASSHOPPER MAKES
7,000–100,000 Hz
HEARS
100–15,000 Hz

THE DECIBEL

Loudness is measured in decibels. The decibel scale is logarithmic, meaning that a sound increase of 10 dB multiplies the intensity by 10 times. So a 20 dB increase corresponds to a sound 10 x 10 = 100 times louder.

Sound quality

If you play the same note on a piano and a guitar, the notes have different sound, because they have a different "tone", or quality. Tone depends on the way an instrument vibrates. "Pitch" is used describe how high or low a sound is. The "acoustics" of a building refers to the way it preserves the quality of sounds made within i

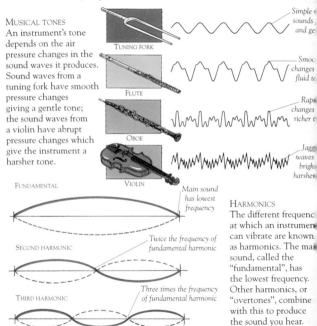

MUSICAL TONES
An instrument's tone depends on the air pressure changes in the sound waves it produces. Sound waves from a tuning fork have smooth pressure changes giving a gentle tone; the sound waves from a violin have abrupt pressure changes which give the instrument a harsher tone.

TUNING FORK

FLUTE

OBOE

VIOLIN

Simple
sounds
and ge

Smoo
changes
fluid to

Rap
changes
richer t

Jagg
waves
brigh
harshe

FUNDAMENTAL

Main sound
has lowest
frequency

SECOND HARMONIC

Twice the frequency of
fundamental harmonic

THIRD HARMONIC

Three times the frequency
of fundamental harmonic

HARMONICS
The different frequenc
at which an instrumen
can vibrate are known
as harmonics. The ma
sound, called the
"fundamental", has
the lowest frequency.
Other harmonics, or
"overtones", combine
with this to produce
the sound you hear.

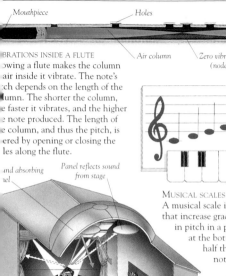

Mouthpiece *Holes*

Air column *Zero vibration (node)* *Peak of vibration (antinode)*

BRATIONS INSIDE A FLUTE
owing a flute makes the column
air inside it vibrate. The note's
ch depends on the length of the
umn. The shorter the column,
e faster it vibrates, and the higher
e note produced. The length of
e column, and thus the pitch, is
ered by opening or closing the
les along the flute.

and absorbing *Panel reflects sound from stage*
nel

MUSICAL SCALES
A musical scale is a sequence of notes
that increase gradually and regularly
in pitch in a pleasing way. The note
at the bottom of the scale has
half the frequency of the
note at the top.

Reflecting panel

ARCHITECTURAL ACOUSTICS
preserve the quality of musical sounds, concert
ls are built so that the echoes of sound waves can
controlled. The building materials absorb just the
nt amount of sound, while special sound panels inside
hall are used to direct the sound towards listeners.

lding materials
carefully chosen

SOUND FACTS

• The science of
architectural acoustics
was founded by an
American physicist
named Wallace Sabine
(1868–1919).

• On a piano, the note
called "middle C" has a
frequency of 256 Hz.

SOUND RECORDING

ALL SOUND RECORDING systems store sound by makin copies of sound waves, either as magnetic patterns or tape, a spiral groove on a record, or as tiny pits in a compact disc. A recording system uses a microphone to convert sound waves into electrical signals.

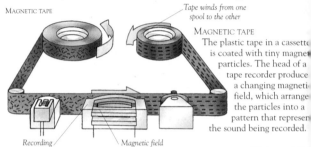

MAGNETIC TAPE

Tape winds from one spool to the other

MAGNETIC TAPE
The plastic tape in a cassette is coated with tiny magnet particles. The head of a tape recorder produce a changing magneti field, which arrange the particles into a pattern that represen the sound being recorded.

Recording head

Magnetic field aligns particles

Wire coil forms electromagnet

Permanent magnet

Diaphragm of thin plastic or metal foil

RECORDING FACTS

• The first sound recording was made by the American inventor Thomas Edison in 1877. His "phonograph" recorded sound as grooves cut into a wax-coated cylinder.

• The first magnetic recording was made in Denmark in 1898.

MICROPHONE
In a moving-coil microphone, sound waves cause a wire coil to vibrate within a magnetic field. This makes an electric current flow through the coil. The current fluctuates in strength as the sound waves change, producing electrical signals that mirror the sound waves.

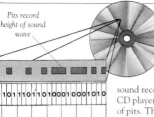

Pits record height of sound wave

101101101010001000101 0

COMPACT DISC

A compact disc (CD) is a plastic disc with pits pressed into its surface. The pits store sound waves as a sequence of binary numbers created by digital sound recording. As the disc spins, a laser in the CD player scans the disc and "reads" the sequence of pits. The CD player translates them into electrical pulses and feeds them to a loudspeaker.

Diaphragm
Electromagnet
Permanent magnet

LOUDSPEAKER

Feeding electrical signals to a loudspeaker generates a varying magnetic field around an electromagnet. The magnet is attached to a diaphragm. The varying field causes the diaphragm to vibrate, producing sound waves.

RECORDS

Stylus *Pick-up head*

Sound can be stored as a continuous wobbling groove around a vinyl record. The stylus of a record player vibrates as it moves along the groove, setting up electrical signals in the pick-up head. The signals are then fed to loudspeakers.

SAMPLING

Sound picked up by microphone

Sound stored in memory

Sound played back on keyboard

A sampling system records sounds and stores them digitally. The sounds are played back through a keyboard. Pressing a key makes the system alter the pitch of a sound to match the pitch of that key. This means that the same sound can be played across a whole musical scale.

MAGNETISM

THERE IS AN invisible force exerted by magnets and electric currents called magnetism. Magnets attract iron and a few other metals, and attract or repel other magnets. Every magnet has two ends, called its north and south poles, where the forces it exerts are strongest.

MAGNETIC FORCES AT WORK

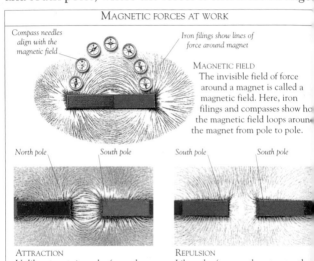

Compass needles align with the magnetic field

Iron filings show lines of force around magnet

MAGNETIC FIELD
The invisible field of force around a magnet is called a magnetic field. Here, iron filings and compasses show how the magnetic field loops around the magnet from pole to pole.

North pole

South pole

South pole

South pole

ATTRACTION
Unlike or opposite poles (a north pole and a south pole) attract each other. Iron filings scattered near the magnets reveal the lines of force running directly between the poles.

REPULSION
Like poles (two north or two south poles) repel each other. The iron filings show how the lines of magnetic force veer sharply away from each other when two like poles meet.

MAGNETIC INDUCTION

Magnetic objects contain "domains" – tiny regions of magnetism, each with two poles. The domains' poles point in all directions, so there is no overall magnetism. A magnetic field lines up the domains, magnetizing the object.

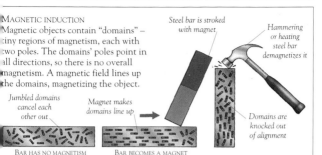

Steel bar is stroked with magnet

Hammering or heating steel bar demagnetizes it

Jumbled domains cancel each other out

Magnet makes domains line up

Domains are knocked out of alignment

BAR HAS NO MAGNETISM

BAR BECOMES A MAGNET

THE EARTH – A GIANT MAGNET

Earth's core of molten iron gives the planet its own magnetic field. The magnetic north and south poles are located near the geographic poles. The north pole of a magnet always points magnetic north.

Magnetic south is near geographic south

Earth's axis runs through geographic poles

Magnetic field is strongest near magnetic poles

MAGNETIC FACTS

• Earth's magnetic poles are at 70° N, 100° W and 68° S, 143° E, but they change constantly.

• The most magnetic substance is neodymium iron boride ($Nd_2Fe_{14}B$).

• The ancient Chinese may have made magnets by heating iron bars and letting them cool while aligned north–south.

NATURALLY MAGNETIC

Lodestone is a natural magnet. It is a form of the mineral magnetite (iron oxide). Its name means "guiding stone" and it was used in compasses 1,500 years ago.

STATIC ELECTRICITY

ELECTRICITY THAT does not flow
is static electricity. A static charge
can be produced by rubbing
a balloon against an object such
as a sweater. Electrons are
transferred from the sweater's
atoms onto the balloon's
atoms. The balloon gains a
negative electric charge and
the sweater a positive one.

BALLOON
CHARGED
RUBBING
(FRICTION)

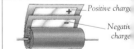

ELECTROSTATIC INDUCTION
This charged balloon can induce a
static electric charge in these pieces
of paper. The balloon's negative
charge repels electrons from the
paper's surface, giving the paper's
surface a positive charge.
Unlike charges attract, so the
balloon picks up the paper.

Balloon
induces
charge in
paper

ELECTRIC FIELD
The area in which a
charged object exerts a
force on other objects is
called an electric field.
Here, a charged plastic
spoon induces an opposite
charge in a nearby flow of
water. Force of attraction
causes the flow to bend.

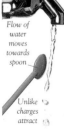

Flow of
water
moves
towards
spoon

Unlike
charges
attract

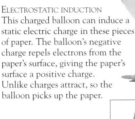

Positive charge

Negative
charge

CAPACITOR
Many electronic devices use
capacitors to build up charge
and store it until it is needed.
Inside a capacitor are two metal
plates separated by an insulator.

N DE GRAAFF GENERATOR
is machine generates static
ctricity. A charged metal comb
uces a positive charge in a moving
t. When the belt reaches the metal
ne, it strips electrons from the metal,
ing the dome a huge positive charge.

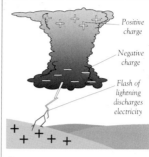

Positive charge

Negative charge

Flash of lightning discharges electricity

LIGHTNING
The tremendous build-up of static
electricity inside a thundercloud
induces a positive charge in the
ground below. Eventually, electricity
discharges from the cloud's base to
the ground and back again (forked
lightning), or within clouds (usually
sheet lightning).

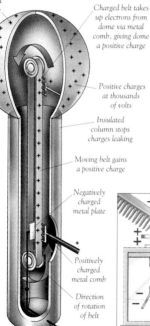

Charged belt takes up electrons from dome via metal comb, giving dome a positive charge

Positive charges at thousands of volts

Insulated column stops charges leaking

Moving belt gains a positive charge

Negatively charged metal plate

Positively charged metal comb

Direction of rotation of belt

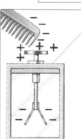

A gold-leaf electroscope detects electric charge

ELECTROSCOPE
A negatively charged comb
touching the rod repels
the rod's electrons to the
leaves. The leaves gain
electrons and each has a
negative charge. The leaves
push each other apart
since like charges repel.

CURRENT ELECTRICITY

AN ELECTRIC CURRENT is a flow of electric charge. In a simple circuit a battery moves negatively charged electrons through metal wires. Electricity can only flow through materials called conductors. Metals are good conductors – they contain free electrons that can move easily.

INSULATED ELECTRIC CABLE

Electrons stay with atoms in insulator *Free electrons in copper wire conductor*

INSULATORS
Electrical insulators block the flow of electric current, because their atoms have no free electrons. Plastics are good insulators and are used to cover conducting wires.

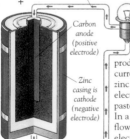

Current flows from negative to positive

+

Carbon anode (positive electrode)

Zinc casing is cathode (negative electrode)

−

Electric current lights bulb

BATTERY
This battery produces an electric current using carbon and zinc conductors called electrodes and a chemical paste called an electrolyte. In a circuit, the current flows from the negative electrode (cathode) to the positive (anode).

CURRENT FACTS
• "Semiconductors" are materials that are insulators when cold, and become conductors when warm.
• "Superconductors" are metals and some ceramics that become very good conductors at temperatures close to absolute zero.

SI UNITS
The **ampere** or **amp** (A) is the SI unit of electric current.

The **coulomb** (C) is the SI unit of electric charge. A current of 1 amp carries a charge of 1 coulomb per second.

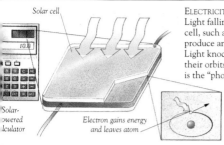

Solar cell

Solar-powered calculator

Electron gains energy and leaves atom

ELECTRICITY FROM SUNLIGHT

Light falling onto a "photovoltaic" cell, such as a solar cell, can produce an electric current. Light knocks electrons out of their orbits around atoms. This is the "photoelectric effect". The electrons move through the cell as an electric current.

TYPES OF CURRENT

Electric current is either direct (d.c.), in which electrons flow in one direction only, or alternating (a.c.), in which electrons change direction many times each second. A battery produces d.c. current.

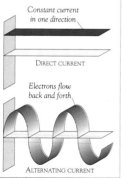

Constant current in one direction

DIRECT CURRENT

Electrons flow back and forth

ALTERNATING CURRENT

RECHARGEABLE BATTERY

A car battery can be recharged by passing an electrical current through it. This reverses the chemical changes that have occurred inside.

Dissolved metal electrodes are restored in recharging

CONDUCTIVITY OF SELECTED SUBSTANCES	
Conductivities are given in units of siemens per metre (S/m): 1 S is the conductivity of a material with a resistance of 1 ohm (Ω).	
SUBSTANCE	CONDUCTIVITY S/M
Copper	58,000,000
Gold	45,000,000
Tungsten	19,000,000
Graphite	70,000
Water (at 20°C)	0.0000025
Diamond	0.00000000001
Air (at sea level)	0.000000000000025

Electrical circuits

An electrical circuit is the path around which an electric current flows. A simple circuit will include a source of electrical energy, such as a battery, and conducting wires linking components, such as switches, bulbs, and resistors, that control the flow of the current.

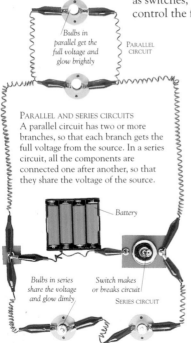

Bulbs in parallel get the full voltage and glow brightly

PARALLEL CIRCUIT

PARALLEL AND SERIES CIRCUITS
A parallel circuit has two or more branches, so that each branch gets the full voltage from the source. In a series circuit, all the components are connected one after another, so that they share the voltage of the source.

Battery

Bulbs in series share the voltage and glow dimly

Switch makes or breaks circuit

SERIES CIRCUIT

CIRCUIT SYMBOLS	
—⌒o⌒—	Switch
—┤⊢—	Single cell
—┤⊦∙┤⊦—	Battery
—(A)—	Ammeter
—(V)—	Voltmeter
—⊗—	Bulb
—▭—	Resistor
—⧄—	Variable resistor

SI UNITS
• The **volt** (V) is the SI un of electromotive force and potential difference: 1 volt makes a current of 1 ampere produce 1 joule of energy per second.
• The **ohm** (Ω) is the SI un of resistance: 1 ohm makes voltage (pd) of 1 volt produe a current of 1 ampere.

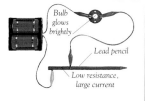

Bulb glows brightly

Lead pencil

Low resistance, large current

RESISTANCE OF A CIRCUIT

Resistance is the degree to which materials resist the flow of current. It can be used to control the flow of current through a circuit. In this circuit, the resistance of a graphite pencil lead controls current flow.

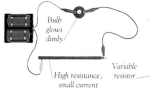

Bulb glows dimly

High resistance, small current

Variable resistor

CIRCUIT EQUATIONS

Several equations can be used to calculate the resistance (R), voltage (V), or current (I) across a conductor in an electrical circuit. These equations are:

To calculate resistance: $R = V/I$

To calculate voltage: $V = IR$

To calculate current: $I = V/R$

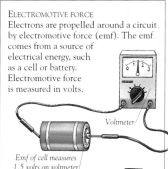

ELECTROMOTIVE FORCE

Electrons are propelled around a circuit by electromotive force (emf). The emf comes from a source of electrical energy, such as a cell or battery. Electromotive force is measured in volts.

Voltmeter

Emf of cell measures 1.5 volts on voltmeter

POTENTIAL DIFFERENCE

The difference in emf between any two points in a circuit is called potential difference (pd) or voltage. Current flows because electrons always move from a point of high potential to a point of low potential.

Voltage (pd) across bulb is 2.2 volts

This "multimeter" can measure current, voltage, or resistance

ELECTROMAGNETISM

MOVING A WIRE in a magnetic field causes a current to flow through the wire. An electric current flowing through a wire generates a magnetic field around the wire. This is electromagnetism.

Electrical connection

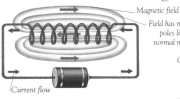

Magnetic field

Field has magnetic poles like a normal magnet

Current flow

FIELD INDUCED BY A WIRE COIL
A coil of current-carrying wire induces a stronger magnetic field than a straight wire. The coil creates a type of electromagnet called a solenoid.

Coils of copper wire around iron core

POWERFUL ELECTROMAGNET
Winding a solenoid around an iron core creates a more powerful magnet field. Here, iron filings show the stro field around this electromagnet.

GENERATORS
Electric current can be produced by rotating a wire coil between the poles of a magnet. Alternatively, a magnet may rotate while the coil remains static. Generators called dynamos give direct current, while alternators are generators that give alternating current.

Galvanometer registers voltage

Electrical connections

Coil spins between magnets

Wires run under board

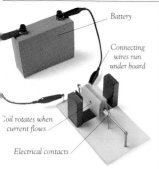

Battery

Connecting wires run under board

Coil rotates when current flows

Electrical contacts

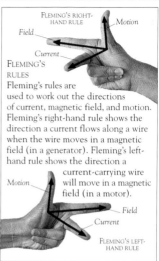

FLEMING'S RIGHT-HAND RULE

Motion

Field

Current

FLEMING'S RULES

Fleming's rules are used to work out the directions of current, magnetic field, and motion. Fleming's right-hand rule shows the direction a current flows along a wire when the wire moves in a magnetic field (in a generator). Fleming's left-hand rule shows the direction a current-carrying wire will move in a magnetic field (in a motor).

Motion

Field

Current

FLEMING'S LEFT-HAND RULE

ELECTRIC MOTORS

In an electric motor, a current flows through a coil of wire between the poles of a magnet. The magnetic field that the coil produces interacts with the field of the magnet, forcing the coil to turn. The rotating coil can be attached to a drive shaft or flywheel to power a machine.

ELECTRIC BELL

Current induces a magnetic field in the electromagnets in this bell, pulling the hammer up to strike the gong. As the hammer moves, it breaks the circuit, then falls back to its original position.

Make-and-break circuit contact

Electromagnets

Drill bit

Pressing the trigger completes the circuit

ELECTRIC DRILL

Many electrical appliances use electric motors. In an electric power drill, gears harness the rotation of the motor to drive the drill bit at high speed. A cooling fan makes sure the motor does not overheat.

ELECTRICITY SUPPLY

ELECTRICITY PRODUCED BY generators in power stations reaches homes via a network of cables known as a grid. Resistance causes some power to be wasted as heat, and electricity is distributed at high voltage and low current to minimize this power loss.

THE ELECTRICITY GRID

PRODUCING ELECTRICITY
Power stations send electricity to substations, where "step-up" transformers increase the voltage for distribution. The power travels along underground cables or overhead lines.

CONSUMING ELECTRICITY
At "step-down" substations, the voltage is reduced by transformers to supply suitable voltages for use in industry or in the home. A local grid takes electricity to these consumers.

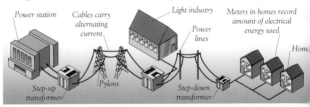

Power station *Cables carry alternating current* *Light industry* *Meters in homes record amount of electrical energy used*

Power lines

Hom

Step-up transformer *Pylons* *Step-down transformer*

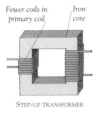

Fewer coils in primary coil *Iron core*

STEP-UP TRANSFORMER

CONTROLLING VOLTAGE
Transformers consist of two wire coils wrapped around an iron core. Step-up transformers have more coils in the secondary coil and increase voltage; step-down transformers have more in the primary coil and reduce voltage.

Fewer coils in secondary coil

STEP-DOWN TRANSFORMER

CIRCUIT BREAKER

FUSE

Fuse wire melts and breaks circuit

CIRCUIT BREAKERS AND FUSES

An electrical fault may allow too much current to flow and cause wires to catch fire. Domestic circuit breakers cut off the current if it reaches dangerous levels. Fuses are the weakest link in a circuit, and burn out if the current is too strong.

TYPES OF PLUG
Electrical appliances are connected to the grid by fitting plugs into sockets. Electrical earth wires direct dangerous currents safely into the ground.

2-PIN PLUG

Earth wire

3-PIN PLUG

Fuse

3-PIN FUSED PLUG

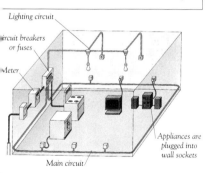

Lighting circuit

ircuit breakers or fuses

Meter

Appliances are plugged into wall sockets

Main circuit

MESTIC CIRCUITS

dern houses have various circuits that supply erent voltages for different purposes. For mple, lighting usually takes power from a erent circuit, or "ring main", to the main power uit. Electric cookers, which use a lot of current, w their electricity from a separate circuit.

ELECTRICITY FACTS

• In 1887, American Nikola Tesla patented an electricity supply system that transmitted alternating current.

• In homes, shops, and offices, voltage must be at 240 volts (110 volts in the USA).

ELECTRONICS

USING COMPONENTS to control electricity is known as
electronics. Integrated circuits and other electronic
components are made of semiconducting materials, such
as silicon. Adding impurities creates two types of silicon:
n-type silicon has extra, free-roaming electrons; p-type
silicon has fewer electrons,
leaving "holes".

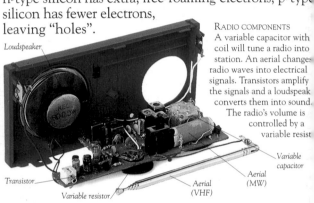

Loudspeaker

RADIO COMPONENTS
A variable capacitor with
coil will tune a radio into
station. An aerial changes
radio waves into electrical
signals. Transistors amplify
the signals and a loudspeaker
converts them into sound.
The radio's volume is
controlled by a
variable resistor

Variable
capacitor

Transistor

Aerial
(MW)

Variable resistor

Aerial
(VHF)

CONTROLLING CURRENT

Electronic circuits
amplify electric current,
change one-way (direct)
current to an oscillating
(alternating) current,
or switch the current
on and off.

*Transmitters are oscillators which
produce an oscillating current*

*Amplifier circuits make a
stronger copy of a weak current*

*Computer circuits use pulses of
on/off current to represent data*

SEMICONDUCTORS

Hole moves

Boron atom

Free electron moves

Arsenic atom

P-TYPE SILICON
Adding boron leaves 'holes' in the silicon, since boron atoms have fewer electrons in their outer shell. The current is carried by the moving holes.

N-TYPE SILICON
Arsenic gives free electrons to the silicon, since arsenic atoms have more electrons in their outer shell. Current is carried by these free electrons.

TRANSISTOR

A transistor is a sandwich of n- and p-type silicon in a p-n-p or n-p-n arrangement. It can boost current or act as a switch. In computers, transistors switch on and off many times each second, enabling rapid calculations to be carried out.

ELECTRICAL COMPONENTS		
COMPONENT	FUNCTION	SYMBOL
Capacitor	Stores charge	
Variable capacitor	Stores varying amounts of charge	
Diode	Permits current to flow in one direction only; can also be used to convert a.c. signals to d.c. signals (a "rectifier")	
Light-emitting diode (LED)	Emits light when current flows through it	
Thermistor	Converts temperature variations into current/voltage	
Aerial	Converts radio waves into a.c. signals (and vice versa)	
Microphone	Converts sound waves into a.c. current/voltage	
Loudspeaker	Converts a.c. signals into sound waves	
p-n transistor	Amplifies electric current, and turns it on and off	
n-p transistor	Amplifies electric current, and turns it on and off	

Integrated circuits

An integrated circuit is a tiny "wafer" of silicon that contains a complete circuit with thousands of components such as transisto and diodes. Integrated circuits, or "microchips", have made electronic devices both smaller and more efficient.

MANUFACTURING

The components of an integrated circuit are ma by building up layers of p-type and n-type semiconductors and other materials on a silicon wafer. They are linked by fine conducting wires. A detailed overlay p is made for each layer and checke for accuracy.

Each plan is a different colour

Transparent overlays

Tiny chi dwarfed packagi

BINARY CODE

Microchips store data as electrical signals in binary code. Binary numbers use only the digits 0 and 1. The decimal number 13, for example, is 1101 in binary form (8+4+0+1). This converts into a binary sequence of on (1) and off (0) electrical pulses. So 1101 is on-on-off-on in binary code.

| (ON) | (ON) | (OFF) | (ON) |
| (1x8) | (1x4) | (0x2) | (1x1) |

ENCASED CHIP

An integrated circuit is also called a microchip. The chip i encased in a tough plastic or ceramic capsule, with pins tha can be soldered or plugged int circuit board. Many chips hav logic gates, which are patterns transistors that process electri signals. Logic gates (see right) add up numbers in calculators

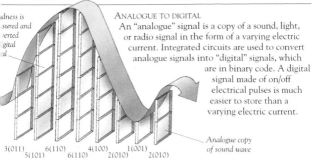

ANALOGUE TO DIGITAL

An "analogue" signal is a copy of a sound, light, or radio signal in the form of a varying electric current. Integrated circuits are used to convert analogue signals into "digital" signals, which are in binary code. A digital signal made of on/off electrical pulses is much easier to store than a varying electric current.

Analogue copy of sound wave

3(011) 6(110) 4(100) 1(001) 2(010)
    5(101)   6(110)   2(010)

LOGIC GATES

gic gates work with digital signals. They switch on off depending on the type of signal they receive. ruth tables" show what happens when signals are her applied (1) or not applied (0) to the gates.

Input A	Input B	Output
0	0	0
1	0	0
0	1	0
1	1	1

AND GATE
Gives an output signal when a signal is applied to one input AND to the other input.

Input A	Input B	Output
0	0	0
1	0	1
0	1	1
1	1	1

OR GATE
Gives an output signal when a signal is applied to one input OR to the other input, OR to both.

Input	Output
0	1
1	0

A symbol used in designing computer circuits

NOT GATE
The NOT gate gives an output signal when a signal is NOT applied to its input.

Weight display

MICROPROCESSOR
A microprocessor is a chip that can store instructions in an electronic memory and act on them. These scales are controlled by a single microchip. The chip converts the weight on the scales into a digital readout. It can convert the weight to or from metric or imperial units.

COMPUTERS

A COMPUTER contains thousands of electronic circu that enable it to store and process vast amounts of information. Although a computer cannot "think" f itself, it can perform a wide variety of tasks extremely quickly. Each task is broker down into a series of simple mathematical calculations.

Monitor screen displays results

Disk drive contains software programs

Keyboard and mouse for inputting data

PERSONAL COMPUTER

The most familiar type of computer is th personal computer (PC), which ca only be used by one person at a time. Most PCs consist of a keyboard and mouse, a disk dri and a monitor screen. Machin such as this is called "hardwar

A wor processi program you write edit tex

COMPUTER PROGRAMS

A program is a set of instructions that tells a computer to carry out a specific task. The instructions may be written as "machine code" (long sets of numbers) or in a computer language such as BASIC or FORTRAN. Computer programs are called "software".

128

SUPERCOMPUTER

Extremely powerful computers able to perform complex tasks are called supercomputers. By performing several processes at once, and by cooling their components so that they conduct electricity more efficiently, they can operate at very high speeds.

computer used in the study of particle physics

CRAY X-MP/48
SUPERCOMPUTER

CAD building plans

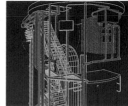

COMPUTER-AIDED DESIGN (CAD)

Information fed into a computer "builds" an object on the screen using computer graphics. CAD allows architects and engineers to test new ideas.

VIRTUAL REALITY

A virtual-reality system enables you to interact with a computer-generated world. A headset supplies you with 3-D images, while a "data glove" lets you "touch" what you see.

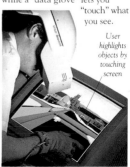

User highlights objects by touching screen

COMPUTER GENERATIONS		
GENERATION	DATE	CHARACTERISTIC
1st	1944–59	Valves (vacuum tubes)
2nd	1959–64	Transistors
3rd	1964–75	Large Scale Integrated circuits (LSIs)
4th	1975–	Very Large Scale Integrated circuits (VLSIs)
5th	Under development	"Artificial Intelligence"-based computers

Inside computers

Memory is crucial to the operation of computers because they need to be able to remember sequences of instructions in order to carry out specific tasks. In a personal computer (PC), there are two memories: read-only memory (ROM) and random access memory (RAM), each consisting of a number of microchips.

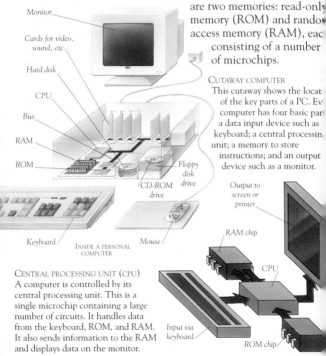

CUTAWAY COMPUTER
This cutaway shows the locat of the key parts of a PC. Ev computer has four basic par a data input device such as keyboard; a central processin unit; a memory to store instructions; and an output device such as a monitor.

Monitor

Cards for video, sound, etc.

Hard disk

CPU

Bus

RAM

ROM

Floppy disk drive

CD-ROM drive

Keyboard

INSIDE A PERSONAL COMPUTER

Mouse

Output to screen or printer

RAM chip

CPU

Input via keyboard

ROM chip

CENTRAL PROCESSING UNIT (CPU)
A computer is controlled by its central processing unit. This is a single microchip containing a large number of circuits. It handles data from the keyboard, ROM, and RAM. It also sends information to the RAM and displays data on the monitor.

Disk coated with magnetic material · Read/write head · Track selector mechanism

...ard disk stores data when a computer ...ff. A floppy disk is used to transfer ...a to other computers. The disks record ...a as magnetic patterns in binary code. ...a is read from a disk by a disk drive.

HELPER BOARDS

Computers contain special circuit boards, or "cards", to carry out specific tasks needing a lot of memory. The computer passes the job on to the card, and is free to handle other tasks.

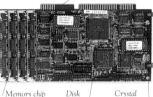

Edge connectors plug into slots

Memory chip · Disk controller · Crystal controls timing

CD-ROM

A CD-ROM is a form of compact-disc player adapted for use in computers. CDs for CD-ROMs can store 50 times more information than a floppy disk, including pictures, text, sound, and video.

CD PAGE

COMPUTER TERMS	
TERM	MEANING
ROM	A computer's permanent memory, whose contents cannot be changed.
RAM	The memory used to store programs being run on the computer.
Buffer	A microchip that stores data temporarily.
Bus	A set of wires or metal strips that carries information from one part of the computer to another.
Operating system	The program that enables a computer to function.
Bit	A digit of binary information (1 or 0).
Byte	A piece of data consisting of eight bits.
Megabyte	One million bytes.
Modem	A device that allows computers to share information via a telephone network.

TELECOMMUNICATIONS

RADIO AND TELEVISION programmes – and even som
telephone conversations – are broadcast by radio
waves. The waves must first be "modulated"
(coded) so that they can carry the sound
and picture signals.

AM RADIO WAVE

Wav
streng
modula

MODULATION
A steady radio (high
frequency) signal is
modulated by a sound
signal in one of two
ways. Its amplitude
(strength) may be
modulated (AM) or its
frequency may change
(FM). The resulting
signal is transmitted
as a radio wave.

FM RADIO WAVE

Frequency of wave
modulated

LONG-RANGE COMMUNICATIONS
Low-frequency radio waves are sent long distances b
bouncing them between the ionosphere (an ion-lade
region of the atmosphere) and the ground. High-
frequency waves pass
through the ionosphere
and are transmitted to
receiving stations on
Earth by orbiting
communications
satellites.

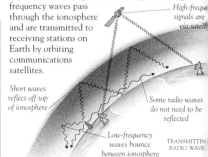

High-freque
signals are
via satell

Short waves
reflect off top
of ionosphere

Some radio waves
do not need to be
reflected

Low-frequency
waves bounce
between ionosphere
and ground

TRANSMITTIN
RADIO WAVE

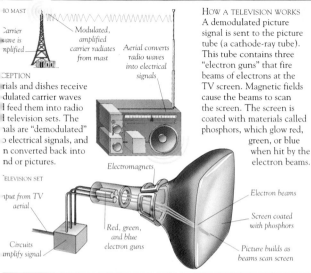

IO MAST

Carrier
wave is
amplified

Modulated,
amplified
carrier radiates
from mast

Aerial converts
radio waves
into electrical
signals

RECEPTION

Aerials and dishes receive
modulated carrier waves
and feed them into radio
and television sets. The
signals are "demodulated"
to electrical signals, and
then converted back into
sound or pictures.

HOW A TELEVISION WORKS
A demodulated picture
signal is sent to the picture
tube (a cathode-ray tube).
This tube contains three
"electron guns" that fire
beams of electrons at the
TV screen. Magnetic fields
cause the beams to scan
the screen. The screen is
coated with materials called
phosphors, which glow red,
green, or blue
when hit by the
electron beams.

Electromagnets

TELEVISION SET

Input from TV
aerial

Circuits
amplify signal

Red, green,
and blue
electron guns

Electron beams

Screen coated
with phosphors

Picture builds as
beams scan screen

TELEPHONES

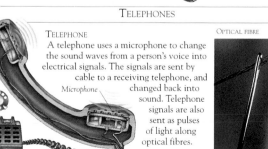

TELEPHONE
A telephone uses a microphone to change
the sound waves from a person's voice into
electrical signals. The signals are sent by
cable to a receiving telephone, and
changed back into
sound. Telephone
signals are also
sent as pulses
of light along
optical fibres.

Microphone

OPTICAL FIBRE

TIMELINE OF SCIENTIFIC DISCOVERIES

THIS CHART CHRONICLES some of the important discoveries in the history of science – from early ideas about the universe and the nature of force and energy to the modern world of particle physics.

c.1000 BC			AD 165
c.1000 BC–c.260 BC	c.259 BC–AD 1599	1600–1640	1641–1650

MATTER

•c.400 BC Greek scientist Democritus suggests that matter is made out of tiny indivisible particles, which he calls atoms. •c.350 BC Aristotle, a Greek philosopher, proposes that matter is made out of four elements: earth, fire, air, and water.	•2 BC Alchemy studied in Egypt, China, and India. Alchemists try to change "base" metals such as lead into precious metals such as gold. Alchemy was the first systematic study of matter. It later reaches Europe.	•1620 A Dutch scientist called Jan van Helmont coins the word "gas". •1620s Francis Bacon, an English philosopher, develops scientific method – science based on experiment.	•1649 French philosopher Pierre Gassendi translates ancient Greek text on the atomic theory, making the idea of the atom popular once again •c.1650 German physicist Otto von Guericke perfects his vacuum pump.

FORCE AND ENERGY

•c.1000 BC Early civilizations rely on wind and muscle power for work and transport, and burn wood and plant matter for heat. •c.260 BC Greek scientist Archimedes discovers principle of flotation and establishes principles of mathematics.	•AD 100 Hero of Alexandria, a Greek engineer, invents the aeolipile, a forerunner of the steam turbine. It uses steam from a boiler to make a metal ball rotate.	•1600 William Gilbert, doctor to Queen Elizabeth I of England, claims that the Earth's core is like a huge magnet. •1638 Italian scientist Galileo Galilei founds mechanics (the study of force and motion). He is the first person to use a telescope.	•1643 Italian physicist Evangelista Torricelli discovers atmospheric pressure and measures it with a mercury barometer – his own invention •1650 Blaise Pascal a French scientist, develops his law of fluid pressures.

1651			1820
1651–1700	1701–1770	1771–1800	1801–1820
•1661 Irish scientist Robert Boyle realizes the nature of elements and compounds. He suggests that the existence of small particles explains chemical reactions. •1670 English physicist Robert Hooke develops the compound microscope.	•1755 Scottish chemist Joseph Black identifies carbon dioxide. Also discovers latent heat. •1766 English chemist Henry Cavendish discovers hydrogen. •1770s French physicist and inventor Charles Coulomb studies electrostatic forces.	•1779 French chemist Antoine Lavoisier names oxygen and shows its role in burning. Proves that air is a mixture of gases, and water a compound of oxygen and hydrogen. •1780s Jean Antoine Chaptal, a chemist from France, sets up a factory to produce sulphuric acid.	•1807–8 Discovery by British chemist Humphry Davy of potassium, sodium, magnesium, barium, and strontium. •1811 Italian physicist Amedeo Avogadro formulates his law which states that equal volumes of different gases contain the same number of particles.
•1665 English mathematician Isaac Newton formulates laws of motion and gravitation. Later discovers that light is made up of a spectrum of colours. •1675 Danish astronomer Olë Römer measures the speed of light by observing Jupiter's moons. •1683 French engineer John Desaguliers introduces the words "conductor" and "insulator".	•1701 French scientist Joseph Sauveur distinguishes between sound waves and vibrations. •1706 English scientist Francis Hawksbee develops a friction machine to generate sparks of electricity. •1752 American scientist Benjamin Franklin proves that lightning is electrical. Also suggests that electricity consists of two types of charge. •1765 James Watt, a Scottish engineer, builds first efficient steam engine.	•1798 Henry Cavendish, English chemist, measures the mass of the Earth with a torsion balance. •1799 Italian chemist Alessandro Volta devises his "voltaic pile" – the world's first battery – using different metals separated by paper discs soaked in salt solution. •1800 André Marie Ampère, a French physicist, explores links between electric current and voltage.	•1803 Englishman John Dalton proposes modern atomic theory – that elements and compounds are made up of atoms and molecules. •1820 Hans Christian Oersted, a Danish physicist, discovers electromagnetism when he notices how a compass needle is deflected by a current-carrying wire.

1821–1840	1841–1860	1861–1880	1881–1899
MATTER			
• 1830 German chemists concentrate their studies on carbon as the basis of the "organic" chemistry of living things. • 1833 English physicist and chemist Michael Faraday discovers the laws of electrolysis.	• 1841 Swedish chemist Jöns Jacob Berzelius discovers allotropy. • 1842 French scientist Eugene-Melchor Peligot discovers uranium. • 1852 English chemist Edward Franklin introduces the concept of valency.	• 1868 Helium discovered by spectroscopic studies of the Sun. • 1869 The Russian schoolteacher Dmitri Mendeleyev classifies elements into groups by atomic weight, and devises the periodic table.	• 1896 Radioactivity discovered by French physicist Antoine Henri Becquerel. • 1897 British physicist Joseph John Thompson, discovers the electron. • 1898 Polish–French chemist Marie Curie and her French husband Pierre Curie isolate radium and polonium.
FORCE AND ENERGY			
• 1831 Scientists Michael Faraday of England and Joseph Henry of the USA independently discover how to use magnetism to create electricity. • 1836 English chemist John Frederic Daniell invents the Daniell cell, the first practical and reliable source of electricity. • 1839 Englishman William Fox Talbot and Frenchman Louis Daguerre independently devise a practical photographic process.	• 1843 English scientist James Joule describes the relationship between heat, power, and work. • 1846 Laws of thermodynamics are established by William Thomson, a British scientist. • 1849 French physicist Hippolyte Fizeau makes an accurate measurement of the speed of light. • 1859 Étienne Lenoir, a Belgian engineer, invents the internal combustion engine.	• 1864 James Maxwell, a Scottish physicist, introduces the idea of the electromagnetic field. Also identifies light as a form of electromagnetic radiation. • 1876 Scottish-born inventor Alexander Graham Bell makes the first telephone. • 1879 American Thomas Edison and Englishman Joseph Swan independently produce the first electric light bulbs. Edison's is the more successful.	• 1884 Charles Parsons, an English engineer, invents the steam turbine for generating electricity. • 1888 Heinrich Hertz, a German physicist, proves the existence of radio waves. • 1888 Croatian-born physicist Nikola Tesla invents the first practical electrical induction motor. • 1894 Young Italian inventor Guglielmo Marconi makes the first radio communication.

1900			1995
1900–1911	1912–1930	1931–1945	1946–1995

MATTER

•1909 Leo Henrick Baekeland, an American chemist, produces the first stable, fully synthetic plastic – "Bakelite". •1911 The atomic nucleus is discovered by New Zealand-born physicist Ernest Rutherford. Later, he learns to convert one element into another.	•1913 Niels Bohr, a Danish physicist, discovers that electrons orbit the nucleus of an atom in shells. •1915 William Bragg and his son Lawrence Bragg invent X-ray crystallography – a way of using X-rays to explore the structure of crystals.	•1931 The neutron is discovered by James Chadwick, a British physicist. •1931 German physicist Ernst Ruska invents the electron microscope. •1939 American chemist Linus Pauling explains the nature of chemical bonds between atoms and molecules.	•1964 American physicist Murray Gell-Mann proposes the existence of quarks. •1984 Genetic fingerprinting is developed by British scientist Alec Jeffreys. •1995 Fifth state of matter, called the "superatom", is found at temperatures close to absolute zero.

FORCE AND ENERGY

•1900 Max Planck, a German physicist, proposes quantum theory – that energy is made up of small units called "quanta". From this theory, scientists deduce that light acts both as waves and as particles. •1905 German-born physicist Albert Einstein publishes his *Special Theory of Relativity*. Together with his *General Theory of Relativity* (1915), it revolutionizes the world of science and shows that mass can be converted to energy.	•1911 Dutch physicist Heike Onnes discovers superconductivity in mercury at near absolute zero. •1912 German physicist Max von Laue discovers that X-rays are electromagnetic radiation, by studying their reflection from crystals. •1912 Austrian-born American physicist Victor Hess discovers high energy cosmic radiation during high-altitude balloon flights.	•1937 First working jet engine is built by British engineer Frank Whittle. •1938 German scientist Otto Hahn and Austrian physicist Lise Meitner discover nuclear fission. •1939 German scientist Hans Bethe explains that the Sun and stars are powered by nuclear fusion. •1942 Enrico Fermi, an Italian–American physicist, builds the first nuclear reactor. •1945 The first electronic computer, ENIAC, is devised in the USA.	•1947 American physicists John Bardeen, Walter Brattain, and William Shockley invent the transistor. •1958 The first integrated circuit consisting of one piece of semiconductor is produced by US electronics engineer Jack Kilby. •1960 The laser is invented by Theodore Maiman, an American physicist. •1971 The first microprocessor, the Intel 4004, is manufactured in the USA.

EARTH AND WEATHER

HOW THE EARTH WAS FORMED

ABOUT 5,000 MILLION years ago our solar system began to take shape. The Sun and the nine planets formed from a cloud of dust and gas swirling in space. Some scientists believe that the centre of this cloud cooled and contracted to form the Sun. Gravity pulled the planets from the rest of the cloud. Other scientists suggest that the dust cloud formed asteroids that joined together to make the Sun and planets

1 FORMING THE SUN
A spinning cloud of gas and dust contracted to form the Sun. Cooler matter from this dust cloud combined to shape the planets.

A dense atmosphere of cosmic gases surrounded the Earth.

2 FORMING THE EARTH
The Earth's radio-activity caused the surface to melt. Lighter minerals floated to the surface and heavier elements, such as iron and nickel, sank to form the Earth's core.

3 THE EARTH'S CRUST
About 4,000 million years ago, the Earth's crust began to form. Blocks of cooling, solid rock floated on a molten rock layer. The rock sometimes sank and remelted before rising again.

EARTH FACTS

• The Earth orbits the Sun at 29.8 km/sec (18.5 miles/sec).

• Oceans cover 70.8% of the Earth's surface.

• Earth is not a sphere – it bulges in the middle.

• The Earth completes a turn on its axis every 23 hours, 56 minutes.

COMPOSITION OF THE EARTH

The elements here are divided by weight. Earth's crust consists mostly of oxygen, silicon, and aluminium. Heavier metals such as iron and nickel are found in the core.

Other elements less than 1%
Aluminium 1.1%
Sulphur 1.9%
Nickel 2.4%
Magnesium 13%
Silicon 15%
Oxygen 30%
Iron 35%

4 MAKING THE ATMOSPHERE
The Earth's crust thickened. It took several million years for volcanic gases to form the atmosphere. Water vapour condensed to make oceans.

6 THE EARTH TODAY
Earth's unique conditions are just right to support a variety of life. Our planet, though, continues to change. Tectonic plates are moving, pulling some continents nearer and pushing others farther apart.

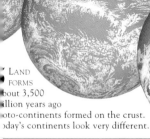

5 LAND FORMS
About 3,500 million years ago proto-continents formed on the crust. Today's continents look very different.

THE EARTH IN SPACE

EARTH IS A DENSE rocky planet, third nearest to the
Sun, and tiny compared with Jupiter and Saturn.
While Earth rotates on its axis each day, it also
orbits the Sun each year, held in orbit by the
Sun's gravity. One moon revolves around the
Earth. From space the Earth looks blue and
calm but under its oceans, deep beneath the
crust, the Earth's core is fiery and white-hot

MERCURY
• 88 days to orbit Sun
• diameter 4,878 km
  (3,032 miles)

EARTH
• 365.25 days to orbit Sun
• diameter 12,756 km
  (7,928 miles)
• 1 moon

MERCURY   EARTH
           VENUS   MARS

MARS
• 687 days to orbit Sun
• diameter 6,786 km
  (4,217 miles)
• 2 moons

VENUS
• 224.7 days to orbit Sun
• diameter 12,102 km
  (7,521 miles)

SUN
• diameter 1,391,980 km (865,121 miles)

THE SOLAR SYSTEM
Our solar system consists of nine p
ets, as well as moons, asteroids,
comets, meteorites, dust, and gas.
of these orbit a central star – the S

JUPITER

*The Great
Red Spot is a
cyclone.*

JUPITER
• 11.86 years to orbit Sun
• diameter 142,984 km
  (88,865 miles)
• 16 moons
• 1 ring

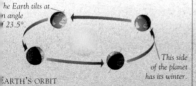

The Earth tilts at an angle of 23.5°.

This side of the planet has its winter.

EARTH'S ORBIT

As the Earth spins on its axis, it also orbits the Sun. When the northern hemisphere faces the Sun it has its summer. At the same time the southern hemisphere faces away from the Sun and has its winter. The equator faces towards the Sun most of the time and there are no significant seasonal changes there.

DISTANCE FROM THE SUN

PLANET	MILLION KM	MILLION MILES
Mercury	57.9	36
Venus	108.2	67.2
Earth	149.6	93
Mars	227.9	141.6
Jupiter	778.3	483.7
Saturn	1,427	886.9
Uranus	2,871	1,784
Neptune	4,497	2,795
Pluto	5,914	3,675

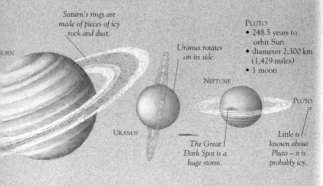

Saturn's rings are made of pieces of icy rock and dust.

Uranus rotates on its side.

PLUTO
• 248.5 years to orbit Sun
• diameter 2,300 km (1,429 miles)
• 1 moon

NEPTUNE

The Great Dark Spot is a huge storm.

Little is known about Pluto – it is probably icy.

SATURN
• 29.46 years to orbit Sun
• diameter 120,536 km (74,914 miles)
• 18 moons
• 7 rings

URANUS
• 84 years to orbit Sun
• diameter 51,118 km (31,770 miles)
• 15 moons
• 11 rings

NEPTUNE
• 164.8 years to orbit Sun
• diameter 49,528 km (30,782 miles)
• 8 moons
• 4 rings

143

EARTH'S MAGNETIC FIELD

THE EARTH BEHAVES like a giant magnet. Molten iron and nickel flow in the Earth's outer core and produce an electric current. This electricity creates a magnetic field, or magnetosphere, that extends into space. Like a magnet, the Earth has two magnetic poles. From time to time, the magnetic poles reverse polarity. The last time they changed was about 700,000 years ago. No one knows why this happens.

MAGNETIC POLES
North and south geographical poles lie at either end of the Earth's axis (the invisible line around which the Earth turns). The magnetic poles' position varies over time. It is the Earth's magnetic field that causes a compass needle to point north.

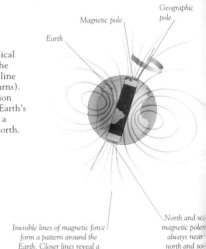

Geographic pole

Magnetic pole

Earth

Invisible lines of magnetic force form a pattern around the Earth. Closer lines reveal a stronger magnetic field.

North and so... magnetic poles always near north and so... geographical p...

MAGNETIC FACTS

• Whales and birds use the Earth's magnetic field to help them navigate.

• Every second the Sun sheds at least a million tonnes (tons) of matter into the solar wind.

MAGNETOSPHERE
Earth's magnetosphere extends about 60,000 km (37,000 miles) into space. It protects the Earth from some of the Sun's most harmful particles.

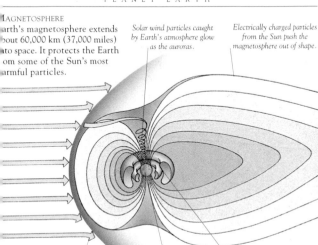

Solar wind particles caught by Earth's atmosphere glow as the auroras.

Electrically charged particles from the Sun push the magnetosphere out of shape.

Solar wind full of charged atomic particles from the Sun

Earth

Atomic particles are trapped in two dense layers called the Van Allen belts.

The polarity of new crust reverses between north and south.

MAGNETIC CRUST
New oceanic crust rises out of the Earth at mid-oceanic ridges. As the rock solidifies, a record of the Earth's magnetism is locked into it. Earth's changing polarities lead to a magnetic pattern in the rock, symmetrical either side of the spreading ridge.

EARTH'S ATMOSPHERE

THE EARTH IS WRAPPED in a blanket of gases called the atmosphere. This thin layer protects the Earth from the Sun's fierce rays and from the hostile conditions of outer space. There are five layers in the Earth's atmosphere before the air merges with outer space. The layers hold air and water vapour that support life, and our weather and climate.

A THIN LAYER
The Earth's atmosphere is actually a thin band around the Earth. If the Earth were an orange, the atmosphere would be as thin as the skin of the orange.

EXOSPHERE
• begins at 900 km (560 miles)
• thin layer before spacecraft reach outer space

THERMOSPHERE
• 80-450 km (50-280 miles)
• reaches 2,000°C (3,632°F)
• contains the ionosphere – electrically-charged air that reflects radio waves

MESOSPHERE
• 50-80 km (30-50 miles)
• meteors burn up and cause shooting stars

STRATOSPHERE
• 20-50 km (12-30 miles)
• ranges from -60°C (-76°F) to just about freezing point at the top
• calm layer where airliners fly
• contains the ozone layer that protects us from the Sun's harmful rays

TROPOSPHERE
• up to 20 km (12 miles) above the Earth
• weather layer, where rain clouds form

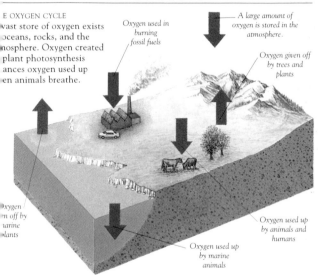

E OXYGEN CYCLE
vast store of oxygen exists
oceans, rocks, and the
nosphere. Oxygen created
plant photosynthesis
ances oxygen used up
en animals breathe.

Oxygen used in
burning
fossil fuels

A large amount of
oxygen is stored in the
atmosphere.

Oxygen given off
by trees and
plants

xygen
n off by
narine
lants

Oxygen used up
by animals and
humans

Oxygen used up
by marine
animals

TMOSPHERE FACTS

The troposphere
ntains 75% of all
e gases of the
mosphere (by mass).

Ozone is a type of
ygen that absorbs
maging ultraviolet
ys from the Sun.

Humans can only live
d breathe normally in
e troposphere layer.

COMPOSITION OF THE
LOWER ATMOSPHERE
Although nitrogen
makes up most of the
air we breathe, oxygen
is the essential gas for
all animal and human
life. Nitrogen is simply
breathed in and out.
Other gases, such as
argon and carbon
dioxide, make up less
than one per cent.

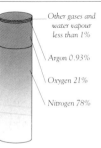

Other gases and
water vapour
less than 1%

Argon 0.93%

Oxygen 21%

Nitrogen 78%

1 4 7

MAPPING THE EARTH

MAPS HELP US TO see what the Earth looks like. A m...
uses symbols to represent different features of the
Earth. A technique called projection can transfer the
curved surface of the globe on to a flat sheet of paper
Aerial photographs help make maps that show valley
and hills. On a larger scal...
satellite photograph
help map-make...
reveal how t...
Earth look...
from space

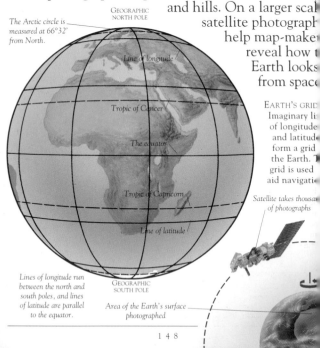

The Arctic circle is measured at 66°32' from North.

GEOGRAPHIC NORTH POLE

Line of longitude

Tropic of Cancer

The equator

Tropic of Capricorn

Line of latitude

EARTH'S GRID
Imaginary li...
of longitude
and latitud...
form a grid
the Earth. T...
grid is used
aid navigatio...

Satellite takes thousan... of photographs

Lines of longitude run between the north and south poles, and lines of latitude are parallel to the equator.

GEOGRAPHIC SOUTH POLE

Area of the Earth's surface photographed

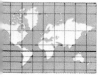

MERCATOR'S PROJECTION

PETERS' PROJECTION

MAP PROJECTIONS
Mercator's map of 1569 distorted the areas of the continents – Greenland appeared larger than Africa. Peters' map shows the right size but wrong shape of the continents.

THE WORLD'S CONTINENTS
he Earth is divided to seven land asses or ntinents.

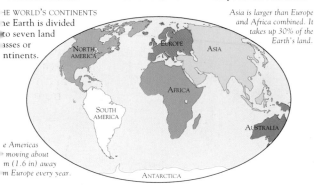

Asia is larger than Europe and Africa combined. It takes up 30% of the Earth's land.

NORTH AMERICA

EUROPE

ASIA

AFRICA

SOUTH AMERICA

AUSTRALIA

ANTARCTICA

e Americas moving about m (1.6 in) away m Europe every year.

TELLITE MAPPING
hile orbiting the Earth, ellites photograph the anet in sections. The parate images are mbined to give a clear cture of the Earth.

Satellite's orbit around the poles

Direction of the Earth's rotation

THE SIZE OF THE CONTINENTS		
CONTINENT	AREA IN SQ KM	AREA IN SQ MILES
Asia	44,485,900	17,176,100
Africa	30, 269,680	11,687,180
North America	24,235,280	9,357,290
South America	17,820,770	6,880,630
Antarctica	13,209,000	5,100,020
Europe	10,530,750	4,065,940
Australia	7,682,300	2,966,368

THE EARTH'S CRUST

EARTH'S SURFACE IS covered by a thin layer of rock called crust. Rocky crust above sea level forms islands and continents. The crust, or lithosphere, is in pieces or plates, that move slowly all the time. Where two plates meet they may slide past each other or one may go under another. New crust forms under the ocean while old crust slips beneath plates.

PLATE FACTS
• Earth's plates "float" on a slushy layer called the asthenosphere.
• The size of the Earth doesn't change – new crust produced equals older crust consumed.

EARTH'S SKIN
Earth's crust, like the skin of an apple, is a thin covering for what is inside. Under the ocean the crust, called oceanic crust, is 6 km (4 miles) thick, but under mountain ranges the continental crust can be 64 km (40 miles) thick.

The rock plates the Earth's crust together like pieces of a jigsaw.

CROSS-SECTION THROUGH THE EARTH'S CRUST
This section through the Earth's crust at the Equator shows the landscape and the direction of plate movement at plate boundaries.

AFRICA

African Rift Valley

INDIAN OCEAN

Indo-Australian plate

African plate

African plate

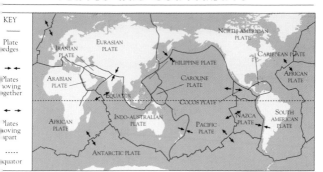

KEY

— Plate edges

Plates moving together

←→ →← Plates moving apart

..... Equator

ATES OF THE WORLD
e surface of the Earth
15 large plates. A
te can include both
ntinental lithosphere
d oceanic lithosphere.
eas such as Australia
in the middle of a
te, while others, like
land, have a plate
ndary through them.

MOVEMENT OF THE EARTH'S PLATES			
PLATE NAMES	DIRECTION OF MOVEMENT	RATE OF MOVEMENT	
		CM PER YEAR	IN PER YEAR
Pacific/Nazca	apart	18.3	7.3
Cocos/Pacific	apart	11.7	4.6
Nazca/South American	together	11.2	4.4
Pacific/Indo-Australian	together	10.5	4.1
Pacific/Antarctic	apart	10.3	4.0

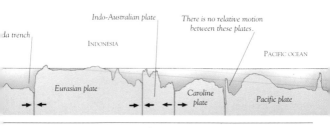

da trench

Indo-Australian plate

There is no relative motion between these plates.

INDONESIA

PACIFIC OCEAN

Eurasian plate

Caroline plate

Pacific plate

MOVING CONTINENTS

EARTH'S CONTINENTS can be rearranged to fit together like pieces of a jigsaw. This idea made scientists think that they once formed a giant landmass, Pangaea. This "supercontinent" broke up, and the continents drifted, over millions of years, to where they are now. This is continental drift or plate tectonics theory. Continents move as the Earth's plates move, sliding along on the asthenosphere, a layer of soft mantle.

250 MILLION YEARS AGO

120 MILLION YEARS AGO

CONTINENTAL DRIFT
When Pangaea broke up, new continents emerged. The outlines of South America and Africa appeared

CROSS-SECTION THROUGH THE EARTH'S CRUST

PACIFIC OCEAN

Pacific plate

Naz

PLATE BOUNDARIES

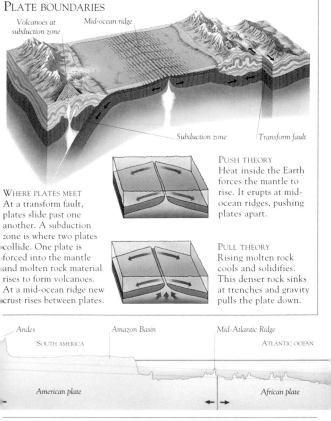

Volcanoes at subduction zone

Mid-ocean ridge

Subduction zone

Transform fault

WHERE PLATES MEET
At a transform fault, plates slide past one another. A subduction zone is where two plates collide. One plate is forced into the mantle and molten rock material rises to form volcanoes. At a mid-ocean ridge new crust rises between plates.

PUSH THEORY
Heat inside the Earth forces the mantle to rise. It erupts at mid-ocean ridges, pushing plates apart.

PULL THEORY
Rising molten rock cools and solidifies. This denser rock sinks at trenches and gravity pulls the plate down.

Andes

Amazon Basin

Mid-Atlantic Ridge

SOUTH AMERICA

ATLANTIC OCEAN

American plate

African plate

INSIDE THE EARTH

THE INTERIOR OF the Earth has four major layers. On the outside is the crust made of familiar soil and rock. Under this is the mantle, which is solid rock with a molten layer at the top. The inside or core of the Earth has two sections: an outer core of thick fluid, and a solid inner core.

The atmosphere stretches about 640 km (400 miles) into space.

The crust varies between about 6 to 64 km (4 to 40 miles) thick.

The mantle is 2,900 km (1,800 miles) thick.

The outer core is 2,000 km (1,240 miles) thick.

The inner core is 2,740 km (1,700 miles) thick.

LAYERS OF THE EARTH
Earth's outer shell is called the lithosphere. It includes the crust and part of the upper mantle. The crust floats on the asthenosphere like an iceberg on the sea. Earth's outer core is mostly oxygen, liquid iron, and nickel. Its inner core, about 4,000°C (7,232°F), is solid iron and nickel.

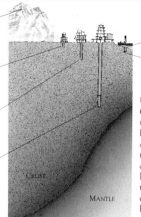

Mount Everest reaches up 8.85 km (5.5 miles).

Sea level

A deep coal mine reaches down less than 1 km (0.62 miles) below sea level.

The deepest ocean drilling has reached 1.7 km (1.05 miles).

The deepest mine reaches down 3.8 km (2.36 miles).

The deepest hole has reached 12 km (7.5 miles).

CRUST

MANTLE

UNDER THE CRUST
Clues to the interior of the Earth come from boreholes. These have only reached as far as the crust. They reveal a dense lower layer and a less dense upper layer to the crust. There is also evidence of a boundary between crust and mantle called the Moho.

CRUST FACTS

• If an excavator could dig a hole through the Earth at 1 m (39 in) per minute, it would take 24 years to reach the other side.

• Western Deep Gold Mine in South Africa is the world's deepest mine. It is 3.8 km (2.36 miles) deep.

• The Earth's crust is mainly granite rock.

COMPOSTION OF THE EARTH'S CRUST

Light elements such as silicon, oxygen, and aluminium make up the Earth's crust. Oceanic crust is mostly basalt (which also contains magnesium and iron). Continental crust is composed of granite-like rocks. These may have been formed from recycled basaltic ocean crust.

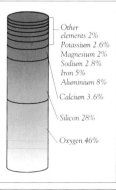

Other elements 2%
Potassium 2.6%
Magnesium 2%
Sodium 2.8%
Iron 5%
Aluminium 8%
Calcium 3.6%

Silicon 28%

Oxygen 46%

DORMANT VOLCANO
If scientists believe a volcano may erupt again, perhaps because it gives off volcanic gases, it is called dormant. Mt. Rainier, U.S.A. is described as dormant.

THE EARTH'S VOLCANOES

MOST VOLCANOES are found near the coast or under the ocean. They usually form at plate edges. Here crust movement allows hot molten rock called magma to rise up from inside the Earth and burst through the crust. Hot magma is called lava when it flows out of a volcano. Ash, steam, and gas also spew out and cause great destruction.

COMPARING ERUPTIONS
One way to compare the size of different volcanic eruptions is to measure the amount of ash thrown out during an eruption.

MT. TAMBORA, INDONESIA, 1815
80 KM³
(19.2 MILES³)

MT. KRAKATOA, INDONESIA, 1883
18 KM³
(4.32 MILES³)

MT. KATMAI, U.S.A., 1912
12 KM³
(2.88 MILES³)

MT. VESUVIUS, ITALY, A.D. 79
3 KM³
(0.72 MILES³)

MT. ST. HELENS, U.S.A. 1980
1 KM³
(0.24 MILES³)

VOLCANO SITES

In general, volcanoes, like earthquakes, occur near plate boundaries. Plate destruction (around the Pacific Ocean) and plate construction (in Hawaii) cause volcanoes.

The chain of volcanoes around the edge of the Pacific Ocean is known as the "Ring of Fire".

Ring of Fire continues through volcanic islands of Japan.

PACIFIC OCEAN

POMPEII

In A.D 79 Mt. Vesuvius erupted burying the town of Pompeii under pumice and ash. The two-day eruption killed 2,000 people with poisonous gases and hot ash.

LARGEST VOLCANIC EXPLOSIONS

The Volcanic Explosivity Index (V.E.I.) grades eruptions from 0 to 8. The scale is based on the height of the dust cloud, the volume of tephra (debris ejected by a volcano), and an account of the severity of the eruption. Any eruption above 5 on the scale is very large and violent. So far, there has never been an eruption of 8.

VOLCANO	DATE	V.E.I.
Crater Lake, Oregon, U.S.A.	c.4895B.C.	7
Towada, Honshu, Japan	915	5
Oraefajokull, Iceland	1362	6
Tambora, Indonesia	1815	7
Krakatoa, Indonesia	1883	6
Santa Maria, Guatemala	1902	6
Katmai, U.S.A.	1912	6
Mt. St. Helens, U.S.A.	1980	5

VOLCANO SHAPES

NOT ALL VOLCANOES are the same. Some are cone-shaped and others are quite flat. The shape of the volcano depends on the kind of lava that comes out of it. Runny lava flows away from the volcano before hardening, but thick, viscous lava forms a hard cone. Volcanoes usually appear near plate boundaries, but they also form at hot spots such as in Hawaii or under the ocean at plate edges.

ICELAND'S RIFT
Skaftar fissure in Iceland lies where two plates are moving apart. It is part of a 27-km (16-mile) rift along the plates' edges.

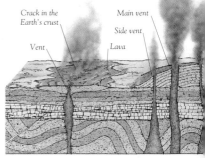

Crack in the Earth's crust

Main vent

Side vent

Vent

Lava

FISSURE VOLCANO
This type of volcano is a long crack in the crust. Runny lava seeps out along its length and forms a plateau.

SHIELD VOLCANO
A shield volcano usually has several sid vents. The lava is runny and produces gently sloping sides.

ORST VOLCANIC ERUPTIONS

Volcano	Date	Number killed
ibora	1815	92,000
Pelée	1902	40,000
ıatoa	1883	36,000
ıdo del Ruiz	1985	23,000

COMPOSITE VOLCANO
Cone-shaped volcanoes build
up from sticky lava. Inside are
layers of thick lava and ash from
previous eruptions. Gas builds
pressure inside the volcano so
that it erupts violently.

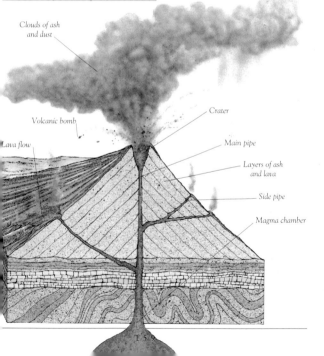

Clouds of ash
and dust

Volcanic bomb

Lava flow

Crater

Main pipe

Layers of ash
and lava

Side pipe

Magma chamber

EXPLOSIVE VOLCANOES

SOMETIMES VOLCANOES explode violently. Volcanoes that form from viscous lava are most likely to do this.

NUÉE ARDENTE
An explosive eruption can cause a glowing ash cloud or *nuée ardente*.

The thick, sticky lava traps gas under it and plugs the volcano's vent. When pressure increases, a violent explosion blows out the lava. Pieces of rock and a great deal of ash are hurled high into the air. Clouds of ash and pumice flow like hot avalanches down the sides of the volcano. Mudflows (also called lahars) are a mixture of water and ash. They travel at great speed and engulf everything in their paths.

MT. ST. HELENS
In the Cascades, U.S.A. a peaceful-looking volcano erupted after 123 years of dormancy. A warning came when one side of the volcano began to bulge as the magma rose. A gas explosion lasting 9 hours and a landslide ensued. An ash cloud over 1,500 km² (580 miles²) caused darkness. Melted snow and ash made mudflows.

BEFORE MT. ST. HELENS ERUPTED

ERUPTION ON 18TH MAY 198

DEVASTATING MUDFLOWS
When Ruiz volcano in Colombia erupted in 1985, the snow melted around its summit. A mixture of water, ash, and pumice fast turned to mud and buried the nearby city of Armero. More than 22,000 people were drowned in the mud.

PRODUCTS OF EXPLOSIVE VOLCANOES

ASH
Particles of lava fall like ash and cover the land.

LAPILLI
Lava ejected in pea-sized pieces is called lapilli.

PUMICE
Pumice is light-weight lava filled with holes.

BOMB
Bomb-shaped lava forms as it flies in the air.

PELE'S HAIR
Sometimes drops of liquid lava blow into fine spiky strands. The threads form needles of volcanic glass. They are named Pele's hair after Pele, the Hawaiian goddess of volcanoes.

NON-EXPLOSIVE VOLCANOES

SOME VOLCANOES ARE cracks in
the ground oozing runny lava.
This type of lava flows for
long distances before it
cools. It builds low-sided
volcanoes and plateaus of
lava. This kind of volcano
forms at plate edges, mostly
under the ocean. A hot spot
volcano bursts through the
middle of a plate; it is not
related to plate margins.

SPREADING RIDGES
The boundary where two plates are
moving apart is usually underwater.
In some places, such as Iceland, the
spreading ridge is above sea level.
Magma rises along this boundary
and lava erupts. The lava may form
mountains at the spreading ridge.

TYPES OF LAVA

PAHOEHOE LAVA
Lava with a wrinkled skin is called
pahoehoe. This is a nonviscous or
runny lava that forms a skin as it
cools, although the inside is still
molten. It is common in Hawaii.

AA LAVA
This is the Hawaiian name for
slow-moving, sticky, viscous
lava. When aa lava solidifies it
has a rough, jagged surface that
is also described as blocky.

HAWAIIAN VOLCANOES
[In] places called hot spots, notably [in] Hawaii, magma rises to create [lava] fountains and fire curtains.

HOT SPOT VOLCANOES
[Th]e Earth's plates move slowly over [hot] spots in the crust. Magma rises, [rea]ching through the crust to form [a n]ew island. In Hawaii, a hot spot [has] built a chain of volcanic islands.

BASALT COLUMNS
Northern Ireland's Giant's Causeway is made of mostly hexagonal columns of basalt rock. At least 60 million years ago, thick lava cooled and shrank to form the blocks.

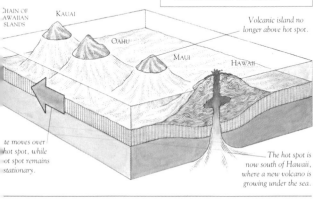

CHAIN OF HAWAIIAN ISLANDS

KAUAI

OAHU

MAUI

HAWAII

Volcanic island no longer above hot spot

[Pla]te moves over [the] hot spot, while [the h]ot spot remains stationary.

The hot spot is now south of Hawaii, where a new volcano is growing under the sea.

VOLCANIC LANDSCAPES

MOVEMENT IN ROCKS undergroun[...] can cause changes to the landscap[...] above. The combination of heat and water in the Earth's rocks produces various phenomena. Molten rock erupting out of the Earth brings gases, mineral deposits, and water with it. Mud pools, hot springs, and geysers for[...] when the gases and water escape. Chemical reactions also occur, changing rocks and depositing minerals in the water near them.

OLD FAITHFUL
This geyser called Old Faithful is in the U.S.A. It shoots out a column of boiling water and steam every hour and has done so for the last 100 years.

THE LANDSCAPE AROUND VOLCANOES

Steaming hot water

Volcanic gases bubble through liquid mud

HOT SPRINGS
Magma heats water stored in cracks in rock. The water returns to the surface as a hot spring.

MUD POOLS
Volcanic gases dissolve rock. Particles of rock mix with water to form bubbling mud pools.

FUMAROLES
As magma rises, it c[...] and gives off gases. S[...] holes or fumaroles i[...] rock let the gases esc[...]

PILLOW LAVA

When lava erupts underwater at spreading ridges, it can produce these rounded shapes called pillow lava. The sea water cools the lava rapidly, so that as it solidifies a crust forms around each lump. The lava formed is typically an igneous rock called basalt.

A NEW ISLAND

In 1963, off the Icelandic coast, a new island rose up from under the sea. Volcanic activity underwater brought magma to the surface. Sea water and hot magma produced explosions and huge amounts of steam. Now, plants grow in the fertile soil.

[GE]YSERS

[Ma]gma inside the Earth [he]ats water in the rocks. [Th]e water shoots from [th]e ground as steam jets.

TERRACES

Hot water stored in rock can dissolve minerals. Minerals are deposited in terraces around a vent.

GEYSER FACTS

• The tallest geyser is Yellowstone National Park's Steamboat Geyser in Wyoming, U.S.A. It reaches 60-115 m (195-380 ft).

• Strokkur Geyser in Iceland spurts every 10 to 15 minutes.

• In 1904, Waimangu Geyser, New Zealand erupted to a height of 460 m (1,500 ft).

WHEN THE EARTH SHAKES

MORE THAN A million times a year, the Earth's crust suddenly shakes during an earthquake. Most of the world's earthquakes are fairly slight. A mild earthquake can feel like a truck passing; a severe one can destroy roads and buildings and cause the sea to rise in huge waves. Earthquakes often happen near volcanoes and young mountain ranges: at the edges of the Earth's plates.

Surface waves radiate from the epicentre.

The focus is inside the Earth.

Shock waves go through the Earth and up to the surface.

A SEVERE EARTHQUAKE
San Francisco, U.S.A. was shaken by a devastating earthquake in 1906. Only the chimney stacks were left standing

CENTRE OF AN EARTHQUA
The earthquake is strongest
the focus. At the epicentre, t
point on the surface above t
focus, the crust shakes and sends o
shock waves. The waves bend as th
travel through layers of rock in the Eart

EARTHQUAKE FAULT ZONES

Earthquakes occur at cracks in the crust called faults. Deep earthquakes take place where one plate is sliding under another.

Many earthquakes occur on the north-east coast of Asia. This is at the boundary of two of the Earth's plates.

Stress builds up in rocks along the fault line.

| BEFORE AN EARTHQUAKE | AFTER AN EARTHQUAKE |

The plates slip into a new position.

SLIDING PLATES

Earthquakes occur at spreading ridges, subduction zones, and transform faults, where two plates slide past each other. Stress builds up in rock and causes a sudden movement as the rock jolts into a new position. Foreshocks may precede an earthquake, and aftershocks follow it.

EARTHQUAKE FACTS

• Before an earthquake it is reported that dogs howl, pandas moan, and well water bubbles.

• A strong earthquake can cause the ground to roll like waves at sea.

• The 1755 earthquake in Lisbon, Portugal lasted 10 minutes. It was felt as far away as north Africa.

• About 90 per cent of earthquakes occur in the Ring of Fire around the Pacific Ocean.

MEASURING EARTHQUAKES

SCIENTISTS WHO STUDY earthquakes are known as seismologists (*seismos* is the Greek word for earthquakes). Seismologists monitor the vibrations or shock waves that pass through the Earth using an instrument called a seismometer. Predicting earthquakes is very difficult. Scientists look for warnings such as bulges in the ground or cracks in surface rocks.

EARTHQUAKE DESTRUCTION
In 1994 in Los Angeles, U.S.A. an earthquake caused devastation. Roads and buildings collapsed, water mains and gas pipes burst, and fires began in the city. Many buildings in Los Angeles were built to be earthquake-proof and so did not suffer very much damage. The earthquake measured 5.7 on the Richter scale.

MERCALLI SCALE
Giuseppe Mercalli (1850-1914) devised a method of grading earthquakes based on the observation of their effects. Using this scale enables the amount of shaking, or intensity, of different earthquakes to be easily compared. On Mercalli's scale earthquakes are graded from 1 to 12.

1 • detected by instruments
2 • felt by people resting
3 • hanging light bulbs sway
4 • felt by people indoors
  • plates, windows rattle
  • parked cars rock

5 • buildings tremble
  • felt by most people
  • liquids spill
6 • movement felt by a
  • pictures fall off wal
  • windows break

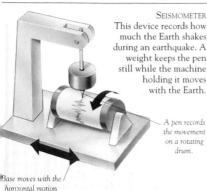

SEISMOMETER

This device records how much the Earth shakes during an earthquake. A weight keeps the pen still while the machine holding it moves with the Earth.

A pen records the movement on a rotating drum.

Base moves with the horizontal motion of the Earth.

The reading from a seismometer is called a seismogram. It indicates the extent of the Earth's shaking, either up and down or from side to side.

RICHTER SCALE		
The amount of energy released by an earth-quake can be measured on the Richter scale. An increase of 1.0 on the scale represents a ten-fold increase in energy.		
EARTHQUAKE	DATE	RICHTER SCALE
North Peru	1970	7.7
Mexico City	1985	7.8
Erzincan	1939	7.9
Tangshan	1976	8.0
Tokyo	1923	8.3
Kansu	1920	8.6

- bricks and tiles fall
- chimneys crack
- difficult to stand
- steering cars difficult
- tree branches snap
- chimneys fall

9
- general panic
- ground cracks
- mud oozes from ground
10
- underground pipes burst
- river water spills out
- most buildings collapse

11
- bridges collapse
- railway lines buckle
- landslides occur
12
- near total destruction
- rivers change course
- waves seen on ground

EARTHQUAKE DAMAGE

IN GENERAL, great loss of life during an earthquake can be avoided. It is often not the Earth's shaking that kills people but falling buildings, particularly poorly constructed ones. Earthquakes can trigger landslides and tsunamis which can be destructive. During an earthquake it is best to stay indoors under a sturdy table. Outdoors, falling masonry is a hazard.

ESTIMATED LIVES LOST AS A RESULT OF RECENT EARTHQUAKES

PLACE	YEAR	ESTIMATED DEATHS
Tangshan, China	1976	695,000
Kansu, China	1920	100,000
Tokyo, Japan	1976	99,000
Messina, Italy	1908	80,000
Armenia	1988	55,000
North-west Iran	1990	40,000
Erzincan, Turkey	1939	30,000

FIRE HAZARD
Fire poses a great danger following an earthquake. Gas leaks and petro spills can lead to large fires like thi in San Francisco, U.S.A. in 1989.

JAPANESE PRINT SHOWING A TSUNAMI TALLER THAN MT. FUJI IN JAPAN.

TSUNAMIS

An earthquake just off the coast can start a wave motion at sea. In the ocean the wave is low but as it nears the shore the front of it slows and water behind builds up to form a huge tsunami.

TSUNAMI FACTS

• The highest tsunami wave was 85 m (279 ft) high. It struck Ishigaki Island, Japan in 1971.

• In the open ocean, a tsunami can travel at speeds of up to 600 km (373 miles) per hour.

EARTHQUAKE-PROOF BUILDINGS

A great deal of damage is caused by buildings collapsing during earthquakes. In earthquake-prone San Francisco and Japan there are safety guidelines that all new buildings must meet. Wooden buildings are replaced with concrete and concrete and steel foundations are used.

NDSLIDES
se rock and debris may be odged by an earthquake cause landslides as here Alaska in 1964. Avalanches may be triggered by the nd shaking. Mudflows or ars can result from rain or snow mixing with loosened soil.

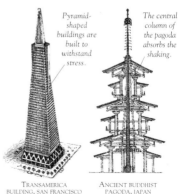

Pyramid-shaped buildings are built to withstand stress.

The central column of the pagoda absorbs the shaking.

TRANSAMERICA BUILDING, SAN FRANCISCO

ANCIENT BUDDHIST PAGODA, JAPAN

LANDSCAPES AND SOIL

THE WEATHER'S EFFECT on rock is what produces soil. This complex process takes many thousands of years. Climate, vegetation, and rock type determine what type of soil forms. As well as rock, soil contains organic matter from decaying plants and animals (humus). Soil covers the landscape and is a medium for plants to grow.

PEAT LANDSCAPE
This landscape is green and low-lying. Spongy peat soil is rich in humus from decayed bog plants. It retains water and nutrients easily.

SANDY LANDSCAPE
In arid (dry) sandy landscapes there is little vegetation. The soil contains hardly any organic material. Winds blow away small particles leaving sand and stones.

TYPES OF SOIL
Chalky soil is thin and stony; water passes through it quickly. Water drains easily through sandy soil, washing out nutrients. Clay soil retains nutrients and moisture but is difficult for plants to take root in. Peat soil is acidic. It holds water and minerals.

CLAY

SAND

PEAT

CHALK

SOIL FACTS

1 m³ (10.8 ft³) of soil may contain more than ?,000 million animals.

Some soils in India, Africa, and Australia are 2 million years old.

It takes about 500 years for 2.5 cm (1 in) of topsoil to form.

SOIL PROFILE

A slice of soil down to the bedrock is called a soil profile. The profile shows several layers, or horizons. The number and thickness of horizons vary with the soil type.

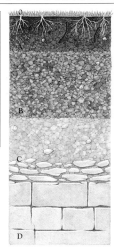

HORIZON 0
- humus layer
- contains live and decaying plants and soil animals

HORIZON A
- topsoil
- dark and fertile
- rich in humus

HORIZON B
- subsoil
- contains minerals washed down from topsoil
- little organic matter

HORIZON C
- infertile layer
- composed of weathered parent rock

HORIZON D
- bedrock (parent rock)
- source of soil's minerals

SOIL CREEP AND EROSION

Gravity and water pull soil down a slope particle by particle. This is called soil creep. Plant roots bind soil and help to prevent it from wearing away, or eroding. Overgrazing and felling forests both lead to soil erosion.

Soil creep is indicated by leaning structures such as walls and telegraph poles.

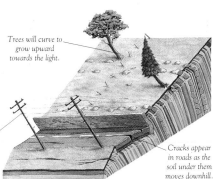

Trees will curve to grow upward towards the light.

Cracks appear in roads as the soil under them moves downhill.

EROSION IN WET CLIMATES

AS SOON AS ROCK is exposed on the Earth's surface, it is attacked by wind, water, or ice – a process known as weathering. This prepares for erosion, when rock is broken down and removed. Weathering can be either physical (wearing away the rock itself) or chemical (attacking the minerals in the rock). Climate and rock type determine the kind of weathering that occurs. In wet climates chemical weathering, mainly by rainwater, is dominant.

MOUNTAIN STREAM
Cascading over steep gradients, a swift-flowing stream wears away softer rocks. Harder rocks remain and create rocky outcrops. These become steep rapids or waterfalls where the water tumbles downhill.

TREE-ROOT ACTION
As trees and other plants grow, their roots push down into small cracks in the rock. The cracks widen as the roots grow and eventually the rock breaks up.

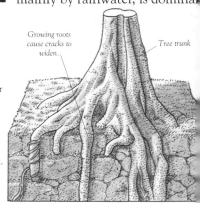

Growing roots cause cracks to widen.

Tree trunk

ST SHATTERING

s type of weathering

urs when water in

ks in the rock

es and expands.

ts in the rock

en and the

shatters.

nents of fallen

called

collect

base of

e.

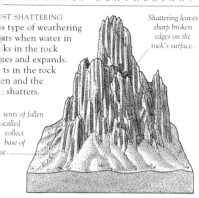

Shattering leaves sharp broken edges on the rock's surface.

EROSION FACTS

• Acid rain can dissolve rock as deep as 30 m (98 ft) below the surface.

• Erosion is fastest in steep, rainy areas and semi-arid areas with little vegetation.

• The rate of erosion for the whole of the world's land area is estimated to be 8.6 cm (3.3 in) every 1,000 years.

TS AND GRIKES

in rainwater seeps

limestone joints and

lves the calcite in the

Ridges known as

s and grooves known

kes form in the rock.

ACID RAIN

Rainwater naturally contains a weak acid called carbonic acid. However, the burning of fossil fuels produces gases such as sulphur dioxide. When this combines with rainwater it produces sulphuric acid – an ingredient of "acid rain". Acid rain damages trees and lake life.

Acid rain slowly dissolves rocks such as limestone and marble.

LIMESTONE STATUES SUFFER EROSION BY ACID RAIN

EROSION IN ARID CLIMATES

IN HOT, DRY, DESERT areas extremes of temperature cause rocks to fragment. By day rock expands in the heat and by night it contracts in the cold. It is mainly physical weathering that occurs in arid climates, chiefly caused by wind. The sand-filled wind blasts rocks and builds shifting sand dunes.

Some rocks break away and fall to the ground.

Larger rock masses split into blocks.

BLOCK DISINTEGRATION
Acute temperature changes can c. rocks to break up. Joints in the ro grow wider with the rock's cycle c expansion and contraction. Large pieces split into small blocks.

ONION-SKIN LAYERING
In the heat of the desert, a rock's surface may expand though the interior stays cool. At night, the surface of the rock cools and contracts. This daily process causes flaking on the surface of the rock, and the outer layers begin to peel and fall away.

SAND DUNES

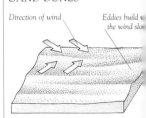

Direction of wind

Eddies build the wind slo

LINEAR OR SEIF DUNE
This type of dune has long parall ridges. It forms where the wind b continually in one direction.

ZEUGENS

...nd carried by the wind
...lpts these strange forms
...ed zeugens. Sand wears
...ay soft rock leaving
...ind areas of harder rock,
...rn into jagged shapes.

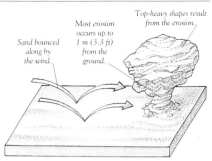

Sand bounced along by the wind.

Most erosion occurs up to 1 m (3.3 ft) from the ground.

Top-heavy shapes result from the erosion.

MUSHROOM ROCKS
The desert wind contains a great deal of sand
which scours away the surface of rocks.
Mushroom-shaped rocks are a result of this action.
Rocks are worn away most at their base by the
sand, leaving behind a landscape of rock pedestals.

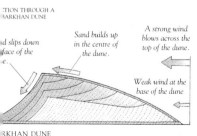

...CTION THROUGH A
...BARKHAN DUNE

...nd slips down ...face of the ...e.

Sand builds up in the centre of the dune.

A strong wind blows across the top of the dune.

Weak wind at the base of the dune

...RKHAN DUNE
...and dune with a crescent-shaped front and a
..., sloping tail is called a barkhan dune. This
...he most common dune shape in sandy deserts.

SAND DUNE FACTS

• Sand is composed
mostly of the hard
mineral quartz.

• Linear or seif dunes
can reach 215 m
(700 ft) high.

• Not all dunes are
made of sand – dunes
can form from salt
crystals, gypsum, or
shell fragments.

• Black sand dunes
form in volcanic areas.

IGNEOUS ROCKS

"FIERY" OR IGNEOUS rocks such as granite and basalt originate from molten magma. The magma is produced deep inside the Earth where rocks melt in the heat of the mantle and crust. Magma that cools and solidifies under the Earth's surface forms intrusive igneous rock. If it erupts as lava from a volcano and then cools on the surface of the Earth, it is known as extrusive igneous rock.

INTRUSIVE IGNEOUS ROCK
Sugar Loaf Mountain, Brazil forme from magma that solidified under ground. Eventually, the surroundi rock eroded leaving this dome sha

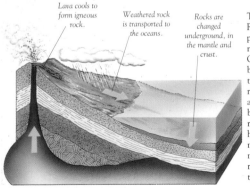

Lava cools to form igneous rock.

Weathered rock is transported to the oceans.

Rocks are changed underground, in the mantle and crust.

THE ROCK CYCLE
Rocks constantl pass through a recycling proces Crustal moveme bring igneous ro to the surface. T rocks weather av and the particle build sedimenta rocks. Pressure a heat undergrour may change, or metamorphose, rocks before they re-emerge.

SYDNEY HARBOUR BRIDGE
The supporting pylons of this famous bridge in Sydney, Australia are built from granite. The span of the bridge is 503 m (1,650 ft) and the arch is made of steel. Granite is often used as a building material because of its strength and availability.

IGNEOUS ROCK FACTS
• Basalt makes up most of the ocean floor.
• Obsidian was used in early jewellery and tools.
• Most continental igneous rocks are quartz, feldspar, and mica.
• Earth's first rocks were igneous rocks.

TYPES OF IGNEOUS ROCK

Shell-like, curved fracture

Granite has coarse grains

OBSIDIAN
This lava forms a natural glass. Its smooth texture is due to rapid cooling.

GABBRO
This intrusive, coarse-grained rock forms from slow-cooled lava.

BASALT
From runny lava that flows great distances, basalt is fine-grained.

PINK GRANITE
Granite is a common intrusive rock. Crystals of pink feldspar, black mica, and grey quartz minerals are visible.

SEDIMENTARY ROCKS

ROCK IS GRADUALLY weakened by
the weather. Particles of rock are
then carried off by rain or wind.
These particles build up into layers
of sediment. Sediment combines
with plant and animal debris and
hardens. Water in the ground can
help to cement the sediment
and turn it into rock (a process
known as lithification). By
studying sedimentary rock
layers, scientists can uncover
the environment of the past.

STRATA
Over millions of years, layer
of sediment are pressed into
bands of rock called strata.
Strata in the Grand Canyon
U.S.A. preserve a record of
the region's history.

FLINT TOOLS
Prehistoric people fashioned
tools from a sedimentary
rock called flint. Flint was
chipped into shape using a
stone. It is a common rock
FLINT
ADZE
that flakes easily, leaving a
sharp edge. Prehistoric
tools such as hand axes
and adzes (for shaping
wood) have been found.

CHALK CLIFFS
These cliffs in Sussex, England
are a type of limestone. They a
calcium carbonate (chalk) and
contain fossils of micro-organis

EYPTIAN PYRAMIDS AT GIZA
borate tombs (begun c.2686) for the Egyptian
araohs, were constructed at Giza, Egypt. They
re built from nummulitic limestone which
ntains many large marine fossils called *nummulites*.

SEDIMENTARY FACTS

• Chalk consists of shells, visible only under a microscope.

• Mudstone forms from compressed mud grains, and sandstone from compressed sand grains.

• Oil is usually found in permeable and porous sandstones.

TYPES OF SEDIMENTARY ROCK

BRECCIA
Fragments of rock cemented together make up breccia.

CHALK
Skeletons of tiny sea animals form this type of limestone. Chalk is fine-grained and soft.

RED SANDSTONE
Cemented sand grains coated with iron oxide make up this sedimentary rock.

SHELLY LIMESTONE
This rock contains a great many fossils cemented together with calcite. Limestone usually forms in a shallow sea, though it can come from a freshwater environment. It is possible to find the source of a specimen by studying the fossils it contains.

FOSSILS

PLANTS AND ANIMALS that lived millions of years ago are preserved in rocks as fossils. A fossil is the remains of an organism, a cast of an animal or plant made from minerals, or even burrows or tracks left by animals and preserved in rock. Sedimentary rocks such as limestone or chalk hold fossils. Palaeontologists are scientists who study fossils.

PLANT FOSSIL
Seed ferns like this one were widespread in the hot swamps of the late Carboniferous period. These primitive land plants, with some adaptations, still exist today.

THE FOSSILIZATION PROCESS

1 When an animal or plant dies underwater, it falls to the seabed. The soft parts of its body decay or are eaten by animals.

2 The organism is buried in layers of sediment. Hard parts of the animal, such as the shell, bones, or teeth, are preserved.

3 Minerals in the s⋯ bed react with th⋯ shell to harden it. S⋯ animals decay, leavi⋯ space where a cast fo⋯

Early dragonflies preserved in limestone have been found in Europe and Australasia. This one dates from the Jurassic period.

DRAGONFLY
(PETALURA)

FISH FOSSIL
Fish are the most primitive vertebrates (animals with backbones). This fish first appeared 30 to 24.5 million years ago, long after the dinosaurs had died out.

SEED FERN
(ALETHOPTERIS)

FISH FROM THE OLIGOCENE PERIOD

Further sediments cover the fossil. Uplift erosion of the crust may actually expose the at the surface.

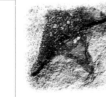

TRACE FOSSILS
Fossilized droppings or tracks are called trace fossils. This dinosaur footprint was left in mud 135 million years ago.

FOSSIL FACTS
• The earliest dinosaur, a *Herrerasaurus*, was found in Argentina in 1989 and dated at 230 million years old.

• The largest fossil footprint was left by a hadrosaurid. It is 1.36 m (4.46 ft) long.

• Fossils of cells are the first evidence of life, 3,200 million years ago.

THE AGES OF THE EARTH

THE EARTH'S HISTORY divides into eras, periods, and epochs. The timescale is marked by the appearance of new lifeforms. Life on Earth is never static – it changes and evolves constantly. Creatures become extinct and others appear. Some creatures may be short-lived and other survive unchanged for millions of years. Using fossil evidence scientists build a picture of life in the past.

JELLYFISH FOSSIL

PRECAMBRIAN FOSSIL
This fossil is about 570 million years old. It is a kind of primitive jellyfish that lived in Australia.

MORE FOSSIL FACTS

• Our species, *Homo sapiens*, first appeared about 40,000 years ago.

• A million Ice Age fossils were found preserved in the tar pits of La Brea, U.S.A.

CARBONIFEROUS SWAMP
Extensive swamps covered the land during the Carboniferous period (363-290 million years ago) It was during this time that forests, containing see plants and ferns, flourished. Some of these were preserved and now form coal deposits. The first reptiles and giant dragonflies lived in these swamp

DILOPHOSAURUS
(WO-RIDGED LIZARD)

*Distinguishing tall,
double crest on
the skull*

THE DINOSAUR AGE
The first land-dwelling
dinosaurs appeared
during the
Triassic, Jurassic,
and Cretaceous
periods. This skeleton is from
Dilophosaurus, an agile, predatory
dinosaur from the Jurassic period.

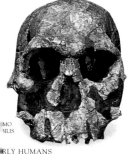

MO
ILIS

RLY HUMANS
mo habilis (handy man) is an
ly human, dating from the
aternary period. The name of
s ancestor comes from the fossil
dence that the early human was
led in using sophisticated tools.

GEOLOGICAL TIMESCALE	
ERA	PERIOD: MILLIONS OF YEARS AGO (MYA)
CENOZOIC	QUATERNARY 2 MYA–PRESENT
	TERTIARY 65–2 MYA
MESOZOIC	CRETACEOUS 146–65 MYA
	JURASSIC 208–146 MYA
	TRIASSIC 245–208 MYA
PALEOZOIC	PERMIAN 290–245 MYA
	CARBONIFEROUS 363–290 MYA
	DEVONIAN 409–363 MYA
	SILURIAN 439–409 MYA
	ORDOVICIAN 510–439 MYA
	CAMBRIAN 570–510 MYA
	PRECAMBRIAN 4,600–570 MYA

METAMORPHIC ROCKS

SEDIMENTARY, metamorphic, or igneous rocks are remade into new metamorphic rocks. The rock doesn't melt but it is changed underground by pressure and heat. During mountain building, in particular, intense pressure over millions of years alters the texture and nature of rocks. Igneous rocks such as granite change into gneiss and sedimentary rocks like limestone into marble.

SLATE MOUNTAINS
Fine-grained slate forms from sedimentary rocks. Rocks such as shale or mudstone are compressed during mountain building and changed into slate. Slate's aligned crystals mean that it splits, or cleaves, easily into flat sheets.

Carved white marble

MARBLE SCULPTURE
Michelangelo's statue of David is carved in marble. Marble comes in many varieties and is often used in buildings. It is also easy to cut.

METAMORPHIC FACTS

• The oldest rock on Earth is a metamorphic rock. It is Amitsoc gneiss from Amitsoc Bay, Greenland.

• Rubies are found in metamorphic limestone in the Himalayas. They formed during mountain building.

REGIONAL METAMORPHISM

Extreme pressure and heat as a result of mountain building lead to regional metamorphism. Metamorphism on this scale can cover a vast area.

Migmatite showing swirls of folded rock

Intrusive igneous rock exposed by weathering.

Aureole (area where metamorphism has taken place)

CONTACT METAMORPHISM

Rocks near to a lava flow or to an intrusion of igneous rock can be altered by contact metamorphism. This metamorphism affects a small area and is generated by heat alone.

TYPES OF METAMORPHIC ROCK

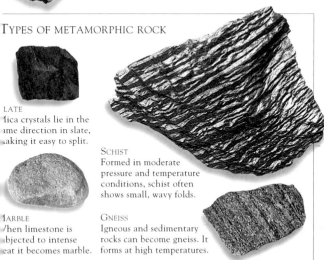

SLATE
Mica crystals lie in the same direction in slate, making it easy to split.

SCHIST
Formed in moderate pressure and temperature conditions, schist often shows small, wavy folds.

MARBLE
When limestone is subjected to intense heat it becomes marble.

GNEISS
Igneous and sedimentary rocks can become gneiss. It forms at high temperatures.

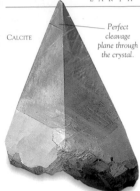

CALCITE

Perfect cleavage plane through the crystal.

CLEAVAGE AND FRACTURE
Diamond and calcite cleave when they break. Cleavage is a smooth break between layers of atoms in a crystal. A fracture is an uneven break, not related to the internal atomic structure. Most minerals fracture and cleave.

MINERALS

ROCKS ARE MADE from non-living, natural substances called minerals, which may be alone or in combination. Marble is pure calcite, for example, but granite is a mixture of quartz, feldspars, and mica. Most minerals are formed from silicates (compounds of oxygen and silicon). Minerals with a regular arrangement of atoms may form crystals. To identify a mineral, properties such as crystal structure, colour, and hardness are tested.

MOHS' SCALE	1	2	3	4
A German mineralogist named Friedrich Mohs devised a scale to compare the hardness of different minerals. A mineral is able to scratch any others below it on the scale and can be scratched by any mineral above it.	TALC	GYPSUM	CALCITE	FLUOR

MINERAL FACTS

• Only a diamond will scratch a diamond.

• Quartz is found in igneous, sedimentary, and metamorphic rock.

• The word "crystal" comes from a Greek word *kyros* meaning "icy cold".

PLAGIOCLASE FELDSPAR

QUARTZ OR ROCK CRYSTAL

FELDSPAR
This abundant rock-forming mineral is in both basalt and granite.

QUARTZ
A common mineral, quartz comes in many different colours. Amethyst and citrine are varieties of quartz.

COLOUR STREAKS
Scratching a mineral on an unglazed tile produces a coloured streak. The colour of the powder left behind is known as the mineral's streak.

ORPIMENT - GOLDEN   HEMATITE - RED/BROWN

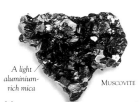

A light aluminium-rich mica

MUSCOVITE

MICA
Found in metamorphic rocks such as schists and slate, flaky mica is also in igneous rocks like granite.

5	6	7	8	9	10
ATITE	ORTHOCLASE FELDSPAR	QUARTZ	TOPAZ	CORUNDUM	DIAMOND

GEMSTONES

ONLY ABOUT 50 OF Earth's 3,000 minerals are valued as gemstones. Minerals such as diamonds, sapphires, emeralds, and rubies are commonly used as gems. They are chosen for their rarity, durability, colour, and optical qualities. Gems may be found embedded in rocks or washed into the gravel of a river. Organic gemstones have a plant or animal origin. They include pearl, amber, and coral.

Red spinels were often mistaken for rubies.

The crown contains more than 3,0 stones

CROWN JEWELS

The British Imperial State Crown contains the Black Prince's ruby (in fact a 170-carat spinel) and the famous Cullinan II diamor

EMERALD

Green beryl crystals called emeralds contain chromium to make them green. Most emeralds are mined in Colombia. They rate 7.5 on Mohs' scale of hardness.

Emerald is fo in granites a pegmatite

KIMBERLITE

Diamonds used to be found mainly in river gravels in India. In 1870 diamonds were discovered in volcanic rock, called kimberlite, in South Africa.

BRILLIANT

Skilled gem cutters, know as lapidaries, cut a rough crystal into a sparkling sto A diamond has 57 facets o faces ground onto it to ma it a brilliant.

SYNTHETIC GEMS

…ne gems can be
…roduced almost
…ctly in a laboratory.
…solved minerals and
…ouring agents
…stallize under strictly
…trolled conditions
…roduce perfect
…stals. Synthetic
…stals are used in
…dicine and the
…ctronics industry.

NATURAL RUBY

SYNTHETIC RUBY

GEMSTONE FACTS

• The Cullinan is the largest diamond ever found. It weighed 3,106 carats (0.6 kg/1.37 lb).

• About one in every 1,000 oysters contains a pearl, and about one in every 3,000 mussels.

• A carat equals 0.2 g (0.007 oz).

IMITATION TURQUOISE

REAL TURQUOISE

IMITATION GEMS

…lass or plastic may be
…ed to imitate gems.
…he optical properties
…such imitations are
…ferent from those
…the genuine gem.

PEARL

Shellfish, such as mussels and oysters, grow pearls in their shells. When a grain of sand lodges in its shell, the animal covers it with nacre, a substance to stop irritation. This creates a pearl.

AMBER

Fossilized tree resin from coniferous trees is called amber. The trees that yielded this amber existed more than 300 million years ago and are extinct. Amber may contain insects trapped in the tree sap.

ORE MINERALS

A ROCK THAT yields metal in sufficient amounts is a metallic ore. Gold and copper can be found as pure metals, that is, uncombined with any other elements. Most other metals, such as iron and tin, are extracted from ores. After mining or quarrying, the ores are crushed, and the metal separated and then purified.

IRON ORE
(HEMATITE)

ALUMINIUM ORE
(BAUXITE)

ALUMINIUM
KITCHEN FOIL

ALUMINIUM

Lightweight aluminium is a good conductor of electricity and resists corrosion. It is extracted from its main ore (bauxite) by passing an electric current through a rock solution. It is used for power lines.

GOLD FACTS

• The largest pure gold nugget weighed 70.9 k (156.3 lb). It was four in Victoria, Australia

• 60 per cent of the world's gold is mined in South Africa.

• Gold never loses its lustre or shine.

• It is said that all the gold ever mined woul fit into an average fou bedroomed house.

MERCURY
THERMOMETER

MERCURY ORE
(CINNABAR)

ON

matite is an important
ore. Iron can be cast,
ged, and alloyed with
er metals. Steel, used in
p-building and industry,
roduced using iron.

MERCURY
The primary mercury ore is called
cinnabar. It is found near volcanic
vents and hot springs, mostly in
China, Spain, and Italy. Mercury is
liquid at room temperature.

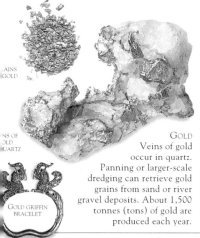

AINS
GOLD

NS OF
OLD
UARTZ

GOLD GRIFFIN
BRACELET

GOLD
Veins of gold
occur in quartz.
Panning or larger-scale
dredging can retrieve gold
grains from sand or river
gravel deposits. About 1,500
tonnes (tons) of gold are
produced each year.

MINING
Blasting and boring
rock in underground
mines allows recovery
of ores such as gold or
tin. Dredging gravel
or quarrying rock also
retrieves ores.

FOSSIL FUELS: COAL

PLANTS THAT GREW millions of years ago slowly changed to form coal. Vegetation in swamp areas, buried under layers of sediment, forms a substance called peat. Peat, in turn, is pressed into a soft coal called lignite. Soft bituminous coal forms under further pressure. Anthracite is the hardest and most compressed coal. When coal burns, the energy of the ancient plants is released. Coal is used to fuel power stations that produce electricity. Coal supplies, like oil, are finite.

PEAT

LIGNITE

BITUMINOUS COAL

ANTHRACITE

FROM PEAT TO COAL
Heat and pressure chang
crumbly brown peat into
shiny black anthracite c

COAL FORMATION

Vegetation

PEAT LAYER
In swamps, when plants decay they form a compact layer called peat. This material is 60 per cent carbon and can be burnt as a fuel.

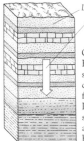

Layers of sediment

Temperature and pressure increases.

COAL LAYER
Buried beneath sediment layers compacted peat forms coal. Lignite is the softest coal and anthracite the hardest coal.

INSIDE A COAL MINE

To reach a seam, or layer, of coal underground, rock must be blasted and bored away. Shafts go down from the surface to tunnels at different levels. Rock pillars and walls support the roof.

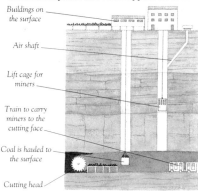

Buildings on the surface

Air shaft

Lift cage for miners

Train to carry miners to the cutting face

Coal is hauled to the surface

Cutting head

⌐AL MINING

⌐ople have mined coal ⌐ce about 500 B.C. ⌐day's miners use drills ⌐l computer-controlled ⌐chines. Special cutting ⌐chines dig out the coal ⌐ the coal face. Deep coal ⌐nes deliver 2,000 tonnes ⌐ns) of coal a day.

⌐P OF COAL DEPOSITS

⌐ampy forests covered parts ⌐Europe, Asia, and North ⌐erica, which were ⌐-lying during the ⌐rboniferous ⌐iod (360-⌐6 million ⌐rs ago). ⌐ese tropical ⌐est areas ⌐vide most of ⌐coal deposits ⌐t are mined today.

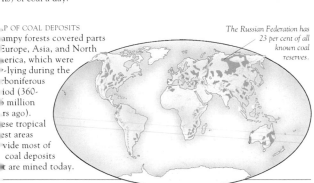

The Russian Federation has 23 per cent of all known coal reserves.

FOSSIL FUELS: OIL AND GAS

MOST SCIENTISTS believe oil and gas are the remains of marine animals. The organisms were broken down over millions of years and compressed to form oil and gas (they are usually found together). The modern world relies heavily on these fuels, especially oil refined into petrol. However, when oil burns it causes pollution.

OIL RIG
An oil production platform floats but is tethered to the seabed. Oil is pumped up lon pipelines to the oil platform

OIL AND GAS FORMATION

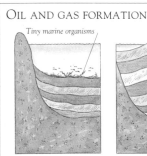

Tiny marine organisms

New layers of sediment

Oil and gas rigs

Fuels colle under so capro

1 Decaying plants and animals sink to the sea floor. They lie buried by accumulating layers of sediment.

2 Heat and pressure increase as the sediments sink deeper. The organic remains become oil and gas.

3 Molecules of gas and oil rise through permeable rock and are held in porous rock.

PRODUCTS MADE FROM OIL
After refining, oil can be separated to produce the substances ethylene (which forms plastics) and ethanol. Ethanol is a solvent used in paint manufacture. With oxygen added, ethanol makes synthetic fibres.

JUMPER MADE FROM
SYNTHETIC FIBRES

INFLATABLE TOY MADE
FROM THIN PLASTIC

PAINT

PLASTIC TOY

OIL USED IN MACHINERY AND VEHICLES

MAP OF OIL AND GAS DEPOSITS
Oil has been found in places such as the Middle East and the Arctic. North and Central America also have large oil and gas fields.

There are large oil deposits
in the North Sea.

The largest gas fields
are in the U.S.A.,
especially Alaska,
and in the Russian
Federation, usually
close to oil deposits.

OTHER SOURCES OF ENERGY

MOST OF THE energy the world uses for cooking, heating, or industry is produced by burning fossil fuels. As well as causing pollution, these fuels will eventually run out. The Sun, wind, or water can be used to create pollution-free energy. This energy is renewable for as long as the Sun shines, the wind blows, and the tides rise and fall. Much of the energy we use in our homes is generated at nuclear power stations.

SOLAR ENERGY
The Sun's light energy is captured by huge mirrors. The energy is used to generate electricity.

TIDAL POWER
Water is held on one side of this power station which is built across an estuary. At high tide water accumulates, then it is allowed to flow through the barrage, or dam. The force of the water-flow drives several turbines.

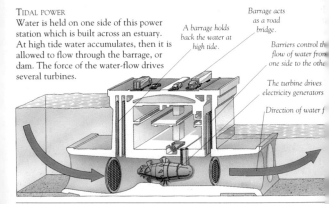

A barrage holds back the water at high tide.

Barrage acts as a road bridge.

Barriers control the flow of water from one side to the other.

The turbine drives electricity generators

Direction of water f

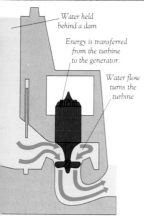

Water held behind a dam

Energy is transferred from the turbine to the generator.

Water flow turns the turbine

NUCLEAR ENERGY

Elements such as plutonium and uranium are used in nuclear power stations to generate energy. An atom of uranium can be split using a particle called a neutron. This produces heat and other neutrons. In turn, these neutrons split more atoms, generating further energy.

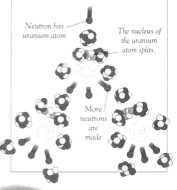

Neutron hits uranium atom

The nucleus of the uranium atom splits.

More neutrons are made

ATER POWER

hydroelectric power station uses ter power to produce electricity. e energy created by falling water ves a turbine. A turbine is then used power an electric generator.

NERGY FACTS

The first tidal power tation opened in La ance, France in 1966.

Nuclear power first roduced electricity in e U.S.A. in 1951.

Hydroelectric power ations generate five er cent of all electricity.

WIND POWER

California, U.S.A. has wind farms that contain thousands of windmills. Wind spins the propellers, which drive electric generators. Each windmill can produce up to four megawatts of power.

THE WORLD'S MOUNTAINS

THE HIGHEST POINTS on Earth result from a collision of Earth's tectonic plates. The highest range of mountains is the Himalayas in Asia. These lofty peaks continue to grow as the Indian plate pushes the Eurasian plate. As the rocky plates fracture and crumple (or fault and fold) a mountain range takes shape. Our planet has had several mountain-building episodes during its history. Some mountains continue to rise though all are being weathered away.

ANCIENT MOUNTAINS
The Scottish Highlands have been eroded into soft rounded hills. The ancient mountains formed more than 250 million years ago.

YOUNG MOUNTAINS
Mountains such as the Himalayas continue to rise. The mountains are 50 or so million years old and have jagged peaks.

TYPES OF MOUNTAIN

FAULT-BLOCK MOUNTAIN
When Earth's plates push into one another, faults or cracks in the crust appear. Huge blocks of rock are forced upwards.

FOLD MOUNTAIN
At the meeting of two of Earth's plates, the crust buckles and bends. The rocky crust is forced up into a mountain range.

MOUNTAINS AND MOUNTAIN RANGES

The world's longest mountain ranges usually follow the edges of the Earth's plates. Where plates collide they crumple and fold.

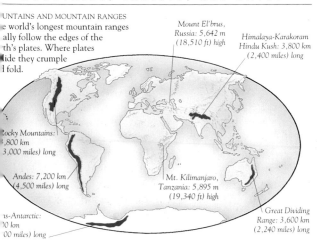

Mount El'brus, Russia: 5,642 m (18,510 ft) high

Himalaya-Karakoram Hindu Kush: 3,800 km (2,400 miles) long

Rocky Mountains: 4,800 km (3,000 miles) long

Andes: 7,200 km (4,500 miles) long

Mt. Kilimanjaro, Tanzania: 5,895 m (19,340 ft) high

Andes-Antarctic: ?0 km (?00 miles) long

Great Dividing Range: 3,600 km (2,240 miles) long

VOLCANO

Magma in a deep magma chamber may erupt to form a volcano. Lava, ash and rock ejected from the volcano, build a tall cone.

DOME MOUNTAIN

Rising magma from under the Earth's crust spreads upwards and forces up rocks near the surface. A dome-shaped mountain is the result.

MOUNTAIN FACTS

• The ten highest mountains in the world are all in the Himalayas.

• Europe's Alps are part of a mountain belt that stretches from the Pyrenees in Europe to the Himalayas in Asia.

• The Himalayas grow at a rate of 1 m (3.3 ft) every 1,000 years.

• The Alps are the youngest of the world's great mountain ranges.

MOUNTAIN FEATURES

CONDITIONS ON MOUNTAINS can be harsh. As altitude increases temperature drops, air becomes thinner, and winds blow harder. Animal and plant life has adapted to survive in this environment. Mountains can be divided into several separate zones. The zones are similar whether the mountain lies in a tropical or temperate area and whether it is an isolated volcanic peak or part of a mountain range.

MOUNT KILIMANJARO
Africa's tallest mountain is Mount Kilimanjaro in Tanzania. It is a solitary peak, not part of a range. In fact, it is a dormant volcanic cone. Despite lying near the equator, Kilimanjaro is permanently snow-capped.

WORLD'S HIGHEST MOUNTAINS			
MOUNTAIN	LOCATION	HEIGHT IN METRES	HEIGHT IN FEET
Mt. Everest, Nepal	Asia	8,848	29,028
Mt. Aconcagua, Argentina	South America	6,960	22,834
Mt. McKinley, Alaska	North America	6,194	20,320
Mt. Kilimanjaro, Tanzania	Africa	5,895	19,340
Mt. El'brus, Russia	Europe	5,642	18,510
Vinson Massif	Antarctica	5,140	16,863
Mt. Wilhelm, Papua New Guinea	Australasia	4,884	16,024

THE ANDES
The world's longest range of mountains is the Andes in South America. The chain stretches for 7,200 km (4,500 miles).

UNDERSEA MOUNTAIN

Measured from the ocean floor, Mauna Kea, Hawaii is taller than Mount Everest. Rising 4,205 m (13,796 ft) above sea level, its base lies in a trough under the sea.

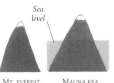

Sea level

MT. EVEREST
8,848 M
(29,028 FT)

MAUNA KEA
10,205 M
(33,480 FT)

MORE MOUNTAIN FACTS

• On a mountain, the temperature drops 0.7°C (1.1° F) for every 100 m (330 ft) climbed.

• In warm equatorial regions trees can grow at heights of 4,000 m (13,124 ft).

MOUNTAIN VEGETATION

As the altitude increases the temperature falls. This effect produces distinct vegetation and climate zones. The plant and animal life of each zone varies. These are the zones of the European Alps.

Rocks permanently covered with snow support no plant or animal life.

Permanent snowline

Loose rock, or scree, fractured by the weathering process

Alpine plants and flowers in pasture land have adapted to survive in the cold air.

Coniferous forest

Deciduous forests grow at the base of the mountain.

VALLEYS

FORCES OF EROSION, especially water, carve out the shape of the landscape. Steep-sided valleys can be cut out by fast-flowing mountain streams. Larger rivers wear a path through the land, shaping wide, flat valleys as they near the sea. Frozen water in glaciers also erodes rock, forming deep, icy gullies. Valleys sometimes form as a result of crustal movement that pull rocks apart at a fault in the Earth's surface.

GORGE
A ravine with steep sides is called a gorge. A canyon is similar to a gorge but it is usually found in desert areas.

Land drops between the plate edges.

RIFT VALLEY
Faults occur in the Earth's crust where two plates are moving apart. A long, straight valley, such as the African Rift Valley, forms between the faults.

Rivers shed their sediments on the flat flood plain.

A fan-shaped delta forms at the river mouth.

FJORD
Steep-sided inlets in Norway and New Zealand are caused by glaciers deepening river valleys. As the ice melts and the sea level rises these fjords become flooded.

VALLEY FACTS

• Africa's Rift Valley stretches for 4,000 km (2,500 miles).

• The longest fjord, in Nordvest, Greenland, is 313 km (194 miles) long.

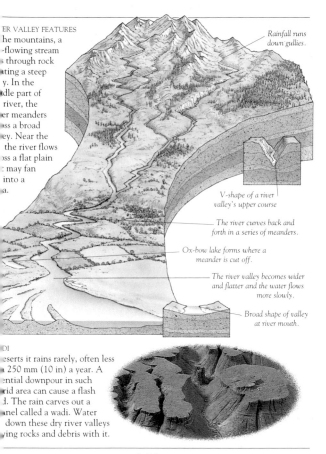

RIVER VALLEY FEATURES

In the mountains, a fast-flowing stream cuts through rock creating a steep valley. In the middle part of the river, the water meanders across a broad valley. Near the sea, the river flows across a flat plain and may fan out into a delta.

Rainfall runs down gullies.

V-shape of a river valley's upper course

The river curves back and forth in a series of meanders.

Ox-bow lake forms where a meander is cut off.

The river valley becomes wider and flatter and the water flows more slowly.

Broad shape of valley at river mouth.

WADI

In deserts it rains rarely, often less than 250 mm (10 in) a year. A torrential downpour in such an arid area can cause a flash flood. The rain carves out a channel called a wadi. Water flows down these dry river valleys carrying rocks and debris with it.

CAVES

UNDERGROUND CAVERNS and caves occur in several types of landscape. Different processes are responsibl for the different sorts of cave. The action of ice, lava, waves, and rainwater cause subterranean openings. In particular, rainwater has a spectacular effect on limestone, producing vast caverns full of unusual shapes.

ICE CAVE
Beneath a glacier there is sometimes a stream of water that has thawed, called meltwater. The water can wear away an cave full of icicles in the glacier.

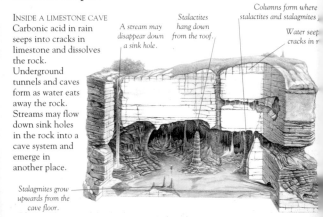

INSIDE A LIMESTONE CAVE
Carbonic acid in rain seeps into cracks in limestone and dissolves the rock. Underground tunnels and caves form as water eats away the rock. Streams may flow down sink holes in the rock into a cave system and emerge in another place.

A stream may disappear down a sink hole.

Stalactites hang down from the roof.

Columns form where stalactites and stalagmites

Water seep cracks in r

Stalagmites grow upwards from the cave floor.

LAVA CAVE
Some lava cools to form a thick crust. Below the crust a tube of molten lava flows. When it empties a cave is left.

CAVE FACTS

• Jean Bernard cave in France is the deepest in the world. It is 1,602 m (5,256 ft) deep.

• The longest stalactite – 6.2 m (20.4 ft) long – is in Co. Clare, Ireland.

• The tallest stalagmite is 32 m (105 ft) high. It is in the Czech Republic.

• America's Mammoth Cave system, Kentucky, is the world's longest cave system. It is 560 km (348 miles) long.

CAVE
...es may form at the base of ...undercut by waves. A ...can be worn through to ...an arch. The top of this ...may eventually ...pse and leave an ...ed stack to be ...ted by the waves.

STALAGMITES AND STALACTITES

STALACTITE
In limestone caves, deposits of calcite in dripping water create distinctive features, such as stalactites. These grow from the ceiling of the cave towards the floor.

COLUMNS
...ineral deposits construct ...alactites and stalagmites in ...ves. If the two shapes ...eet, they form a column.

STALAGMITE
It may take several thousand years for a stalagmite to grow 2.5 cm (1 in) – drip by drip from a cave floor to the roof.

THE WORLD'S GLACIERS

A GLACIER IS a moving ice mass that results from mo
snow falling in winter than melts in the summer. In
mountain regions glaciers form when snow builds up
pressing down on older snow and squeezing out the a

The compressed ice will eventually
begin to move downhill. This froze
"river" carries a great deal of debris
Surrounding rock is scoured by the
ice and sediment as it travels down
the valley. In this way glaciers leav
their mark on
the landscape.

GLACIAL DEBRIS
Rocks are smoothed
when they are plucked
up and carried along by
a glacier. This rock has
scratches, or striae, too.

*Ridge or arête
between two
glaciers*

*Medial moraine –
debris carried in the
middle of the glacier*

*When the ice moves
a sharp incline, it cr
to form crevasses*

THE WORLD'S LONGEST GLACIERS		
GLACIERS	LENGTH IN KM	LENGTH IN MILES
Lambert-Fisher Ice Passage, Antarctica	515	320
Novaya Zemlya, Russia	418	260
Arctic Institute Ice Passage, Antarctica	362	225
Nimrod-Lennox-King, Antarctica	289	180
Denman Glacier, Antarctica	241	150
Beardmore Glacier, Antarctica	225	140
Recovery Glacier, Antarctica	200	124

FORE GLACIATION
e mountain valley
ved out by a river is
ally steep and shaped
e a letter V.

AFTER GLACIATION
A mountain glacier flows
along the path of a river.
The V-shape is eroded by
the glacier into a U-shape.

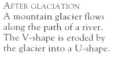

GLACIER FACTS
• Eight of the ten
longest glaciers in the
world are found in the
Antarctic.

• About 10 per cent of
Earth's land surface is
permanently glaciated.

• The fastest-moving
glacier is the Quarayaq
glacier in Greenland.
It flows 20-24 m
(65-80 ft) per day.

• Most glaciers move
at a rate of about 2 m
(6 ft) per day.

OSS-SECTION
A GLACIER

*Cirque or corrie – hollow
where glacier begins*

Compact snow called firn

FEATURES OF A GLACIER
A glacier begins high in the mountains in
hollows called cirques. New snow builds up
and becomes compacted, forming denser ice
called firn. As the glacier moves downhill it
collects rock from the floor and sides of the
valley and carries it along. Eventually the
glacier reaches a point where it melts and
drops its load of rocky debris, or moraine.

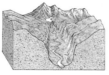

*The snout or front
of the glacier*

*Meltwater
flows from the
snout*

*Pile of rocks and
boulders called
terminal moraine*

ICE CAPS AND ICE AGES

ANTARCTICA AND GREENLAND are blanketed in ice sheets up to 3,500 m (11,500 ft) thick. Many winters of snowfall accumulate to produce an ice cap, which eventually moves downhill as a broad glacier. In Earth's history, periods of extreme cold, called ice ages, brought glacial conditions as far south as Europe and North America. Our mild climate may only be an interval between ice ages.

ICE CAP
Vast ice sheets covering Antarctic and Greenland are known as ice caps. This type of glacier originate in cold regions of the world; other glaciers are in mountainous areas.

FORMATION OF AN ICE CAP
Layers of snow build up during the winter months and become icy firn. Over several years, the result is a thick ice cap. Gravity pulls the ice down to the edges of the land.

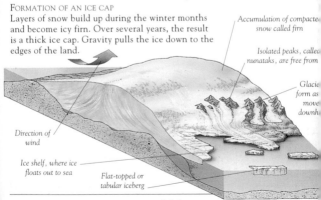

Accumulation of compacte
snow called firn

Isolated peaks, called
nunataks, are free from

Glacie
form as
move
downh

Direction of
wind

Ice shelf, where ice
floats out to sea

Flat-topped or
tabular iceberg

...APH OF THE EARTH'S TEMPERATURE
...low points on the graph show the last
...occasions when the average temperature
...Earth was cold enough to allow major
...ial advances.

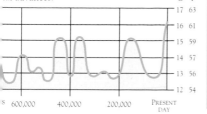

	Climate	
	°C	°F
	17	63
	16	61
	15	59
	14	57
	13	56
	12	54

...s   600,000   400,000   200,000   PRESENT
                                              DAY

...AGES

...ing the last ice age,
...ut 30,000 years ago, ice
...ts covered a large part
...e planet, particularly
...th America and Europe.
...ice ages are interspersed
...warmer periods called
...rglacials. Ice advanced
...retreated with each
...or temperature change.

PLEISTOCENE EPOCH
– THE LAST ICE AGE

EXTENT OF ICE IN
THE WORLD TODAY

SCIENTISTS EXAMINE
A BABY MAMMOTH
FOUND IN THE ICE

WOOLLY MAMMOTH
In Siberia, the remains of extinct animals called mammoths have been found in ice. They froze so quickly that their bodies were preserved virtually intact. These elephant-like mammals had curled tusks and woolly coats and lived during the last ice age.

AVALANCHES AND ICEBERGS

MOUNTAINS ARE inhospitable places. Winter snowstorms pile up layers of ice and snow. The layers may become unstable and rush down the mountain in an avalanche, sweeping away anything in their path. Ships at sea must contend with another icy hazard: icebergs, formed when large chunks of ice break off coastal glaciers or ice shelves and float out to sea.

SEA ICE
Seawater freezes when it reaches −1.9°C (28°F). Sea ice is never more than abou 5 m (16 ft) thick. It can be used as a source of fresh wat because the salt is left behin in the sea.

A heavy snowfall adds weight to the snow cover.

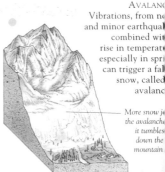

AVALAN
Vibrations, from ne and minor earthqua combined wit rise in temperat especially in spr can trigger a fa snow, called avalanc

More snow j the avalanch it tumbles down the mountain

SNOWLINE

There is an imaginary line on a
mountainside, called the snowline,
below which snow melts
during summer. Above
this line the snow
remains throughout
the year. The
snowline is higher
in areas nearer
the equator.

*In Antarctica, the
snowline is at or
near sea level.*

*The snowline in the
European Alps is at about
2,700 m (9,000 ft) high.*

*On the equator
the snowline
is 4,900 m
(16,000 ft) high.*

ICEBERGS

Glaciers and the floating edges of ice caps lose
chunks of ice called icebergs into the sea, a
process known as calving. All icebergs are frozen
fresh water, rather than frozen sea water.

THE WORLD'S OCEANS

SEEN FROM SPACE, the Earth looks blue and watery. This is because two-thirds of it is covered with water. The water is held in oceans and seas. (Seas are surrounded by land.) Three of the five oceans are in the southern hemisphere. Major currents circulate the oceans anti-clockwise in the southern hemisphere and clockwise in the northern hemisphere.

THE WORLD'S LARGEST OCEANS AND SEAS		
OCEAN OR SEA	AREA IN KM²	AREA IN MILES²
Pacific Ocean	166,229,000	64,181,000
Atlantic Ocean	86,551,000	33,417,000
Indian Ocean	73,422,000	28,348,000
Arctic Ocean	13,223,000	5,105,000
South China Sea	2,975,000	1,149,000
Caribbean Sea	2,516,000	917,000
Mediterranean Sea	2,509,000	969,000
Bering Sea	2,261,000	873,000

FORMATION OF OCEANS

THE ATMOSPHERE FORMS
The semi-molten surface of the Earth was covered by volcanoes. Hot gases and water vapour emitted by volcanoes formed the Earth's early atmosphere.

THE RAINS FALL
The water vapour in this early atmosphere condensed as rain. Rainstorms poured down on the planet and filled the vast hollows on the Earth's surface.

THE OCEANS FORM
These huge pools became the oceans. The water was hot and acidic. Later, plant life evolved and produced oxygen for the atmosphere and oceans.

OCEAN ZONES
Oceanographers split
the oceans into zones
according to depth.
Only water near the
surface is sunlit. At
greater depths the
water is colder and
darker. Pressure also
increases with depth.
Sea creatures have
adapted to conditions
in the different zones.

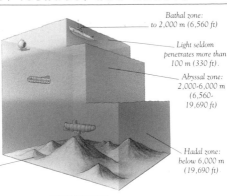

Bathal zone:
to 2,000 m (6,560 ft).

Light seldom
penetrates more than
100 m (330 ft).

Abyssal zone:
2,000-6,000 m
(6,560-
19,690 ft)

Hadal zone:
below 6,000 m
(19,690 ft)

The temperature
deep in the ocean is
nearly freezing.

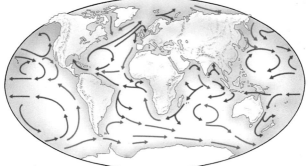

THE OCEANS' CURRENTS
Currents may be warm or cold. They flow across the
surface or deep beneath it. The wind controls surface
currents, which flow in circular directions. Currents
carry some of the Sun's heat around the planet,
warming polar areas and cooling tropical areas.

KEY	
COLD CURRENT	→
WARM CURRENT	→

WAVES AND TIDES

THE OCEANS AND seas are always moving. Buffeted by the wind and heated by the Sun, waves and currents form in the oceans. Ripples on the surface of the water grow into waves that pound the shore and shape coastlines. The Moon's and Sun's gravity pull the oceans, causing a daily and monthly cycle of tides.

WHIRLPOOL
An uneven seafloor can cause several tidal flows to collide. The currents surge upwards and rush into each other. Eddies and whirlpools form at the surface.

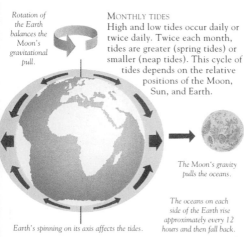

Rotation of the Earth balances the Moon's gravitational pull.

MONTHLY TIDES
High and low tides occur daily or twice daily. Twice each month, tides are greater (spring tides) or smaller (neap tides). This cycle of tides depends on the relative positions of the Moon, Sun, and Earth.

The Moon's gravity pulls the oceans.

The oceans on each side of the Earth rise approximately every 12 hours and then fall back.

Earth's spinning on its axis affects the tides.

SPRING TIDES
The Sun, Earth, and Moon are aligned to create spring tides.

NEAP TIDES
Opposing pulls of Sun and Moon cause neap tides.

LF STREAM
urrent of warm water called the
lf Stream moves from the Gulf
Mexico across the Atlantic,
nging mild winter weather to
western coasts of Europe.
e a huge river at sea, the
lf Stream flows 160 km
0 miles) a day. This current
gyre is 60 km (37 miles) wide
600 m (2,000 ft) deep. As
Gulf Stream nears Europe it is
ed the North Atlantic Drift.

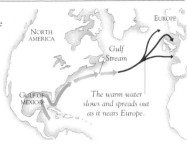

EUROPE

NORTH
AMERICA

Gulf
Stream

GULF OF
MEXICO

*The warm water
slows and spreads out
as it nears Europe.*

*top part of the wave,
e crest, continues up
the beach.*

*Particles near the surface
turn over and over*

*e beach slows
n the base of
the wave.*

WAVE MOVEMENT
The wind blows waves
towards the shore. But it
is not the water particles
that travel, only the
wave form. The particles
rotate as each wave
passes and return to their
original position.

AVE FACTS

The highest recorded
ave was seen in the
estern Pacific. It was
m (112 ft) high from
ugh to crest.

The Antarctic
rcumpolar Current
ws at a rate of
0 million m³ (4,600
llion ft³) per second.

Hawaiian tides rise
cm (12 in) a day.

COMPOSITION OF
SEAWATER
The oceans contain
dissolved minerals,
some washed from
the land by rivers.
The predominant
constituents of sea-
water are sodium
and chloride which
together form salt.
The oceans are
about 35 parts water
to one part salt.

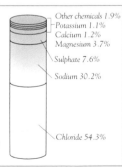

Other chemicals 1.9%
Potassium 1.1%
Calcium 1.2%
Magnesium 3.7%

Sulphate 7.6%

Sodium 30.2%

Chloride 54.3%

THE OCEAN FLOOR

THE WORLD UNDER the oceans has both strange and familiar features. Similar to a landscape on dry ground, mountains, valleys, and volcanoes dot the ocean floor. Once scientists had equipment to explore the ocean bed, they discovered that tectonic plate movement had caused many ocean floor features, including trenches, seamounts, and submarine canyons.

MAPPING THE OCEAN
Oceanographers use
echo-sounding, which
bounces signals off the
ocean bed, to map the
ocean floor's contours

FEATURES OF THE OCEAN FLOOR

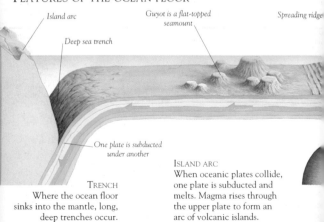

Island arc

Guyot is a flat-topped
seamount

Spreading ridge

Deep sea trench

One plate is subducted
under another

TRENCH
Where the ocean floor
sinks into the mantle, long,
deep trenches occur.

ISLAND ARC
When oceanic plates collide,
one plate is subducted and
melts. Magma rises through
the upper plate to form an
arc of volcanic islands.

DEEP-SEA EXPLORATION

DIVERS AND VEHICLES	DEPTH IN METRES	DEPTH IN FEET
Sponge diver holding breath	15	49
SCUBA sports diver	50	164
Oil rig divers with diving bell	250	820
Deepest experimental dive	500	1,640
Barton's benthoscope	1,370	4,494
Cousteau diving saucer	3,350	11,000
Shinkai submersible	6,500	21,325
Trieste bathyscape	10,911	35,800

BATHYSCAPE
The deepest dive was made by the bathyscape *Trieste* in 1960. It dived in the world's deepest trench, the Mariana Trench.

SEAMOUNT
An underwater volcano that rises over 1,000 m (3,280 ft) is a seamount.

ABYSSAL PLAIN
This sediment-covered plain lies at a depth of about 4,000 m (15,000 ft).

SUBMARINE CANYON
Rivers of sediment flowing from the continental shelf can erode deep canyons.

Two of the Earth's tectonic plates are moving apart

Seamount

Submarine canyon

Continental shelf

Abyssal plain

Continental slope

Magma rises between the plates

Continental rise

MID-OCEANIC RIDGE
Magma rising between two tectonic plates forms a ridge.

CONTINENTAL SLOPE
The continental slope descends steeply from the continental shelf towards the abyssal plain, flattening out along the gently sloping continental rise.

CONTINENTAL SHELF
Stretching from the edge of the land like a vast ledge under the sea, the continental shelf can be 70 km (43 miles) wide. The ocean here is about 250 m (1,600 ft) deep.

OCEAN FEATURES

OCEANS ARE a rich source of many useful substances.
Seawater contains nutrients and minerals. Deposits of
oil and gas are found in continental
shelf sediment. Metals such as gold
and manganese are present in
sediments on the ocean
floor. Near ocean
ridges, the sea may
contain minerals from
inside the Earth.

BLACK SMOKERS

In 1977, scientists discovered
strange chimneys, formed from
minerals on the ocean floor,
called black smokers.
In rift valleys
between spreading
ridges, they eject
water as hot as 300°C
(572°F) and minerals
such as sulphur.

*The vent
minerals
colour the
water black.*

*Jets of hot
water shoot
from the
chimneys.*

*Smokers can
grow as tall
as 10 m
(33 ft).*

*Tube worms
and giant
clams live on
bacteria near
the vents.*

THE WORLD'S DEEPEST SEA TRENCHES		
TRENCH	DEPTH IN METRES	DEPTH IN FEET
Mariana Trench, West Pacific	10,920	35,827
Tonga Trench, South Pacific	10,800	35,433
Philippine Trench, West Pacific	10,057	32,995
Kermadec Trench, South Pacific	10,047	32,961
Izu-Ogasawara Trench, West Pacific	9,780	32,087

OCEAN PRODUCT FACTS

• There are 0.000004
parts per million of gold
in the ocean.

• It takes a million
years for a manganese
nodule to grow 2 mm
(0.08 in) in diameter.

OCEAN PRODUCTS

MANGANESE
Nodules from the seabed are used in industry.

OIL
This is a non-renewable fossil fuel. It is pumped from rocks in the continental shelf.

SAND
Rock pounded by waves becomes sand. In volcanic areas it is black.

LIMESTONE
Like sand, limestone is found mostly in coastal waters.

Diamonds in gravel are known as alluvial diamonds.

Diamond

DIAMONDS IN GRAVEL
In shallow waters off the coasts of Africa and Indonesia, diamonds can be found in continental shelf gravels. Most have been washed down by rivers into the sea.

OCEAN FLOOR SEDIMENT
The continental shelf is covered with sand, mud, and silt washed onto it from rivers. In the deep ocean, the floor is covered with ooze. This contains remains of dead marine life.

Rock is carried 500 km (311 miles) from the ridge over 5 million years. Sediment gathers.

After 10 million years the rock has moved farther from the ridge. It is now covered with thick sediment.

Rock erupted from the mantle at mid-ocean ridges has no sediment cover.

ISLANDS

A PIECE OF LAND smaller than a
continent and surrounded by
water is called an island. Magma
rising from volcanic vents in the
crust creates islands in the sea.
An arc of islands appears where
a tectonic plate is subducted.
Some islands exist only when
the tide is high; at low tide it is
possible to walk to these islands.
Small islands may exist in rivers
and lakes. In warmer regions
coral reefs may grow from the
sea, built by living
organisms.

Causeway

A narrow s
of land lin
the island
the shore

CAUSEWAY
A change in sea level
can create an island.
Land may be accessible
only at low tide by a
causeway. At high tide
the island is cut off.

ISLAND FACTS

• Bouvet Island is the
most remote island –
about 1,700 km (1,056
miles) from the nearest
landmass (Antarctica).

• Kwejalein in the
Marshall Islands, in the
Pacific Ocean is the
largest coral atoll. Its
reef measures 283 km
(176 miles) long.

ISLAND ARC
On one side of a subduction zone, a curved chain
arc of volcanic islands may be pushed up from un
the ocean floor. From space the numerous volcan
peaks on the islands of Indonesia are clearly visib

E WORLD'S LARGEST ISLANDS

ISLAND	AREA IN KM ^{2}	AREA IN MILES ^{2}
nland	2,175,219	839,852
Guinea	792,493	305,981
co	725,416	280,083
agascar	587,009	226,644
n Island, Canada	507,423	195,916
atra, Indonesia	427,325	104,990
hu, Japan	227,401	87,799
t Britain	218,065	84,195

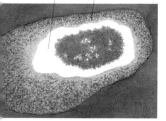

d builds up more e side of the reef.

New coral organisms grow on old coral skeletons.

AL ISLAND

ds such as the Maldives in the Indian
an are known as coral islands. Tiny
ne organisms called corals grow on
nerged rock formations such as under-
olcanoes (seamounts) in warm, salty
The coral grows slowly up to the
n's surface and, when sea level drops,
tes a firm platform above sea level.

FORMATION OF A CORAL ATOLL

Volcanic island

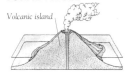

1 A FRINGING REEF
Where a volcano has
emerged from under the
ocean, coral begins to grow on
its fringes, around the base of
the volcano.

Barrier reef

2 A BARRIER REEF
When volcanic activity
subsides, the peak erodes. The
coral forms a reef around the
edge of the volcano.

Lagoon

3 AN ATOLL FORMS
Eventually, the volcano
sinks beneath the sea. A ring
of coral known as an atoll
remains on the surface.

COASTS

WHERE THE LAND meets the sea there is the coast.
Coasts may have cliffs, or sandy or pebble beaches.
There is a continual battle between sea and coast
as rock is broken down by pounding waves, and
sand carried about by wind. Some coasts retreat
but new coast is always being deposited in other
areas. Beaches alter with the
seasons, as sand shifts along
the shore or out to sea.

*Longshore drift car
sand across a bay
river mouth.*

*Waves slow at
the end of the tail
or spit of sand.*

Sand spit

LONGSHORE DRIFT

*A pebble moves in a zig-
zagged path along the beach.*

BEACH FORMATION
Sand and shingle deposited along
the shore form a beach. Its shape
is determined by the angle of the
waves. This process is called
longshore drift. Storms hurl beach
debris about, but eventually most
ends up on the seabed.

*Waves strike the
beach at an angle.*

*Wind and
wave direction*

·AST FACTS

The largest pleasure
·ch is Virginia Beach,
·.S.A. with an area of
·3 km² (310 miles²).

·he world has about
·4,000 km (312,000
·les) of coastline.

·he highest sea cliffs
· at Molokai, Hawaii.
·ey descend 1,010 m
·300 ft) to the sea.

· At Martha's Vineyard,
·.S.A. the cliffs retreat
·m (5.6 ft) per year.

TYPES OF COAST

Direction of waves

TOMBOLO
This type of coastline
links an island to the
shore by a strip of sand.

BARRIER BEACH
A lagoon forms behind
a barrier of sand built
by onshore waves.

Direction of waves

BAYHEAD BEACH
Waves striking a head-
land at an angle leave
a protected arc of sand.

FJORD COASTLINE
A submerged glacial
valley with steep sides
forms a fjord coastline.

*Groynes or fences built
into the sea prevent
longshore drift.*

*Sand builds up
against the
groyne.*

SEA STACKS
Waves, carrying
sand and pebbles,
gradually wear away
a headland. First, a
cave appears, which
is enlarged to form
an arch. Then, the
arch falls, leaving
an isolated stack.

*Sea cave eroded
by sea until
arch forms*

*Top of arch
collapses leaving
pillar or stack*

·d and shingle

2 2 5

THE WORLD'S RIVERS

WHEREVER THEY occur, rivers are
a key part of the Earth's water
cycle. They carry rainwater
from high areas down to the
sea, filling up lakes and pools
on the way. In some parts of
the world, rivers do not exist
all year round. During the dry
season they can disappear
altogether but reappear once
the wetter season begins.

PERENNIAL RIVER
In temperate and tropical areas
reliable supply of rainwater crea
perennial rivers. Rivers such as
Nile, in Africa, flow all year ro

THE WATER CYCLE
Water is constantly circulating between
land, sea, and air. The Sun's heat causes
evaporation from seas, lakes, and rivers.
Tiny droplets of water vapour
rise and form clouds. The
droplets cool and condense
to fall as rain. The water
fills rivers and lakes and
flows to the sea.

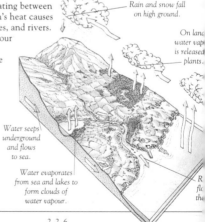

*Rain and snow fall
on high ground.*

*On land
water vap
is released
plants.*

*Water seeps
underground
and flows
to sea.*

*Water evaporates
from sea and lakes to
form clouds of
water vapour.*

RIVER FACTS
• The River Nile is
longer, but the Amazon
carries more water.

• China's Yangtze
carries 1,600,000 tonnes
(tons) of silt a year.

SEASONAL RIVER

This dry river bed belongs to a Spanish seasonal river. In the hot summer many rivers dry up, but during the wet winter season rain will fill them up.

THE WORLD'S LONGEST RIVERS		
RIVER AND CONTINENT	LENGTH IN KM	LENGTH IN MILES
Nile, Africa	6,695	4,160
Amazon, S. America	6,437	4,000
Yangtze/Chang Jiang, Asia	6,379	3,964
Mississippi-Missouri, N. America	6,264	3,892
Ob-Irtysh, Asia	5,411	3,362
Yellow/Huang He, Asia	4,672	2,903
Congo/Zaire, Africa	4,662	2,897
Amur, Asia	4,416	2,744
Lena, Asia	4,400	2,734
Mackenzie-Peace, N. America	4,241	2,635

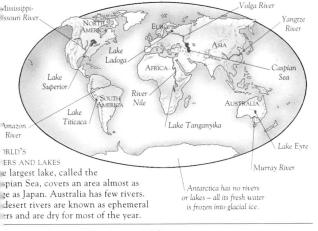

Mississippi-Missouri River

Volga River

Yangtze River

Lake Ladoga

Lake Superior

Caspian Sea

Lake Titicaca

River Nile

Amazon River

Lake Tanganyika

Lake Eyre

Murray River

Antarctica has no rivers or lakes – all its fresh water is frozen into glacial ice.

WORLD'S RIVERS AND LAKES

The largest lake, called the Caspian Sea, covers an area almost as large as Japan. Australia has few rivers. Its desert rivers are known as ephemeral rivers and are dry for most of the year.

RIVER FEATURES

FROM ITS SOURCE in the mountains, the snow or rainwater that fills a stream cuts a path through rock on its way to the sea. Streams join and form a river that flows more slowly, meandering across the land. A river may carry a large amount of sediment, which it deposits on the low, flat river valley and the floor of the sea.

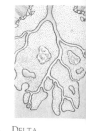

DELTA
At the river's mou[th] it sheds its sedime[nt] to form a broad fan of swampy land.

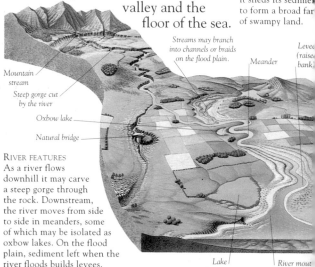

Streams may branch into channels or braids on the flood plain.

Meander

Leve[e]
(raise[d]
bank[)]

Mountain stream

Steep gorge cut by the river

Oxbow lake

Natural bridge

Lake

River mout[h]

RIVER FEATURES
As a river flows downhill it may carve a steep gorge through the rock. Downstream, the river moves from side to side in meanders, some of which may be isolated as oxbow lakes. On the flood plain, sediment left when the river floods builds levees.

MELTWATER

A river may begin its life in a glaciated part of the world. Melting ice and snow from a glacier feed mountain streams.

OVERLAND FLOW

Rainwater running downhill gathers into small streams called tributaries, which join to form a river.

SPRING

A rock layer called the aquifer stores rainwater. The water may appear as a spring when the aquifer is near the surface.

MORE RIVER FACTS

• The Ganges and Brahmaputra delta, India, is the largest in the world. Its area is about 75,000 km² (30,000 miles²).

• The widest waterfall is Khone Falls in Laos. They are 10.8 km (6.7 miles) wide.

• Each year rivers unload 20,000 million tonnes (tons) of sediment into the sea.

Softer rock undercut by rock and water

Swirling rocks and water

Hard rock

...od plain ...re sediment ...deposited

Most rivers run into the sea.

WATERFALLS

A river flows swiftly near its source cutting through soft rocks more easily than hard. A sheer face of hard rock is exposed where water plunges, undercutting the rock below.

...iment on seabed

THE WORLD'S HIGHEST WATERFALLS		
WATERFALL AND COUNTRY	HEIGHT IN METRES	HEIGHT IN FEET
Angel Falls, Venezuela	979	3,212
Tugela Falls, S. Africa	853	2,799
Utgaard, Norway	800	2,625
Mongefossen, Norway	774	2,539
Yosemite Falls, U.S.A.	739	2,425

LAKES

AN INLAND BODY of fresh water or
salt water, collected in a hollow, is
called a lake. In geological terms,
lakes are short-lived; they can dry
up or become clogged in a few
thousand years. Lakes form when
depressions resulting from crustal
movement, erosion, or volcanic
craters fill up with water. The
Caspian Sea, in the former Soviet
Union, the world's largest lake,
and Lake Baikal, Siberia, the
world's deepest lake, were both
produced when the crust lifted,
cutting off areas of the sea.

SWAMP
The Everglades, U.S.A.
are mangrove swamps. I
warm climates, mangrov
trees grow in the salty
(brackish) water of mud
estuaries. The trees form
islands in the mud.

TYPES OF LAKE

KETTLE LAKE
Melting glaciers leave
behind ice blocks and
debris. Melted ice fills
depressions between the
debris to form kettle lakes.

TARN
A circular mountain lake
is known as a tarn. These
lakes form in hollows worn
by glacial erosion or
blocked by ice debris.

VOLCANIC LAKE
The craters of ancien
volcanoes fill up with
water and produce la
such as Crater Lake,
Oregon, U.S.A.

VANISHING LAKES

SEDIMENT BUILDS
Lakes begin to fill up with
sediment, washed into them
by rivers. The mud and silt
create a delta in the lake,
which has areas of dry land.

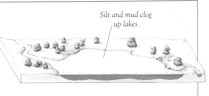

Silt and mud clog
up lakes.

Channels become narrow.

SWAMP FORMS
The lake area gets smaller
and shallower. Islands of
dry land fan out into the
lake. Reeds grow, turning
the lake into a swamp.

LAKE DISAPPEARS
Eventually, the lake
area is colonized by
plants, forming a
wetland environment.

Plants grow in the sediment.

OXBOW LAKE
This curved lake appears
when a river cuts off a
meander loop. The lake
eventually fills with
sediment and vegetation.

THE WORLD'S LARGEST LAKES AND INLAND SEAS		
LAKE AND CONTINENT	AREA IN KM²	AREA IN MILES²
Caspian Sea, Asia/ Europe	370,980	143,235
Lake Superior, N. America	82,098	31,698
Lake Victoria, Africa	69,480	26,826
Lake Huron, N. America	59,566	22,998
Lake Michigan, N. America	57,754	22,299
Aral Sea, Asia	37,056	14,307
Lake Tanganyika, Africa	32,891	12,699
Lake Baikal, Asia	31,498	12,161
Great Bear Lake, N. America	31,197	12,045

WEATHER AND CLIMATE

CLIMATE IS A LONG-ESTABLISHED PATTERN of weather. This pattern may vary, or it may remain the same throughout the year. Climate is usually defined in terms of temperature and rainfall.

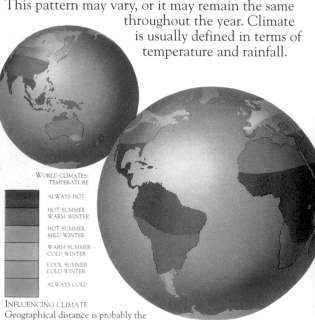

WORLD CLIMATES: TEMPERATURE

ALWAYS HOT

HOT SUMMER WARM WINTER

HOT SUMMER MILD WINTER

WARM SUMMER COLD WINTER

COOL SUMMER COLD WINTER

ALWAYS COLD

INFLUENCING CLIMATE

Geographical distance is probably the main factor influencing the climate in any particular part of the world. Distance from the equator affects temperature, as does altitude (distance above sea-level). Distance from a coastline affects both temperature and rainfall, while distance from a mountain range can increase or decrease rainfall.

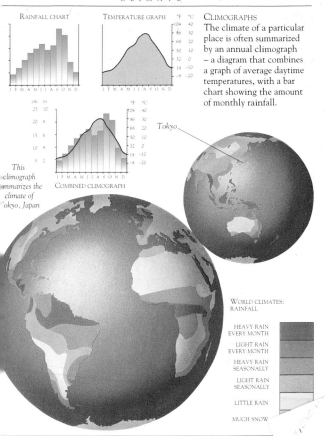

RAINFALL CHART

TEMPERATURE GRAPH

J F M A M J J A S O N D

°F °C
104 40
86 30
68 20
32 0
14 -10
-4 -20

J F M A M J J A S O N D

CLIMOGRAPHS
The climate of a particular place is often summarized by an annual climograph – a diagram that combines a graph of average daytime temperatures, with a bar chart showing the amount of monthly rainfall.

cm in
25 10
20 8
15 6
10 4
5 2

°F °C
104 40
86 30
68 20
32 0
14 -10
-4 -20

J F M A M J J A S O N D

COMBINED CLIMOGRAPH

Tokyo

This climograph summarizes the climate of Tokyo, Japan

WORLD CLIMATES: RAINFALL

HEAVY RAIN EVERY MONTH

LIGHT RAIN EVERY MONTH

HEAVY RAIN SEASONALLY

LIGHT RAIN SEASONALLY

LITTLE RAIN

MUCH SNOW

TROPICAL

YEAR-ROUND HIGH TEMPERATURES combined with
heavy rainfall are characteristic of a tropical climate
Near the equator, the rainfall is distributed fairly
evenly throughout the year. Farther to the north an
south, the rainfall tends to be concentrated into a
distinct wet season. Altogether, about half of the
world's population lives in regions of tropical climat

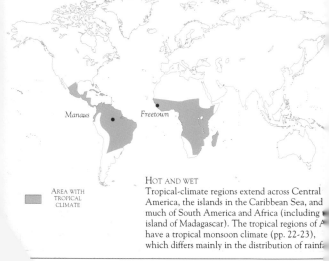

Manaus

Freetown

AREA WITH
TROPICAL
CLIMATE

HOT AND WET
Tropical-climate regions extend across Central
America, the islands in the Caribbean Sea, and
much of South America and Africa (including
island of Madagascar). The tropical regions of A
have a tropical monsoon climate (pp. 22-23),
which differs mainly in the distribution of rainf

TROPICAL CONDITIONS
High temperatures, heavy rainfall, and lush vegetation make most tropical regions extremely humid (humidity measures the amount of water vapour in the air). Frequent rainfall means that the sky is often filled with clouds, and sunshine is fairly limited. In general, winds are light but tropical thunderstorms and cyclones (hurricanes) can cause considerable destruction.

LANDSCAPE
Tropical climates produce a characteristic natural vegetation known as tropical rainforest. The largest remaining rainforest is in the Amazon Basin, Brazil.

ANNUAL RAINFALL 190 CM (74.8 IN)	ANNUAL RAINFALL 343.6 CM (135.3 IN)

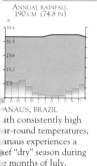

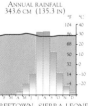

MANAUS, BRAZIL
With consistently high year-round temperatures, Manaus experiences a brief "dry" season during the months of July, August, and September.

FREETOWN, SIERRA LEONE
Situated on the coast, Freetown has six months of heavy rain each year. During the wet season, sunshine is limited to only 2-3 hours per day.

CLIMATE FACTS
• The kinetic energy of the raindrops in a tropical rainstorm is equivalent to 5,500 watts per hectare (2,200 watts per acre).

• In geography, the "tropics" lie between the Tropic of Cancer (23°30N) and the Tropic of Capricorn (23°30S). Tropical climates extend beyond this strict definition.

TROPICAL MONSOON

TORRENTIAL MONSOON rains
dominate the climate in the
tropical regions of Asia and
Australasia. Twice a year, the
prevailing winds reverse their
direction completely. This shift
in the wind divides the year into
a rainy season followed by a
predominantly dry season.

WET SEASON
In parts of India, the
monsoon rains regularly
produce flooding.

Bombay

Darwin

AREA WITH
TROPICAL
MONSOON
CLIMATE

MONSOON ZONE
The area affected by the monsoon extends from
the Horn of Africa, across the Indian subcontinent
and Southeast Asia, to the northern coast of
Australia. Seasonal monsoon-type weather also affec
parts of Africa, and Central and South America.

NORTHEAST MONSOON
With the onset of winter (below), Central Asia becomes a high-pressure region, and the winds reverse direction. Cool dry winds blow from the northeast towards the equator, lowering temperatures.

THWEST MONSOON
ng early summer (above), low
ure over Central Asia produces
hwesterly winds that carry warm
ture-laden air from the Indian
n. These winds bring the heavy
soon rains.

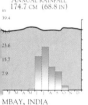

ANNUAL RAINFALL
174.7 CM (68.8 IN)

MBAY, INDIA
arly all of Bombay's
nfall occurs in the
r months of the
nsoon wet season –
e, July, August,
September.

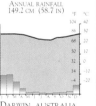

ANNUAL RAINFALL
149.2 CM (58.7 IN)

DARWIN, AUSTRALIA
Situated to the south of the equator, Darwin has a dry season at the same time as Bombay has a wet season.

CLIMATE FACTS
• The word monsoon comes from the Arabic word mausin, which means "seasonal wind".
• Monsoon rains advance across Asia at a rate of about 100 km (60 miles) per day.
• At Cherrapungi in northern India, 22 m (864 in) of rain fell during the 1861 monsoon season.

DRY

LITTLE OR NO RAINFALL is the main characteristic
of the dry climate found in desert and semi-desert
regions. Most deserts also experience high daytime
temperatures, but some are cool or even cold.
The large mid-latitude deserts – the Sahara and
Arabian deserts – are the result of the global pattern
of air circulation. Dry air descends on these regions
bringing clear skies and hot sunshine.

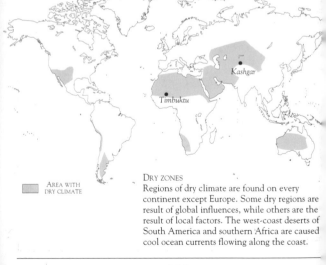

Kashgar

Timbuktu

AREA WITH
DRY CLIMATE

DRY ZONES
Regions of dry climate are found on every
continent except Europe. Some dry regions are
result of global influences, while others are the
result of local factors. The west-coast deserts of
South America and southern Africa are caused
cool ocean currents flowing along the coast.

DRY CONDITIONS
Desert skies are usually cloudless with strong sunlight. Although the air above the desert surface heats up, it remains relatively cool compared with the ground. Sand or rocks in direct sunlight will easily reach 60-70°C (140-160°F). At night, temperatures may drop to below freezing point. Occasional thunderstorms can sometimes produce local sandstorms.

...DSCAPE
...e areas of the driest ...rts are seas of sand ...s. The constantly ...ing dunes prevent ... the most drought-...ant plants from ...ing a foothold.

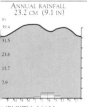

ANNUAL RAINFALL
23.2 CM (9.1 IN)

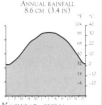

ANNUAL RAINFALL
8.6 CM (3.4 IN)

...MBUKTU, MALI
...cated in the southern ...hara, Timbuktu has ...ar-round high ...nperatures. All of the ...nfall occurs during the ...mmer months.

KASHGAR, CHINA
Situated more than 1,600 km (1,000 miles) from the sea, Kashgar is hot in summer, cold in winter, and very dry throughout the year.

CLIMATE FACTS
• The world's driest place is the Atacama Desert in northern Chile. Between 1903 and 1917, the town of Arica received no rain at all for a period of 5,206 days.

• The sunniest place in the world is the town of Yuma, in Arizona, U.S.A. with an average of 4,127 hours of bright sunshine each year.

WARM

COMFORTABLE TEMPERATURES and moderate rainfall throughout the year are found in warm-climate regions. Some of these regions are described as having a "Mediterranean" climate, but this term can be misleading. Geographical conditions around the Mediterranean Sea have created an especially mild climate. Some warm-climate regions have more extreme temperatures in both winter and summer.

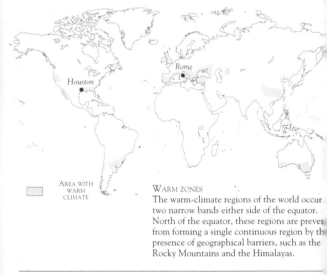

Houston

Rome

AREA WITH
WARM
CLIMATE

WARM ZONES
The warm-climate regions of the world occur two narrow bands either side of the equator. North of the equator, these regions are prevent from forming a single continuous region by the presence of geographical barriers, such as the Rocky Mountains and the Himalayas.

WARM CONDITIONS

With mild winters and a long frost-free growing period, warm-climate regions are ideally suited to most types of agriculture. In California and the Mediterranean region, citrus fruits, grapes, and olives are important cash crops. In China, the warm-climate region is the most productive rice-growing area.

OSCAPE
t of the natural
tation has been
ed from warm-
ate regions to
e way for human
ements and
ulture.

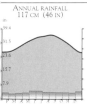

ANNUAL RAINFALL 117 CM (46 IN)

ANNUAL RAINFALL 74.4 CM (29.3 IN)

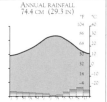

OUSTON, U.S.A.
e climograph for
uston shows a short
ld winter and a long
rm summer. Rainfall is
tributed fairly evenly
er the year.

ROME, ITALY
Situated slightly farther north, Rome has a shorter summer than Houston. Rainfall is more seasonal, and is highest during the autumn.

CLIMATE FACTS

• A warm climate is no guarantee of a mild winter. In January 1932, 5 cm (2 in) of snow fell on central Los Angeles, U.S.A.

• Europe's highest temperature of 50.5°C (123°F) was recorded in southern Portugal.

• The Mediterranean region has more than 30 individually named local winds.

COOL

COLD WINTERS with frequent night-time frosts are characteristic of cool-climate regions. These regions have much more changeable weather than elsewher Cool-climate regions are strongly influenced by larg moving weather systems called depressions, or "lows and anticyclones, or "highs". As one of these system passes over a particular location, it produces a series of changing weather conditions.

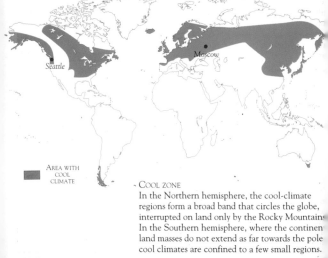

AREA WITH
COOL
CLIMATE

COOL ZONE
In the Northern hemisphere, the cool-climate regions form a broad band that circles the globe, interrupted on land only by the Rocky Mountain In the Southern hemisphere, where the continen land masses do not extend as far towards the pole cool climates are confined to a few small regions.

COOL CONDITIONS

There is considerable variation across cool-climate regions because of their great geographical extent. Coastal regions often have a less extreme climate than regions farther inland. Deciduous trees, which lose their leaves in winter, are confined to the warmer regions. In general, human settlement and agriculture are similarly restricted by temperature.

LANDSCAPE
In most cool-climate regions, the landscape is still dominated by natural vegetation. Forests of needleleaf (coniferous) trees encircle the globe.

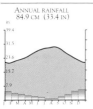

ANNUAL RAINFALL
84.9 CM (33.4 IN)

SEATTLE, U.S.A.
Situated on the coast, Seattle's climate is moderated by the sea, which keeps temperatures relatively high during the winter months.

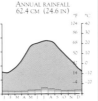

ANNUAL RAINFALL
62.4 CM (24.6 IN)

MOSCOW, RUSSIA
Moscow's inland climate is more extreme than that of Seattle. Rainfall also follows a different pattern, with a summer maximum.

CLIMATE FACTS

• The lowest recorded temperature in the Northern hemisphere, –71°C (–96°F), was measured in the cool-climate region at Oimyakon, Siberia.

• The highest recorded temperature in Britain is 37.1°C (98.8°F) in August 1990; and the lowest on record is –27.2°C (–17.0°F) in January 1982.

MOUNTAIN AND POLAR

MOUNTAINS CREATE THEIR OWN CLIMATE, no matter where they are located. The climate of a mountain or mountain range can be divided vertically into a number of sub-zones. While foothills may have a tropical climate, peaks may be covered in ice. Near the North and South Poles, the polar climate is dominated by low temperatures, irregular strong winds, and year-round snow cover.

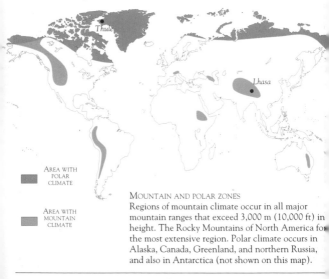

AREA WITH
POLAR
CLIMATE

AREA WITH
MOUNTAIN
CLIMATE

MOUNTAIN AND POLAR ZONES
Regions of mountain climate occur in all major mountain ranges that exceed 3,000 m (10,000 ft) in height. The Rocky Mountains of North America for the most extensive region. Polar climate occurs in Alaska, Canada, Greenland, and northern Russia, and also in Antarctica (not shown on this map).

MOUNTAIN CONDITIONS

The sub-zones of a mountain climate get progressively colder with increased altitude. The vegetation on the lower slopes largely depends upon which climate zone the mountain is in. On the upper slopes, needleleaf trees reach to the tree-line. Above this level are found alpine plants which can withstand the harsh conditions. The uppermost level is bare rock and snow.

...AR LANDSCAPE
...r regions are
...inated by snow
... ice. Some parts of
...arctica are covered
... a layer of ice
... than 3,000 m
...000 ft) thick.

ANNUAL RAINFALL
40.8 CM (16 IN)

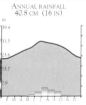

ANNUAL RAINFALL
6.7 CM (2.6 IN)

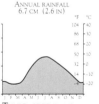

CLIMATE FACTS

• The highest recorded temperature inside the Arctic Circle is 37.8°C (100°F), at Fort Yukon, Alaska, in June 1915.

• The highest recorded Antarctic temperature is 14.4°C (58°F) in October 1958.

• Mount Kilimanjaro in Tanzania is the only permanent snowcap within sight of the equator.

...ASA, TIBET
...uated some 3,600 m
...,000 ft) above sea
...el, Lhasa has
...prisingly warm
...mmers thanks to clear
...es and strong sun.

THULE, GREENLAND
Temperatures at Thule only rise above freezing during the middle of summer. The annual "rainfall" consists entirely of snow.

WEATHER AND SEASONS

IN SOME PARTS OF THE WORLD, weather is seasonal; it changes according to the time of year. Seasons depend on varying amounts of sunlight reaching different parts of the Earth's surface. These variation are the result of the Earth's orbit around the Sun on a tilted axis. In general, seasons become more noticeable with increasing distance from the equato

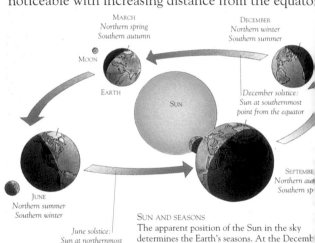

MARCH
*Northern spring
Southern autumn*

DECEMBER
*Northern winter
Southern summer*

MOON

EARTH

SUN

*December solstice:
Sun at southernmost
point from the equator*

JUNE
*Northern summer
Southern winter*

*June solstice:
Sun at northernmost
point from the equator*

SEPTEMBE
*Northern au
Southern sp*

SUN AND SEASONS

The apparent position of the Sun in the sky determines the Earth's seasons. At the Decemb solstice, in the middle of summer in the Southe hemisphere, the Sun appears to be directly ove Tropic of Capricorn. At the June solstice, the S appears to be directly over the Tropic of Cance

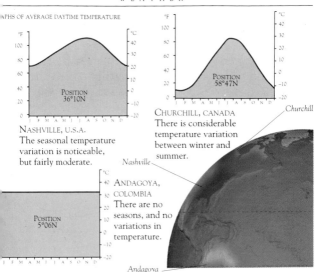

GRAPHS OF AVERAGE DAYTIME TEMPERATURE

POSITION 36°10N

NASHVILLE, U.S.A.
The seasonal temperature variation is noticeable, but fairly moderate.

POSITION 58°47N

CHURCHILL, CANADA
There is considerable temperature variation between winter and summer.

POSITION 5°06N

ANDAGOYA, COLOMBIA
There are no seasons, and no variations in temperature.

DATA: SEASONS AND DAYLIGHT (HOURS AND MINUTES)			
Date	Andagoya	Nashville	Churchill
1	11:51	10:00	6:38
2	11:58	10:56	9:11
3	12:06	11:55	11:41
4	12:14	12:45	14:31
5	12:20	14:00	17:04
6	12:23	14:32	18:49
7	12:21	14:26	17:31
8	12:17	13:32	15:46
9	12:09	12:27	13:00
10	12:01	11:19	10:11
11	11:53	10:21	7:37
12	11:49	9:46	5:54

SOLSTICE FACTS
• The June solstice (mid-summer in the Northern hemisphere) takes place around 21-22 June.
• The December solstice (mid-winter in the Northern hemisphere) takes place around 22-23 December.

WIND AND WEATHER

WINDS CIRCULATE air around the planet. They carry warm air from the equator to the poles and cold air in the opposite direction. This process balances the Earth's temperature. Some global winds (known as prevailing winds), such as polar easterlies and trade winds, are an important part of the world's weather systems.

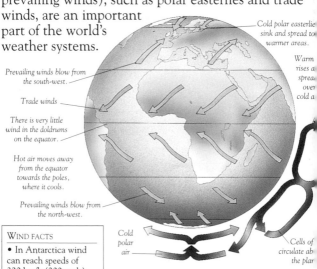

Cold polar easterlie sink and spread to warmer areas.

Warm rises a sprea over cold a

Prevailing winds blow from the south-west.

Trade winds

There is very little wind in the doldrums on the equator.

Hot air moves away from the equator towards the poles, where it cools.

Prevailing winds blow from the north-west.

Cold polar air

Cells of circulate ab the plar

WIND FACTS

• In Antarctica wind can reach speeds of 320 km/h (200 mph).

• Highest wind speed recorded at ground level is 371 km/h (230 mph).

WINDS OF THE WORLD

Three prevailing winds blow around the planet at ground level, on either side of the equator. Trade wind bring dry weather, westerly winds are damp and warm and polar easterlies carry dry, cold polar air.

ORMATION OF A ROSSBY WAVE

SNAKING WIND
he Earth's rotation
uses curling, high
titude winds called
ossby waves.

DEEPENING WAVE
The wave deepens along
the polar front. It forms
a meander 2,000 km
(1,250 miles) long.

DEVELOPED LOOPS
The curls become loops
and the hot and cold air
separate to produce
swirling frontal storms.

Earth's rotation
deflects winds on
the ground.

Trade winds
near the equator

DE WINDS
e area either side of the
tor (the tropics) the
ailing winds are called the
 winds. In the northern
isphere the winds blow
 the north-east, and in
outhern hemisphere they
 from the south-east.

SEA BREEZES AND LAND BREEZES
On sunny days the land warms up during the
day. Warm air rises from the land and cool air is
drawn in from the sea. At night the land cools
down quickly and cold air sinks out to sea.

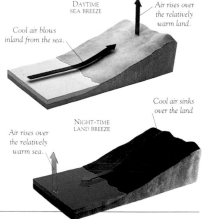

DAYTIME
SEA BREEZE

Air rises over
the relatively
warm land.

Cool air blows
inland from the sea.

Cool air sinks
over the land

NIGHT-TIME
LAND BREEZE

Air rises over
the relatively
warm sea.

TEMPERATURE AND PRESSURE

WE THINK OF temperature in
terms of whether it is a hot or
cold day – the temperature close
to the Earth's surface. We cannot
feel air pressure in the same way,
but it is equally important to us.
The uneven distribution of
temperature and pressure in the
atmosphere provides the energy
to drive the weather machine.

A WARM DAY?
On the beach it is warm.
3,000 m (10,000 ft) over
however, the temperatur
well below the freezing p

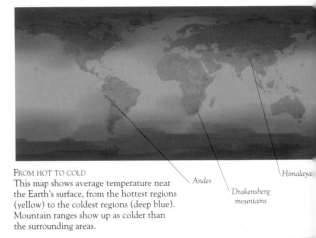

FROM HOT TO COLD
This map shows average temperature near
the Earth's surface, from the hottest regions
(yellow) to the coldest regions (deep blue).
Mountain ranges show up as colder than
the surrounding areas.

Andes

Drakensberg
mountains

Himalaya

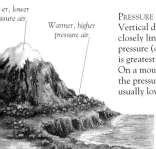

er, lower
sure air

Warmer, higher
pressure air

PRESSURE AND TEMPERATURE

Vertical differences in air temperature are
closely linked to air pressure. In general, air
pressure (often called atmospheric pressure)
is greatest at sea-level, where the air is densest.
On a mountain peak, the air is less dense and
the pressure is lower. The air temperature is
usually lower than it would be at sea-level.

ATMOSPHERIC MOTION

Like other fluids, air tends towards a
state where all regions at the same
altitude have equal pressure. As a result,
air flows from regions of high pressure to
regions of low pressure. The difference
between two adjoining regions can be
described as a pressure gradient, and air
flows "down" the gradient.

*A pressure gradient exists
between high pressure at A and
low pressure at B*

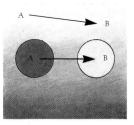

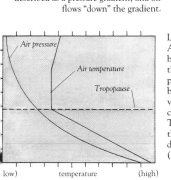

Air pressure

Air temperature

Tropopause

low)   temperature   (high)

LAPSE RATE

Air pressure and air temperature
both decrease steadily away from
the Earth's surface. The rate of
pressure decrease is constant,
but the temperature decrease is
variable and depends on the water
content (humidity) of the air.
The rate of decrease is known as
the "lapse rate". The lapse rate for
dry air is about 1.0°C per 100 m
(5.5°F per 1,000 ft).

AIR MASSES

PROLONGED HIGH PRESSURE can cause parts of the atmosphere to become stagnant. The resulting air masses take on the weather characteristics of the region in which they formed. When these air masses start moving, they carry their weather with them, especially to the mid-latitudes.

AIR MASS MARKERS
Cumulus clouds like thes[e] are typical of a maritime polar air mass.

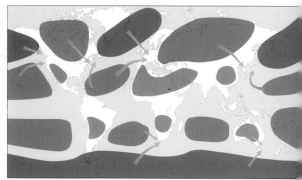

MAIN MASSES
This map shows the basic distribution of the different air masses that influence the weather. The size and locations of individual air masses are approximate because they change constantly.

MARITIME POLAR
CONTINENTAL POLAR
CONTINENTAL TROPICAL
MARITIME TROPICAL

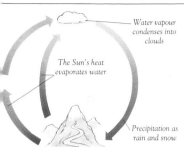

The Sun's heat evaporates water

Water vapour condenses into clouds

Precipitation as rain and snow

CLOSED CYCLE

Water circulates through the atmosphere as vapour, evaporating from land and oceans, and condensing to fall as precipitation. The amount of water vapour in a given air mass is called its humidity. Warm air can hold more water vapour than cold air. Air that cannot hold any more water vapour is said to be saturated.

ITCZ

The ITCZ (inter-tropical [con]vergence zone), is marked by a narrow zone of cloud clusters that bring heavy [r]ainfall. The ITCZ occurs [where] air streams from higher [la]titudes converge near the [equat]or, forcing warm moist air [up] cool, and condense into rain-bearing clouds.

A: AIR MASSES	
[air] mass	Description
[mar]itime tropical (mT)	warm and very moist
[mar]itime polar (mP)	cool and fairly moist
[mar]itime arctic (mA)	cold and quite moist
[mar]itime antarctic (mAA)	very cold and fairly dry
[cont]inental tropical (cT)	hot and dry
[cont]inental polar (cP)	cold and dry
[cont]inental arctic (cA)	very cold and dry
[cont]inental antarctic (cAA)	very cold and dry

ATMOSPHERE FACTS

- Water has an average "residence period" in the atmosphere of 11 days before it falls as rain or snow.
- A tropical air mass contains about 5-10 times more water than a polar air mass of similar size.

HIGHS AND LOWS

WEATHER IN THE mid-latitudes is controlled by a sequence of high-pressure and low-pressure frontal weather systems. High-pressure systems, called anticyclones or "highs", usually bring fine, settled weather. Low-pressure systems, called depressions or "lows", usually bring rain and very changeable conditions.

JET-STREAM CLOUDS
These clouds have been blown into elongated shapes by the jet stream.

FAMILY OF DEPRESSIONS
This illustration shows a family of three depressions at different stages of development. The upper picture shows the shape of the depressions viewed from above. The lower picture shows the systems in cross-section along the line A-B.

Cold front

Jet stream

A

Rain
(green shading)

Cloud
(brown shading)

Low pressure
at centre of
depression

Rain clouds

A

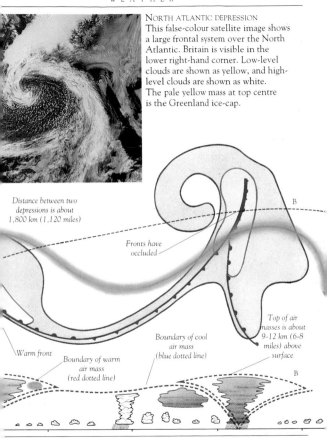

NORTH ATLANTIC DEPRESSION
This false-colour satellite image shows
a large frontal system over the North
Atlantic. Britain is visible in the
lower right-hand corner. Low-level
clouds are shown as yellow, and high-
level clouds are shown as white.
The pale yellow mass at top centre
is the Greenland ice-cap.

*Distance between two
depressions is about
1,800 km (1,120 miles)*

B

*Fronts have
occluded*

*Top of air
masses is about
9-12 km (6-8
miles) above
surface*

*Boundary of cool
air mass
(blue dotted line)*

Warm front

*Boundary of warm
air mass
(red dotted line)*

B

CLOUDS

AIR RISES as it warms, as it passes over mountains, or when it is blown upwards by cool air. Rising air cools, condenses, and forms clouds of water droplets. There are three cloud levels: cirrus form at the highest level, alto in the middle, and stratus at the lowest level.

FOGGY AIR
Clouds that form at ground level are known as fog. Fog, mixed with smoke from burning fuels, produces smog. Earlier this century, London, England, suffered from severe smog.

CLOUD FORMATION

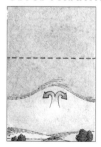

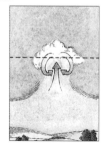

THE LAND WARMS
The Sun warms the land on a clear day. Air near the ground is warmed and rises.

A CLOUD FORMS
As the warm air rises, it cools. The moisture it contains condenses and forms a cloud.

GROWING CLOUDS
Fleecy clouds appear in the sky. They get bigger and cool air circulates inside them.

CLOUD AND AIR FACTS

Cirrus are the highest clouds – they may reach 12,000 m (39,370 ft).

Glider pilots and birds use pockets of rising air called thermals to help them stay in the air.

OKTAS

Cloud cover is measured in oktas. On weather maps a partially shaded circle represents cover.

CLEAR   1   2

3   4   5   6   7   8

CLOUD TYPES

CIRRUS (A)
• wisps of cloud made of ice crystals
• about 12,000 m (39,370 ft) high

CIRROCUMULUS (B)
• forms at about 9,000 m (29,528 ft)
• rippled ice crystal cloud

CUMULONIMBUS (C)
• dark, storm cloud with rain

ALTOCUMULUS (D)
• layers or rolls of fluffy cloud

ALTOSTRATUS (E)
• grey or white sheet of cloud
• forms between 2,000 m and 6,000 m (6,562 ft and 19,685 ft)

STRATOCUMULUS (F)
• layer at the top of cumulus cloud

CUMULUS (G)
• large, white, heaped, fluffy cloud

NIMBOSTRATUS (H)
• low, rain cloud
• under 2,000 m (6,562 ft)

STRATUS (I)
• low-level, flat, grey sheet of cloud

RAIN AND THUNDERSTORMS

EARTH'S WATER CYCLE relies on rain. Rain fills rivers and lakes and provides water for plants and animals. Tiny water droplets in the air form rain when they gather into larger drops inside clouds. Raindrops can be moved about by warm and cold air currents. Inside cumulonimbus clouds, droplets are tossed around until they produce the electric spark we know as lightning.

Droplets of more than 0.5 mm (0.02 in) fall as rain.

Smaller drops of water fall as drizzle.

Rising air

HOW RAIN FORMS

In tropical areas, rising air currents agitate the water droplets in clouds until they join into raindrops. In temperate regions, ice crystals in the clouds above freezing level melt on their way down and form rain.

MONSOON

Seasonal winds called monsoons draw moist air inland, bringing summer rain to southern Asia. In winter, a cold, dry wind blows over the land and out to the ocean.

IN FACTS

A record 1,870 mm
(.62 in) of rain fell in
e month in 1861 in
errapunji, India.

utunendo, Colombia,
world's wettest place,
an annual rainfall of
770 mm (463.4 in).

LIGHTNING

Water droplets and ice in a
storm cloud collide and
build up electric charges.
Positive charges gather
at the top of the cloud
and negative ones at the
base. When the electricity is
released it flashes between
clouds or sparks to the
ground and back again.

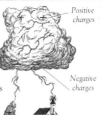

Positive charges

Negative charges

RAINBOWS

Sunlight striking raindrops is
refracted, reflected by the backs
of the droplets, and refracted
again. This causes the white light
to split into its seven constituent
colours: red, orange, yellow,
green, blue, indigo, and violet.

RAINFALL MAP

Around the world rainfall
varies greatly. Warm seas in
the tropics evaporate and
bring lots of rain. Near the
sea land is wetter but
mountains may block rain.

KEY TO ANNUAL RAINFALL

○ Less than 250 mm (10 in)

○ 250-500 mm (10-20 in)

○ 500-1,000 mm (20-39 in)

● 1,000-2,000 mm (39-79 in)

● 2,000-3,000 mm (79-118 in)

● More than 3,000 mm (118 in)

SNOW, HAIL, AND FROST

WHEN THE WEATHER is very cold, snow, hail, or frost leave a white coating on the landscape. Snow and hail fall from clouds. They are a result of water freezing in the cloud. Frost forms when water in the air condenses and freezes as it touches a cold surface. It leaves an icy glaze on windows, trees, and roads.

SNOWY WEATHER
In the European Alps the snow the winter months does not m because the ground temperatur low. Strong winds sometimes the snow into deep snowdrifts.

HOW SNOW FORMS
High up in the atmosphere, above the freezing level, water droplets in clouds form ice crystals, which collide and combine. As they fall, the ice crystals form snowflakes.

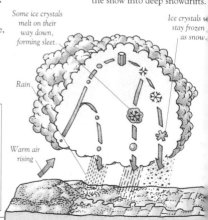

Some ice crystals melt on their way down, forming sleet.

Rain

Warm air rising

Ice crystals u stay frozen as snow

SNOW FACTS

• The largest recorded hailstone weighed 765 g (1.7 lb) and fell in Kansas, U.S.A. in 1970.

• In 1921, in Colorado, U.S.A., 1,930 mm (76 in) of snow fell in one day.

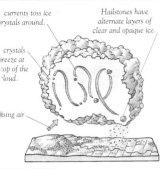

currents toss ice crystals around.

Hailstones have alternate layers of clear and opaque ice.

crystals freeze at top of the cloud.

rising air

HAIL FORMS
cumulonimbus clouds above 10 km
miles) the temperature is freezing. Water
plets blown to the top of the cloud freeze.
ers of ice build up around the hailstone
repeatedly melts and refreezes.

ZEN RIVER
e Zanskar River in the Himalayas is frozen
ng the winter months. The frozen river makes
elling in the region easier, as local people can
k up and downstream on the ice. Under the
fish can survive in the unfrozen water. In
mer, the river is a fast-flowing torrent.

ICICLES
Spectacular ice shapes, such as
icicles, form when water freezes in
cold weather. Icicles grow as drips
of melting snow or ice refreeze.

The outside of an icicle freezes before the inside.

Icicles often hang from leaking pipes.

HOAR FROST
Below freezing point, water
vapour in the air freezes. It
leaves spiky crystals of hoar
frost on cold surfaces.

HURRICANES AND TORNADOE

WINDS SUCH AS hurricanes (cyclones) and tornado
occur when warm air masses encounter cold air
masses. Winds reach high speeds
and bring torrential rain and
huge dark clouds. A
tornado concentrates its
havoc on a fairly narrow
trail whereas a hurricane
destroys a much larger area
and can last for many days.

BEAUFORT SCALE	
NUMBER	DESCRIPTION
0	Calm, smoke rises straight up
1	Light air, smoke drifts gently
2	Light breeze, leaves rustle
3	Gentle breeze, flags flutter
4	Moderate wind, twigs move
5	Fresh wind, small trees sway
6	Strong wind, large branches move
7	Near gale, whole tree sways
8	Gale, difficult to walk in wind
9	Severe wind, slates and branches break
10	Storm, houses damaged, trees blown down
11	Severe storm, buildings seriously damaged
12	Hurricane, devastating damage

SATELLITE PHOTOGRAPH
Hurricanes can be tracked easily
from space using satellites. The
swirling clouds accumulate from
tropical thunderstorms. They bui
into tight bands of spiralling clou

HURRICANE
Coasts, in particular, are damage
by hurricanes. Large waves are
whipped up by the storms which
lash coastlines and can cause flo

s and
...ratus
...around
...ge of
...rm

...icanes
...as wide
...0 km
...miles).

Bands of wind
and rain spiral.

At the eye
the sky is
clear and
winds light.

Currents rise
and spread
outwards.

HOW A HURRICANE FORMS

A cluster of tropical storms can become a hurricane. Bands of cumulonimbus and cumulus clouds spiral towards the centre of the storm. Warm air rises and cools, building huge storm clouds that bring rain. At the centre, or eye, of the hurricane, the pressure is low and the weather is calm.

...TERSPOUT

...tornado occurs over
...ocean it is known as
...terspout. Water is
...ed up in a column by
...ds reaching speeds of
...m/h (50 mph), less
...n those of a tornado.

A violent
updraught
sucks up dust
and vehicles.

Winds in the
tornado may
reach speeds of
450 km/h
(280 mph).

...RRICANE FACTS

...Winds up to 320 km/h
...0 mph) have been
...orded in a hurricane.

...Hurricanes spin anti-
...ckwise north of the
...uator and clockwise
...th of the equator.

...Waterspouts are
...ally between
...and 100 m
...4-328 ft) high.

TORNADO

If a mass of cool, dry air collides with a mass of warm, damp air it may form a tornado. This dark funnel of whirling air picks up debris from the ground. The storm may last only a few minutes but its spinning winds are very destructive.

BLIZZARDS AND SANDSTORMS

WINDBLOWN PARTICLES of snow and sand are a normal part of weather in polar and desert regions. In remote areas, they cause little disruption. However, when blizzards and sandstorms occur in highly populated areas, they can cause chaos. Visibility is greatly reduced, and most forms of transport are paralyzed.

BLIZZARD
A blizzard is snow blown by winds that have an average speed of at least 52 km/h (32 mph).

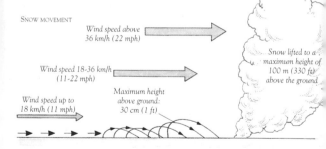

SNOW MOVEMENT

Wind speed above 36 km/h (22 mph)

Wind speed 18-36 km/h (11-22 mph)

Wind speed up to 18 km/h (11 mph)

Maximum height above ground: 30 cm (1 ft)

Snow lifted to a maximum height of 100 m (330 ft) above the ground

SNOW CREEP
Under gentle winds, snow particles roll along the ground, rising no more than 2.5 cm (1 in) above the surface.

SALTATION
Under moderate winds, snow particles jump and bounce along the ground in a form of movement called saltation.

TURBULENT DIFFUSION
In strong winds, the w[...] has enough force to lif[...] fallen snow back into [...] air in a process called turbulent diffusion.

SANDSTORM

A sandstorm darkens the sky in sub-Saharan Africa. There are two main types of sandstorm. A small sandstorm (haboob) is formed by the downdraught winds of a thunderstorm. A large sandstorm (khamsin) is formed by strong winds that blow for several days.

DUST STORM

With dramatic suddenness, a dust storm sweeps across a Canadian airport. Dust particles are smaller and lighter than sand and are lifted into the atmosphere more easily. This particular storm was raised by the strong winds at the leading edge of a cold front.

FREEZING RAIN

Rain falling through very cold air, or onto cold objects, can freeze into a coating of clear ice. This is also known as glaze.

DATA BOX: WIND CHILL EFFECT		
Air	Wind speed	
temperature	6 km/h (10 mph)	32 km/h (20 mph)
0°C (32°F)	–3°C (27°F)	–6°C (21°F)
–2°C (28°F)	–5°C (23°F)	–9°C (15°F)
–4°C (24°F)	–7°C (19°F)	–12°C (10°F)
–7°C (20°F)	–10°C (14°F)	–15°C (5°F)
–9°C (16°F)	–12°C (10°F)	–19°C (0°F)
–12°C (12°F)	–14°C (6°F)	–20°C (–5°F)
–14°C (8°F)	–17°C (1°F)	–24°C (–11°F)
–16°C (4°F)	–19°C (–3°F)	–27°C (–16°F)

WEATHER MAPPING

MILLIONS OF PEOPLE listen to the weather forecast each day. The forecast is compiled using data collected from all around the world and even from weather satellites in space. Meteorologists study the movements of warm and cold air masses and the fronts where they meet. Using this information they plot weather charts and predict the coming weather.

SATELLITE IMAGES
From space, the Earth appears to be surrounded by swirling clouds. Africa desert has no cloud cove

WEATHER MAP
A picture of the weather at a given time can be shown on a weather map, known as a synoptic chart. Standard symbols are used, such as lines to show fronts (where one body of air – an air mass – meets another).

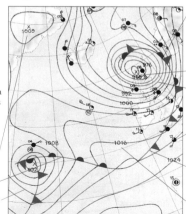

Occluded fron – merged war and cold fron

A depression a centre of lo pressure

Closer isoba indicate stronger win

Shows wind strength and direction

Cold front – cold air is advancing.

Air pressure millibars

Centre of high pressure

Warm front – warm air is advancing.

Isobars link points with the same air pressure.

FORMATION OF A DEPRESSION

AIR MASSES
Air masses are a vast area of wet or dry, warm or cold air. At the polar front, a warm air mass and a cold one collide.

FORMING A BULGE
The warm tropical air mass pushes into the cold polar air along the polar front. The front begins to bulge.

DIVIDING INTO TWO
The Earth's rotation spins the air masses. Cold air pursues warm air in a spiral formation. The polar front splits.

OCCLUDED FRONT
When the cold front catches up with the warm front, it pushes under the warm air. An occluded front results.

WEATHER FACTS

• A cold front travels up to 50 km/h (30 mph) and may overtake a warm front ahead of it.

• The first television weather chart was broadcast in Britain on 11th November, 1936.

• An air mass can cover an area as large as Brazil.

BAROMETER
The air around the Earth has mass and exerts pressure. A barometer measures air pressure in units called millibars.

TEMPERATURE PEAKS
This chart shows five ice ages in Earth's history, when the temperature fell and ice sheets covered much of the planet. These cold periods were separated by interglacials when the average temperature rose.

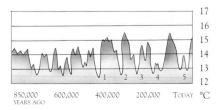

850,000 600,000 400,000 200,000 TODAY °C
YEARS AGO

17
16
15
14
13
12

SPACE

WHAT IS THE UNIVERSE?

THE UNIVERSE IS EVERYTHING that exists. From
the Earth beneath our feet to the farthest
stars, everything is a part of the universe. The
universe is so large that it contains countless
billions of stars. However, most of
it consists of nothing
but empty space.

Galax

*Comet –
dirty snow*

*Galaxy containing
billions of stars*

*Supernova – the
death of a large star*

LOOKING TO THE SKIES

From Earth, we can look into space and study the
universe. In every direction we look there are stars.
There are more stars in the universe than any
other type of object – stars in enormous groups
called galaxies and stars at different stages of their
lives, including at least one star that has planets.
Despite the huge size of the universe, we know of
only one place where life exists – planet Earth.

UNIVERSE FACTS

• There are about
100,000 million galaxies
in the universe; each
contains approximately
1,000 million stars.

• The most distant
objects we can detect
are 139,000 million
million million km
(87,000 million million
million miles) away.

RSEHEAD IN SPACE

king like a chess knight, the Horsehead
ula (centre left) is a gigantic cloud of dark-
oured dust. It is visible because the dust blocks
light from behind the nebula, so that we see it
ilhouette. The universe contains many similar
ids that block our view of different regions.

Pulsar – a rapidly rotating neutron star

The Sun – an ordinary middle-aged star

Cluster of stars

Quasar – a very bright and distant object

Planets – balls of rock, ice, or gas

Nebula – a cloud of gas and dust

VISUALISING THE UNIVERSE

The easiest way to think of the universe
is as a sphere which is constantly
expanding so that everything is getting
farther away from everything else. There
is nothing beyond the universe, because
the universe contains all of time and
space within it.

SCALE OF THE UNIVERSE

DISTANCES IN THE UNIVERSE are so great that the light year is used as a unit of measurement. Light travels at about 300,000 km/s (186,000 miles/s), and a light year (ly) is the distance light travels in one year. A galaxy can measure thousands of light years across and be millions of light years distant.

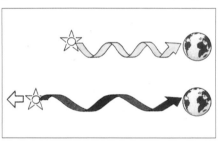

LIGHT AND MOTION

A star's light can tell u about its motion. If th star is moving away fr Earth, its light is stretc by comparison with stationary stars. Light from a star moving aw also shifted towards th red end of the spectru Stars approaching Ear have compressed light shifted towards blue.

SCALE OF SIZES

The human world, the world of everyday experience, is dwarfed by the scale of the universe. Earth is one of nine planets orbiting the Sun, which is one of about 500,000 million stars in the Milky Way galaxy.

The Sun is just one st among billions in the Milky Way galaxy.

Earth is the third of nine planets orbiting the Sun.

More than 5,000 million people live on Earth.

The human scale is the familiar one of everyday objects.

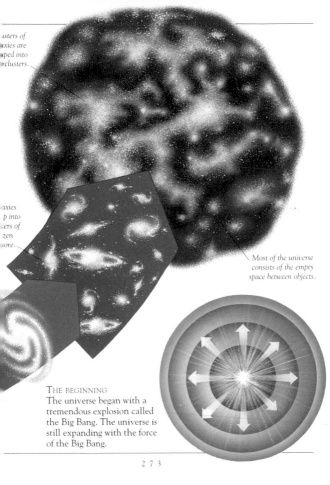

usters of
axies are
ped into
rclusters.

axies
p into
ers of
zen
ore.

Most of the universe
consists of the empty
space between objects.

THE BEGINNING
The universe began with a
tremendous explosion called
the Big Bang. The universe is
still expanding with the force
of the Big Bang.

LIFE STORY OF THE UNIVERSE

ALL MATTER, ENERGY, SPACE, and time were created in the Big Bang around 15,000 million years ago. At first the universe was small and very hot. Atomic particles joined to form hydrogen and helium and the universe expanded and cooled. Over millions of years these gases have produced galaxies, stars, planets, and us.

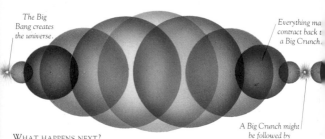

The Big Bang creates the universe.

Everything may contract back to a Big Crunch.

A Big Crunch might be followed by another Big Bang.

WHAT HAPPENS NEXT?
There are two theories about the future of the universe. Either it will stop expanding and shrink back in a process called a Big Crunch, or carry on expanding forever.

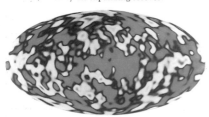

BIG BANG RIPPLES
This map of the whole sky is based on tiny variations in the temperature of space. Red is warmer than average and blue is colder. These tiny variations are faint traces of the Big Bang explosion. The information for the map was obtained the Cosmic Background Explorer Satellite (COBE

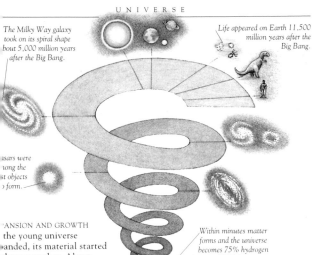

The Milky Way galaxy took on its spiral shape about 5,000 million years after the Big Bang.

Life appeared on Earth 11,500 million years after the Big Bang.

Quasars were among the first objects to form.

EXPANSION AND GROWTH
As the young universe expanded, its material started to clump together. About 500 million years after the Big Bang, galaxies started to take shape. The solar system formed about 10,000 million years after the Big Bang.

Within minutes matter forms and the universe becomes 75% hydrogen and 25% helium.

The initial temperature of the universe was about 10,000 million million million degrees

UNIVERSE: COOLING DATA

Time after Big Bang	Temperature
10^{-6} secs	$10^{13}°C$ ($1.8 \times 10^{13}°F$)
3 minutes	$10^{8}°C$ ($1.8 \times 10^{8}°F$)
300,000 years	$10^{4}°C$ ($10,000°C$-$18,000°F$)
1 million years	$3,000°C$ ($5,400°F$)
5,000 million years	$-170°C$ ($-275°F$)
15,000 million years	$-270°C$ ($-454°F$)

UNIVERSE FACT
• Scientists can trace the life story of the universe back to what is called the Planck time, 10^{-43} seconds after the Big Bang. 10^{-43} means a decimal point followed by 42 zeros and then a one.

WHAT IS A GALAXY?

A GALAXY IS an enormous group of stars. A large galaxy may have billions, a small galaxy only a few hundred thousand. Even small galaxies are so big that it takes light thousands of years to cross them. Galaxies formed from vast spinning clouds of gas, and they continue to spin. The speed of rotation affects their shape.

DISTANT STAR CITY
The Andromeda galaxy is s
far away that its light takes
2,200,000 years to travel to
Earth. We see the galaxy as
was 2,200,000 years ago.

GALAXIES: THE FOUR
BASIC TYPES

ELLIPTICAL
These range from ball-shaped to egg-shaped. They contain mainly old stars, and are the most common type.

SPIRAL
These are disc-shaped. Most material is in the spiral arms where new stars are formed. Old stars are in the nucleus.

BARRED-SPIRAL
These are like spira galaxies, but the nu is elongated into a The spiral arms ext from the ends of the

BRIGHTEST LIGHTS
...is is an X-ray image of a
...asi-stellar object, one of the
... brightest, and remotest
...ects. The most distant
... about 15,000 million
...t years away. Known as
...asars, they are probably
... cores of the first
...axies to be formed.

BRIGHT GALAXIES: DATA		
Galaxy	Distance	Type
Andromeda (M31)	2,200,000 ly	Sb
M32	2,300,000 ly	E2
M33	2,400,000 ly	Sc
Wolf-Lundmark	4,290,000 ly	Irr
M81	9,450,000 ly	Sb
Centaurus A	13,040,000 ly	E0
Pinwheel (M101)	23,790,000 ly	Sc
Whirlpool (M51)	29,340,000 ly	Sc
NGC2841	37,490,000 ly	Sb
NGC1023	39,120,000 ly	E7
NGC3184	42,380,000 ly	Sc
NGC5866	42,380,000 ly	E6
M100	48,900,000 ly	Sc
NGC6643	74,980,000 ly	Sc
M77	81,500,000 ly	Sb
NGC3938	94,540,000 ly	Sc
NGC2207	114,100,000 ly	Sc

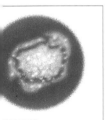

...IREGULAR
...ome of these have a
...nt of spiral structure;
...hile others do not fit
...ny known pattern.
...hey are the rarest type.

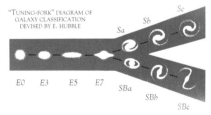

"TUNING-FORK" DIAGRAM OF
GALAXY CLASSIFICATION
DEVISED BY E. HUBBLE

E0   E3   E5   E7   SBa   SBb   SBc   Sa   Sb   Sc

CLASSIFYING GALAXIES BY SHAPE
Elliptical galaxies are classified from E0 (spherical)
to E7 (very flattened). Spirals (S) and barred spirals
(SB) are graded from a to c, according to the
compactness of the central nucleus and the tightness
of the arms. Irregular galaxies (Irr) are not shown
here, but can be divided into types I and II.

CLUSTERS AND SUPERCLUSTERS

GALAXIES OCCUR TOGETHER in
clusters that range in size from
a few to a few thousand galaxies.
Clusters themselves also occur
in groups called superclusters
which are the largest structures
in the universe.

NEIGHBOURING CLUSTER
The Virgo cluster is about 60
million light years away, but
it is the nearest major cluster
to our own Local Group.

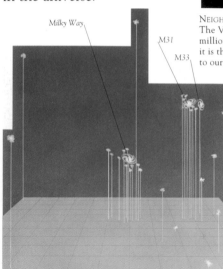

Milky Way

M31

M33

THE LOCAL GROUP
Our own cluster is
about five million
light-years across
and contains about
30 galaxies. The
largest galaxies in
the Local Group are
Andromeda (M31),
Triangulum (M33),
and our own Milky
Way galaxy.

SUPERCLUSTER FACTS

The average distance between galaxies in a cluster is about ten galaxy diameters.

The Local Group is just one small part of a giant supercluster about 100 million light years in diameter.

SOME LOCAL GROUP GALAXIES: DATA

Name	Diameter	Distance
Andromeda	150,000 ly	2,200,000 ly
M33	40,000 ly	2,400,000 ly
Large Magellanic Cloud (LMC)	30,000 ly	170,000 ly
Small Magellanic Cloud (SMC)	20,000 ly	190,000 ly
NGC 6822	15,000 ly	1,800,000 ly
NGC 205	11,000 ly	2,200,000 ly

HONEYCOMB SPACE

Superclusters tend to be flattened into discs or sheets, or elongated into filaments. These shapes cannot be seen through a telescope, but scientists now know that the large-scale structure of the universe is basically a honeycomb arrangement. Superclusters are arranged on the surface of immense "bubbles". These bubbles are almost completely empty of matter. They are huge voids that contain only a few atoms of gas.

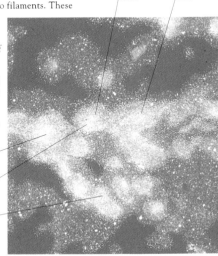

Coma cluster

Ursa Major cluster

Local Group

Virgo cluster

Leo cloud

LOCAL SUPERCLUSTER

THE MILKY WAY

THE SUN IS JUST ONE of about 500,000 million stars in our own galaxy – the Milky Way. Ours is a spiral galaxy, with a nucleus of old stars surrounded by a halo of even older stars. All the young stars, such as the Sun, are located in the spiral arms. The Milky Way is so large that it takes light 100,000 years to travel from edge to edge. All the stars we see at night are in the Milky Way.

SAGITTARIUS STAR CLOUD
This photograph shows young stars in a small part of the Sagittarius arm of the Milky Way. Clouds of dust obscure our view of most of that region of the galaxy.

From the side the spiral arms look like a flattened disc.

Galactic halo con the oldest stars

MILKY WAY GALAXY:
EXTERNAL SIDE VIEW

Nucleus is the brightest region of the galaxy

SIDE-ON SPIRAL
Viewed sideways-on, from a distance of about a million light years, the Milky Way galaxy would look like a giant lens – with flattened edges and a bright central nucleus. Around the nucleus is a roughly spherical halo that contains the oldest stars in the galaxy.

THE MILKY WAY
AS SEEN FROM
EARTH

...OVE THE SPIRAL
...om above, or below, the spiral arms of
...e Milky Way galaxy would be clearly
...ible. These contain most of the galaxy's
...s and dust, and this is where
...r-forming regions
...e found.

...x-Centaurus arm

Galactic
nucleus

...ation of
...solar system

...rion arm
...Local Arm)

Sagittarius
arm

MILKY WAY GALAXY:
EXTERNAL OVERHEAD VIEW

THE LOCAL ARM

THE SOLAR SYSTEM is situated about two-thirds of the
way from the galaxy's centre, at the edge of a spiral
arm called the Local Arm or the Orion arm. From
this viewpoint, we see the galaxy as a great milky
river of stars across
the night sky.

*The galactic nucleus
about 6,000 ly acr*

POSITION OF THE
LOCAL ARM IN
THE GALAXY

SEVEN STARRY SISTERS
The Pleiades is a cluster of bright stars,
seven of which can be seen with the naked
eye, hence their popular name – the Seven
Sisters – which has been in use for at least
2,000 years. In fact there are more than 200
stars in the cluster, which formed about 60
million years ago – shortly after the
dinosaurs died out on Earth.

• From edge to edge the Dumbbell Nebula is two light years in diameter.
• Some stars in Canis Major are only about 300,000 years old – mere star babies compared with our 5,000 million-year-old Sun.
• The nearest bright star cluster to the Sun is the Hyades about 150 light years away. The Hyades forms the V-shape of the bull's head in the constellation of Taurus.

CTACULAR END
e Dumbbell Nebula, about 1,000 light years
n the Sun, is a single star nearing the end of
ife. Spherical shells of gas are blown out
n the star's surface, making a spectacular
t. Gradually all the gas will disperse, and
eventually be used to form new stars
where in the galaxy.

THE LOCAL REGION OF SPACE WITHIN 1,000 LIGHT YEARS OF THE SUN

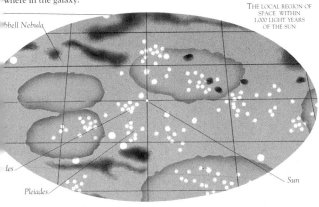

bbell Nebula

les

Pleiades

Sun

WHAT IS A STAR?

A STAR IS an enormous spinning
ball of hot and luminous gas.
Most stars contain two main
gases – hydrogen and helium.
These gases are held together by
gravity, and at the core they are
very densely packed. Within
the core, immense amounts of
energy are produced.

STAR CLUSTER
The cluster M13 in the
constellation of Hercules
contains hundreds of
thousands of stars
arranged in a
compact ball

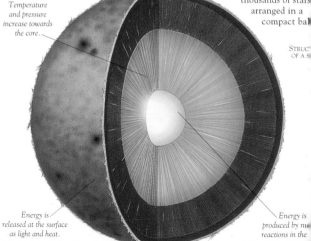

STRUC
OF A S

*Temperature
and pressure
increase towards
the core*

*Energy is
released at the surface
as light and heat.*

*Energy is
produced by nu
reactions in the*

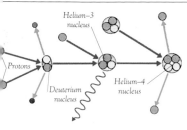

CORE FUSION

A star produces energy by nuclear fusion. Within the core, hydrogen nuclei (protons) collide and fuse to form first deuterium (heavy hydrogen) and then two forms of helium. During fusion, energy is given off. This type of reaction, which is found in most stars, is called the proton-proton chain.

Helium-3 nucleus

Protons

Deuterium nucleus

Helium-4 nucleus

⌐YING SIZES

s differ greatly in amount of gas they ⌐tain, and in their The largest stars ⌐,000 times the ⌐eter of the Sun, ⌐e the smallest are a fraction of its size ⌐t much bigger than ⌐planet Jupiter.

PROXIMA CENTAURI

BROWN DWARF

SUN

SIRIUS

η (ETA) ORIONIS

⌐OMINENT STARS: DATA

⌐ame	Designation	Distance
⌐ega	α Lyrae	26 ly
⌐llux	β Geminorum	36 ly
⌐pella	α Aurigae	45 ly
⌐debaran	α Tauri	68 ly
⌐gulus	α Leonis	84 ly
⌐nopus	α Carinae	98 ly
⌐ica	α Virginis	260 ly
⌐telgeuse	α Orionis	520 ly
⌐laris	α Ursa Minoris	700 ly

STAR FACTS

• All the chemical elements heavier than hydrogen, helium, and lithium were made by nuclear reactions inside stars.
• The mass of the Sun – (1 solar mass) – is used as a standard for measuring other stars.

STAR BIRTH

STARS FOLLOW a life cycle that lasts millions or billions of years. All stars begin in the same way – as material in a nebula, a cloud of gas and dust. Stars are not born individually, but in groups called clusters. Initially, the stars in a cluster have roughly the same composition. Despite these early similarities, the stars usually develop at different rates, and most clusters drift apart before very long.

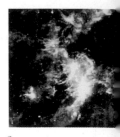

STELLAR BIRTHPLACE
In the Orion Nebula light from new stars illuminates the dust clouds. The stars themselves remain hidden by the dust. One of these young stars is 10,000 times brighter than the Sun.

FORMATION AND EARLY DEVELOPMENT OF A STAR

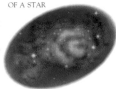

Inside a nebula, gravity causes spinning balls of gas to form – these are known as protostars.

The protostar (seen here in cross-section) shrinks, and its core becomes denser. An outer halo of gas and dust develops.

When the core reac[h]es critical density, nuc[lear] reactions start. The energy released blow[s] away most of the ha[lo]

SINGLE OR DOUBLE

The Sun is unusual – it is a solitary star. In most cases a protostar spins fast enough to form a double or multiple star (1). Multiple stars may orbit around a common centre of gravity (2), and may also orbit around one another (3). Double stars often appear to be variable in their light output because one star regularly blocks the light of the other.

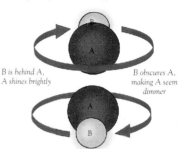

B is behind A, A shines brightly

B obscures A, making A seem dimmer

the young star ntinues to spin pidly, the remaining s and dust become ttened into a disc.

In at least one case (the star we call the Sun) this disc of gas and dust has formed into a system of orbiting planets.

With or without planets, the new star now shines steadily, converting hydrogen to helium by nuclear fusion.

LIFE CYCLE OF A STAR

A STAR'S LIFE CYCLE depends on its mass. Stars of the same mass as the Sun shine steadily for about 10,000 million years. More massive stars convert their hydrogen more quickly, and have shorter lives. The Sun is half way through its life. In about 5,000 million years, it will expand to become a red giant star, and then collapse and end as a dwarf star.

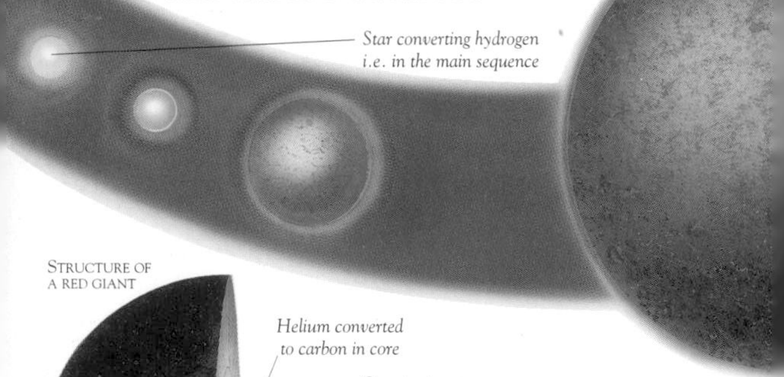

Star converting hydrogen
i.e. in the main sequence

STRUCTURE OF
A RED GIANT

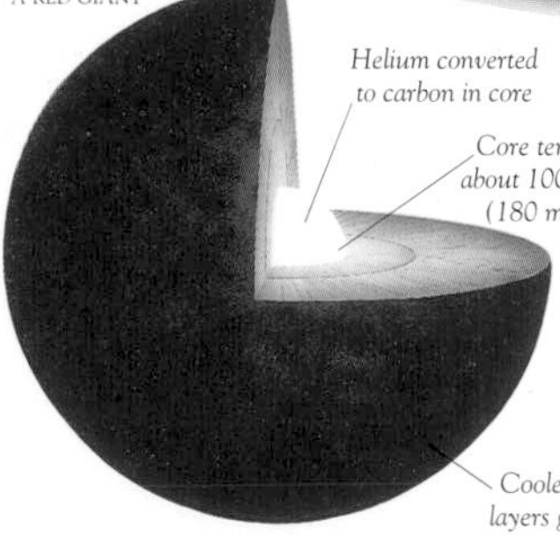

Helium converted
to carbon in core

Core temperature
about 100 million°C
(180 million°F)

Cooler outer
layers glow red

RED GIANTS
When most of the hydrogen
has been converted to heliu
the star becomes a red giant
converting helium to carbon
The core heats up causing th
surface to expand and cool.
red giant may expand to mo
than 100 times its former siz

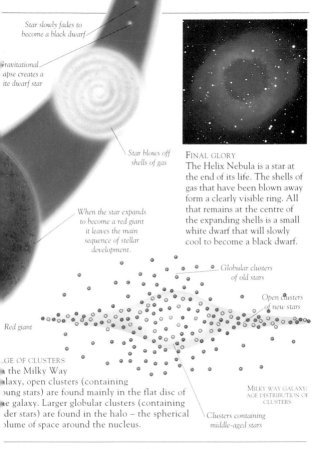

Star slowly fades to
become a black dwarf

Gravitational
collapse creates a
white dwarf star

Star blows off
shells of gas

When the star expands
to become a red giant
it leaves the main
sequence of stellar
development.

FINAL GLORY
The Helix Nebula is a star at
the end of its life. The shells of
gas that have been blown away
form a clearly visible ring. All
that remains at the centre of
the expanding shells is a small
white dwarf that will slowly
cool to become a black dwarf.

Globular clusters
of old stars

Open clusters
of new stars

Red giant

AGE OF CLUSTERS
In the Milky Way
Galaxy, open clusters (containing
young stars) are found mainly in the flat disc of
the galaxy. Larger globular clusters (containing
older stars) are found in the halo – the spherical
volume of space around the nucleus.

MILKY WAY GALAXY:
AGE DISTRIBUTION OF
CLUSTERS

Clusters containing
middle-aged stars

DEATH OF MASSIVE STARS

THE WAY A STAR DIES depends on its mass. The most massive stars end their lives by simply exploding. This huge explosion is called a supernova, and may be bright enough to briefly outshine an entire galaxy. What happens next depends on how much stellar material is left after the supernova.

EXPLOSIVE COLLAPSE
Stars of at least eight solar masses end as supernovae. Gravity causes them to collapse with incredible force producing shock waves.

SUPERNOVA
EXPLOSION

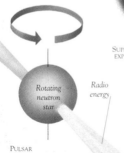

Radio
energy

Rotating
neutron
star

PULSAR

Temperature at
10,000 millio
(18,000 millio

NEUTRON SPINNER
If the core that remains after a supernova is between 1.4 and 3.0 solar masses, it forms what called a neutron star. Composed of super-dense material, neutron stars spin very quickly and produce beams of radio energy that appear to fla on and off very rapidly. These are called pulsa

A RARE AND SPECTACULAR SIGHT
Although supernovae are fairly
common in the universe, they are
rarely seen from Earth. In 1987 a
supernova was observed in the
Large Magellanic Cloud, a nearby
galaxy. The left-hand photograph
shows the normal appearance of
the star (arrowed). The supernova
(designated SN 1987A) is clearly
visible in the right-hand picture.
After shining brightly for a few
months, it slowly faded from view.

...CK HOLES

...e core left after a supernova
...eds three solar masses, it
...collapse until it becomes a
...k hole – something so
...se that its gravity will
... in even light. By
...nition black holes
...nvisible, but they are
...eved to be surrounded
...spinning accretion disc
...aterial being drawn into
...lack hole.

...LAR THEFT

...black hole forms near
...her star, it may
... in gas from the
...gradually stealing
...ass. Astronomers
...ve that the object
...wn as Cygnus X-1 is
...r/black hole pair.

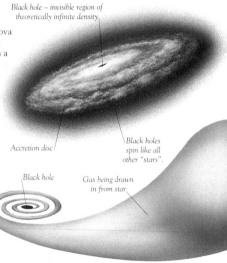

*Black hole – invisible region of
theoretically infinite density*

Accretion disc

*Black holes
spin like all
other "stars".*

Black hole

*Gas being drawn
in from star*

STELLAR CLASSIFICATION

THE MASS OF A STAR affects its
other properties – its colour,
temperature, and luminosity.
Each star is different, but by
studying their properties,
astronomers have been able to
devise a system that enables
them to classify all stars.

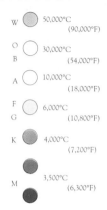

W 50,000°C (90,000°F)

O
B 30,000°C (54,000°F)

A 10,000°C (18,000°F)

F
G 6,000°C (10,800°F)

K 4,000°C (7,200°F)

M 3,500°C (6,300°F)

HEAT AND LIGHT

A star's colour is usually a good indicator of its
temperature. Blue stars are the hottest, and red
the coolest. The Harvard system uses letters of
the alphabet to classify stars according to their
surface temperature. This diagram shows the
colour and temperature range of the main types.

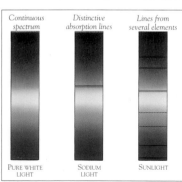

Continuous spectrum

Distinctive absorption lines

Lines from several elements

PURE WHITE LIGHT

SODIUM LIGHT

SUNLIGHT

CHEMICAL LINES

Each star emits its own
particular light. Splitting thi
light into a spectrum reveals
the chemical elements that
make up the star. The differe
elements are indicated by da
absorption lines that
run across the spectrum.
Sodium atoms absorb light
only in the yellow part of th
spectrum. Sunlight displays
hundreds of absorption lines
but only the most prominen
are shown here.

HERTZSPRUNG-RUSSELL (HR) DIAGRAM OF STELLAR CLASSIFICATION

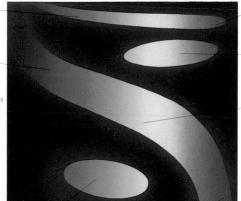

Supergiant
stars e.g.
Deneb

Betelgeuse
is a red
supergiant.

Main
sequence
stars, e.g.
Sirius A,
which convert
hydrogen to
helium

Arcturus is
a red giant.

The Sun
is a main
sequence
yellow dwarf.

White dwarf
stars e.g.
Sirius B

Barnard's Star is
a main sequence
red dwarf.

COLOUR-CODED DIAGRAM

The HR diagram plots a star's temperature
against its absolute magnitude (the amount of
light it gives off). The brightest stars are at the
top, and the dimmest are near the bottom. The
hottest stars are to the left and the coolest to
the right. Most stars spend some part of their
lives in the main sequence which runs from top
left to bottom right across the diagram. Giant
stars are found above the main sequence and
dwarf stars below.

STAR FACTS
• The hottest type W
stars are very rare and
are also known as Wolf-
Rayet stars.
• By the standards of
space, the Sun is very
small. Astronomers
refer to it as a type G
dwarf star.
• Clusters of types O
and B stars (known as
OB1 clusters) contain
hot, bright, young stars.

BRIGHTNESS

HOW BRIGHTLY A STAR shines in
the sky depends on its luminosity
(amount of light energy produced),
and on its distance from Earth.
Astronomers use two different
scales to measure a star's magnitude
(brightness). Absolute magnitude
compares stars from a standard
distance. Apparent magnitude
describes how bright a star appears
as viewed from Earth.

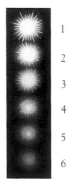

1
2
3
4
5
6

OBSERVED BRIGHTNESS
The scale of apparent
magnitude for naked-eye
stars. Brighter stars have
lower numerical values.

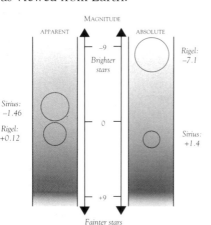

MAGNITUDE

APPARENT

ABSOLUTE

−9

*Brighter
stars*

Rigel:
−7.1

Sirius:
−1.46

Rigel:
+0.12

0

Sirius:
+1.4

+9

Fainter stars

APPARENT VS ABSOLUTE
Sirius is the brightest star
in our sky (apparent
magnitude −1.46) brighter
than Rigel (apparent
magnitude +0.12). Yet in
reality, Rigel is by far the
brighter star with an
absolute magnitude of
−7.1, as opposed to Sirius
which has an absolute
magnitude of +1.4.

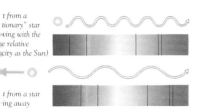

...t from a ...tionary" star ...ving with the ...e relative ...city as the Sun)

...t from a star ...ing away

...IFTING LIGHT

...l objects in the universe are moving. In light from ...rs moving away from the Sun, the dark absorption ...es are shifted towards the red end of the spectrum – ...so-called "red shift".

...W FAR?

...culating a star's absolute magnitude ...ns knowing its distance. For fairly ...se stars (within a few hundred light ...rs) astronomers can measure distance ...g the parallax method. Earth's orbit ...und the Sun enables astronomers to ...e two sightings of a star from opposite ...s of the orbit. The apparent shift in ...ition of the star between the two ...tings is called the parallax. ...e greater the parallax, the ...rer the star. In this case, star ...as the greater shift and ...e closer.

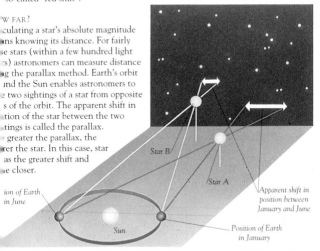

...ion of Earth ...in June

Star B

Star A

Apparent shift in position between January and June

Position of Earth in January

Sun

ABOVE OUR HEADS

OUR KNOWLEDGE of the universe
has been gained from our unique
position on Earth. By day the
sky is dominated by the Sun. At
night the blackness of space is
studded with stars and galaxies
which form an unchanging
backdrop. However, our view of
them changes throughout the
year as Earth orbits the Sun.

CIRCULAR STAR TRAILS
Earth's daily rotation causes
the stars to appear to circle
around the sky. This effect
can be captured by a long-
exposure photograph.

*Stars appear
as patterns
against the
sphere.*

CELESTIAL SPHERE
From Earth the stars
appear to be set against
giant celestial sphere.
the Earth travels on i
yearly orbit around t
Sun, different section
of the sphere are
exposed to our view.
At any particular tim
about half the sphere i
hidden by the Sun's gla
The motion of other obje
such as the planets, are also
plotted against the sphere.

*The Sun's
path is called
the ecliptic.*

GALAXY

All the stars we
can see in the sky, including
our Sun, are in the Milky Way galaxy.
This panoramic view of the Milky
Way (looking towards the centre of
our galaxy), was photographed from
Christchurch, New Zealand.

MARTIAN MOTION

Planets, which have their own
orbits around the Sun, appear to
move across the sky against the
backdrop of stars. The name
"planet" is in fact taken from an
ancient Greek word meaning
"wanderer". Of all the planets,
Mars seems to wander the most –
sometimes it appears to change
direction and move backwards
across Earth's sky. This backward
motion is in fact an optical
illusion caused by the Earth
overtaking Mars as it travels
around the Sun.

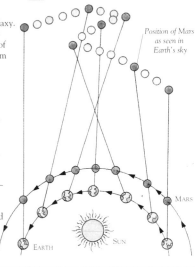

*Position of Mars
as seen in
Earth's sky*

MARS

EARTH

SUN

SPECIAL EFFECTS

FROM EARTH it is possible to see several "special effects" in the sky. Some of these effects are due to peculiarities of the Earth's magnetic field and atmosphere. Other effects depend on the position of the objects in the solar system, especially the Sun, Earth, and Moon. Meteor showers are an effect produced by space dust burning up in the atmosphere.

AURORA BOREALIS
Charged particles from the Sun, carried by the solar wind, cause dramatic light shows when they enter Earth's atmosphere.

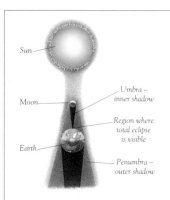

Sun

Moon

Earth

Umbra – inner shadow

Region where total eclipse is visible

Penumbra – outer shadow

ECLIPSE OF THE SUN
Occasionally, the Moon comes into perfect alignment between the Sun and the Earth. When this occurs, the Moon blocks out the Sun's light causing what is called a solar eclipse. From some parts of Earth's surface, the disc of the Moon appears to cover completely the Sun's face, and there is a brief period of darkness. Although the Moon is a great deal smaller than the Sun, it is able to block the light totally because it is so much nearer to the Earth.

HALO AROUND THE MOON

On some winter nights a halo appears around the Moon, but this has nothing to do with the Moon itself. Sunlight reflected towards Earth by the Moon is refracted (bent) by ice crystals high in Earth's atmosphere. This refraction of light creates a circular halo.

METEOR RADIANT

Dust particles from space are seen as meteors when they burn up in the atmosphere. In a meteor shower, which is caused by dust from a comet, all the meteors appear to come from a single point in the sky. This point is known as the radiant of the meteor shower.

SPECIAL EFFECT FACTS

Aurora borealis ("northern lights") are best observed from locations near the north magnetic pole. Similar displays in the southern hemisphere are called aurora australis "southern lights".

A lunar eclipse occurs when the Earth comes directly between the Sun and the Moon. The Earth's shadow can be seen crossing the Moon.

A meteor radiant is an optical illusion. In fact the meteors travel along parallel tracks.

CONSTELLATIONS

SEEN FROM EARTH, the stars
seem to form patterns in the
sky. These patterns are known
as constellations. The skies
around Earth have been
divided into 88 different
constellations, each one of
which is supposed to represent
a mythological person,
creature, or object.

CONSTELLATION OF ORION
In Greek myth, Orion was
mighty hunter. The three
bright stars in a row for
Orion's Belt, an
easily located
"skymark"

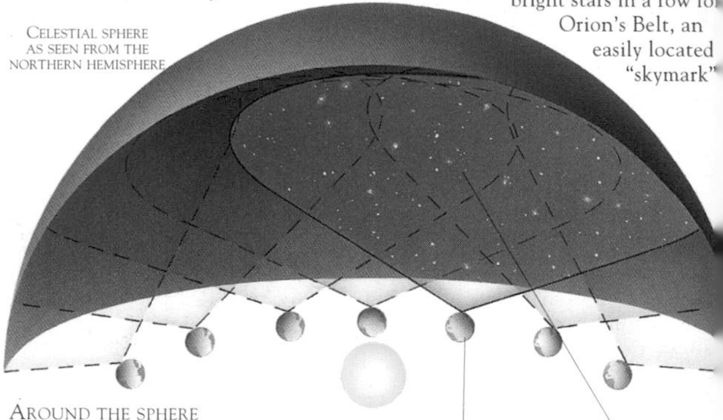

CELESTIAL SPHERE
AS SEEN FROM THE
NORTHERN HEMISPHERE

AROUND THE SPHERE
As the Earth makes its yearly orbit around
the Sun, different portions of the celestial
sphere come into view, presenting the
constellations in an annual sequence.

Position of
Earth
in March

Constellati
visible from I
in Marcl

100,000 YEARS AGO

TODAY

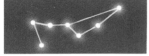

100,000 YEARS FROM NOW

CHANGING SHAPE
The constellations appear fixed, but
in fact they change very slowly. The
changes to the Plough can only be
seen over very long periods of time.

- A constellation is a
two-dimensional view
of objects in three-
dimensional space.

- The Plough (the Big
Dipper in the United
States) is not a separate
constellation but is part
of Ursa Major (the
Great Bear).

- Aboriginal Australians
have their own view of
constellations – they see
patterns in the dark
spaces between stars.

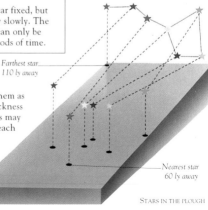

Farthest star
110 ly away

Nearest star
60 ly away

STARS IN THE PLOUGH

ES OF SIGHT
e constellations are a
nan invention. We see them as
patterns against the blackness
pace, but in fact the stars may
arther in distance from each
er than they are from
ch. The stars in the
ugh seem to be close
ether. However,
y are more
tered than
y appear.

CATALOGUING STARS

STARS ARE catalogued according to the constellation in which they appear. Within each constellation, the individual stars are identified by means of letters or numbers. Other objects are catalogued separately.

ORION

The constellation "figure" is drawn around the stars.

ORION NEBULA
In Earth's sky, the nebula appears as a faint, fuzzy patch of light just below Orion's Be

POSSESSIVE NAMES
All the constellations have been given Latin names. When referring to a particular star, the possessive case of the Latin name is used. For example, stars in the constellation of Orion are designated Orionis.

MAPPING THE SKIES
The constellations fit together to map the sky. All the stars inside a constellation's boundaries belong to that constellation, even if they appear to be unconnected to the star making up the main "title" figure.

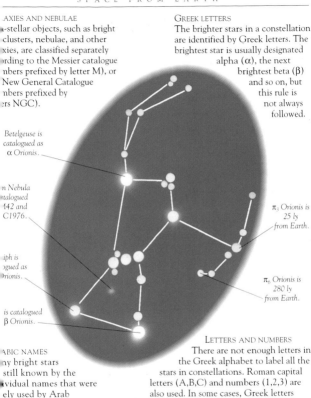

GALAXIES AND NEBULAE

...-stellar objects, such as bright ...clusters, nebulae, and other ...xies, are classified separately ...rding to the Messier catalogue ...nbers prefixed by letter M), or ... New General Catalogue ...nbers prefixed by ...rs NGC).

GREEK LETTERS

The brighter stars in a constellation are identified by Greek letters. The brightest star is usually designated alpha (α), the next brightest beta (β) and so on, but this rule is not always followed.

Betelgeuse is catalogued as α Orionis.

...n Nebula ...talogued ...142 and ...C1976.

...iph is ...ogued as ...rionis.

...is catalogued ... β Orionis.

π_3 Orionis is 25 ly from Earth.

π_6 Orionis is 280 ly from Earth.

ARABIC NAMES

...ny bright stars ...still known by the ...ividual names that were ...ely used by Arab ...onomers more than 800 ...rs ago – e.g. Betelgeuse, ...ph, and Rigel.

LETTERS AND NUMBERS

There are not enough letters in the Greek alphabet to label all the stars in constellations. Roman capital letters (A,B,C) and numbers (1,2,3) are also used. In some cases, Greek letters are used with subscript numbers to identify stars that are near to each other, for example π_3 and π_6 Orionis.

NEAR OR FAR?

STARS ARE VAST DISTANCES from
us and from each other. Light,
which travels faster than
anything else, takes 8.3 minutes
to travel from the Sun to the
Earth. Light from the next
nearest star, Proxima Centauri,
takes 4.3 years. People cannot
tell the distances to stars just by
looking at them. But they can
see subtle differences in colour
and apparent brightness.

LIGHT YEARS APART
All the stars in this distant
cluster may look as if they a
the same distance from Ear
Yet in fact the stars are ma
light years apart.

HOW BRIGHT? HOW FAR?
Stars that have similar apparent magnitude
(brightness) can lie at hugely different
distances from Earth. Objects in the
constellation of Orion are between
70 and 2,300 light years (ly)
from Earth. The brightest
star, Rigel, is more
than 900 ly away.

RELATIVE PO
OF STARS IN

Orion Nebula

Each main
represents
light yea

Rigel

Mir

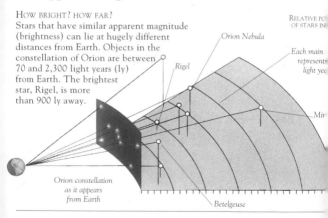

Orion constellation
as it appears
from Earth

Betelgeuse

STELLAR DATA: NEAREST STARS TO THE SUN

Name	Distance	Colour
Proxima Centauri	4.2 ly	red
α Centauri A	4.3 ly	yellow
α Centauri B	4.3 ly	orange
Barnard's Star	5.9 ly	red
Wolf 359	7.6 ly	red
Lalande 21185	8.1 ly	red
Sirius A	8.6 ly	white
Sirius B	8.6 ly	white

STAR FACTS
• Proxima Centauri is part of a triple star system along with α Centauri A and α Centauri B.
• The brightest star, Sirius A, has a faint white dwarf companion, Sirius B.

NEIGHBOURING STARS

Many of the stars within 40 light years of the Sun are dim red dwarfs like Barnard's Star, which cannot be seen with the naked eye. Others, such as Vega, are 50 times more luminous than the Sun.

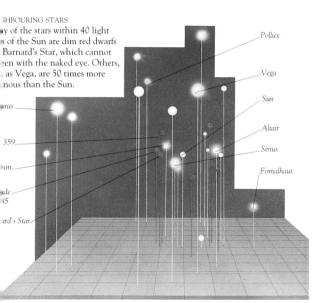

Pollux

Vega

Sun

Altair

Sirius

Fomalhaut

Sirius

Wolf 359

Procyon

Lalande 21185

Barnard's Star

THE NORTHERN SKY

PEOPLE LIVING IN the northern hemisphere see the northern half of the celestial sphere. The stars visible on a particular night depend on the observer's latitude, the time of year, and the time of night. The stars near the centre of the sky-map are called circumpolar and can be seen throughout the year. Polaris (the North Star) appears to remain directly over the North Pole.

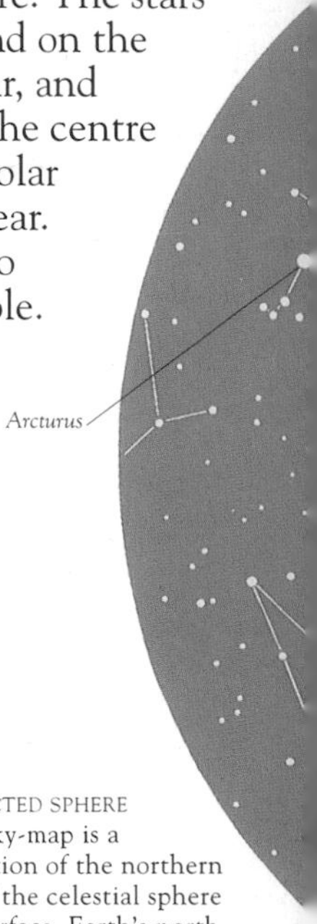

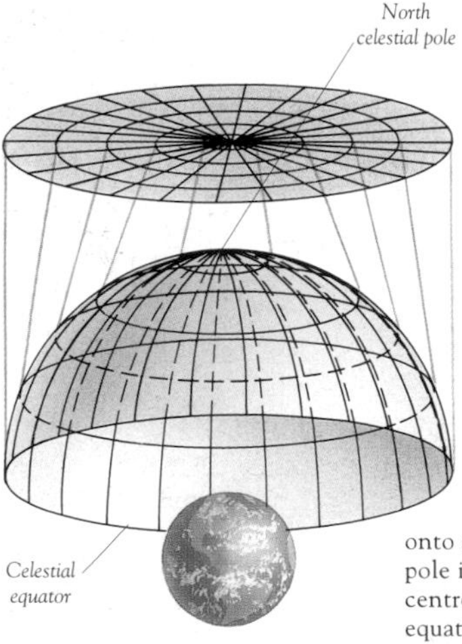

North celestial pole

Arcturus

Celestial equator

PROJECTED SPHERE
This sky-map is a projection of the northern half of the celestial sphere onto a flat surface. Earth's north pole is situated directly below the centre of the map. The celestial equator is a projection of Earth's equator out into space.

The edge of the map marks
the celestial equator – stars
here can also be seen by
southern hemisphere
observers.

Polaris

The Plough

The stars around
the edge come into
view month by month
during the year.

Betelgeuse

THE SOUTHERN SKY

PEOPLE LIVING IN the southern hemisphere see the southern half of the celestial sphere. The stars visible on a particular night depend on the observer's latitude, the time of year, and the time of night. The stars near the centre of the sky-map are called circumpolar and can be seen all year round. Alpha Centauri, one of the nearest stars to the Sun, is a southern hemisphere star.

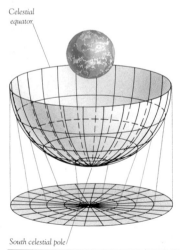

Celestial equator

Alpha Centauri

Antares

South celestial pole

PROJECTED SPHERE
This sky-map is a projection of the southern half of the celestial sphere onto a flat surface. Earth's south pole is situated directly below the centre of the map. The celestial equator is a projection of Earth's equator out into space.

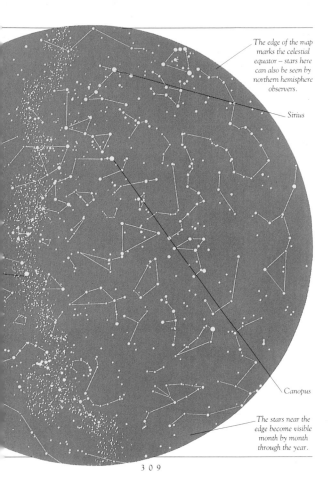

The edge of the map marks the celestial equator – stars here can also be seen by northern hemisphere observers.

Sirius

Canopus

The stars near the edge become visible month by month through the year.

WHAT IS THE SOLAR SYSTEM?

THE SOLAR SYSTEM consists of the Sun and the many objects that orbit around it – nine planets, over 60 moons, and countless asteroids and comets. The system occupies a disc-shaped volume of space more than 12,000 million kilometres (7,458 million miles) across. At the centre is the Sun which contains more than 99 per cent of the solar system's mass.

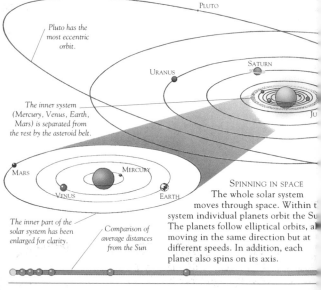

PLUTO

Pluto has the most eccentric orbit.

URANUS

SATURN

The inner system (Mercury, Venus, Earth, Mars) is separated from the rest by the asteroid belt.

JU

MARS

MERCURY

VENUS

EARTH

The inner part of the solar system has been enlarged for clarity.

Comparison of average distances from the Sun

SPINNING IN SPACE
The whole solar system moves through space. Within t system individual planets orbit the Su The planets follow elliptical orbits, a moving in the same direction but at different speeds. In addition, each planet also spins on its axis.

MERCURY

VENUS

EARTH

MARS

JUPITER

SATURN

URANUS

NEPTUNE

PLUTO

SOLAR SYSTEM FACTS

Images obtained with the latest telescopes strongly suggest that some other stars (e.g. Pictoris) are forming planetary systems.

The solar system has a total of 61 moons by the latest count. Future space probes are almost certain to discover extra moons orbiting the outer planets.

Each of the four gas planets has a ring system around it – the rings have been omitted from this illustration for ease of comparison.

Orbits are elliptical (oval) rather than circular

The time taken for a planet to make one orbit of the Sun is called the orbital period.

Pluto is the smallest and least known planet.

THE PLANETS

The planets form two main groups – the inner four are composed of rock, while the next four are larger and are composed mostly of liquefied gas. The outermost planet, Pluto, is mainly rock.

SOLAR GRAVITY

ABOUT 4,600 MILLION years ago, the solar system formed from a cloud of gas and dust. The Sun formed first and the other objects formed from the leftovers. The Sun's gravity dominates the system because it is so massive by comparison with the planets.

CONDENSING INTO PLACE
The young Sun was surrounded by a cloud of gas, snow, and dust that flattened into a disc. Dust clumped together to form the four inner rock planets. The giant outer planets formed from a mixture of gas, snow, and dust. Pluto's origin is a mystery.

ORBITAL PATHS
Most of the planets orbit close to the plane of the Earth's orbit (the ecliptic). Pluto has the most inclined orbit, possibly because it is the most distant planet and is the least influenced by the Sun's gravity. However the next most inclined planet is Mercury (7°), which is the nearest planet to the Sun.

THE PLANETS:
ORBITAL INCLINATION
TO THE ECLIPTIC

Pluto: 17.2°
Mercury: 7°
Venus: 3.39°
Saturn: 2.49°
Mars: 1.85°
Neptune: 1.77°
Jupiter: 1.3°
Uranus: 0.77°
Earth: 0°

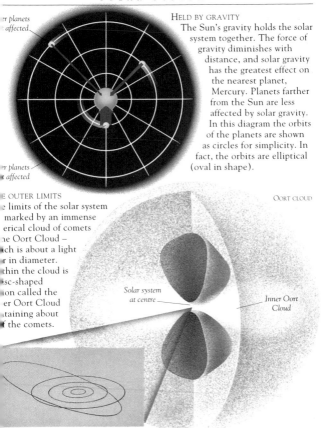

r planets
affected

r planets
affected

HELD BY GRAVITY

The Sun's gravity holds the solar
system together. The force of
gravity diminishes with
distance, and solar gravity
has the greatest effect on
the nearest planet,
Mercury. Planets farther
from the Sun are less
affected by solar gravity.
In this diagram the orbits
of the planets are shown
as circles for simplicity. In
fact, the orbits are elliptical
(oval in shape).

E OUTER LIMITS

e limits of the solar system
marked by an immense
erical cloud of comets
ne Oort Cloud –
ch is about a light
r in diameter.
hin the cloud is
sc-shaped
ion called the
er Oort Cloud
taining about
the comets.

OORT CLOUD

Solar system
at centre

Inner Oort
Cloud

THE SUN

LIKE OTHER STARS, the Sun is a huge ball of spinning gas. Nuclear reactions take place at its core giving off energy. The Sun is the only star close enough to be studied in detail. Its surface features, such as sunspots and prominences, can be observed from Earth. Satellites and space probes are able to get a closer view and obtain even more information.

ECLIPSE OF THE SUN
During an eclipse, the outer layer of the Sun, the corona becomes visible. Normally the corona is hidden by glare

Year 1   Year 4   Year 7   Year 10   Year 12

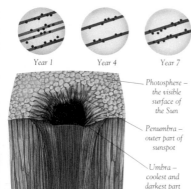

Photosphere – the visible surface of the Sun

Penumbra – outer part of sunspot

Umbra – coolest and darkest part

COOL AND DARK
Sunspots, dark patches on the surface, are regions of cooler ga caused by disturbances in the Sun's magnetic field. Sunspots follow an 11-year cycle that begins with the Sun being spo free. The spots appear at high latitude and gradually increase in number, moving towards th Sun's equator during the cycle

OLAR DATA

Average distance from Earth	149,680,000 km (93,026,724 miles)
Distance from centre of galaxy	30,000 light years
Diameter (at equator)	1,391,980 km (865,121 miles)
Rotation period (at equator)	25.04 Earth days
Mass (Earth = 1)	330,000
Gravity (Earth = 1)	27.9
Average density (water = 1)	1.41
Absolute magnitude	4.83

SOLAR FACTS

• Never look directly at the Sun. Even with sunglasses, camera film, or smoked glass you risk damaging your eyesight.

• The safe way is to project the Sun's image on to a piece of paper using a hand lens.

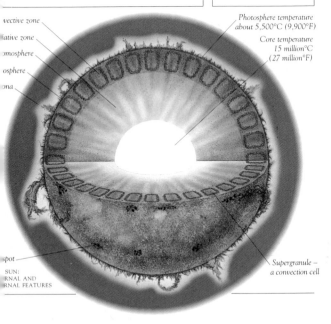

vective zone

ative zone

omosphere

osphere

ona

Photosphere temperature about 5,500°C (9,900°F)

Core temperature 15 million°C (27 million°F)

spot

SUN:
RNAL AND
RNAL FEATURES

Supergranule – a convection cell

SOLAR ENERGY AND INFLUENCE

AT ITS CORE, the Sun converts hydrogen to helium a rate of 600 million tonnes (to every second. The energy produced eventually reaches the surface an travels through spac

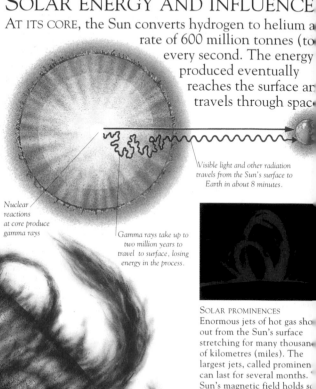

Visible light and other radiation travels from the Sun's surface to Earth in about 8 minutes.

Nuclear reactions at core produce gamma rays

Gamma rays take up to two million years to travel to surface, losing energy in the process.

SOLAR PROMINENCES
Enormous jets of hot gas sho out from the Sun's surface stretching for many thousan of kilometres (miles). The largest jets, called prominen can last for several months. Sun's magnetic field holds sc prominences in gigantic loo

Solar wind deflects interstellar gas

The solar wind takes about five days to reach Earth.

Around Earth the solar wind blows at about 500 km/s (311 miles/sec).

Solar wind deflects most cosmic rays

ULYSSES
SOLAR PROBE

Sensors located on hinged boom

EXTENT OF INFLUENCE

The Sun influences an enormous volume of space around it. Gases streaming from the corona become the high-speed solar wind. The solar wind carries a magnetic field from the Sun. As the Sun rotates, the field takes on a spiral shape. The volume of space swept by the solar wind is called the heliosphere.

TO THE SOLAR POLES

Earth's orbit in the Sun's equatorial plane means that the Sun's poles cannot be studied from Earth. The Ulysses probe was launched in 1990 to study these hard-to-observe regions.

SOLAR ENERGY FACTS

• Converting hydrogen to helium means that the Sun loses at least a million tonnes (tons) of its mass every second.

• The amount of the Sun's energy reaching Earth's surface (known as the solar constant) is equivalent to 1.37 kw (kilowatts) of electricity per square metre (square yard) per second.

MERCURY

A SMALL ROCK WORLD with a large dense core, Mercury is the closest planet to the Sun. There is no real atmosphere and much of the surface is marked by numerous impact craters. Dominated by the Sun, Mercury experiences the greatest variation in surface temperature of any planet in the solar system. Differences between day and night can be more than 600°C (1,080°F).

DIFFICULT TO SEE
Photographs taken from Earth show Mercury as a fuzzy disc, difficult to observe against the Sun. This image was put together from photographs taken by the Mariner 10 probe

Earth

Mercury

MERCURY: PLANETARY DATA	
Average distance from the Sun	57.9 million km (36 million miles)
Orbital period	88 Earth days
Orbital velocity	47.9 km/s (29.7 miles/sec)
Rotation period	58.7 Earth days
Diameter at equator	4,878 km (3,032 miles)
Surface temperature	–180°C to +430°C (–292°F to +806°F)
Mass (Earth = 1)	0.055
Gravity (Earth = 1)	0.38
Number of moons	0

MERCURY FACTS
• Mercury was named after the fleet-footed messenger of the Roman gods because it travels so quickly across Earth's sky.

• Mercury's largest crater, Caloris Planitia measures 1,400 km (875 miles) across.

6% oxygen

5% sodium

8% helium

% potassium and hydrogen

CURY:
OSITION OF ATMOSPHERE

THIN AIR

Mercury's atmosphere is extremely thin – less than one trillionth of Earth's. Sodium and potassium occur in the daytime only. At night these elements are absorbed back into the surface rocks.

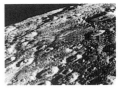

PROBE'S EYE VIEW
Craters cover about 60 per cent of Mercury's surface; the other 40 per cent consists of relatively smooth plains.

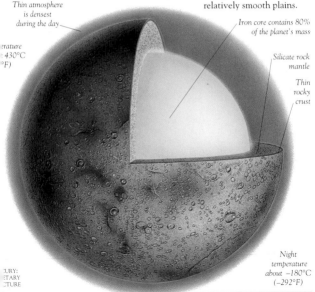

Thin atmosphere is densest during the day

erature
: 430°C
°F)

Iron core contains 80% of the planet's mass

Silicate rock mantle

Thin rocky crust

Night temperature about −180°C (−292°F)

CURY:
ETARY
CTURE

LONG DAYS

Mercury rotates very slowly on an almost upright axis. The axis is tilted at just 2° from the normal (at 90°) to the plane of its orbit. A single day on Mercury (sunrise to sunrise) lasts for 176 Earth days. Although days are very long, the Mercurian year is very short. The planet takes only 88 Earth days to complete one orbit around the Sun.

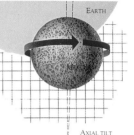

EARTH

MERCURY

AXIAL TILT
2°

ECCENTRIC ORBIT

A combination of long da[ys] and short years would cre[ate] strange effects for any inhabitants. While Mercury completes two orbits of the Sun (show[n] here separately for clarit[y]) an observer on the surfac[e] (marked by a dot) would experience only one Mercur[ian] day. Birthdays would happen more often than sunrise.

SURFACE MAP

The Mariner 1[0] photographs we[re] used to produce maps of Mercur[y]. Each square of t[he] grid covers abo[ut] 80 x 80 km (50 x 50 miles)

MPACT CRATER FORMATION ON ROCK PLANETS

A meteorite impact blasts out a circular crater, and ejected material falls back to form a circular rim.

Rock compressed by the initial impact may bounce back from the sides to form a roughly conical central peak.

The crater profile is gradually reduced as rock fragments and debris slip from the walls and peak.

TARY VISITOR

ner 10 is the only probe to have made a led study of Mercury. Launched in ember 1973, the probe took five ths to reach the planet. During three approaches the probe photographed t 40 per cent of the surface area. At its st approach, Mariner 10 was 300 km miles) above the surface.

High resolution cameras

MARINER 10 PROBE

RCURY: CREATIVE CRATER NAMES

rcury's craters commemorate creative people:

riters	Composers	Painters	Architects
nte	Bach	Brueghel	Bernini
rvantes	Chopin	Cezanne	Bramante
kens	Grieg	Dürer	Imhotep
ethe	Handel	Holbein	Mansart
Po	Liszt	Monet	Michelangelo
lville	Mozart	Renoir	Sinan
elley	Stravinsky	Titian	Sullivan
stoy	Verdi	Van Gogh	Wren

FACTS

• Mercury can only be seen from Earth at twilight – either just before dawn or just after sunset.

• Parts of Mercury's surface have a wrinkled appearance – the result of the planet shrinking as its core cooled.

VENUS

A ROCK PLANET with a dense
atmosphere, Venus is almost
the same size as the Earth.
The two share some surface
features, but conditions on
Venus are very different from
those on Earth. The surface
environment of Venus is
extremely hostile – intense
heat, crushing pressure, and
unbreathable air. Overhead
there are thick clouds of
sulphuric acid droplets.

OBSCURED BY CLOUDS
The surface features of Venus
are hidden by a permanent
blanket of thick cloud. The
dark swirls are high-altitude
wind systems.

Venus

Earth

VENUS: PLANETARY DATA	
Average distance from the Sun	108.2 million km (67.2 million miles)
Orbital period	224.7 Earth days
Orbital velocity	35 km/s (21.7 miles/sec)
Rotation period	243 Earth days
Diameter at equator	12,102 km (7,521 miles)
Surface temperature	480°C (896°F)
Mass (Earth = 1)	0.81
Gravity (Earth = 1)	0.88
Number of moons	0

VENUS FACTS

• Venus shines bright
in Earth's sky because
the cloud layer reflects
most of the sunlight.

• Venus has phases like
the Moon. You need a
telescope to see them
clearly, but binoculars
will enable you to see
the crescent phase.

er haze

ud layer
0 km
5 miles)
hick

er haze

JS: ATMOSPHERE
CTURE AND COMPOSITION

BENEATH THE CLOUDS

Below the clouds is a clear carbon-dioxide atmosphere. At the surface, atmospheric pressure is 90 times that of Earth at sea-level.

96%	carbon dioxide
3.5%	nitrogen
0.5%	sulphur dioxide, argon, and carbon monoxide

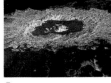

COMPUTER IMAGE

This is a computer-generated image of the Howe meteorite crater 37 km (23 miles) in diameter. The image was produced from radar-mapping data.

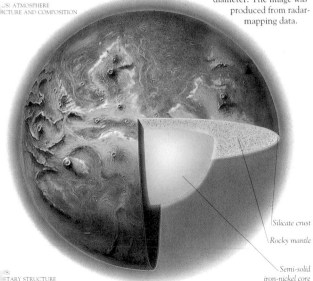

JS:
ETARY STRUCTURE

Silicate crust

Rocky mantle

Semi-solid
iron-nickel core

BACKWARD ROTATION

Venus is one of only two planets to rotate on its axis in a backward direction (the other is remote Pluto). Venus' backward rotation is so slow that a Venusian day lasts longer (243 Earth days) than a Venusian year (224.7 Earth days). Driven by powerful winds, Venus' atmosphere moves at its own, much faster, pace. The upper levels of the cloud layer take just four Earth days to travel right around the planet.

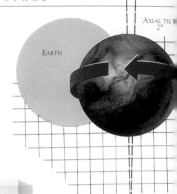

EARTH

AXIAL TILT
2°

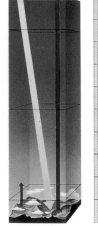

100 km
(62 miles)

Sunlight reflected
by cloud layer

EARTH

VENUS

GREENHOUSE PLANET

At 480°C (896 °F), Venus has a higher average surface temperature than any other planet in the solar system. The heating of Venus is the result of a "greenhouse effect" run wild. Although the cloud layer reflects much of the sunlight that hits it, some solar heat energy does reach the surface. But instead of being radiated back into space, the heat energy is trapped by the cloud layer causing temperatures to rise. On Earth the cloud layer allows much more heat to escape.

[AE]RIAL VIEW

[M]at Mons is an extinct volcano
[abo]ut 8 km (5 miles) high. This
[ima]ge was produced by the
[Ma]gellan probe's radar-mapping
[tech]niques that can penetrate
[Ven]us' thick clouds. The data
[has] been processed to give a
[vie]wpoint located about
[1.6] km (1 mile) above
[the] planet's surface.

Solar panels

Propulsion module

Radar signal reflected by surface features

Radio signal measures altitude

[V]ENUS: SELECTED EXPLORATION EVENTS

[Pr]obe	Date	Result
[M]ariner 2	14/12/62	Successful fly-by
[V]enera 4	18/10/67	Sampled atmosphere
[V]enera 7	15/12/70	Sent data from surface
[M]ariner 10	5/2/74	Fly-by on way to Mercury
[V]enera 9	23/10/75	First orbit and soft landing and first surface image
[V]enera 15	10/10/83	First radar mapping
[Pi]oneer-Venus 2	9/12/78	Multiple descent probes investigate atmosphere
[M]agellan	10/8/90	Complete radar mapping

MORE FACTS

• The facts that Venus
has a small axial tilt
and backward rotation
are just popular
convention. According
to the rules of the
IAU (International
Astronomical Union),
Venus rotates in a
normal direction
around an axis tilted at
177.9° to the vertical.

EARTH

THE THIRD PLANET from the
Sun, Earth, is unique in the
solar system and is possibly
unique in the universe.
Only Earth has the range of
temperatures that permit
liquid water to exist, and
Earth alone has developed
an oxygen-rich atmosphere.
These two factors have
enabled the rocky planet
Earth to evolve the myriad
varieties of life.

JEWEL IN SPACE
Photographed by Apollo
astronauts returning from the
Moon, planet Earth looks like
brightly coloured jewel – blue
oceans, white clouds, and gree
brown land masses.

Earth

EARTH: PLANETARY DATA	
Average distance from the Sun	149.6 million km (93 million miles)
Orbital period	365.25 days
Orbital velocity	29.8 km/s (18.5 miles/sec)
Rotation period	23.93 hours
Diameter at equator	12,756 km (7,928 miles)
Surface temperature	−70°C to +55°C (−94°F to +131°F)
Gravity (Earth = 1)	1
Number of moons	1

EARTH FACTS
• The oldest rocks so
far discovered in the
Earth's crust date bac
3,900 million years.
• The oxygen in
Earth's atmosphere is
the result of life. The
process of oxygenatio
began with bacteria
about 2,000 million
years ago.

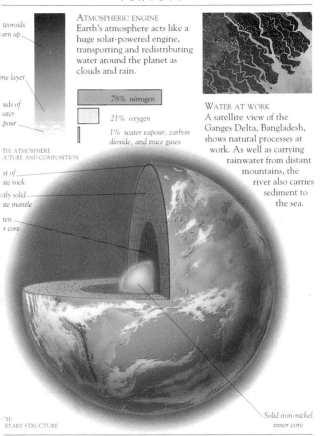

teoroids
rn up

ne layer

uds of
ater
pour

ATMOSPHERIC ENGINE
Earth's atmosphere acts like a huge solar-powered engine, transporting and redistributing water around the planet as clouds and rain.

| 78% nitrogen |
| 21% oxygen |
| 1% water vapour, carbon dioxide, and trace gases |

TH: ATMOSPHERE
UCTURE AND COMPOSITION

WATER AT WORK
A satellite view of the Ganges Delta, Bangladesh, shows natural processes at work. As well as carrying rainwater from distant mountains, the river also carries sediment to the sea.

st of
te rock

tly solid
te mantle

ten
r core

TH:
ETARY STRUCTURE

Solid iron-nickel
inner core

UNEQUAL HEATING

Earth's axis of rotation is tilted at 23.5° to the vertical. As the planet travels around the Sun during the year, the tilt causes seasonal variations in climate. These variations are most noticeable in the high latitudes away from the equator. Spinning on a tilted axis gives rise to unequal heating of the surface by the Sun. This differential heating produces differences in atmospheric pressure which create the wind systems that drive Earth's climate.

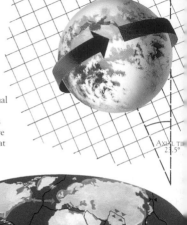

AXIAL TILT
23.5°

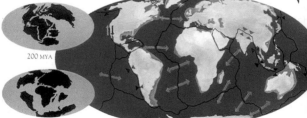

200 MYA

60 MYA

200 MILLION YEARS AGO
The continents were grouped closer together.

60 MILLION YEARS AGO
The landmasses had moved some way towards their present locations.

CONTINENTS IN MOTION

The continents "float" on the surface of the Earth's crust, which is made up of a number of separate plates. These plates are in constant slow-motion, pushed apart as new crust is produced at mid-ocean ridges. The result is that the continents are also gradually moving. Areas where plates are in collision have many volcanoes and earthquakes.

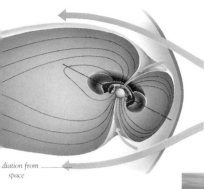

SPINNING MAGNET
Earth has a much stronger magnetic field than any of the other rock planets. Produced by the rapid rotation of the nickel-iron core, the magnetic field extends far into space and deflects harmful radiation away from the planet. Despite its elongated ovoid shape, this magnetic field is called the magnetosphere.

diation from
space

WATER OF LIFE
ter only exists in its liquid form between
C (32°F) and 100°C (212°F), which is about
same range of temperatures found on Earth.
uid water is absolutely essential to practically
forms of life. Along with carbon dioxide, it is
of the two raw materials used by plants to
duce their own food and provide the oxygen
n which animal life depends.

ARTH: PHYSICAL LIMITS

ge	4,600 million years
lass	59,760 million million tonnes (tons)
urface area	510 million km²
	(317 million sq miles)
overed by water	70.8 per cent
ighest mountain	8,848 metres (29,028 ft)
eepest ocean trench	10,924 metres (35,842 ft)
ldest evidence of life	3,500 million years ago
otal number of living species	at least 10 million

MORE FACTS
• The Atlantic Ocean increases in width by about 3 cm (1.2 in) each year.
• Earth has periodic magnetic reversals when the north pole becomes the south pole, and the south becomes north.

EARTH'S MOON

EARTH HAS A single satellite, the Moon, which is about one quarter the size of our planet. Although the Earth and the Moon are closely linked, there are many striking contrasts. The Moon is a waterless, airless, and lifeless place. Its surface is covered by craters, the scars of a massive meteorite bombardment that took place billions of years ago.

FAMILIAR SIGHT
Some of the features on the Moon can be identified with the naked eye. Binoculars, or small telescope, will reveal a considerable amount of detail

The Moon's distance from Earth varies during its orbit.

Minimum   Average   Maximum

THE MOON: DATA	
Average distance from the Earth	384,400 km (238,906 miles)
Orbital period	27.3 Earth days
Orbital velocity	1 km/s (0.6 miles/sec)
Rotation period	27.3 Earth days
Diameter at equator	3,476 km (2,160 miles)
Surface temperature	−155°C to +105°C (−247°F to +221°F)
Mass (Earth = 1)	0.012
Gravity (Earth = 1)	0.16
Escape velocity	2.38 km/s (1.48 miles/sec)

MOON FACTS

• The Moon has approximately the same surface area as the continents of North and South America.

• The pull of the Moon's gravity is largely responsible for the twice daily rise and fall of tides in Earth's seas and oceans.

URE IN A MOONSCAPE

e Moon remains unique as the only
raterrestrial object upon which
nan beings have walked. Protected
a spacesuit from the airless lunar
vironment, one of the Apollo 17
ronauts investigates a large boulder.
disturbed by the effects of wind or
n, his footprints should remain
ible for millions of years.

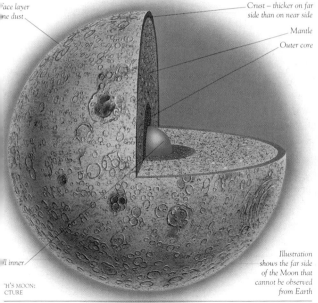

face layer
ne dust

Crust – thicker on far
side than on near side

Mantle

Outer core

l inner

H'S MOON:
CTURE

Illustration
shows the far side
of the Moon that
cannot be observed
from Earth

HELD IN PLACE

Earth is larger and more massive than the Moon, and has a powerful effect on its smaller neighbour. Under the influence of Earth's gravity the Moon's motion through space has been moderated so that its rotation period is the same as its orbital period – 27.3 days. This synchronisation of motion means that the same face of the Moon is always turned towards the Earth – the near side. The other side is always turned away from us – the far side.

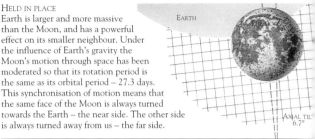

EARTH

THE MOON

AXIAL TILT 6.7°

BATTERED SURFACE

About 3,800 million years ago, the Moon's surface received an intense meteorite bombardment.

Some 1,000 million years later, the largest craters gradually filled up with dark lava, and formed the lunar seas.

Since that time, the appearance of the lunar surface has hardly changed apart from a few recent ray craters.

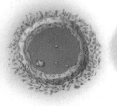

OLD CRATER

RAY CRATER

CHANGING MOONSCAPE
Most of the craters were made about 3,0 million years ago, a many are only fain visible. Some newer craters are identifiabl by conspicuous rays of pa ejected material fanning o from the crater wall.

⟨MO⟩ON ROCK

⟨ab⟩out 380 kg (836 lb) of moon rock have been brought
⟨bac⟩k to Earth. There are no sedimentary or metamorphic
⟨roc⟩ks on the Moon – all the samples brought
⟨bac⟩k are either igneous lavas
⟨ma⟩inly basalt) or breccias
⟨pro⟩duced by the heat
⟨an⟩d force of meteorite
⟨imp⟩acts. Most of the
⟨mo⟩on's surface is
⟨cov⟩ered with a layer of
⟨cru⟩shed and broken rock
⟨cal⟩led "regolith") which
⟨is ab⟩out 20 m (65 ft) deep .

MOON ROCK COLLECTED
BY APOLLO ASTRONAUTS

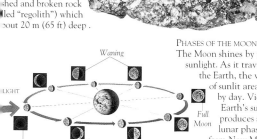

Waning

⟨SUN⟩LIGHT

*Full
Moon*

New Moon

Waxing

PHASES OF THE MOON
The Moon shines by reflected
sunlight. As it travels around
the Earth, the visible amount
of sunlit area changes day
by day. Viewed from
Earth's surface, this
produces a cycle of
lunar phases – waxing
from New Moon to Full
Moon, and then waning
back to New Moon once more.

⟨EA⟩RTH'S MOON: SELECTED EXPLORATION EVENTS

⟨Ve⟩hicle	Date	Result
⟨Lu⟩na 3	10/10/59	First images of far side
⟨Lu⟩na 9	3/2/66	First soft landing
⟨Su⟩rveyor 3	17/4/67	Landing site soil studies
⟨Ap⟩ollo 11	20/7/69	Humans first land on Moon
⟨Lun⟩a 16	24/9/70	Robot returns with samples
⟨Lun⟩a 17	17/11/70	Mobile robot landed
⟨Ap⟩ollo 15	30/7/71	Lunar Roving Vehicle used
⟨Ap⟩ollo 17	11/12/72	Last Apollo mission lands

MORE FACTS
• The first person to
step on to the Moon
was the astronaut Neil
Armstrong early on
21 July 1969.
• His historic first
words were, "That's
one small step for a
man, one giant leap
for mankind."

MARS

A RED-HUED ROCK PLANET,
Mars is a cold, barren world
with a thin atmosphere. There
are many Earthlike features,
such as polar ice caps and
water-carved valleys, but there
are many important differences.
Temperatures rarely rise above
freezing point, the air is
unbreathable, and huge dust-
storms scour the surface. The
planet's red colour is caused by
the presence of iron oxide.

LONG RANGE VIEW
This image was obtained by an
Earth-orbiting telescope at a
distance of 85 million km
(53 million miles) from Mars.
Bluish clouds can be seen
above the north pole region.

Earth

Mars

MARS: PLANETARY DATA	
Average distance from the Sun	227.9 million km (141.6 million miles)
Orbital period	687 Earth days
Orbital velocity	24.1 km/s (15 miles/sec)
Rotation period	24.62 hours
Diameter at equator	6,786 km (4,217 miles)
Surface temperature	−120°C to +25°C (−184°F to +77°F)
Mass (Earth = 1)	0.107
Gravity (Earth = 1)	0.38
Moons:	2

MARS FACTS
• Mars was named
after the Roman god
of war because it
appears the colour of
spilled blood.
• The south polar ice
cap on Mars is much
larger than the north
polar ice cap, and the
southern winter is
considerably longer.

ALMOST WATERLESS

On Mars, water vapour is found
only in the lowest part of the
atmosphere, as clouds or fog
along valley floors.

95% carbon dioxide
2.7% nitrogen
1.6 % argon
0.7% oxygen, carbon monoxide, and water vapour

GRANDEST CANYON

Valles Marineris, largest of
the Martian canyons, has a
length of about 4,500 km
(2,800 miles) and a
maximum depth of
7 km (4 miles).

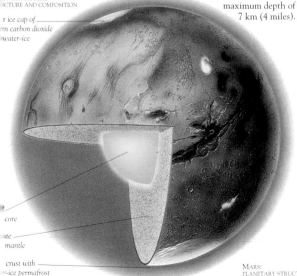

r ice cap of
n carbon dioxide
water-ice

core

te
mantle

crust with
-ice permafrost

MARS:
PLANETARY STRUCTURE

EARTHLIKE SEASONS

Mars is smaller than the Earth, but turns on its axis more slowly, so that the day lengths are almost identical. A day on Mars is just 41 minutes longer. A similar axial tilt gives Mars the same pattern of seasons as we experience on Earth. However, because of the greater orbital period (687 Earth days), the length of each season is nearly twice as long.

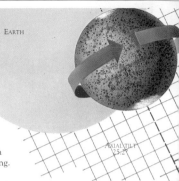

EARTH

AXIAL TILT
25.2°

DESERT SURFACE

This is a view of the Martian surface photographed by the Viking I lander. Part of the lander is seen here in the foreground. The rocks in the middle of the picture are about 30 cm (1 ft) across and this "stony desert" appearance is typical of about 40 per cent of Mars' surface area. Some Martian landforms, however, are more dramatic. Olympus Mons towers 25 km (15.5 miles) high.

*Olympus Mons, a giant
shield volcano, is the tallest
mountain in the
solar system.*

*Earth's Mauna Kea volcano
dwarfed by compari...*

Hawaiian Islands   *Ocean floor*   *Sea level*

'S OF MARS' MOONS

Deimos

Phobos

7   6   5   4   3   2   1

N RADIUSES OF MARS

LL MOONS

has two tiny moons, Phobos
Deimos, neither of them more
30 km (18.5 miles) in length.
are irregularly shaped and have
appearance of being asteroids
were captured by Mars' gravity.
os orbits Mars at a distance of
km (5,830 miles) every 7 hours
40 minutes. Deimos orbits three
farther away, at a distance of
62 km (14,581 miles), and takes
t 30 hours to circle the planet.

*Smaller and darker
than its companion*

DEIMOS

PHOBOS

*The crater Stickney is nearly
10 km (6.2 miles) across*

ARS: SELECTED EXPLORATION EVENTS

hicle	Date	Result
riner 4	14/7/65	First fly-by images
riner 9	13/11/71	Photomapped surface from Martian orbit
rs 3	2/12/71	Orbit achieved, lander failed after 20 seconds
king 1 nd	20/7/76	Successful soft landings provide images and soil data
king 2	3/9/76	but no evidence of life

MORE FACTS

• Phobos means "fear",
and Deimos means
"terror" – suitable
companions for the
planet named after a
god of war.
• Viewed from the
surface of Mars, Phobos
crosses the sky three
times each day.

JUPITER

THE LARGEST of the planets,
Jupiter has two and a half
times more mass than all
the other planets together.
Jupiter has a small rock
core, but consists mainly
of gas in various physical
states. The mantle of cold
liquefied gas merges into a
dense atmosphere. Giant
wind systems give Jupiter
a banded appearance.

GAS GIANT
Voyager I photographed Jup
from a distance of 28.4 milli
(17.5 million miles). The m
is just visible against a backg
of Jupiter's stormy atmosphe

Earth   Jupiter

JUPITER: PLANETARY DATA	
Average distance from the Sun	778.3 million km (483.7 million miles)
Orbital period	11.86 Earth years
Orbital velocity	13.1 km/s (8.1 miles/sec)
Rotation period	9.84 hours
Diameter at equator	142,984 km (88,865 miles)
Cloud-top temperature	–150°C (–238°F)
Mass (Earth = 1)	318
Gravity (Earth = 1)	2.34
Number of moons	16

JUPITER FACTS

• The pressure in
Jupiter's interior is s
great that hydrogen
gas exists naturally in
a semi-solid metallic
form not yet made
on Earth.

• Jupiter can be seer
with the naked eye a
a bright silver "star"
in Earth's night sky.

AMMONIA CLOUDS
The atmosphere consists
mostly of hydrogen and
helium. Small quantities
of other gases are found
only in the cloud layers.

| 90% hydrogen |
| 10% helium |
| Traces of methane, ammonia, and water vapour |

...e clouds
...mmonia

...e clouds
...monium
... sulphide

... clouds
...ter ice

...R: ATMOSPHERE
...TURE AND COMPOSITION

TROUBLED SPOT
The most prominent feature
on Jupiter is the Great Red
Spot, a gigantic rotating
storm bigger than the Earth.

Liquid hydrogen and helium outer mantle

Metallic hydrogen inner mantle

Rock core about twice the size of Earth

...h-altitude
...e clouds

...Narrow ring
system

...TER:
...ETARY STRUCTURE

RINGS:
STRUCTURE

Halo
ring

Main ring

FASTEST SPINNER

Despite its enormous size, 11 times the diameter of Earth, Jupiter rotates on its axis faster than any other planet. This high-speed rotation causes the gas giant to bulge around the equator, giving it a slightly oval shape. The rapid rotation also produces the powerful wind systems which divide Jupiter's atmosphere into bands that lie parallel with the equator. The most powerful winds move at speeds of several hundred kilometres (miles) per hour.

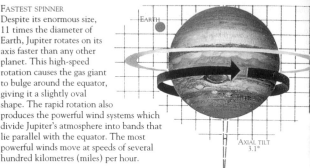

EARTH

JUPITER

AXIAL TILT
3.1°

THE GALILEAN MOONS:

EUROPA
Covered by a smooth layer of solid ice, Europa has sufficient internal heat to have seas of liquid water lying beneath its featureless surface.

CALLISTO
Covered with cracked and dirty ice around a rock core, Callisto is scarred by many craters. The largest i named Valhalla, with a diameter of 3,000 km (1,865 miles).

GANYMEDE
The largest moon in the solar system, Ganymede is larger than the planets Pluto and Mercury. Believed to consist mainly of ice and slush, Ganymede may have a silicate rock core.

IO
Debris from man volcanoes gives Io's surface an orange colour. The interior is still molten, and Io has the first active volcanoes to be discovered outside the Earth.

MOONS OF JUPITER

The four largest moons were discovered by Galileo, hence their collective name. The others have been discovered subsequently, some of them by the Voyager I probe. The four innermost moons orbit in the opposite direction to all the other moons.

Inner moons (left to right): Io; Thebe; Almathea; Adrastea; Metis

Outer moons (left to right): Sinope; Pasiphae; Carme; Ananke; Elara; Lysithea; Himalia; Leda; Callisto; Ganymede; Europa; Io (also shown above)   SCALE IN RADIUSES OF JUPITER

JUPITER: SATELLITE DATA				
	Diameter		Distance from Jupiter	
	km	miles	km	miles
Metis	40	25	127,960	79,528
Adrastea	20	12.5	128,980	80,162
Almathea	200	124	181,300	112,679
Thebe	100	62	221,900	137,912
Io	3,630	2,256	421,600	262,026
Europa	3,138	1,950	670,900	416,967
Ganymede	5,262	3,270	1,070,000	665,009
Callisto	4,800	2,983	1,883,000	1,170,292
Leda	16	10	11,094,000	6,894,966
Himalia	180	112	11,480,000	7,134,866
Lysithea	40	25	11,720,000	7,284,027
Elara	80	50	11,737,000	7,294,592
Ananke	30	19	21,200,000	13,175,885
Carme	44	27	22,600,000	14,045,991
Pasiphae	70	43	23,500,000	14,605,344
Sinope	40	25	23,700,000	14,729,645

MORE FACTS

• The orbital periods of planetary satellites increase according to their distance from the planet. Innermost Metis orbits Jupiter in 0.295 Earth days, while Sinope takes 758 days.

• The Voyager probes obtained 30,000 images of Jupiter and its moons.

• The volcanoes on Io eject material at speeds up to 1,000 m/s (3,285 ft per sec). This is about 20 times faster than material from volcanoes on Earth.

SATURN

FAMED FOR ITS magnificent ring system, Saturn is the second largest of the planets. Like its nearest neighbour Jupiter, Saturn is a gas giant. However, the mass is so spread out that on average the planet is less dense than water. Saturn has more moons than any other planet – at least 18. The largest moon, Titan, has an unusually thick atmosphere.

RINGED WORLD
Saturn is at the limit of easy telescopic viewing from Earth. This photograph was taken at a distance of 17.5 million km (11 million miles) by Voyager 2.

Earth   Saturn

SATURN: PLANETARY DATA	
Average distance from the Sun:	1,427 million km (886.9 million miles)
Orbital period	29.46 Earth years
Orbital velocity	9.6 km/s (6 miles/sec)
Rotation period	10.23 hours
Diameter at equator	120,536 km (74,914 miles)
Cloud-top temperature	−180°C (−292°F)
Mass (Earth = 1)	95
Gravity (Earth = 1)	0.93
Number of moons	18

SATURN FACTS

• Saturn's rings are less than 200 m (656 ft) thick, but over 270,000 km (167,800 miles) in diameter.

• The rings consist of billions of ice-covered rock fragments and dust particles.

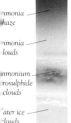

ammonia
haze

ammonia
clouds

ammonium
rosulphide
clouds

ater ice
clouds

TURN: ATMOSPHERE STRUCTURE AND COMPOSITION

MUTED APPEARANCE
Saturn's atmosphere is
very similar to Jupiter's,
but it is colder. The cloud
layers are much thicker,
and have muted bands.

94% hydrogen

6% helium

Traces of methane,
ammonia, and water vapour

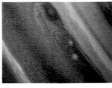

CYCLONIC STORM
False-colour images show
cyclonic activity in Saturn's
atmosphere. The pale ovals
are rotating storms shaped
by powerful jet
streams.

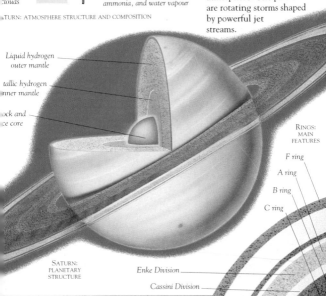

Liquid hydrogen
outer mantle

tallic hydrogen
nner mantle

ock and
ce core

SATURN:
PLANETARY
STRUCTURE

RINGS:
MAIN
FEATURES

F ring

A ring

B ring

C ring

Enke Division

Cassini Division

TILTED SYSTEM

Saturn rotates very rapidly on an axis
that is tilted at 26.7° to the vertical.
The orbits of the rings and moons are
all aligned with this rotation, and lie
in the same plane as the planet's
equator, giving the whole system a
tilted appearance. Like the other
giant gas planets, Saturn bulges
noticeably at the equator where
the speed of rotation is faster than
at the poles. Inside the atmosphere,
winds sweep around the equator at
1,800 km/h (1120 mph).

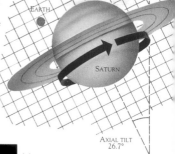

EARTH

SATURN

AXIAL TILT
26.7°

MANY MOONS

Saturn has 18 moons; one (Titan) is ver
large, seven are of average size, and the
rest are small and irregularly shaped.
Some of the small moons are co-orbital:
they share an orbit with another moon.
Mimas, the closest of the larger moons,
dominated by the huge crater Herschel,
perhaps the result of a co-orbital collisio

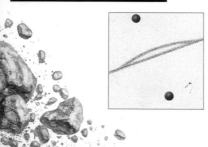

BRAIDED RINGS

Some of the inner moons orbi
within the rings, creating gaps
and braids. Pan sweeps the En
Division clear of ring material
while Prometheus and Pandor
twist and braid the F ring wit
their gravitational effect. The
moons are sometimes said to
"shepherd" the rings in the
same way that dogs keep a floc
of sheep together.

CROWDED SPACE

Saturn has both a pair and a triplet of co-orbital moons. In addition, two other moons, Janus and Epithemus, have orbits that are extremely close to each other. Astronomers believe that these two were once a single moon that broke up.

Inner moons (left to right): Helene and Dione (co-orbital); Calypso, Telesto, and Tethys (co-orbital); Enceladus; Mimas; Janus; Epithemus; Pandora; Prometheus; Atlas; Pan

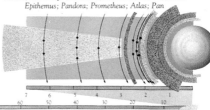

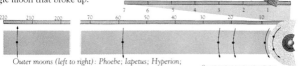

Outer moons (left to right): Phoebe; Iapetus; Hyperion; Titan; Rhea; Helene; and Dione (also shown above)

SCALE IN RADIUSES OF SATURN

SATURN: SATELLITE FACTS — Moons

	Diameter		Distance from Saturn	
	km	miles	km	miles
Pan	20	12	133,600	83,033
Atlas	34	21	137,640	85,544
Prometheus	110	68	139,350	86,607
Pandora	88	55	141,700	88,067
Epimetheus	120	75	151,422	94,109
Janus	190	118	151,472	94,140
Mimas	390	242	185,520	115,301
Enceladus	500	311	238,020	147,930
Tethys	1,050	653	294,660	183,132
Telesto	25	15	294,660	183,132
Calypso	26	16	294,660	183,132
Dione	1,120	696	377,400	234,555
Helene	33	20	377,400	234,555
Rhea	1,530	951	527,040	327,557
Titan	5,150	3,201	1,221,850	759,385
Hyperion	280	174	1,481,000	920,447
Iapetus	1,440	895	3,561,300	2,213,362
Phoebe	220	137	12,952,000	8,049,720

MORE FACTS

• The rings of Saturn seem to be neatly graded, with the largest fragments found in the inner rings closest to the planet, while fine dust accumulates in the outer rings.

• Saturn is the only planet that has three moons sharing the same orbit – Tethys, Telesto, and Calypso.

• Mimas was to have been named "Arthur". Although this did not happen, many of its features are named after characters in the legend of King Arthur.

URANUS

A COLD GAS giant, Uranus is
the seventh planet from the
Sun. Little surface detail can
be seen, and even close-up
pictures show only a few
clouds of frozen methane
gas. Despite its featureless
appearance, Uranus has one
interesting peculiarity. The
planet, and its rings and
moons, are all tilted by more
than 90°, travelling around
the Sun on their side.

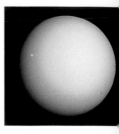

BLANK FACE
Faintly visible from Earth as a
"star" in the night sky, Uranus
was not identified as a planet
until 1781. The ring system was
not discovered until 1977 –
almost 200 years later.

Earth

Uranus

URANUS: PLANETARY DATA	
Average distance from the Sun	2,871 million km (1,784 million miles)
Orbital period	84 Earth years
Orbital velocity	6.8 km/s (4.2 miles/sec)
Rotation period	17.9 hours
Diameter at equator	51,118 km (31,770 miles)
Cloud-top temperature	–210°C (–346°F)
Mass (Earth = 1)	14.5
Gravity (Earth = 1)	0.79
Number of moons	15

URANUS FACTS
• Uranus is named after
Urania, the Ancient
Greek muse (patron
goddess) of astronomy.
• Light from the Sun,
which takes about eight
minutes to reach Earth,
takes more than 2 hours
30 minutes to travel as
far as Uranus.

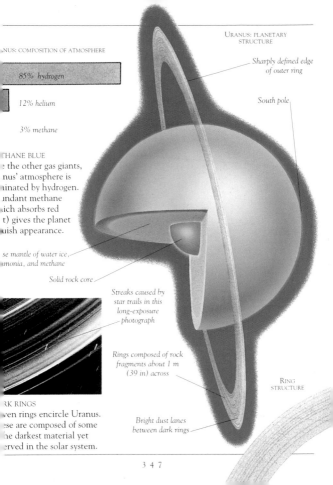

URANUS: COMPOSITION OF ATMOSPHERE

85% hydrogen

12% helium

3% methane

METHANE BLUE

Like the other gas giants,
Uranus' atmosphere is
dominated by hydrogen. The
abundant methane
(which absorbs red
light) gives the planet
a bluish appearance.

Dense mantle of water ice,
ammonia, and methane

Solid rock core

DARK RINGS

Eleven rings encircle Uranus.
These are composed of some
of the darkest material yet
observed in the solar system.

Sharply defined edge
of outer ring

South pole

Streaks caused by
star trails in this
long-exposure
photograph

Rings composed of rock
fragments about 1 m
(39 in) across

RING
STRUCTURE

Bright dust lanes
between dark rings

SIDEWAYS ORBIT

Uranus' axis of rotation is tilted at 98° to the vertical – the equator runs through the "top" and "bottom" of the planet. This extreme tilt also extends to the rings and moons. Uranus' sideways stance may have been the result of a collision with another celestial body at some time in the distant past.

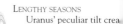

EARTH

AXIAL TIL 98°

URANUS

LENGTHY SEASONS

Uranus' peculiar tilt crea extremely long seasons. the planet travels arou the Sun, each pole receives 42 Earth years sunlight, followed by t same period of total darkness. However, the temperature does not vary wit the seasons because Uranus is s far away from the Sun.

STRANGE MAGNETISM

Uranus generates a magnetic field which is tilted, but not the same way as the planet. The magnetic field is tilted at 60° to the axis of rotation, which means that the magnetosphere has a fairly normal shape. To make the situation even more extraordinary, Uranus' magnetic field is offset from the planet's centre.

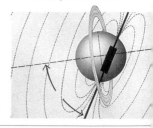

GS AND MOONS
ly the innermost
on, Cordelia,
ts within the ring
em. Miranda is
haps the most
usual moon in the
r system – it
ws every sign of
e having been
ted apart and
n reassembled.

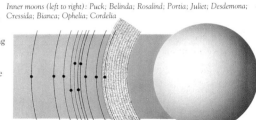

Inner moons (left to right): Puck; Belinda; Rosalind; Portia; Juliet; Desdemona; Cressida; Bianca; Ophelia; Cordelia

Outer moons (left to right): Oberon; Titania; Umbriel; Ariel; Miranda; Puck (also shown above)

RANUS: SATELLITE DATA

	Diameter		Distance from Uranus	
	km	miles	km	miles
ordelia	30	19	49,750	30,920
phelia	30	19	53,760	33,412
anca	40	25	59,160	36,768
ressida	70	43	61,770	38,390
esdemona	60	37	62,660	38,943
liet	80	50	64,360	40,000
rtia	110	68	66,100	41,081
salind	60	37	69,930	43,462
linda	70	43	75,260	46,774
ck	150	93	86,010	53,456
iranda	470	292	129,780	80,659
iel	1,160	721	191,240	118,856
mbriel	1,170	727	265,970	165,301
tania	1,580	982	435,840	270,876
beron	1,520	945	582,600	362,088

MORE FACTS

• Before Voyager 2, Uranus was believed to have five moons. The accepted total is now 15, and there may be more waiting to be discovered.

• The Uranian moons are all named after characters in plays by William Shakespeare.

• In contrast to Saturn, the outermost Uranian ring has no fragments less than about 20 cm (8 in) across.

NEPTUNE

THE OUTERMOST of the gas
giants, Neptune is a near twin
to Uranus. Too faint to be seen
easily from Earth, its position
was calculated mathematically.
Neptune was first observed in
1846 exactly where it was
predicted to be. Methane in
the atmosphere gives Neptune
a deep blue coloration. The
rings and six of the moons
were discovered by the
Voyager 2 probe.

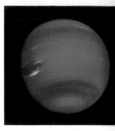

DARK STORMS
Photographed by the second
Voyager probe, the atmosphe
of Neptune shows several cle
features including the Great
Dark Spot, which is a huge
cyclonic storm.

Earth

Neptune

NEPTUNE: PLANETARY DATA	
Average distance from the Sun	4,497 million km (2,795 million miles)
Orbital period	164.8 Earth years
Orbital velocity	5.4 km/s (3.4 miles/sec)
Rotation period	19.2 hours
Diameter at equator	49,528 km (30,782 miles)
Cloud-top temperature	–220°C (–364°F)
Mass (Earth = 1)	17
Gravity (Earth = 1)	1.2
Number of moons	8

NEPTUNE FACTS
• Neptune is named
after the Roman god o
the sea.
• Neptune
radiates 2.6
times more
heat than it
receives from the Sun
– a sign of an internal
source of heat.

PTUNE: COMPOSITION OF ATMOSPHERE

85% hydrogen

13% helium

2% methane

DROCARBON HAZE
herwise very similar to that of Uranus,
ptune's atmosphere has a deeper blue
our. The highest level contains a
n hydrocarbon haze.

CIRRUS CLOUDS
High-altitude cirrus clouds of frozen
methane crystals. These clouds
are situated about 40 km
(25 miles) above the
main cloud layer.

thane, ammonia, and
water-ice mantle

cate rock
core

Adam's
ring

Le Verrier
ring

Galle
ring

Great Dark
Spot

TUNE:
NETARY STRUCTURE

Dark low-altitude clouds
of hydrogen sulphide

RING STRUCTURE

LACK OF SEASONS

Neptune rotates on its axis at approximately the same angle of tilt as Earth. However, Neptune is far too distant from the Sun for the tilt to result in a similar cycle of seasons. Conditions in the atmosphere are dominated by winds blowing at up to 2,000 km/s (1,250 mph) which carry the dark storms around the planet in a backward direction.

AXIAL TILT
29.6°

GREAT DARK SPOT

The largest storm on Neptune, the Great Dark Spot is about the same size as Earth. The storm rotates in an anti-clockwise direction. This photograph has been processed to give a red colour to high-altitude features.

TRITON

The largest of Neptune's moons, Triton is the coldest place in the solar system at –235°C (–391°F). It has a thin atmosphere, mainly of nitrogen, and a large south polar ice cap composed of methane ice. Photographs show the ice to have a pink tinge, which is believed to be due to the presence of organic chemicals formed by the action of sunlight.

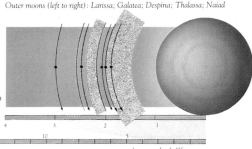

Outer moons (left to right): Larissa; Galatea; Despina; Thalassa; Naiad

LING NEPTUNE
four innermost
s orbit within
ing system.
n is the only
moon in the
system that
s in a backward
tion compared to
planet's rotation.

N RADIUSES OF NEPTUNE

moons (left to right): Nereid; Triton; Proteus; Larissa; and inner moons (also shown above)

ANT EXPLORER

ger 2 is the only probe that has so far visited
us and Neptune. The journey to Neptune took 12
, and information from Voyager 2 (transmitted at
peed of light) took more than four hours to reach
. Among Voyager 2's many discoveries were six of
une's eight moons and ice volcanoes on Triton.

VOYAGER 2

EPTUNE: SATELLITE DATA

	Diameter		Distance from Neptune	
	km	miles	km	miles
aiad	50	31	48,000	29,832
halassa	80	50	50,000	31,075
espina	180	112	52,500	32,629
alatea	150	93	62,000	38,533
rissa	190	118	73,600	45,743
oteus	400	249	117,600	73,088
riton	2,700	1,678	354,800	220,510
ereid	340	211	5,513,400	3,426,600

FACT
• The outermost moon,
Nereid, has the most
eccentric orbit of any
known satellite. During
a single orbit, Nereid's
distance from Neptune
varies between
1,300,000 km (800,000
miles) and 9,700,000 km
(6,000,000 miles).

PLUTO

THE MOST DISTANT of all the planets, Pluto, is also the least understood. Pluto's orbit around the Sun is uniquely tilted at 17°, and is highly unusual in other ways. For about ten per cent of its long orbital path, Pluto is closer to the Sun than Neptune. Pluto has a single large moon, Charon, and together they form a two-object system.

BLURRED IMAGE
The clearest image of Pluto a[nd] Charon has been obtained by the Hubble Space Telescope orbiting Earth. Ground-based photographs show a single bl[ur]

Earth   Pluto

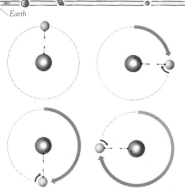

CLOSELY LINKED SYSTEM
Pluto and Charon exhibit a powerful effect on each othe[r]. Charon's orbit around Pluto become synchronized with Pluto's own rotation, so that both have the same period – [6.4] Earth days. As a result, the s[ame] face of Charon is always turn[ed] to the same face of Pluto. Fr[om] one side of Pluto, Charon is always visible in the sky. Fr[om] the other side of the planet, [the] moon cannot be seen at all.

UTO: PLANETARY DATA

verage distance	5,913.5 million km
from the Sun	(3,675 million miles)
rbital period	248.5 Earth years
rbital velocity	4.7 km/s (2.9 miles/sec)
otation period	6.38 Earth days
iameter at equator	2,300 km (1,429 miles)
urface temperature	–230°C (–382°F)
ass (Earth = 1)	0.002
ravity (Earth = 1)	0.04 Moons: 1

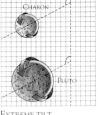

EXTREME TILT
Pluto and Charon both
rotate on axes that are
tilted at 122.6° to the
vertical – the least
upright of all the
planets.

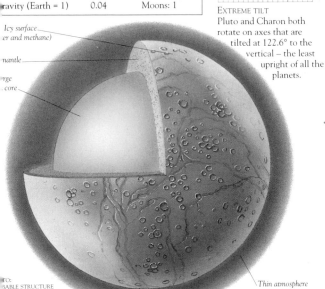

Icy surface
(. er and methane)

mantle

rge
. core

TO:
ABLE STRUCTURE

Thin atmosphere
containing methane
and nitrogen

COMETS

A COMET IS a "dirty snowball" composed of snow and dust. Billions of comets orbit the Sun at a distance of about one light year. A few comets have orbits that take them closer to the Sun. As they near the Sun and are heated, the snow turns to gas and forms a long bright tail.

COMET HALLEY
Most comets that approach the Sun are seen only once, but a few return periodically. Comet Halley returns every 76 years.

ORBITING THE SUN
A periodic comet has a regular orbit that brings it close to the Sun. For most of its orbit, the comet has no tail. The tail only develops as the comet nears the Sun and its surface is heated. The tail gets longer and longer, and then disappears as the comet moves away from the Sun.

Tail develops as the comet approaches the Sun

SUN

Tail is longer near the Sun

For most of its orbit, a comet is a tailless dirty snowball.

Tail shrinks as comet moves away

[FLO]WING GAS

[Th]e nucleus of a typical comet [is a]bout 20 km (12.5 miles) [acr]oss. When heated by the [Sun], jets of gas and dust [shoot] from the surface of [the] nucleus to form a [glo]wing cloud called a [com]a, which surrounds [the] nucleus. The coma [can] be ten times [larg]er than the Earth. [The] comet's tail [may] be millions of [kilo]metres (miles) long.

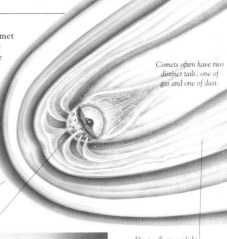

Comets often have two distinct tails, one of gas and one of dust.

Coma

Nucleus made of dust and frozen gases

Dust reflects sunlight

[HE]ART OF A COMET

[Thi]s photograph of the nucleus of Comet [Hal]ley was taken by the Giotto probe from a [dist]ance of about 1,700 km (1,050 miles). [Bri]ght gas jets can be seen on the sunlit [(upp]er) surface. Instruments aboard Giotto [sho]wed that the main constituent of the [nuc]leus was water-ice.

METEORS

EVERY DAY, thousands of dust particles and rock fragments from space enter the Earth's atmosphere. Most burn up due to friction with the air. The streaks of light they produce are called meteors. Very rarely a larger fragment survives the atmosphere and hits Earth's surface. These "space-rocks" are called meteorites.

METEOR SHOWER
This is a a false-colour photograph of a Leonid meteor shower (yellow streaks), which is associated with Comet Tempel Tuttle.

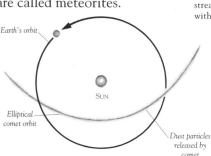

Earth's orbit

SUN

Elliptical comet orbit

Dust particles released by comet

CROSSING ORBITS
Most meteors are caused by dust and debris shed by comets as they pass close to the Sun. The debris stays in the path of the comet's orbit; and when the Earth's orbit crosses that of the comet, we experience a meteor shower. Some showers are regular annual events.

METEOR FACTS

• Each year about 28,000 tonnes (tons) of extraterrestrial material enters our atmosphere

• Most meteors are vapourized at altitudes above 80 km (50 miles)

• Meteor showers are named after the constellation in which the radiant appears, e.g. the Perseids.

• The heaviest showers have meteors falling at 60,000 per hour.

STONY
METEORITE

Fragments of
nickel-iron embedded
in a matrix of rock

Heat-blackened
surface

STONY-IRON
METEORITE

STONES AND IRONS FROM SPACE

There are two main types of meteorite – those
composed mainly of rock (called "stones") and
those made mostly of metal (called "irons").
Rocky meteorites are far more common than
"irons", but the rarest meteorites on Earth (less
than one in every hundred found) are "stony-
irons" that contain both metal and rock.

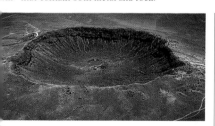

IMPACT CRATER

Meteorite Crater in Arizona, U.S.A., measures
1.3 km (0.8 miles) across. It was formed about
25,000 years ago when a meteorite about 45 m
(150 ft) in diameter struck the surface at a
speed of around 11 km/s (6.8 miles/sec).
Meteorite hunters have found several "iron"
fragments in the crater.

METEORITE FACTS

• More than 90% of
identified meteorites
that strike the Earth
are "stones".

• The world's largest
known meteorite still
lies where it fell at
Hoba West in southern
Africa. Its weight is
estimated at over 60
tonnes (tons).

• Last century, Tsar
Alexander of Russia
had a sword made from
an "iron" meteorite.

ASTEROIDS

MILLIONS OF CHUNKS of rock
orbit the Sun. These are the
asteroids, sometimes called
the minor planets. Asteroids
range in size from a few metres
(feet) across, to those that are
hundreds of kilometres (miles)
in diameter. Most of the
asteroids are found in a wide
belt between the orbits of
Mars and Jupiter.

SPACE ROCK
Ida is a typical asteroid – small
and irregular in shape with a
maximum length of 52 km
(32 miles). Its surface is heavily
cratered and covered by a thin
layer of dust.

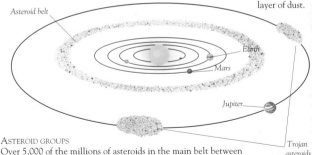

Asteroid belt

Earth

Mars

Jupiter

Trojan
asteroids

ASTEROID GROUPS
Over 5,000 of the millions of asteroids in the main belt between
Mars and Jupiter have so far been located and identified. Other
groups of asteroids follow different orbits. Trojan asteroids are
co-orbital with Jupiter, held in place by the giant planet's
powerful gravity.

*Craters due to
meteorite impacts*

*Most asteroids are
irregular in shape.*

ASTEROID ORIGINS

The larger asteroids are spherical and
were formed in the same way as the
planets. The smaller irregular asteroids are
either remnants of the original material that
formed the solar system, or the result of
collisions between two or more large asteroids.

*coloration
se surface is
ed in rust*

FAILED PLANET

The asteroid belt was probably
formed at the same time as the rest
of the solar system. Rock fragments
and dust particles in this part of the
system were prevented from
clumping together to form a
planet by Jupiter's gravity.
But if all the asteroids were
put together, their mass
would be only a tiny
fraction of
the Earth's.

TEROID FACTS

he first asteroid to
discovered was Ceres
ich has a diameter of
3 km (580 miles).

Asteroids which have
average distance
m the Sun less than
rth's are known as
en asteroids.

Earth has been struck
several asteroids in
e past, and it is only a
tter of time before
other asteroid strikes
planet.

INFORMATION FROM SPACE

GATHERING AND STUDYING starlight is just
one way that we learn about the universe
Visible light is only a small part of the
electromagnetic spectrum, which
covers all forms of radiation. By
studying different types of radiatio
we learn more about both the
visible and the invisible parts
of the universe.

ATMOSPHERIC SHIELD
The atmosphere shields Earth again
radiation from space. Gamma ray
X-rays, and most ultraviolet (U
rays are stopped. Only visible
light, some infrared and U
radiation, and some radio
signals reach the surface

*Ozone
layer*

*Gamma
rays
and
X-rays*

UV rays

*Most infrared
stopped here*

*Visible light and short-
wave radio reach surface*

INFORMATION SPECTRUM
Electromagnetic radiation travels
through space as waves of
varying length (the distance
between wave crests). Gamma
rays have the shortest wavelength,
then X-rays, and so on through
the spectrum to the longest radio
waves. Visible light, which is all
that we can see naturally, occupies
a very narrow portion (less than
0.00001 per cent) of the spectrum.

10^{-13} m
0.0000000000001 metres

X-RAYS

GAMMA RAYS

CRAB NEBULA IN DIFFERENT LIGHTS

The Crab Nebula is the remnant of a supernova explosion seen in 1054. In UV light (right) the nebula has an eerie glow produced by highly energetic particles from the explosion interacting with the surrounding space environment.

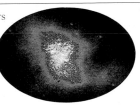

VISIBLE LIGHT

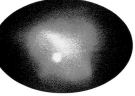

This visible light image of the nebula has been computer-processed to show the presence of hydrogen (red) and sulphur (blue) in the filaments of gas still streaming out from the explosion.

X-RAY

X-rays emitted by the Crab Nebula produce a picture (right) that shows a bright object at the centre of the nebula – the pulsar that is the remains of the pre-supernova star.

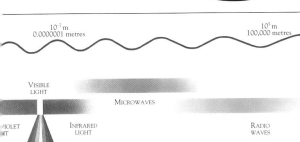

10^{-7} m
0.0000001 metres

10^{5} m
100,000 metres

VISIBLE
LIGHT

MICROWAVES

VIOLET
GHT

INFRARED
LIGHT

RADIO
WAVES

OPTICAL TELESCOPES

THE OPTICAL TELESCOPE is one of the main tools of astronomy. But little time is spent looking through a telescope eyepiece – modern instruments collect and store visual information electronically. The optical telescope remains an important tool because it gathers basic information.

PALOMAR DOME
The protective dome of the H Telescope at the Mount Palom Observatory, California, U.S. shields the telescope from the effects of weather.

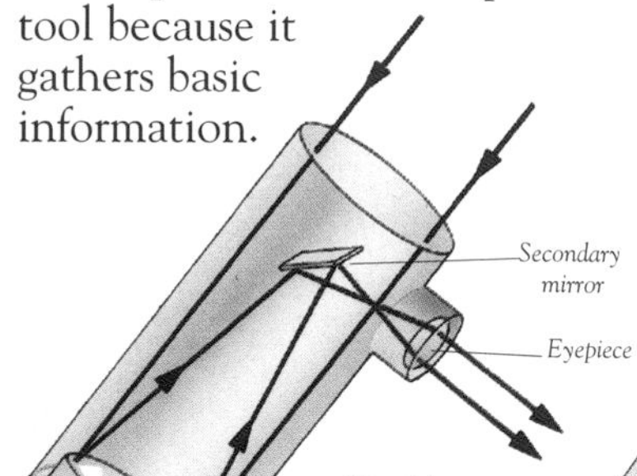

Secondary mirror

Eyepiece

Main light-gathering mirror

Main light-gathering ler

Eyepiece lens

REFLECTOR TELESCOPES
Telescopes use lenses and mirrors to gather light and produce an image. Reflector telescopes, which make use of curved mirrors, are the most useful type for astronomy.

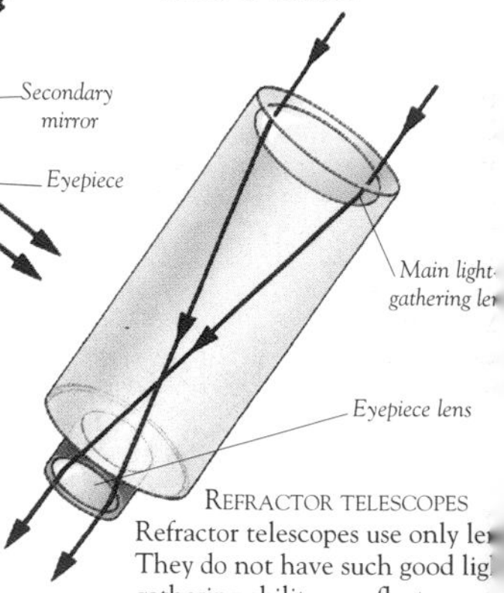

REFRACTOR TELESCOPES
Refractor telescopes use only le They do not have such good ligl gathering ability as reflector telescopes, but they remain very popular with amateur astronom

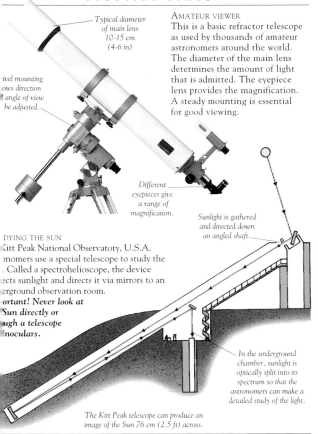

Typical diameter of main lens 10-15 cm (4-6 in)

*ivel mounting
ows direction
l angle of view
be adjusted.*

AMATEUR VIEWER
This is a basic refractor telescope as used by thousands of amateur astronomers around the world. The diameter of the main lens determines the amount of light that is admitted. The eyepiece lens provides the magnification. A steady mounting is essential for good viewing.

Different eyepieces give a range of magnification.

Sunlight is gathered and directed down an angled shaft.

DYING THE SUN
itt Peak National Observatory, U.S.A.
nomers use a special telescope to study the
. Called a spectrohelioscope, the device
ects sunlight and directs it via mirrors to an
erground observation room.
**ortant! Never look at
Sun directly or
ugh a telescope
noculars.**

In the underground chamber, sunlight is optically split into its spectrum so that the astronomers can make a detailed study of the light.

The Kitt Peak telescope can produce an image of the Sun 76 cm (2.5 ft) across.

RADIO ASTRONOMY

WE HAVE BEEN LISTENING in to the radio energy of the universe for about 50 years. Radio astronomy can obtain additional information about familiar objects, as well as seek out new ones. Two major discoveries – quasars and pulsars – were made by radio astronomers.

VERY LARGE ARRAY
A radio telescope consists of large metal dish. In order to gather more information, rad astronomers sometimes use a number of small dishes linke together. The Very Large Ar (VLA) in New Mexico, U uses up to 27 linked dish each one 25 m (82 f across, to collect ra signals from spa

The VLA d are arrange a Y-shap

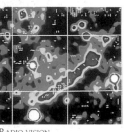

Radio waves

RADIO VISION
Radio telescopes, like ordinary radio sets, can be tuned to a particular wavelength, and the intensity of the radio energy can be measured. Computers are then used to produce "radio-maps" of the sky, such as this image of the bar-shaped radio source known as 1952+28.

LARGEST DISH

The world's largest radio telescope, the 305 m (1,000 ft) Arecibo dish, is built into a natural hollow in the hills of Puerto Rico. The dish is "steered" using the Earth's own rotation. Arecibo has also been used to send a radio message out into space.

Simple processing of the Arecibo message produces this visual image which contains a representation of a human being.

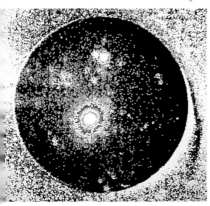

RADIO GALAXIES

Many galaxies that are quite faint visually are very "bright" at radio wavelengths. These are often called radio galaxies, or active galaxies. This optical image of radio galaxy 3C 33 has been colour-coded according to intensity of light in the visible part of the spectrum ranging from white (most intense) to blue (the least).

IMAGES OF SPACE

MUCH OF THE information that astronomers obtain through their instruments is presented as visual images. Conventional and electronic cameras are used to record these images. The information is usually stored on computers which can process images to improve the picture and bring out details.

PIXELATED VIEW
Electronic cameras make image with a grid of tiny picture-elements (pixels). This view of dim and distant star cluster wa obtained with a ground-based telescope. The individual pixel are clearly visible, although it takes a trained eye to identify image as a star cluster.

MARTIAN CHEMICAL PHOTOMAP
This image of the surface of Mars, with the Martian equator running across the middle of the picture, was produced by cameras aboard the Viking orbiter space probes. The image has been colour-coded by computer according to the chemical composition of the surface. Craters and other surface features are also visible.

Frost is shown in turquoise

Red identifies h concentrations iron oxide

FALSE COLOUR GIVES A TRUER VIEW
Astronomers have several techniques for
analysing the information contained in
images. One of the most important is
adding false colour to the image.
Saturn has a fairly muted appearance
in ordinary photographs. This
image has been colour coded to
emphasize the banding of
the planet's upper
atmosphere.

COLOURING THE CORONA
This image of the normally
invisible solar corona (the Sun's
outer atmosphere) was produced
from data obtained by the Solar
Maximum Mission satellite. The
image has been computer-
processed and enhanced with
false colours, in order to identify
zones of differing gas density
within the solar corona.

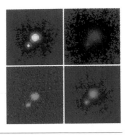

SEPARATE THEN COMBINE
Images of space are often obtained through a series
of coloured filters. The object is photographed
through each filter in turn, and the resulting
images are then combined to give a much fuller
picture than with any single ordinary photograph.
This series was taken with the Hubble Space
Telescope, and shows Pluto and its moon Charon.

OBSERVATORIES

OPTICAL TELESCOPES are usually installed in mountain-top observatories, where they suffer least interference from Earth's atmosphere. Radio telescopes can be situated almost anywhere, and are usually located near universities. The high cost of telescopes which use the latest technology means that observatories are often shared between countries.

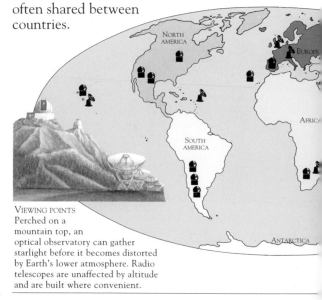

NORTH AMERICA

EUROPE

AFRICA

SOUTH AMERICA

ANTARCTICA

VIEWING POINTS
Perched on a mountain top, an optical observatory can gather starlight before it becomes distorted by Earth's lower atmosphere. Radio telescopes are unaffected by altitude and are built where convenient.

HIGH AND DRY

The domes of the Cerro Tololo Inter-American Observatory are sited in the Andes foothills of Chile. A dry climate with cloud-free nights and a steady atmosphere makes this an ideal location for clear viewing.

AUSTRALIA

MAP KEY

OPTICAL TELESCOPE

RADIO TELESCOPE

HIGH-TECH TELESCOPE

The Keck Telescope situated on Mauna Kea, Hawaii, is the world's largest optical telescope. The main mirror is made up of 36 computer-controlled hexagonal segments.

TELESCOPES IN SPACE

BY PLACING THEIR TELESCOPES in orbit above Earth's atmosphere, astronomers get a much better view. They can see farther and can collect information from wavelengths that are absorbed by the atmosphere. Information and images gathered in orbit are transmitted back to Earth for study and analysis.

ORBITING TELESCOPE
The US space station Skylab carried a total of eight telescopes on the X-shaped Apollo Telescope Mount

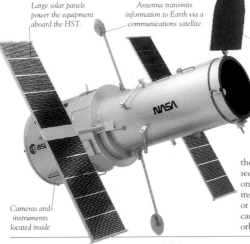

Large solar panels power the equipment aboard the HST.

Antenna transmits information to Earth via a communications satellite

Protective hinged cover

HUBBLE
The Hubble Space Telescope (HST) uses a large mirror to gather light. The light is then directed by a secondary mirror into one of the scientific instrument packages or high-resolution cameras aboard this orbiting space telescope.

Cameras and instruments located inside

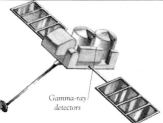

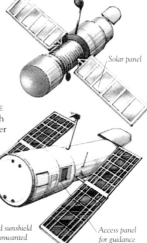

DIRECTION FINDER
Orbiting gamma-ray telescopes (left) have been in use since the mid-1970s. Although gamma rays cannot be focused to produce an image, they can be used to plot the direction and intensity of gamma-ray sources.

Gamma-ray detectors

Solar panel

CIAL TELESCOPES
biting X-ray satellites (right) enable
entists to pinpoint areas of intense activity
distant galaxies. Special telescopes, known
grazing incidence telescopes, are used
ause X-rays pass straight through
venTional lenses and mirrors.

DUAL USE
The HST (right) operates at the wavelength
of visible light, and also at the slightly shorter
ultraviolet (UV) wavelength. This
feature makes the HST doubly useful
to astronomers as data and images
obtained at two different
wavelengths can be compared.

Access panel for guidance package

Gold-plated sunshield cuts out unwanted infrared radiation

CLEARER VIEW
From orbit, infrared telescopes (left) gather infrared light before it can be absorbed by Earth's lower atmosphere. Infrared satellites are also used to study the Earth's surface.

ROCKETS

SATELLITES, SPACE PROBES, and
astronauts are lifted into space
by rockets. There are two main
types. The conventional tall,
thin rocket is made from several
stages stacked on top of each
other. The newer Space Shuttle
design lifts off with the aid of
massive booster rockets. But
when it returns from space, the
Shuttle lands like an aircraft.

LIFT OFF
A Saturn V rocket stand
poised on the launch-pa
Its engines burn fuel at a
rate of thousands of litre
(gallons) per second.

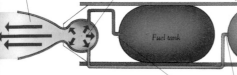

*Nozzle shapes the
stream of hot
exhaust gases*

*Liquid fuel and oxygen
are combined in the
combustion chamber.*

Fuel tank

Oxygen tank

*Fuel and oxygen
stored in reinforced
pressurised tanks*

*Pumps control the flow
of fuel and oxygen to the
combustion chamber.*

ROCKET POWER
A rocket is propelled upwards by hot exhaust
gases streaming from nozzles at the tail. These
gases are the result of burning a mixture of liquid
oxygen and fuel (such as liquid hydrogen) inside
a combustion chamber. Carrying its own oxygen
supply enables a rocket engine to function in the
airless vacuum of space.

ESCAPE VELOCITY

A rocket, or any other object, is held on the Earth's surface by the force of gravity. To escape the effects of Earth's gravity and enter space, a rocket needs to achieve a speed of 40,000 km/h (24,840 mph) – this is the "escape velocity" of planet Earth. On the Moon, where the force of gravity is only one sixth as powerful as on Earth, the escape velocity is lower – only about 8,500 km/h (5,300 mph).

Payload – satellite or space probe

Third stage rocket engines

ARIANE: A TYPICAL
THREE-STAGE LAUNCH VEHICLE

Second stage rocket engines

First stage rocket engines

External booster rockets assist first stage engines at lift-off

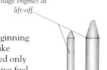

~USABLE SPACE CRAFT

streaming exhaust trail marks the beginning
another Space Shuttle mission. Unlike
nventional rockets, which can be used only
ce, the Shuttle is reusable. The massive fuel
k and booster rockets are jettisoned shortly
er launch and recovered. The Shuttle's own
gines carry it on into orbit, and small thruster
kets are used to manoeuvre it into position.

FLY-BYS

LIFTED INTO SPACE by rockets, space probes are computer-controlled robots packed with scientific instruments. Probes are sent to fly by a planet, or even orbit around it, sending data and images back to Earth. After they have completed their planned missions, some probes continue on into space.

VOLCANIC DISCOVERY
The probe Voyager I obtained this image of Io which shows the first active volcano seen outside Earth.

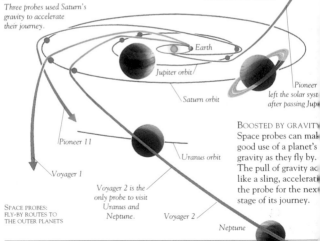

Three probes used Saturn's gravity to accelerate their journey.

Earth

Jupiter orbit

Saturn orbit

Pioneer left the solar syst after passing Jup

BOOSTED BY GRAVIT
Space probes can mak good use of a planet's gravity as they fly by. The pull of gravity ac like a sling, acceleratir the probe for the next stage of its journey.

Pioneer 11

Uranus orbit

Voyager 1

Voyager 2 is the only probe to visit Uranus and Neptune.

SPACE PROBES:
FLY-BY ROUTES TO
THE OUTER PLANETS

Voyager 2

Neptune

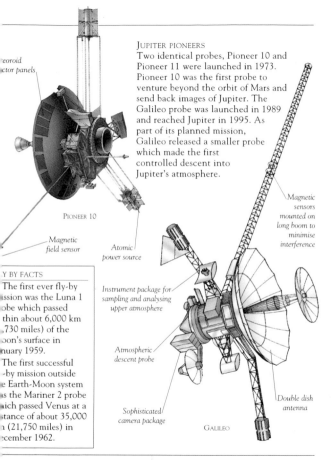

JUPITER PIONEERS
Two identical probes, Pioneer 10 and Pioneer 11 were launched in 1973. Pioneer 10 was the first probe to venture beyond the orbit of Mars and send back images of Jupiter. The Galileo probe was launched in 1989 and reached Jupiter in 1995. As part of its planned mission, Galileo released a smaller probe which made the first controlled descent into Jupiter's atmosphere.

eoroid
ctor panels

PIONEER 10

Magnetic field sensor

Atomic power source

Magnetic sensors mounted on long boom to minimise interference

Instrument package for sampling and analysing upper atmosphere

Atmospheric descent probe

Double dish antenna

Sophisticated camera package

GALILEO

LANDERS

SPACE PROBES SENT to orbit a
planet can release a second
craft to land on the surface.
The lander, a scientific robot,
carries out its pre-programmed
tasks and then relays the data
it has obtained back to Earth.
So far, landers have provided
information about the Moon,
Venus, and Mars.

COMING IN TO LAND
This dramatic photograph of
lunar craters was taken from
one of the Apollo landers
during its low-altitude descent
to the Moon's surface.

IS THERE LIFE ON MARS?
Two Viking orbiter craft each
released a lander that descended
safely to the Martian surface. In total
about 3,000 photographic images
were sent back to Earth. The landers
also tested the Martian soil with four
different experiments to check for
any sign of life – none
was found.

VIKING LANDER CRAFT

Television cameras

Sensors for
testing atmospheric
conditions

Robot arm to
take soil samples

VENERA 9 LANDER CRAFT

The two parts separate
and the lander
begins its descent
through the atmosphere.

The protective
atmospheric shield
is jettisoned

On-board braking
engines begin to slow
Venera 9

LANDER FACTS

The first successful
lander was Luna 9
which soft-landed on
the Moon in 1966.

Venera 7 became the
first lander to transmit
data from the surface of
Venus in 1970.

The Viking landers
analysed Mars' soil and
found that it contained
the following chemical
elements:

silica	14%
iron	18%
aluminium	2.7%
titanium	0.9%
potassium	0.3%

HOT LANDING

A series of Venera space
probes was sent to Venus.
Each consisted of two parts,
one of which descended to
the surface. Conditions on
Venus – very high temperature
and pressure – meant that
the landers could function
for only a few minutes.

Parachutes
further slow the
descent

Venera 9 obtains
and transmits
several images
before failing

WORKING IN SPACE

ASTRONAUTS NOW WORK in
space on a regular basis. Many
experiments are carried out
aboard orbiting laboratories;
and satellites are launched,
retrieved, and repaired while
in Earth orbit.

WORKING ON THE MOON
Buzz Aldrin (the second man
to walk on the Moon) sets
up one of the scientific
experiment packages that
the Apollo 11 crew left
behind on the lunar surface.

Television
camera

Steering
control

Antenna

Equipment
storage rack

Wire-mesh
wheels

LUNAR ROVING VEHICLE
(LRV)

MOON BUGGY
Crew members of the
Apollo 15, 16, and 17
missions made effective
use of the LRV. This
"moon-buggy" enabled
them to travel tens of
kilometres (miles)
across the lunar surface
collecting samples over
a wide area.

SELF-PROPELLED
Powered by small jets
of nitrogen gas, the
Manned Maneuvering
Unit enables astronauts
to move about freely
outside their spacecraft.

MAN
MANEUVER
L

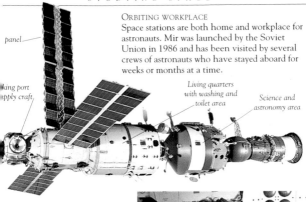

panel

king port
pply craft

ORBITING WORKPLACE
Space stations are both home and workplace for astronauts. Mir was launched by the Soviet Union in 1986 and has been visited by several crews of astronauts who have stayed aboard for weeks or months at a time.

Living quarters with washing and toilet area

Science and astronomy area

LABORATORY CONDITIONS
 crew member places a specimen inside one of the zero-gravity periment chambers located in the ace Shuttle's crew compartment. Larger scale experiments can be carried out in the cargo bay using computer-controlled equipment.

RUNNING REPAIRS
The Space Shuttle lets astronauts position themselves alongside a faulty satellite and either repair it in space, or bring it back to Earth for overhaul. The most successful repair mission to date was in December 1993, when new optical equipment was installed on the Hubble Space Telescope.

MILESTONES IN ASTRONOMY

The astronomer's job is to observe, describe, and explain objects in space. The story of astronomy is marked by a series of milestone achievements. Advances in technology have led to better descriptions and more comprehensive explanations.

EUDOXUS OF CNIDUS (408-355 B.C.) was a Greek thinker who studied at Athens under the philosopher Plato. In later life he developed the theory of crystal spheres – the first scientific attempt to explain the observed motion of the planets, and stars.

MILESTONE
According to Eudoxus, the Earth was at the centre of the universe. The stars and planets were set into a series of transparent crystal spheres that surrounded the Earth in space.

PTOLEMY (c.A.D. 120-180) lived in Alexandria, Egypt, at the height of the Roman Empire. Although little is known about him, he has become famous as the "father of astronomy". The idea that the Earth is at the centre of the universe is often referred to as the "Ptolemaic System".

MILESTONE
He compiled a compendium, known as the "Almagest", of Ancient Greek astronomical knowledge. Handed down over the centuries, Ptolemy's book continued to provide the basis of scientific astronomy for more than 1,000 years.

AL-SUFI (903-86) was a Persian nobleman, and one of the leading astronomers of his time. His "Book of Fixed Stars" listed the position and brightness of more than 1,000 stars, and beautifully illustrated the main constellations.

MILESTONE
During the Dark Ages, scientific astronomy was kept alive in the Islamic empire. Our knowledge of the works of Ptolemy is entirely due to Arab translators.

NICOLAUS COPERNICUS (1473-1543) worked as a church lawyer in Poland. Near the end of his life he published an exciting new view of the universe which replaced Ptolemy's.

MILESTONE

Copernicus removed the Earth from its traditional place at the centre of the universe, and replaced it with the Sun. This was considered to be a revolutionary view, and the "Copernican Revolution" was strongly opposed by the Christian Church.

GALILEO GALILEI (1564-1642) was an Italian scientist and astronomer who supported Copernicus' new theory. As a result, he was put on trial by the Church, and he remained a virtual prisoner for the rest of his life.

MILESTONE

Galileo pioneered the use of the refractor telescope for astronomy. He made several major discoveries, including mountains on the Moon, the phases of Venus, and the four largest moons of Jupiter.

ISAAC NEWTON (1643-1727) was a professor of mathematics and a great scientist. He is supposed to have had the idea for his theory of gravity after seeing an apple fall from a tree.

MILESTONE

The theory of gravity explained why apples fall, and why planets orbit around the Sun. Newton was able to establish the scientific laws that apply to the motion of objects in space. He also experimented with optics – splitting sunlight into its spectrum – and designed a reflecting telescope.

EDMOND HALLEY (1656-1742) became Britain's Astronomer Royal – one of the first official government scientists. As a young man he voyaged to the remote island of St Helena, and charted the stars of the southern hemisphere.

MILESTONE

Halley is famous for predicting the return of the periodic comet that now bears his name. His work reinforced the idea that astronomy is a very precise science that can make accurate predictions.

WILLIAM HERSCHEL (1738-1822) was born in Hanover, Germany, but moved to England where he at first worked as a professional musician. His interest in astronomy led him to design and build his own telescopes.

MILESTONE
Herschel became famous for his discovery of the planet Uranus in 1781 Today he is remembered as one of the greatest astronomical observers. By studying the Milky Way over many years, he was able to make the first reasonably accurate estimate of its size and shape.

JOSEPH VON FRAUNHOFER (1787-1826) was an orphan who eventually became the director of a scientific institute in Germany. He was a trained optical worker who made some of the world's highest-quality telescope lenses.

MILESTONE
Fraunhofer identified and studied the dark absorption lines (now called Fraunhofer lines) in the solar spectrum. These lines enable scientists to tell which chemical elements are present in a source of light.

NEPTUNE (FIRST LOCATED 1846) The position of a new planet in the solar system was predicted mathematically. But its existence could not be confirmed until it had been observed.

MILESTONE
The "discovery" of Neptune was made possible by astronomers' increased understanding of the universe. Following the work of Newton and Halley, they were able to make increasingly accurate predictions about the behaviour of objects in space.

WILLIAM HUGGINS (1824-1910) was an English astronomer who had his own private observatory in London. He was a pioneer of the technique of stellar spectroscopy (analysing the spectra produced by starlight).

MILESTONE
Huggins studied the light from many different stars. As a result of his work, he was able to show that stars are made of the same chemical elements that are found on Earth. He also showed that some nebulae are composed of gas.

GIOVANNI SCHIAPARELLI (1835-1910) was an Italian astronomer who became director of the Brera Observatory at Turin. He made headlines in 1877, when he claimed to have seen a network of straight lines or "canals" on Mars.

MILESTONE
Schiaparelli's most famous discovery was mistaken, but it did focus popular interest and attention on astronomy. He also established the link between comets and meteor showers.

EJNAR HERTZSPRUNG (1873-1967) and HENRY RUSSELL (1877-1957) were two scientists who working independently came to the same conclusions about the colour and temperature of stars.

MILESTONE
The Hertzsprung-Russell (HR) diagram shows the relationship between surface temperature and colour. Astronomers can identify the so-called "main sequence" of stellar development. Giant, supergiant, and dwarf stars are also located on the diagram.

ARTHUR EDDINGTON (1882-1945) was born in the north of England and became Professor of Astronomy at Cambridge. He was interested in the origin of stars, and he wrote science books for a general audience.

MILESTONE
Eddington was able to describe the structure of a star. He also explained how a star stays in one piece – balanced by the forces of gravity (pulling in), and gas pressure and radiation pressure (pushing out).

HARLOW SHAPLEY (1885-1972) was an American astronomer who became director of Harvard College Observatory. He used variable stars as markers to study the distance and distribution of star clusters.

MILESTONE
Shapley was able to give the first accurate estimate of the size and shape of the Milky Way galaxy. He also showed that the Sun is located a very long way from the centre of the galaxy.

CECILIA PAYNE-GAPOSCHKIN (1900-79) was born in England, but spent most of her working life at Harvard Observatory in America. She is thought by many people to have been the greatest-ever woman astronomer.

MILESTONE
By analysing the spectra of many different stars, Payne-Gaposchkin was able to show that all stars in the main sequence of development (the Sun for example) are composed almost entirely of the chemical elements hydrogen and helium.

EDWIN HUBBLE (1889-1953) was an American who began his working life as a lawyer before becoming a professional astronomer. He showed that the Andromeda spiral was definitely not part of the Milky Way galaxy.

MILESTONE
By showing that some objects are located outside the Milky Way, Hubble proved the existence of other galaxies. He also discovered that the universe appears to be constantly expanding.

GEORGES LEMAITRE (1894-1966) was a Belgian mathematician who worked in Britain and America. His work had an important influence on the way that astronomers think about the universe.

MILESTONE
Lemaitre proposed and developed the Big Bang theory about the origin of the universe. According to this theory, all matter and energy were created simultaneously by a huge explosion. This theory explains why many galaxies appear to be speeding away from us.

KARL JANSKY (1905-49) was an American radio engineer. While trying to solve the problem of static and interference with radio broadcasts, he discovered radio waves coming from the Milky Way.

MILESTONE
Without realising it, Jansky discovered the basic techniques of radio astronomy. As a result of his work, astronomers have been able to gather information from other parts of the electromagnetic spectrum, and not just from visible light.

RED HOYLE (b. 1915)
a British astronomer
ho began his career as
mathematician. He
ecame famous for his
heory that life on Earth
as the result of infection
y bacteria from space
arried by comets.

MILESTONE
Hoyle's most important
work concerned the basic
nuclear reactions at work
deep inside stars. He
explained the processes
by which stars convert
hydrogen into helium and
other heavier elements.

RED WHIPPLE (b. 1906)
as appointed professor of
stronomy at Harvard in
945, and became director
f the Smithsonian
Astrophysical Observatory
n 1955. He is best known
or his studies of comets
nd the solar system.

MILESTONE
His theory that comets
are "dirty snowballs" has
recently been proved
correct by space probes
such as Giotto. It now
seems likely that comets
are "leftovers" from the
formation of the solar system.

ARNO PENZIAS (b. 1933) and
ROBERT WILSON (b. 1936) are
American scientists. In
978 they received the
Nobel prize for physics
or discovering the
ackground radio energy
f the universe – energy
hat is left over from the Big Bang.

MILESTONE
This radio energy ("the
microwave background")
gives the universe an
average temperature
about 3°C (5°F) above
absolute zero. Many
people believe that its
discovery confirmed the Big Bang theory.

UPERNOVA 1987A
he observation of a
right supernova
uring 1987 gave
stronomers their first
pportunity to study a
upernova event with
odern telescopes and
her equipment.

MILESTONE
Analysis of the energy and
particles produced by the
event, confirmed the theory
that all chemical elements
heavier than iron are made
by very high-temperature
nuclear reactions during
supernova explosions.

SPACE MISSIONS I

THE SPACE AGE began in 1957
with the launch of the
first satellite. Four years later
Yuri Gagarin became the
world's first astronaut. The
next 20 years saw a surge of
interest in space exploration.

FIRST SPACE VEHICLE
A model of Vostok I, the
craft in which Yuri Gagarin
made his historic first orbit
the Earth on 12 April 1961

CONTROLLED LANDING
The probe Luna 9 was the first to make a
successful soft landing on the Moon in
February 1966. Luna 9 sent back the
first panoramic images taken from
the surface of the Moon.

*Lower part left
behind on Moon's
surface*

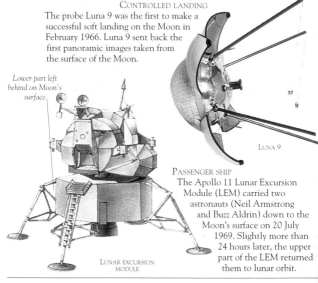

LUNA 9

PASSENGER SHIP
The Apollo 11 Lunar Excursion
Module (LEM) carried two
astronauts (Neil Armstrong
and Buzz Aldrin) down to the
Moon's surface on 20 July
1969. Slightly more than
24 hours later, the upper
part of the LEM returned
them to lunar orbit.

LUNAR EXCURSION
MODULE

ROBOT MOON ROVER
Two Lunokhod robot vehicles
were sent to the Moon in the
early 1970s. Equipped with
television cameras that enabled
them to be driven from a control
room on Earth, the two vehicles
travelled a total of 47.5 km
(29.5 miles) across the Moon.

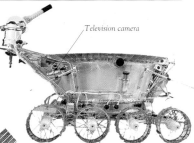

Television camera

LUNOKHOD I

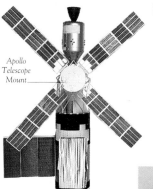

*Apollo
Telescope
Mount*

SKYLAB

SCIENTIFIC PLATFORM
Launched in 1973, the Skylab
orbiting laboratory and observatory
gave astronauts the opportunity to
work in space for weeks at a time.
Skylab also enabled scientists to
study the workings of Earth's
atmosphere and climate systems
from the viewpoint of space.

MESSAGE TO THE STARS
The two Pioneer probes each
carry a gold-covered plaque that
shows a visual representation of
human beings, as well as simple
directions for locating the solar
system and planet Earth.

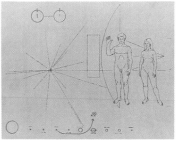

SPACE MISSIONS II

WORKING IN ORBIT became much easier with the introduction of the Space Shuttle in 1981. Probes have now visited all but one of the outer planets, and further exploration is planned.

The Shuttle has a mechanical arm which can be used to launch or retrieve satellites.

The external fuel tank breaks away at a height of 110 km (70 miles)

The booster rockets operate for about two minutes and are jettisoned at a height of 45 km (28 miles).

The Shuttle can lift-off with eight crew and up to 29 tonnes (tons) of cargo.

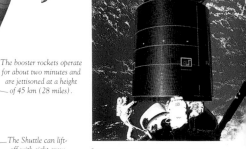

INCREASING COMMUNICATIONS
The communications satellite Intelsat was launched by astronauts on the 49th Space Shuttle mission in May 1992. Improved communications is just one of the benefits of space technology now enjoyed by the general public.

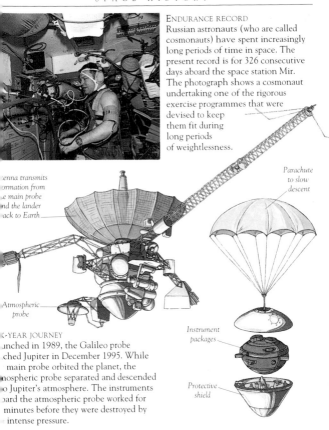

ENDURANCE RECORD
Russian astronauts (who are called cosmonauts) have spent increasingly long periods of time in space. The present record is for 326 consecutive days aboard the space station Mir. The photograph shows a cosmonaut undertaking one of the rigorous exercise programmes that were devised to keep them fit during long periods of weightlessness.

...enna transmits ...ormation from ...e main probe ...nd the lander ...ack to Earth

Parachute to slow descent

Atmospheric probe

Instrument packages

Protective shield

...K-YEAR JOURNEY
...unched in 1989, the Galileo probe ...ched Jupiter in December 1995. While ...main probe orbited the planet, the ...nospheric probe separated and descended ...o Jupiter's atmosphere. The instruments ...ard the atmospheric probe worked for ... minutes before they were destroyed by ... intense pressure.

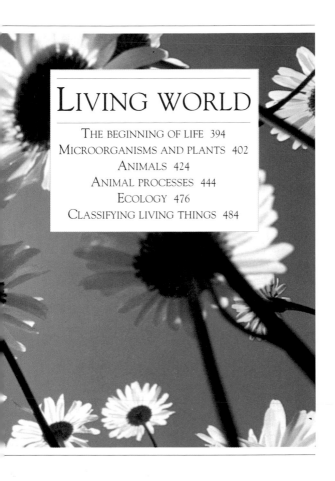

LIVING WORLD

WHAT IS NATURE?

Humans are the most intelligent of all animals

MOST SCIENTISTS divide nature into five kingdoms: animals, plants, fungi and two kingdoms called Monera and Protista. Monerans and protists include single-celled forms of life, such as bacteria and algae. Animals, plants, and most fungi are multi-cellular.

HUMANS

Humans are mammals, and more specifically primates, along with apes and monkeys. Like most mammals, humans give birth to live young.

Some fungi absorb nutrients from dead matter

FUNGI AND LICHENS

Fungi and lichens were considered plants. Now, more is known about how they live, and they are thought of as a separate kingdom.

FUNGI

LARKSPUR

Flowering plants are very successful

PLANTS

Early plants lived in water and then adapted to conditions on land. Nearly all plants are able to use sunlight to turn simple materials into food.

CHARACTERISTICS OF LIVING THINGS

• Able to use energy

• Able to take in raw materials

• Able to get rid of waste

• Able to respond to the outside world

• Able to reproduce

• Able to grow and develop

GIRAFFE
WEEVIL

*Flying insects
can travel
to find food*

MONERANS AND PROTISTS

The Monera kingdom includes
the simplest forms of life, such as
bacteria. It has at least 4,000 species.
The Protista kingdom is more varied.
It includes simple forms of algae and
protozoa (animal-like organisms
such as amoebas). It comprises at
least 50,000 species.

COCCI
BACTERIA

SPIRAL
BACTERIA

AMOEBA

...ECTS

...e most successful
...nals on Earth are
...cts. There are more
...cies of insect than any
...er group of animals on
...h. Insects are able to
...ive in almost all
...itats except the sea.

*Mammals, like
the lion, are
warm-blooded*

ANIMALS

The animal kingdom includes
simple creatures such as sponges
...nd complex mammals such as lions
...and humans. Animals cannot make
...r own food as plants do; they must
...nd it and eat it. They are able to
...vive in many different habitats.

LION

HOW LIFE BEGAN

THROUGHOUT HISTORY, people have wondered how life on Earth began. Some people believe it was specially created. Scientists think that the first simple life forms were the result of chemical reactions four billion years ago.

EARTH'S
STEAMING
SURFACE

THE BEGINNING OF THE EARTH
In the early days of the Earth, the planet was a fiery mass of molten rock. Earth's surface cracked and hot lava poured out filling the atmosphere with steam and gases. The lava hardened and the steam cooled to rain, creating steaming, muddy pools.

Surface covered with sizzling lava

Steam rises to condense and fall again as rain

MIXTURE OF GASES
Scientists have filled this flask with a mixture of gases like those that existed in the early days of the Earth. To simulate lightning, electric sparks are added. The gases combine and produce compounds that are found in all living things.

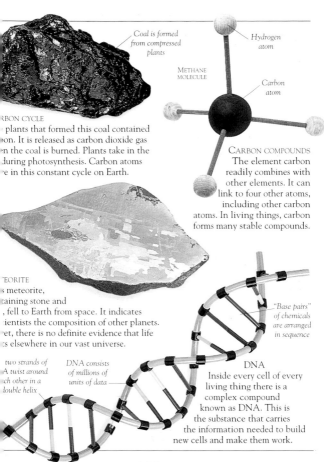

Coal is formed
from compressed
plants

Hydrogen
atom

METHANE
MOLECULE

Carbon
atom

RBON CYCLE

plants that formed this coal contained
on. It is released as carbon dioxide gas
n the coal is burned. Plants take in the
during photosynthesis. Carbon atoms
e in this constant cycle on Earth.

CARBON COMPOUNDS
The element carbon
readily combines with
other elements. It can
link to four other atoms,
including other carbon
atoms. In living things, carbon
forms many stable compounds.

EORITE
s meteorite,
aining stone and
, fell to Earth from space. It indicates
ientists the composition of other planets.
et, there is no definite evidence that life
s elsewhere in our vast universe.

"Base pairs"
of chemicals
are arranged
in sequence

two strands of
A twist around
ch other in a
double helix

DNA consists
of millions of
units of data

DNA
Inside every cell of every
living thing there is a
complex compound
known as DNA. This is
the substance that carries
the information needed to build
new cells and make them work.

EVOLUTION

FOSSILS SHOW THAT certain life forms have altered or "evolved" over time and that others have died ou British naturalists Charles Darwin a Alfred Russel Wallace formed the theory of evolution. It is based on "natural selection", a process th favours the best adapt members of a species

AN EVOLUTIONARY LINK
This fossil is *Archaeopteryx* – a bird-dinosaur with wings. It may show a li between reptiles and birds. This kind of link is important to scientists because it is evidence of ho one species may have evolved from another.

GALÁPAGOS FINCHES

GATHERING EVIDENCE
When Charles Darwin visited the Galápagos Islands in 1832, he found 13 species of finch. He noticed that the birds had different beak shapes suited to their particular eating habits. Darwin believed that the finches had gradually evolved from a single species long ago.

WARBLER FINCH

Strong, heavy beak for crushing big seeds

The sharp point of this beak catches small insects

LARGE GROUND FINCH

Insect and seed eater has a small beak

SMALL TREE FINCH

This finch uses a cactus spine to pick up insects

WOODPEC FINCH

...acotherium
...d 50 million
...s ago. It had
... toes on its
...ront feet

Mesohippus, which
lived 30 million years
ago, had three toes
on its front feet

Merychippus existed
20 million years ago.
One of its three toes
formed a large hoof

Equus is the
modern horse

Equus evolved about
two million years ago.
It has a single toe or
hoof on each foot

...LUTION OF THE HORSE
... earliest fossils of a horse-like animal, called Hyracotherium,
... a small mammal, about the size of a dog, that ate leaves.
... time, descendants became larger with longer legs and
...fferent diet. Modern horses are larger still and eat grass.

NATURAL SELECTION

Darwin believed evolution favoured
individuals that were best suited to
their environment. Less successful
individuals of the same species would
naturally die out. In 19th-century
England, dark peppered moths
became more common than pale
peppered moths. Pollution meant that
dark moths were better camouflaged
from birds on the blackened trees.

PEPPERED MOTHS
ON LIGHT BARK

ARTIFICIAL SELECTION

... size, colour, and shape of animals
...uch as horses, dogs, and cats can
... modified artificially through
...lective breeding. Breeders
...oose individuals with the
...desired qualities and reject the rest.

Sphynx is
bred to be
hairless

SPHYNX
CAT

Human evolution

Apes are humans' closest relatives. Apes and humans together are known as hominoids. Humans and their direct ancestors are called hominids. The earliest hominid fossils are from about 3.5 million years ago. One such fossil, found in Ethiopia, is called "Lucy". She had a small brain but walked upright. The most recent hominids belong to the group *Homo* and appeared about two million years ago. These include *Homo habilis*, who used too

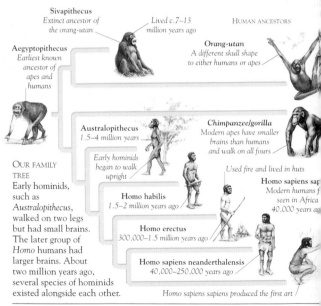

Sivapithecus
Extinct ancestor of the orang-utan

Lived c.7–13 million years ago

HUMAN ANCESTORS

Aegyptopithecus
Earliest known ancestor of apes and humans

Orang-utan
A different skull shape to either humans or apes

Australopithecus
1.5–4 million years

Early hominids began to walk upright

Chimpanzee/gorilla
Modern apes have smaller brains than humans and walk on all fours

OUR FAMILY TREE
Early hominids, such as *Australopithecus*, walked on two legs but had small brains. The later group of *Homo* humans had larger brains. About two million years ago, several species of hominids existed alongside each other.

Used fire and lived in huts

Homo sapiens sap
Modern humans f seen in Africa 40,000 years a

Homo habilis
1.5–2 million years ago

Homo erectus
300,000–1.5 million years ago

Homo sapiens neanderthalensis
40,000–250,000 years ago

Homo sapiens sapiens produced the first art

SKELETON SHAPES
[Gor]illas walk on [thei]r feet and hands. [The] human skeleton [is ad]apted for upright [wal]king. It has a [forw]ard-pointing [big t]oe, whereas the [goril]la's toe is angled [for g]rasping. Human [leg b]ones are [wider] to make [walk]ing easier.

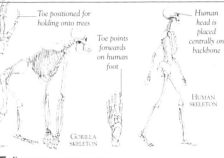

Toe positioned for holding onto trees

Toe points forwards on human foot

GORILLA SKELETON

Human head is placed centrally on backbone

HUMAN SKELETON

FIRST HUMAN FOOTPRINTS
Mary Leakey, a British fossil expert, unearthed these fossilized footprints in Africa in 1977. They were left by three hominids in volcanic ash nearly four million years ago.

Apes evolved 30 million years ago

Hominids appeared only around 5 million years ago

Earth was formed 4.6 billion years ago

Dinosaurs lived 200 million years ago

Reptiles appear

If you imagine Earth's history in one hour, then humans appear just before the hour strikes

Land plants emerge

Plant life in the oceans began 1.5 billion years ago

Bacteria appeared 3.8 billion years ago

EVOLUTIONARY CLOCK
Scientists believe simple life forms first appeared on Earth 3.8 billion years ago. It was not until about five million years ago that the first hominids appeared.

ARRIVAL TIMES OF HUMANS

[H]umans originated in Africa, but spread [to] many other regions much more recently.

REGION	APPROXIMATE ARRIVAL TIME
[Aust]ralia	At least 40,000 years ago
[Nort]h America	At least 12,000 years ago
[Mad]agascar	2,000 years ago
[New] Zealand	1,000 years ago
[Anta]rctica	150 years ago

MICROSCOPIC LIFE

THERE ARE MANY kinds of life that are so tiny they a
invisible except through a microscope. These includ
billions of bacteria and viruses, some of which live i
the human body. Another group of small organisms,
called protists,
also consist of
just a single cell.

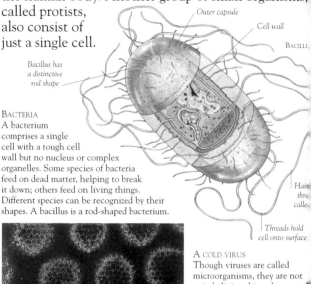

Outer capsule

Cell wall

BACILLU

*Bacillus has
a distinctive
rod shape*

BACTERIA
A bacterium
comprises a single
cell with a tough cell
wall but no nucleus or complex
organelles. Some species of bacteria
feed on dead matter, helping to break
it down; others feed on living things.
Different species can be recognized by their
shapes. A bacillus is a rod-shaped bacterium.

*Hai
thre
calle*

*Threads hold
cell onto surface*

A COLD VIRUS
Though viruses are called
microorganisms, they are not
strictly living things because t
cannot reproduce without the
help of living cells. In animals
viruses can cause colds and flu
or diseases such as AIDS.

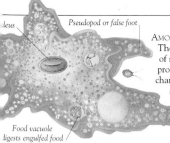

ıleus — Pseudopod or false foot

AMOEBA
The jelly-like amoeba belongs to a group of single-celled organisms known as protists. Amoebas move by constantly changing shape. They take in food by surrounding and engulfing it. Food is stored and digested in a structure called a food vacuole.

Food vacuole
ligests engulfed food

CELLS

ₙNIMAL CELL
he flexible skin around
ₙ animal cell allows
ome chemicals
ₙto the cell but
ot others. The
ell is controlled
y the nucleus.
ₙ the fluid around
ₑe nucleus, called
ₜtoplasm, lie tiny
ₒrganelles that perform specific tasks.

Plasma membrane

Cytoplasm

Nucleus – the cell's command centre

Energy-producing organelle

ₕloroplasts
o the energy
ₙ sunlight

Plasma
embrane

Cell wall

Vacuole used to store cell sap

Nucleus

ₗLANT CELL
plant cell differs from an animal cell in two
ₙportant ways. It has an additional rigid cell wall as
ℓll as a plasma membrane around it and it contains
ℓen organelles called chloroplasts.

Slug forms into fruiting body

Fruiting body releases spores

Spores germinate

Amoeba grows from spore

Amoebas come together into slug

Slug migrates

LIFE OF A SLIME MOULD
A slime mould reproduces in an unusual way. First, slime mould amoebas gather together to form a mass called a slug. The slug moves towards the light. Eventually, it forms a tall, fruiting body that releases spores. The spores produce new amoebas.

FUNGI AND LICHENS

FUNGI ARE NEITHER plants nor animals but members of a separate kingdom that includes mushrooms, moulds, and yeasts. Many fungi exist as tiny threads that form large fruiting bodies. Lichens are living partnerships between fungi and alga

Fruiting body releases spores

Spores form hyphae

Network called mycelium

Fruiting body begins to form

Mycelium spreads

LIFE CYCLE OF A FUNGUS
For most of its life a fungus is a network of threads, called hyphae, in the fungus's food source. Fungi form fruiting bodies to release their spores.

FLY AGARIC TOADSTOOL (POISONOUS)

Brightly colour poisonous ca

Spores form in gill

Stalk is made up of many threads meshed together

BUDDING YEAST
Microscopic fungi called yeast exist as individual cells. During their reproduction process, known as budding, new cells begin as buds that grow and eventually separate from the parent cell.

TOADST
The life cycle of n fungi includes a frui body such as a toads or mushroom. fruiting body prov a way for the fung reproduce. Sp (seed-like spe are made in under the and released w conditions are ri

The fruiting body of the puffball puffs out spores

PUFFBALL

A puffball fungus starts out as a solid head of cells. Gradually, the cells dry out and form a papery bag. When drops of rain or an animal brush the bag, a cloud of spores is released into the air. The spores are very light and can be carried long distances.

FUNGI FACTS

• The fungus *Penicillium notatum* produces the well-known antibiotic drug, penicillin.

• A giant puffball can release seven million million spores in its life.

• The seeds of many orchids will not germinate without the presence of a fungus.

TYPES OF LICHEN

lichen is not a plant, but a partner-ip between a fungus and an alga that xists as one organism. Lichens grow n rocks and tree trunks. The fungus ssolves substances that the alga uses; and the alga supplies the fungus with food made by photosynthesis. Lichens grow in five forms, of which three – leafy (foliose), crusty and flat (crustose), and mixed (squamulose) – are shown here.

Leafy type of lichen

Tree bark

Lichens will eventually dissolve minerals from the rock

Spore-producing body

CLADONIA LOERKEANA

HYPOGYMNIA PHYSODES

Flat and crusty lichens

CALOPLACA HEPPIANA

Mixture of shrubby and leafy lichen

ALGAE AND SIMPLE PLANTS

PLANTS EVOLVED FROM ALGAE, which consist of either
one cell or many cells. Algae do not have true roots
or leaves, and they also lack flowe
Liverworts and mosses were some
of the earliest plants on Earth. Th
grow in damp, shady places. Ferns a
horsetails were among the first plan
to develop water-carrying systems.
They are known as vascular plants

EXAMPLES OF ALGAE

New
colonies
growing

Adult
colony

VOLVOX
Volvox is a freshwater
alga. It consists of
many cells and is
often found in ponds.

Cap

Stalk

GREEN
ALGA
ACETABULARIA

ACETABULARIA
This is a single-celled,
cup-shaped alga found
in shallow sea water.

SEAWEEDS
A seaweed is a plant-like marine alga ma
of many cells. It usually anch
itself to the sea bed n
the shore, and its le
like fronds trap
energy in sunlig

Kelp is a
brown
seaweed

Bladderwrack
has air
bladders to
make it float
on the
surface

Sugar k
has from
long, le
like fla

Carrageen

Dulse
is a red
seaweed

Liverworts grow close to the ground

LIVERWORT

Liverworts usually grow in damp areas where there is shade. Like mosses, liverworts are bryophytes, a group of simple plants that have no true stems, leaves, or roots. Liverworts are flat, ribbon-like plants. Their life cycle, like that of ferns, has two stages.

Moss grows on rotting wood

MOSSY LOG

Other simple plants, mosses, live mostly in damp places. Mosses do not have true roots but only thread-like rhizoids. Mosses are also non-vascular, meaning that they lack a system for carrying water.

LIFE CYCLE OF A FERN

The life cycle of a fern has two quite different stages. During the first stage, a leafy plant (the sporophyte) creates spores. These produce the small, heart-shaped second stage (the gametophyte). This makes male and female cells that fuse, forming a new sporophyte.

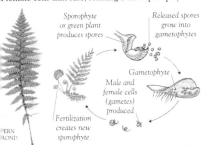

Sporophyte or green plant produces spores

Released spores grow into gametophytes

Gametophyte

Male and female cells (gametes) produced

Fertilization creates new sporophyte

FERN FROND

Side branches in circles from the stem

HORSETAIL

Common in damp places, horsetails are an ancient, brush-like plant. They spread by spores and have creeping underground stems.

CONIFERS

PINES, CEDARS, AND CYPRESSES are examples of conifers. Conifers form part of a group of plants called gymnosperms. These were the first land plants to reproduce with seeds rather than spores. Conife usually grow their seeds in hard, woo cones. Most conifers, including firs and pines, are evergreen, which mear that they keep their leaves throughout the year

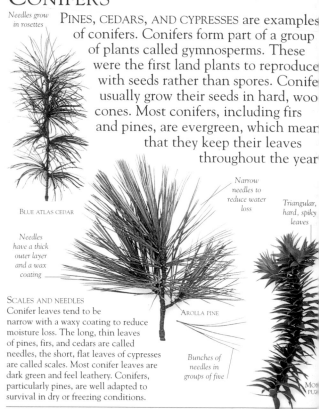

Needles grow in rosettes

BLUE ATLAS CEDAR

Needles have a thick outer layer and a wax coating

Narrow needles to reduce water loss

Triangular, hard, spiky leaves

AROLLA PINE

Bunches of needles in groups of five

MO
PUZ

SCALES AND NEEDLES
Conifer leaves tend to be narrow with a waxy coating to reduce moisture loss. The long, thin leaves of pines, firs, and cedars are called needles, the short, flat leaves of cypresses are called scales. Most conifer leaves are dark green and feel leathery. Conifers, particularly pines, are well adapted to survival in dry or freezing conditions.

ature cones
release
seeds

Female
and male
cones grow
separately

Male cone
releases pollen
to fertilize
female

_ds
one

E CYCLE OF A CONIFER
onifer grows male and
ale cones. Pollen from
e cones fertilizes female
es that later form seeds.

ure
ale
sits
ght
ree

EDAR
ONES

es break
er a few
nths

TALLEST AND HEAVIEST TREES

TALLEST TREE
Coast redwoods are the
world's tallest trees,
reaching 111 m (364 ft).

HEAVIEST TREE
Another redwood, the
giant sequoia, is the
world's heaviest tree.

CEDAR CONE
The seed scales inside the
mature cedar cone
peel away and
the cone
disintegrates
while still
on the tree.

SCOTS PINE CONE
The mature female cone
of the Scots
pine opens
up and the
seeds flutter
away into
the air.

AMBER
Some conifers
produce resin to protect
themselves from insects,
which get trapped in the
sticky sap. Prehistoric
insects have been
preserved in fossilized
resin, called amber.

FLOWERING PLANTS

THE MOST SUCCESSFUL PLANTS on Earth are the flowering plants. They can survive in many kinds of habitat, from mountainsides to deserts. There are more than 250,000 species of flowering plants and nearly all produce food by a process called photosynthesis. Most of these plants have green leaves and live in soil.

Leaves reduced to spines

CACTUS FAMILY
Cactus family (Cactaceae) plants live in dry places. They have no leaves and store water in their stems.

Flowers form distinctive, five-petal shape

PEA FAMILY
The pea family (Leguminosae) includes the food plants, beans and peas. The flowers have five petals and produce a fruit known as a legume. The legume holds one or more seeds.

FLOWERING PLANT FACTS
• The Tallipot palm *Corypha umbraculifera* takes about 100 years to flower and then dies.

• Potatoes, peppers, and tomatoes are members of the nightshade family, which also includes many poisonous plants.

GRASS FAMILY
The most widespread flowering plants are grasses (Gramineae). Many are grown for their seeds (grain), such as wheat, rice, maize, and oats.

Flowers have five petals

ROSE FAMILY

In the rose family, (Rosaceae) many plants, such as roses, apples, cherries, and strawberries, are cultivated. Some rose family species are trees or shrubs. The flowers usually have four or five petals and many stamens at the centre.

Thorns grow on stems

...CH FAMILY

...e beech family (...aceae) includes trees ...h as sweet chestnuts, ...s, and beeches. Their ...ts are nuts and their ...ers are frequently ...kins. In the northern ...misphere beech trees are ...d as a source of timber.

Many pollen-producing stamens

Adapted flowers attract animals

ORCHID FAMILY

The second-largest family of flowering plants is the orchid family (Orchidaceae). Their specialized flowers attract animal pollinators. Orchids rely on a special relationship with fungi to grow.

LARGEST FAMILIES OF FLOWERING PLANTS

SCIENTIFIC NAME	COMMON NAME	NUMBER OF SPECIES
...mpositae	Daisy family	25,000
...chidaceae	Orchid family	18,000
...guminosae	Pea family	17,000
...amineae	Grass family	9,000
...biaceae	Coffee family	7,000
...phorbiaceae	Spurge family	5,000
...peraceae	Rush family	4,000

Plants and leaves

A plant's stem supports its buds, leaves, and flowers. Inside the stem are cells that carry water, minerals, and food to different parts of the plant. Roots anchor the plant and absorb water and minerals from the soil. Leaves use the Sun's energy to make food.

Stigma — Petal — Flower

Stamen

Bract (le
like struct

Sepal — Receptr

Node

Petiole

Lamir

Branch — Stem

Lateral
bud

Midrib

HIBISCUS — Main root

L
r

LEAVES

LEAF SHAPES

A simple leaf has a single blade (lamina), but a compound leaf is divided into separate leaflets. In a bipinnate compound leaf, the leaflets are divided.

SIMPLE LEAF — Apex

Leaf vein

Lamina
or blade
– from
apex
to base

Midrib

Base — Petiole or
leaf stalk

BIPINNATE

LINEAR

PALMATE

PINNATE

BITERNATE

PLANT ANATOMY

The visible part of the pla
the shoot. It consists of a s
supporting buds (undevelc
shoots), leaves, and flowe
The shoot grows towards
light. Roots fix the plant
the ground and collect w

Waxy cuticle

...er
...rmis

...plasts
...re the
...t's
...d is
...de

...gy
...phyll
...ls

...ace

Guard cell

Stoma
– opening in the leaf

Tightly packed
mesophyll
palisade cells

Maple leaves
change from
green to
yellow to
orange to red

INSIDE A LEAF

Both sides of a leaf
have a thin outer
layer, called an
epidermis, which
is often covered
by wax or hairs.
Between these two
layers are mesophyll
cells and air spaces.

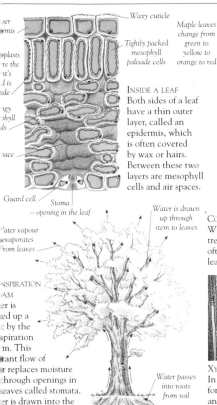

...ater vapour
...evaporates
...from leaves

...NSPIRATION
...AM
...er is
...ed up a
...by the
...spiration
...m. This
...tant flow of
...r replaces moisture
...hrough openings in
...eaves called stomata.
...er is drawn into the
...'s roots and pulled
...rough the stem.

Water is drawn
up through
stem to leaves

Water passes
into roots
from soil

COLOURFUL LEAVES

When leaves of deciduous
trees die, chemical changes
often occur, turning the
leaves bright colours.

XYLEM AND PHLOEM

In the stem, xylem cells
form tubes that carry water
and minerals from the roots
to the leaves. Phloem cells
take food to all parts.

PHOTOSYNTHESIS

PLANTS MAKE THEIR FOOD by a process known as photosynthesis. It requires sunlight, water, and carbon dioxide. Photosynthesis is carried out mostly in the leaves, where the pigment that gives leaves their green colour, called chlorophyll, is stored. Oxygen is released during this process.

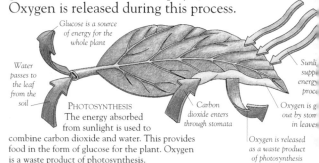

Glucose is a source of energy for the whole plant

Water passes to the leaf from the soil

Sunli supp energy proce

PHOTOSYNTHESIS
The energy absorbed from sunlight is used to combine carbon dioxide and water. This provides food in the form of glucose for the plant. Oxygen is a waste product of photosynthesis.

Carbon dioxide enters through stomata

Oxygen is g out by stom in leaves

Oxygen is released as a waste product of photosynthesis

PHOTOSYNTHESIS FACTS

• If photosynthesis stopped, almost all life on Earth would cease.

• Each year, plants make about 100 billion tonnes of glucose by harnessing the light of the Sun.

• Earth's atmosphere would contain no oxygen without photosynthesis.

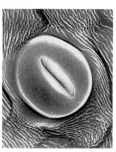

STOMATA
On the underside of leaves are microscopi pores called stomata. These openings allow the gases carbon diox and oxygen to pass in and out of the leaf. Guard cells are situat on either side of each pore and control its opening and closing.

DE A CHLOROPLAST
:osynthesis takes
e in structures
d chloroplasts.
se are inside
t cells, mostly
e leaves.
y contain
rophyll, a green
ent that absorbs
gy from sunlight.

CHLOROPLAST

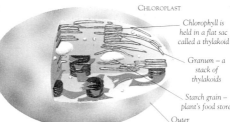

Chlorophyll is
held in a flat sac
called a thylakoid

Granum – a
stack of
thylakoids

Starch grain –
plant's food store

Outer
membrane

aytime: plant
ives out more
gen than it uses

Twilight: plant
releases equal
amounts of gases

Night-time: plant
releases more
carbon dioxide

CHLOROPHYLL
When sunlight reaches a
plant, red and blue light is
absorbed and green light is
reflected, making the plant
appear green. The pigment
chlorophyll, in chloroplasts,
reflects the green colour.

TOSYNTHESIS AND RESPIRATION
ng the day, plants make food by
osynthesis. They take in carbon dioxide
release oxygen. At night, photosynthesis
s and plants respire. They break
n food, taking in oxygen and
sing carbon dioxide.

Enzymes inside
leaf digest insects

VENUS FLY
TRAP

Trap sealed with
interlocking
spines

Lobes of trap formed
from modified leaves

Insects nudge
trigger hairs on the
edge of the trap

US FLY TRAP
e plants living in acid, boggy
make food by photosynthesis
get some nutrients from animals.
Venus fly trap has a spring-trap
nanism that allows it to catch insects.

PLANT GROWTH

WHEN A PLANT BEGINS TO GROW, its shoot reaches u
so its leaves can absorb sunlight, and its roots grow do
to absorb water and nutrients from the soil. Once a pla
is mature, it reproduces by flowering or in other way
Many plants store food for the next growing season.

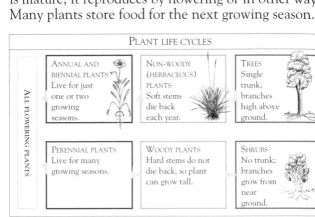

PLANT LIFE CYCLES

ALL FLOWERING PLANTS

ANNUAL AND
BIENNIAL PLANTS
Live for just
one or two
growing
seasons.

NON-WOODY
(HERBACEOUS)
PLANTS
Soft stems
die back
each year.

TREES
Single
trunk,
branches
high above
ground.

PERENNIAL PLANTS
Live for many
growing seasons.

WOODY PLANTS
Hard stems do not
die back, so plant
can grow tall.

SHRUBS
No trunk;
branches
grow from
near
ground.

*Seed provides food
for young plant*

Roots

*Leaves begin to
photosynthesize*

Shoot

*Seedling's leav
now make foo
to fuel growt*

1 GERMINATION
Once the
seed coat (testa) has
split and the roots have
begun to grow down,
the first shoot reaches
up towards the light.

2 GROWING
Growth
takes place at
the tips of the
seedling's roots and
shoot. The shoot
reaches upwards.

3 SEEDLI
Leaves
provide th
plant with f
by photosynthesis.
Roots take in nutri
and water from the

REPRODUCING WITHOUT SEEDS

Many plants, including this strawberry, can reproduce without making seeds. To do this, they grow parts that can take root and grow. This is asexual reproduction, because only one parent is involved.

Parent plant produces two ways it also makes seeds

New plant begins to grow in different place

Parent plant sends out runners over the ground

STORAGE SYSTEMS

SWEET POTATO
Plants such as the sweet potato store food from one growing season to the next. The food is held in a swollen underground stem called a tuber.

GRAPE HYACINTH
The bulb produced by plants such as the grape hyacinth is another type of storage system. Food is stored in layers of fleshy scales packed into the bulb.

A bulb is a type of short underground stem

HOW TREES GROW

TREE RINGS
Wood is a strong material that supports trees and shrubs. It consists of layers of xylem cells toughened with a substance called lignin. Each growing season a new ring of xylem is added.

Young tree has smooth bark

Cracked bark of mature tree

BARK
The layer on the outside of a woody plant's stem is known as bark. The outer layer of bark is dead, but under this there are living phloem cells. Tiny pores in the bark, called lenticels, allow gases to pass through.

FLOWERS

FLOWERS ENABLE A PLANT to be pollinated and then form seeds. Flowers consist of male and female organs surrounded by petals that may be coloured and scented to attract visiting animals. The male parts of a flower (stamens) make pollen; the female parts (carpels) make cells that form seeds.

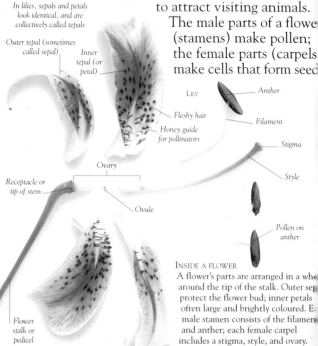

In lilies, sepals and petals look identical, and are collectively called tepals

Outer tepal (sometimes called sepal)

Inner tepal (or petal)

LILY

Fleshy hair

Honey guide for pollinators

Anther

Filament

Stigma

Style

Ovary

Receptacle or tip of stem

Ovule

Pollen on anther

Flower stalk or pedicel

INSIDE A FLOWER

A flower's parts are arranged in a wh[...] around the tip of the stalk. Outer se[...] protect the flower bud; inner petals [...] often large and brightly coloured. E[...] male stamen consists of the filament[...] and anther; each female carpel [...] includes a stigma, style, and ovary.

GIANT FLOWER
The giant rafflesia (*Rafflesia arnoldii*) is the world's largest flower. It can grow up to 105 cm (3.5 ft) across and weigh up to 7 kg (15.4 lb). It is at risk from the destruction of its habitat in the rainforests of Sumatra.

CAPITULUM

UMBEL

SPIKE

RACEME

INFLORESCENCE
Inflorescences are groups of flowers arranged on a single stem. Sunflowers and their relatives form a capitulum, which contains many flowers but looks like one flower. A spike consists of stalkless flowers on a straight stem; a raceme has flowers with stalks. An umbel is umbrella-shaped.

ENDANGERED FLOWERING PLANTS

Of the 300,000 or so species identified, about six per cent are endangered. Plants are at risk from over-collection or destruction of their habitat. This is a selection of key endangered species.

CONTINENT	SPECIES	THREATENED BY
North America	Saguaro cactus *Carnegia gigantea*	Over-collection
South America	Chilean wine palm *Juba chilensis*	Land clearance
Africa	African violet *Saintpaulia ionantha*	Forest clearance
Asia	Orchid *Paphiopedilum rothschildianum*	Over-collection
Europe	Madonna lily *Lilium candidum*	Over-collection
Australia	Lobster claw *Clianthus puniceus*	Browsing from livestock

POLLINATION

POLLINATION ENSURES that a plant
can develop seeds and so reproduce.
The process can be carried out
by animals, usually insects, or
by the wind or water. Pollen is
transferred from the male part
of one flower to the female
part of another. Both flowers
must be of the same species.

SUNFLOWER UNDER
ULTRAVIOLET LIGHT

Outer pe
look pa

ANIMAL POLLINATION

When an insect, such as a bee, visits a flower,
pollen from the flower's anthers is brushed onto it.
The bee collects nectar and pollen to take to the
hive, and may visit other flowers of the same species,
transferring
pollen grains
between
flowers as
it feeds.

ATTRACTING INSECTS

Seen under ultraviolet light, t
centre of this sunflower looks
dark and the petals look pale.
Honeybees see this contrast,
and are attracted to the necta
rich, dark centre of the flower

BUMBLEBEE ON
A DOG ROSE

Pollen is
stored in
sacs on the
bee's legs

Bee collects
nectar from inside
the flower

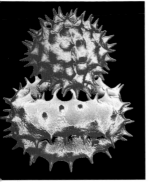

WIND POLLINATION
The flowers of wind-pollinated plants are often small and dull. When the flowers are mature, their dry, dusty pollen is scattered by the wind to other flowers. Many grasses, in particular, are wind-pollinated.

SWEET CHESTNUT (MALE)

Filament

Anther

Hanging flowers are called catkins

LEN GRAINS
e pollen grains above are enlarged
ny times. Unmagnified, they look like
ticles of yellow dust. Pollen is produced
he anthers of a flower. It contains the
le sex cells.

*ticky pollen grains
attach themselves
to feathers*

HUMMINGBIRD FROM THE AMAZON RAINFOREST

MMINGBIRD
ne flowers are
linated by birds or bats.
hummingbird drinks nectar
m inside a flower and picks up
len grains on its feathers. It then
ies this pollen to other flowers.

POLLINATION FACTS

• The smallest pollen grains are only 0.02 mm (0.0008 in) across.

• Ribbonweed, a water plant, has pollen that floats in "boats" to female flowers.

• A species of orchid in Madagascar is pollinated by a moth with a 30 cm (1 ft) long tongue.

FERTILIZATION AND FRUITS

AFTER A FLOWER IS POLLINATED, male and female cells join to produce seeds. To do this, nuclei from pollen grains travel down special tubes to the female ovules, and fertilization takes place. The plant's ovaries then expand around the developing seeds, forming fruits.

Pollen grain

Pollen tube

Ovule

Ovum (female sex cell)

FERTILIZATION

Fertilization occurs after a pollen grain containing male cells reaches a flower's stigma. A tube grows down from the grain to the ovule. Male nuclei travel along the tube to join a female cell.

SEED FACTS

• The coco-de-mer palm *Laodicea maldivica* has the largest seeds. Each fruit weighs up to 20 kg (44 lb) and has one seed.

• Orchids have the smallest seeds. A billion can weigh 1 g (0.035 oz).

DEVELOPMENT OF A SUCCULENT FRUIT

FLOWER BLOOMS
A flower in full bloom attracts pollinators by its fragrance and colour.

Stamen

Ovary

OVARY SWELLING
Stamens wither and the ovaries enlarge as ovules develop into seeds.

Ovary

MATURING FRUIT
Ovaries grow and their walls become fleshy. They begin to change colour.

Drupelet

RIPE FRUIT
The ovaries darken as they become ripe. Each contains a single seed.

MON

lemon is a succulent
icy) fruit. It is brightly
oloured to attract animals
at it and disperse its seeds.

g
e fig is a false fruit. Its
sh surrounds tiny internal
wers that form seeds.

SEED DISPERSAL

LESSER BURDOCK
This fruit of the lesser
burdock has a coat
covered in hooked
burrs. The hooks
fasten onto the fur
of passing animals and
are dispersed in this way.

SYCAMORE
The dry
fruit of the
sycamore has
become flat and elongated. It forms
a double wing shape that enables
the seed to be carried by the wind.

Seed

Fruit
flattened
into wings

Remains
of the
flower

PEA
A pea pod is a
e of dry fruit called a
ume. It splits along two
es to release its seeds.

CHESTNUT
Nuts, a dry fruit with a hard
wall around the seed, are
"indehiscent", meaning
that they do not split
open to release the seeds.

STRAWBERRY
A strawberry is a
swollen flower base
studded with achenes
(hard, one-seeded fruits).

HONESTY
This "dehiscent" dry
fruit has a fruit wall
that splits so that
the seeds can be
carried by the wind.

SIMPLE INVERTEBRATES

AN ANIMAL WITHOUT a backbone is known as an invertebrate. Invertebrates make up over nine-tenths of all animal species. Some are simple, microscopic creatures; others larger and more complex.

Digestive cavity in the middle of the bell

Plankton trapped in mucus

Adult jellyfish

Fleshy arms collect food

The ephyrae break free

JELLYFISH

A jellyfish moves by contracting its bell-shaped body. It has trailing tentacles that pull food into the digestive cavity, which is in the middle of the jellyfish.

Polyp splits into eight-armed buds called ephyrae

Small polyps form

LIFE CYCLE OF A JELLYFISH

Adult jellyfish release fertilized larvae that rest on the sea bed. The larvae grow into small polyps that divide into buds and swim away as tiny adults.

MUSHROOM CORAL FUNGIA

TYPES OF SIMPLE INVERTEBRATE

There are more than a million known species of invertebrate divided into 30 phyla (types). These are two of the simplest.

INVERTEBRATE	NAME OF PHYLUM	FEATURES	NUMBER OF SPECIES
	Poriferans (sponges)	Simple animals that filter food from water	5,000
	Cnidarians (sea anemones, corals, jellyfish)	Simple animals with stinging threads	10,000

CORAL

A coral is a polyp with a cylindrical shape. Most corals live together in colonies. Corals may build hard cases of calcium carbonate. When they die these may form coral reefs.

TAPEWORM AND ITS HEAD

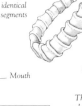

Hooks and suckers
on the head

EARTHWORM

An earthworm has a
segmented body, which it
moves using two sets of
muscles. The muscles
change the shape of the
[seg]ments. Earthworms feed
[o]n the organic matter in
soil. An earthworm is
both male and female
(hermaphroditic).

*Body is
formed from
identical
segments*

*Gizzard (part
of the stomach)*

*Earthworms have
several "hearts"*

Mouth

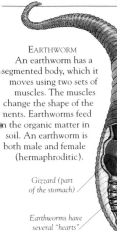

INSIDE AN EARTHWORM

*The worm
releases eggs
in packets*

TAPEWORM

A tapeworm
is a type of
parasitic flatworm
that lives inside
the intestines of
animals such as
pigs, cats, or even
humans. The worm's
head has hooks and suckers
that grasp the intestines.
Food is absorbed from
the host animal's gut.

TYPES OF INVERTEBRATE (WORMS)

Worms are often divided up into repeated segments.
Most are free-living, but some are parasitic.

VERTEBRATE	NAME OF PHYLUM	FEATURES	NUMBER OF SPECIES
	Annelids (worms, leeches)	Worms with a segmented body	12,000
	Platyhelminthes (flatworms, flukes, tapeworms)	Worms with a simple flattened body	10,000
	Nematodes (roundworms)	Worms with an unsegmented cylindrical body	15,000

MOLLUSCS AND ECHINODERM

THE SOFT BODY of a mollusc is usually covered by a
hard shell. Molluscs include gastropods, such as snai
bivalves, such as oysters; and cephalopods, such as
squids. Echinoderms have a five
part body and live in the sea.

Reproductive organ

Mantle

Mucus gland

Eye

INSIDE A SNAIL
A snail's body has three
parts: the head, the muscu
foot, and the body, whic
covered by a mantle of s
and contains the main org

Muscular foot

Lung

Sensory tentacle

Mollusc sinks to
a suitable spot
on the sea bed

Egg hatches into
free-swimming
larvae

Sperm
cells fertilize
egg cells
outside the
adult's body

The veliger
larvae stage

Shell
forms

LIFE CYCLE OF AN OYSTER
Molluscs usually lay eggs
that hatch into larvae.
As a larva grows, its shell
develops. The young adult
then settles on the sea
bed. Some snails hatch
out as miniature adults.

TYPES OF MOLLUSC

There are more than 50,000 species of mollusc. These are
divided into seven classes. Five are listed below.

MOLLUSC	NAME OF CLASS	FEATURES	NUMBE OF SPEC
	Bivalves (clams and relatives)	Shells in two parts, which hinge together	8,00
	Polyplacophorans (chitons)	Shell made of several plates	500
	Gastropods (slugs, snails, and relatives)	Molluscs with a muscular sucker-like foot	35,0
	Scaphopods (tusk shells)	Molluscs with tapering tubular shells	350
	Cephalopods (octopus, squid, cuttlefish)	Molluscs with a head and ring of tentacles	600

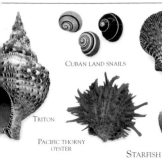

CUBAN LAND SNAILS

MOLLUSC SHELLS

Mollusc shells have a huge variety of colours and shapes. They are formed from calcium carbonate, which is secreted by the mantle. Bivalves have a two-part shell with a hinge.

SCALLOP

TRITON

PACIFIC THORNY OYSTER

A starfish can grow a new arm to replace a damaged limb

STARFISH

...arfish is a typical echinoderm. It has a spiny-
...nned body with five equal parts, tiny sucker
...feet, and an internal skeleton made from
...rd plates called ossicles. It lives in the
...ea. Starfish prise open the shells of
...alves to eat the soft body inside.

SCARLET
STARFISH

TYPES OF ECHINODERM

...hinoderms are a distinctive group of invertebrates that live in
...e sea. There are 6,500 species in six classes (four listed below).

...HINODERM	NAME OF CLASS	FEATURES	NUMBER OF SPECIES
	Asteroids (starfish)	Central mouth surrounded by arms	1,500
	Echinoids (sea urchins)	Body surrounded by a case bearing spines	1,000
	Crinoids (feather stars)	Mouth surrounded by feathery arms	600
	Holothuroidea (sea cucumbers)	Worm-like body with feeding tentacles	1,100

MOLLUSC FACTS

• The world's most venomous gastropod is the geographer cone in the Pacific Ocean. Its venom can kill a human.

• The largest land snail is the giant African land snail *Achatina achatina*. It can grow up to 39 cm (15.4 in) from head to tail.

ARTHROPODS

ARACHNIDS, CRUSTACEANS, and insects are part of the arthropod group of invertebrates. Insects are by far the largest of these three groups. All arthropods have a jointed body with a tough body case. The case is shed as the animal grows.

The egg is laid in a silk sac to protect it

Spiderlings resemble the adult spider

Spiderling moults

LIFE CYCLE OF A SPIDER
Arachnids such as spide lay eggs that hatch into tiny versions of adults. They moult several tim before they are mature.

IMPERIAL SCORPION

Poison gland
Sting
Heart
Intestine
Cephalothorax
Pedipalps – a pair of pincers for feeding
Abdomen
Spiracle – air hole

INSIDE AN ARACH
The body of arachnid is divided into a front middle part (cephalothor and a rear part (abdome Arachnids have pairs of walking l

TYPES OF ARACHNID

The class Arachnida includes spiders, mites, and scorpions. It contains 73,000 species, which are grouped into ten orders. Six orders are listed below.

ARACHNID	NAME OF ORDER	NUMBER OF SPECIES	ARACHNID	NAME OF ORDER	NUMB OF SPEC
	Scorpiones (scorpions)	2,000		Uropygi (whip scorpions)	60
	Solifugae (camel spiders)	900		Opiliones (harvestmen)	4,50
	Acari (mites and ticks)	30,000		Araneae (spiders)	40,00

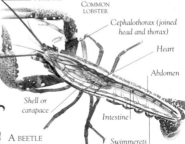

INSIDE A CRUSTACEAN
A typical crustacean has a hard body case with a head, thorax, abdomen. It has compound eyes, two pairs of antennae, many pairs of jointed legs.

COMMON LOBSTER

Antenna

Cephalothorax (joined head and thorax)

Heart

Abdomen

Shell or carapace

Intestine

Swimmerets

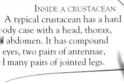

GOLIATH BEETLE

Strong legs used for fighting

A BEETLE
The Goliath beetle is the world's heaviest. It weighs up to 100 g (3.5 oz). Beetles are very well armoured. Their forewings are hardened, curved plates called elytra. The elytra protect the fragile hind wings that are used for flying.

TYPES OF CRUSTACEAN

There are more than 55,000 species of crustaceans divided into eight classes. These include the four classes below.

CRUSTACEAN	NAME OF CLASS	FEATURES	NUMBER OF SPECIES
	Branchiopods (fairy shrimps, water fleas)	Small animals of freshwater and salty lakes	1,000
	Cirripedia (barnacles)	Immobile animals with a box-like case	1,220
	Copepods (cyclopoids and relatives)	Small animals often found in plankton	13,000
	Malacostracans (shrimps, crabs, lobsters)	Many-legged animals, often with pincers	30,000

Mature adult

Egg is fertilized outside body

First larval stage

Second larval stage

Post-larval stage

LIFE CYCLE OF A SHRIMP
Crustaceans usually lay their eggs in water. Once hatched, the egg begins its first larval stage. After two more larval stages, there is a final post-larval stage before adulthood.

INSECTS

INSECTS MAKE UP over four-fifths of all the animal species on Earth. About 800,000 species are known, and many thousands more are discovered each year. Insects live in almost every habitat on land, from rainforest to desert. Many live in fresh water, but hardly any live in the sea. Most insects can fly, and many change shape as they mature.

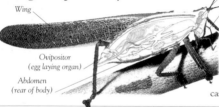

Antenn

KATYDID (FEMAL

Brain

Mandibles (mouthpar

Wing

Ovipositor
(egg laying organ)

Abdomen
(rear of body)

INSIDE
AN INSECT

An insect's body is s
into three parts: the
head, the thorax, and
the abdomen. It has
jointed legs, a hard b
case, and it usually has w

TYPES OF INSECT

Insects are part of the phylum Arthropoda. There are 800,000 known species of insect in the class Insecta. They are grouped into 32 orders, six of which are shown below.

INSECT	NAME OF ORDER	NUMBER OF SPECIES	INSECT	NAME OF ORDER	NUMBE OF SPEC
	Odonata (dragonflies)	5,000		Hemiptera (bugs)	82,00
	Orthoptera (grasshoppers and crickets)	20,000		Coleoptera (beetles)	350,00
	Lepidoptera (butterflies and moths)	170,000		Hymenoptera (ants, bees, and wasps)	110,00

Final moult produces adult with wings

The nymph resembles the adult

CYCLE OF GRASSHOPPER
...oung grasshopper
...ches as a wingless
...ph. It moults several
...es as it grows bigger.

...hatch as
...pillars

Caterpillar sheds its skin as it grows

Fully grown larvae spin cap to close cell

Only one egg is laid in each cell

Wood fibres are mixed with saliva to produce "paper"

...ale
...rfly
...ggs

Larva becomes pupa

Worker wasps extend the nest and collect food

CYCLE OF A BUTTERFLY
... mature caterpillar
...s a chrysalis (pupa).
...de the chrysalis, the
...rfly's body develops.

Feathery hairs deter predators

WASP NEST
Wasps make their nests from wood fibres, which they collect and chew into pulp. Inside the nest, the queen lays her eggs in a comb of cells, one egg in each cell.

CATERPILLAR
To discourage predators,
...ch as birds, many caterpillars have spiky bodies that
...make them unpleasant to eat. Other caterpillars are
camouflaged and difficult to see among the leaves.

INSECT FACTS

• Columns of army ants in South America can be up to 100 m (328 ft) long, 1 m (3.3 ft) wide.

• A cat flea can reach a height of 34 cm (13.4 in) in a single jump.

• The world's largest bee is a female, Wallace's giant bee – it can grow to 3.9 cm (1.5 in) long.

FISH

WITH MORE THAN 20,000 species, fish are more numero
than all other vertebrates (animals with backbones).
Fish are very well suited to life in the water. They ha
streamlined bodies, and most have slippery scales an
a special organ that helps them float. There are three
distinct types of fish; bony fish are the most widespre:

INSIDE A FISH
Bony fish have a skeleton
made of bone. They
swim using their tail
and are covered by
slimy scales. Fish
have gills to obtain
oxygen and a gas-
filled swim bladder
to keep them buoyant.

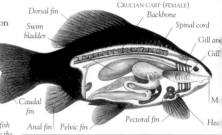

CRUCIAN CARP (FEMALE)
Backbone
Dorsal fin
Swim
bladder
Spinal cord
Gill are
Gill
Caudal
fin
M
Anal fin   Pelvic fin
Pectoral fin
Hea

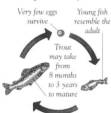

Very few eggs
survive

Young fish
resemble the
adult

Trout
may take
from
8 months
to 3 years
to mature

LIFE CYCLE OF A TROUT
Some fish give birth to
fully formed young but
most release eggs, often
thousands at a time. The
young fish are called fry.

TYPES OF FISH			
There are more than 20,000 species of fish. These are divid into three groups. The largest group is made up of bony fis.			
FISH	NAME OF CLASS	FEATURES	NUM OF SPE
	Agnatha (jawless fish)	Fish with sucker-like mouths	75
	Chondrichthyes (cartilaginous fish)	Fish with skeletons of cartilage	80
	Osteichthyes (bony fish)	Fish with skeletons of bone	22,0

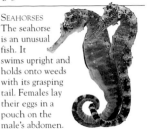

SEAHORSES
The seahorse
is an unusual
fish. It
swims upright and
holds onto weeds
with its grasping
tail. Females lay
their eggs in a
pouch on the
male's abdomen.

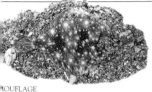

CAMOUFLAGE
Fish such as plaice or sole gradually
their skin colour and pattern to
in with their sea-bed background.

LOACH

UPSIDE-DOWN
CATFISH

FISH HABITATS
Fish can live almost anywhere there
is water. They have adapted to life in
the deepest oceans as well as along the
shore and even in underwater caves.

Mountain lakes and streams
such as loach and salmon
live at altitudes of up to
4,900 m (16,000 ft).

Lakes and rivers
In freshwater lakes
and rivers live carp,
characins, and catfish.

Shoreline
Along the shoreline
are fish, such as the
mudskipper, that spend
some time out of water.

MUDSKIPPER

Coastal waters
Coral reefs in tropical
coastal waters are home
to many brightly
coloured fish.

MANDARIN FISH

PACIFIC MANTA RAY

Open ocean
In the open ocean, fish
such as rays and skates can
grow to a large size. Sharks
hunt in this environment.

cave-dwelling
ave no eyes
use they spend
lives in darkness.

Deep ocean
The large mouths and
expanding stomachs of
deep-sea fish trap more of
the food available.

CAVE CHARACIN

GULPER EEL

Middle-ocean depths
With little sunlight
reaching these depths
and the water cooler,
few fish live here.

OARFISH

AMPHIBIANS

AMPHIBIANS WERE THE FIRST GROUP of animals to move from water to live on land. Most amphibians spend the early part of their lives in water. Later, they grow legs, lose their gills, and can live both on land and in water.

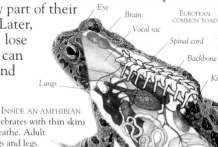

Eye

Brain

EUROPEAN COMMON TOAD

Vocal sac

Spinal cord

Backbone

Ki

Lungs

Intestine

INSIDE AN AMPHIBIAN
Amphibians are vertebrates with thin skins through which they breathe. Adult amphibians have lungs and legs. Frogs and toads lose their tails; newts and salamanders do not.

Adult has lungs and lives on land and in water

Back legs grow

After three weeks front legs appear

LIFE CYCLE OF A NEWT
Larvae, called tadpoles, hatch out in water. They breathe through gills. After about eight weeks, the tadpoles develop legs and their gills disappear.

TYPES OF AMPHIBIAN			
There are about 3,000 species of amphibian that make up the class Amphibia. They are divided into three orders.			
AMPHIBIANS	NAME OF ORDER		NUMBER OF SPEC
	Apoda (caecilians)		170
	Anura (frogs and toads)		3,70
	Urodela (newts and salamanders)		350

AXOLOTL

This unusual Mexican salamander does not mature. It stays in its tadpole stage, breathing through gills and living in water. Axolotls can reproduce in their immature state.

Axolotls keep their feathery red gills

AMPHIBIAN FACTS

• Female marine or cane toads lay 30,000 – 35,000 eggs during each spawning.

• A golden poison-arrow frog from Colombia is the most poisonous frog. An adult frog has enough poison to kill 1,000 humans.

Yellow and black coloration warns predators

Skin can ooze poisons

SALAMANDER

The tiger salamander, like many salamanders, has brightly patterned skin. This warns predators that it is poisonous. Adult salamanders breathe through their skin.

Salamanders have long, slim bodies

Thin skin absorbs oxygen

Mottled colours hide frog

Strong back legs help the frog leap away from danger

ASIAN LEAF FROG

Amphibians have developed many ways to avoid being eaten. The Asian leaf frog has the colour and shape of a dead leaf. It blends in perfectly with the debris on the forest floor.

Rough, dry skin

Male wraps eggs around his back legs

MALE MIDWIFE TOAD

Midwife toads mate on land, which is unusual for amphibians. When the female has laid her eggs and they have been fertilized, the male carries the eggs on his back legs for at least a month.

REPTILES

MILLIONS OF YEARS AGO, reptiles dominated Earth. Some of these reptiles – including dinosaurs – died out, but other kinds are still alive today. Unlike amphibians, reptiles may live entirely on dry land, but they are also cold-blooded, and so need warmth to become active. Most reptiles lay eggs.

INSIDE A REPTILE
Reptiles are vertebrates with scaly skins. Except for snakes and some lizards, most reptiles have four legs. A reptile's skin is tough and waterproof, and helps it to retain water in hot, dry conditions.

Nostril
Brain
Heart
Stomach
Bladder
Kidney
Backbone

EYED-LIZARD
(FEMALE)

TYPES OF REPTILE		
There are about 6,000 species of reptile in the class Reptilia. These are divided into four orders.		
REPTILE	NAME OF ORDER	NUMBER OF SPECIES
	Squamata (lizards and snakes)	5,700
	Crocodilia (crocodilians)	23
	Rhynochocephalia (tuataras)	2
	Chelonia (turtles, tortoises, and terrapins)	200

Egg sealed with membrane to prevent drying out

Young resemble adult

Mature adult continues to grow

LIFE CYCLE OF A GECKO
Many reptiles lay eggs that are sealed with a strong membrane. The young hatch out as miniature versions of their parents.

CROCODILES

The ancient Crocodilia order includes crocodiles, alligators, and gavials, which have narrower jaws. Crocodiles spend a lot of time in water and can shut their nostrils when they dive. Despite their ferocious appearance (sharp teeth, strong jaws, and a powerful tail) they are careful parents.

Crocodiles carry their young in their mouth

FEMALE
NILE CROCODILE

BOA CONSTRICTOR

Pythons, boa constrictors, and anacondas are snakes that feed mainly on mammals that they kill by constriction. The snake coils around its prey, and as the animal struggles, it squeezes tighter until the animal suffocates. Then the snake swallows it.

The snake opens its special hinged jaws to swallow its victim

KOMODO
DRAGON

Wrinkly, loose fitting skin

LARGEST LIZARD

The world's largest lizard is a monitor lizard called the Komodo dragon. It can grow up to 3 m (10 ft) long and weigh up to 166 kg (365 lb). There are fewer than 5,000 Komodo dragons left. They live on a few islands in Indonesia, including Komodo Island.

BIRDS

BIRDS ARE THE LARGEST ANIMALS capable of powered flight. Their streamlined bodies are covered with feathers, and many bones are hollow to save weight. Birds live in different habitats, and reproduce by laying hard-shelled eggs. Some species have lost the ability to fly.

INSIDE A BIRD
Birds are warm-blooded vertebrates. Their feathers give them a lightweight, warm covering. They have beaks (or bills) and lay eggs that have hard shells.

Brain
Backbone
Beak
Crop – store fo tempora
Stomach
SPECKLED PIGEON
Liver
Rectum
Tail feathers
Foot with claws

TYPES OF BIRD

About 9,000 species of bird have been discovered. These divide into 28 orders. Perching bird (Passeriformes) make up the largest order (5,414 species). Six other orders are listed here.

BIRD	NAME OF ORDER	NUMBER OF SPECIES	BIRD	NAME OF ORDER	NUMBE OF SPECI
	Rheiformes (rheas)	2		Anseriformes (waterfowl)	150
	Piciformes (woodpeckers, toucans, barbets)	381		Falconiformes (birds of prey)	290
	Psittaciformes (parrots, lories, cockatoos)	342		Strigiformes (owls)	174

eggs have
hard shells

Chick uses
special tooth to
escape egg

Bird has
adult plumage
after six weeks
and can then fly

Chick has
soft down
feathers

LIFE CYCLE OF A MOORHEN
A moorhen's eggs are
incubated by both parents.
After 21 days, the chicks
hatch, using a special tooth
to chip their way out. The
young can swim and feed
a few hours after hatching.

TYPES OF FEATHER

FEATHER FUNCTIONS
Feathers are strong and flexible. They are
made of strands of a protein called keratin. The
strands are often hooked together to
form a flat surface. A bird has several kinds
of feathers, suited to particular purposes.

WING FEATHER

DOWN
FEATHER

*Soft, fluffy
down keeps
bird warm*

*Tail
feathers
are long
and stiff
for flight*

*These cover bird's
body and keep
it streamlined*

*Barbs
hook together
to keep
surface flat*

CONTOUR
FEATHERS

TAIL
FEATHER

TYPES OF BEAK

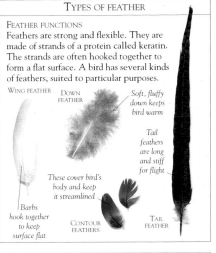

BEAKS FOR A PURPOSE
A bird's beak, or bill, is bone with a
covering of horn. The shape of the
beak is suited to the bird's feeding habits.
Birds of prey, such as kestrels, have sharp,
hooked beaks for tearing flesh and macaws have
beaks with a pointed end to pierce fruit.

GREEN-WINGED
MACAW

KESTREL

GREATER
FLAMINGO

AVOCET

*Lower beak pumps
water through
upper sieve in beak*

*Upturned beak swings
back and forth in water*

MAMMALS

MAMMALS ARE A VERY DIVERSE GROUP of animals. They range from tiny shrews to huge rhinos and from whales that spend their lives in the oceans to bats that spend time in the air. Mammals can live in nearly all habitats – jungles, rivers, and deserts. Humans belong to this group of animals.

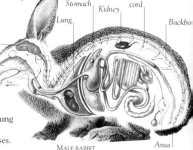

Brain

Nasal cavity

Stomach

Lung

Kidney

Spinal cord

Backbone

MALE RABBIT

Anus

INSIDE A MAMMAL
All mammals are warm-blooded. Most mammals have hair of some sort on their bodies. Female mammals suckle their young with their own supply of milk. A mammal has well-developed senses.

TYPES OF MAMMAL

There are about 4,000 species in the class Mammalia. They are divided into 21 orders. The largest order is the Rodentia, which includes 2,021 species of rodent. Six orders are listed here.

MAMMAL	NAME OF ORDER	NUMBER OF SPECIES	MAMMAL	NAME OF ORDER	NUMBER OF SPECIES
	Monotremes (egg-laying mammals)	3		Artiodactyla (even-toed, hoofed mammals)	220
	Marsupials (mammals that grow in a pouch)	272		Carnivora (meat eaters)	237
	Insectivora (insect eaters)	428		Cetacea (whales and dolphins)	78

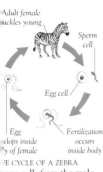

Adult female
suckles young

Sperm
cell

Egg cell

Egg
develops inside
body of female

Fertilization
occurs
inside body

LIFE CYCLE OF A ZEBRA
Sperm cells from the male
must join an egg cell in
the female for fertilization
to take place. This occurs
inside the female mammal.
Most mammals develop in
the womb of their mother
and all are fed on her milk.

MARSUPIALS
Wallabies, kangaroos,
and koalas are
marsupials. Their
young are born in a
very immature state
after a short gestation
time. They crawl
into the mother's
pouch and spend
time suckling there
while they develop.

INDIAN FRUIT BAT

FLYING MAMMALS
Bats are the only
mammals capable of
powered flight. A bat flies by
flapping a thin membrane
of skin stretched between
each of its front and back
legs. The largest bat may
have a wingspan of 2 m (6.5 ft).

Mother squirrel
suckles young for
first few weeks

SQUIRREL WITH YOUNG
A mammal whose baby develops inside the
mother's womb (uterus) is known as a
placental mammal. Inside the womb,
the babies are protected while they
develop and are fed with oxygen and
food via the placenta.

Young are well-
developed at birth
and grow rapidly

Baby squirrels
can soon
find their
own food

PRIMATES

THIS GROUP OF MAMMALS includes monkeys, apes, and humans. The primates form the most intelligent group of animals. With forward-facing eyes for judging distances, grasping fingers, and long limbs, primates are ideally suited to life in the trees. Some primates also have prehensile tails that grip onto branches.

PATAS MONKEY

Closely se
nostrils of C
World mon?

OLD WORLD MONKEY
Monkeys from the Old World, which includes Europe, Africa, and Asia, have long noses and closely set nostrils. The Patas monkey lives in groups of up to 20 females and one male on the plains, where it eats grass and seeds.

SQUIRREL MONKEY

NEW WORLD MONKEY
New World monkeys live in scrub and forest in Central and South America. Most of these monk? have flat faces and nostrils set wide apart, a many also have prehensile tails that can wra? around branches like an extra limb. Howler and squirrel monkeys are both New World monkeys.

LORIS

Animals such as lemurs, lorises, and bushbabies are known as prosimians, or primitive primates. They are almost all nocturnal (active at night) and they have excellent eyesight. Most eat leaves, insects, and birds.

Large eyes provide good night vision

Grasping hands cling to branches

GORILLA

The fearsome-looking gorilla is actually a vegetarian. Gorillas walk on their feet and front knuckles and spend most of their time on the ground. Some gorillas live in lowland rainforests and others in the mountains.

ORANG-UTAN

Like gorillas, chimpanzees, and gibbons, orang-utans are not monkeys but apes. These shy and solitary primates live in the rainforests of Borneo and Sumatra, and spend their life in the trees.

AVERAGE PRIMATE WEIGHTS

The 233 species of primate vary in size from the tiny pygmy marmoset to the mighty gorilla and between males and females.

SPECIES	AVERAGE WEIGHT (FEMALE)	AVERAGE WEIGHT (MALE)
Gorilla	105 kg (231 lb)	205 kg (452 lb)
Human	52 kg (115 lb)	75 kg (165 lb)
Proboscis monkey	9 kg (20 lb)	19 kg (42 lb)
Patas monkey	5.5 kg (12 lb)	10 kg (22 lb)
Pygmy marmoset	120 g (4.2 oz)	140 g (5 oz)

NUTRITION AND DIGESTION

ANIMALS LIVE BY TAKING IN FOOD and breaking it down into simple substances. It fuels their muscles and body processes and provides the raw materials for growth. Herbivores are animals that feed only on plants. Carnivores eat meat, while omnivores eat a variety of foods.

MEAT EATER

Like all cats, the tiger feeds almost exclusive on meat. Meat is easy to digest, and it contains a lot of useful nutrients, so a single meal will last a tiger for several days. However, meat has t be caught and a tiger uses a large amount of energy tracking its pre

CHEWING THE CUD

Cows feed on grass, which is easy to find but difficult to digest. They break it down with the help of microorganisms in a digestive chamber called the rumen. When the grass is partially broken down, a cow regurgitates it and chews it again – "chewing the cud".

Cows belong to a group of animals called ruminants

Omasum (third stomach chamber)

Rumen (first stomach chamber)

Intestine absorb nutrients a water fro digested fo

Digestion is completed i abomasum (fourth stoma chamber)

Reticulum (second stomach chamber)

FLUID FEEDERS

Many adult insects survive entirely on liquid food. They include mosquitoes that feed on blood, and aphids and cicadas that feed on plant sap. Butterflies feed mainly on nectar from flowers, using a long drinking tube that coils up when not used.

Sugary nectar is a good source of energy

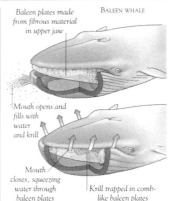

BALEEN WHALE

Baleen plates made from fibrous material in upper jaw

Mouth opens and fills with water and krill

Mouth closes, squeezing water through baleen plates

Krill trapped in comb-like baleen plates

FILTER FEEDING

Small animals called krill are abundant in the sea but are difficult to collect in any quantity. Whales filter them from the water using rows of baleen plates.

EGG-EATING SNAKE

Some snakes specialize in a diet of eggs. An African egg-eating snake works its jaws around its food, and swallows it. As the egg travels down the snake's throat, tiny spines break it open. It spits out the broken shell.

TEETH AND JAWS

ANIMALS USE THEIR TEETH to grip their food and to cut or chew it so that it is easier to digest. Teeth, brought together by powerful jaw muscles, are tough enough to withstand pressure without breaking. Human teeth stop growing when they are fully formed but some animals' teeth – such as those of rodents – grow all their life.

CROCODILE TEETH
Like all reptiles, crocodiles have simple teeth with a roughly conical shape. Their teeth are constantly replaced so they do not get a chance to wear out. The teeth fall out and may be replaced over 40 times.

Crocodile rips prey apart before swallowing chunks

Teeth grip and tear prey but cannot chew

GRAZING TEETH
Most of a sheep's teeth are towards the back of its jaws. Molars have hard ridges that grind up grass. The sheep cuts grass with sharp teeth at the front of its lower jaw. These bite up against a hard pad.

Hard pad

Cutting teeth

SHEEP SKULL

Grinding teeth

THE DENTAL TOOLKIT

A VARIETY OF TEETH
Unlike other animals, mammals have several kinds of teeth that work together. In a dog, incisors and canines grab hold of food. Carnassials slice through it, and molars and premolars chew the food.

DOG'S TEETH

MOLAR   CARNASSIAL   PREMOLAR   INCISOR

CANINE

BITING AND CUTTING TEETH
A dog usually has a total of 42 teeth (10 more than an adult human). For dogs, biting is more important than chewing, and most of their teeth have sharp points or edges.

ony ridge
nchors jaw
muscles   DOG'S SKULL   Molars in angle of jaw

PECIALIZED TEETH
usks are unusually long teeth that rotrude beyond a mammal's jaws. lephant tusks are specialized ncisors, teeth that other ammals use for biting. lephants use them mainly o dig up food, to strip bark om trees, and for fighting.

Upper part of
tusk is solid

Lower part of
tusk has a soft
pulpy centre

ELEPHANT'S
TUSKS

TEETH FACTS

• Shark's teeth constantly move to the edge of its jaw. Each one falls out after about two weeks to be replaced by one behind it.

• An adult elephant chews with four huge teeth. The teeth are replaced slowly. This stops when 24 teeth have been replaced.

• Turtles and tortoises are completely toothless.

BREATHING

ALL ANIMALS NEED TO TAKE IN OXYGEN, and at the same time they have to get rid of a waste gas called carbon dioxide. Very small animals do this through the surface of their bodies, but most larger animals do it with the help of special organs, such as gills or lungs.

Water flows out

BREATHING IN WATER
A fish's gills are arches that support stacks of thin flaps, which are supplied with blood. When water flows past the flaps, oxygen travels into the blood and carbon dioxide flows into the water.

Water enters through mouth

Water flows past gill flaps

Water leaves throu gill flaps

Mudskippers are careful to stay damp

FISH OUT OF WATER
Mudskippers are small fish that live in mangrove swamps. They can survive underwater as well as in air. In the air, they breathe by taking gulps of water to keep some water in their gills. They probably absorb some oxygen through their gills and some through the lining of their mouths.

Air sac in head

Air sac in thorax

GRASSHOPPER'S
TRACHEAL SYSTEM

Trachea

Spiracle

TRACHEAL SYSTEM
Openings called spiracles let air into an insect's body, and link to tiny tubes called tracheae that split to supply each cell. Large insects have sacs to pump air around their bodies.

BIRD'S ONE-WAY LUNGS
Birds need a lot of oxygen to fly. They are very efficient at extracting it from the air they breathe. Special air sacs allow air to move straight through their lungs, which ensures they get as much oxygen as possible from the air.

...achea
...dpipe)

Air sacs

Lungs

...RD'S RESPIRATORY SYSTEM

LUNGS

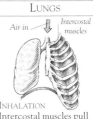

Air in

Intercostal muscles

INHALATION
Intercostal muscles pull ribs up while diaphragm moves down; ribcage expands and air flows in.

Air out

Diaphragm

EXHALATION
Intercostal muscles and diaphragm relax, lungs and ribcage deflate. Air is forced out of lungs.

...OMING UP FOR AIR
...e all mammals, whales have lungs and they breathe
... They have a "blowhole" on the top of their head
...her than nostrils. Some whales can hold their breath
... over an hour
...en they dive.

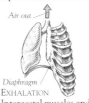

Blowhole

BLOOD AND CIRCULATION

BLOOD DELIVERS SUBSTANCES that cells need, and takes away their waste. In simple animals, such as molluscs and insects, it flows mainly through open spaces inside the body, but in vertebrates, including mammals, it flows through a system of tubes called blood vessels. Blood is pumped around by the heart.

EUROPEAN LOBSTER

BLUE-BLOODED CRUSTACEAN
In many animals, blood is coloured red because it contains a red substance called haemoglobin that carries oxygen. In lobsters and other crustaceans, the oxygen-carri[ng] is blue

Lobster's blood contains a blue pigment – haemocyanin

MOVING HEAT
As well as moving dissolved chemicals, blood also moves heat. When a lizard basks in the sunshine, the blood beneath its skin warms up. The blood carries this heat to its internal organs.

Blood absorbs heat from skin

Body begins to warm up, enabling lizard to become active

OCELLATED LIZARD BASKING IN SUN

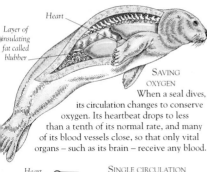

Heart

Layer of insulating fat called blubber

SAVING OXYGEN

When a seal dives, its circulation changes to conserve oxygen. Its heartbeat drops to less than a tenth of its normal rate, and many of its blood vessels close, so that only vital organs – such as its brain – receive any blood.

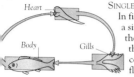

Heart

Body

Gills

SINGLE CIRCULATION

In fish, blood flows in a single circuit. From the heart, it flows through the gills, collects oxygen, and flows on to the body.

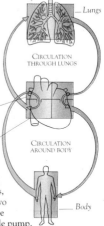

Lungs

CIRCULATION THROUGH LUNGS

Heart pumps blood around two circuits

Blood returns to other side of heart

CIRCULATION AROUND BODY

Body

ANIMAL HEART RATES

Animals with small bodies have much faster heartbeats than larger ones.

ANIMAL	BEATS PER MINUTE
Grey whale	9
Harbour seal (diving)	10
Elephant	25
Human	70
Harbour seal (at surface)	140
Sparrow	500
Shrew	600
Hummingbird (hovering)	1,200

DOUBLE CIRCULATION

In humans and other mammals, blood makes two circuits, and the heart is a double pump. In the first circuit, it flows from the heart to the lungs and back. In the second, it flows around the rest of the body.

SKELETONS

ANIMALS SUCH AS JELLYFISH have completely soft bodie
that work well in water, but create problems on land.
Other animals have a solid framework, or skeleton.
This gives them their shape, and provides
something for their
muscles to pull against.
Skeletons can be inside
the body or surround it
from the outside.

*Armoured
thorax*

*Tubula
legs*

AN OUTSIDE SKELETON
An insect's body is
covered by an exoskeleton
made of separate plates that
hinge together at flexible joints.
The advantage of this skeleton
is that it is very tough, and helps
to stop insects from drying out.
To grow, an insect sheds its
exoskeleton from time to time
and grows a larger one in its place.

*All organs
are inside
the skeleton*

*Hard
forewing
(elytron)*

JEWEL BEETLE'S
EXOSKELETON

*Separate plates
on abdomen*

NAUTILUS
SHELL

AN OUTER SHELL
A shell is a hard case that protects
a soft-bodied animal. Unlike an
insect's exoskeleton, it can grow,
so the animal inside never has to
shed it. This nautilus shell has gas-
filled compartments to help the
mollusc control its depth in water.

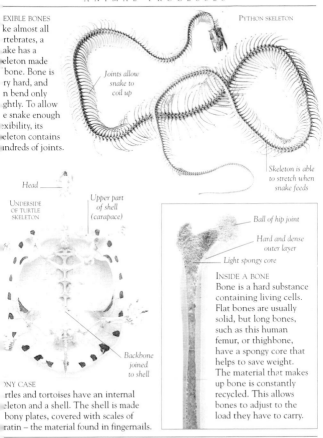

PYTHON SKELETON

EXIBLE BONES

ke almost all
rtebrates, a
ake has a
eleton made
bone. Bone is
ry hard, and
n bend only
ghtly. To allow
e snake enough
exibility, its
eleton contains
ndreds of joints.

*Joints allow
snake to
coil up*

*Skeleton is able
to stretch when
snake feeds*

Head

UNDERSIDE
OF TURTLE
SKELETON

*Upper part
of shell
(carapace)*

*Backbone
joined
to shell*

ONY CASE

rtles and tortoises have an internal
eleton and a shell. The shell is made
bony plates, covered with scales of
ratin – the material found in fingernails.

Ball of hip joint

*Hard and dense
outer layer*

Light spongy core

INSIDE A BONE

Bone is a hard substance
containing living cells.
Flat bones are usually
solid, but long bones,
such as this human
femur, or thighbone,
have a spongy core that
helps to save weight.
The material that makes
up bone is constantly
recycled. This allows
bones to adjust to the
load they have to carry.

More skeletons

The skeletons of vertebrates,
or animals with backbones,
all follow the same underlying plan, but
over millions of years they have become
modified for many different ways of life.
For some animals – particularly birds –
lightness is important; for others, such as
elephants, the emphasis is on strength; and
for others, such as fish, flexibility is vital.

Paper-thin skull

Highly flexible neck

CROW SKELETON

Keel anchors wing muscles

Ribs anchor muscles used in swimming

COD SKELETON

Backbone

SUPPORTED IN WATER

A fish's body is buoyed up by water, so its skeleton
does not have to be as strong as that of an animal that
lives on land. Fish have a large number of vertebrae,
and many pairs of thin and flexible ribs.

Slend[er] leg bo[nes]

LIGHT BON[ES]
Compared to other la[rge]
animals, birds ha[ve]
lightweight skeletons wi[th]
few bones. Many of t[he]
bones are honeycombed w[ith]
air spaces (reducing bon[e]
weight), and some of the[se]
spaces connect to the air s[acs]
that a bird uses to breath[e.]

FOUR-LEGGED
SKELETON
A salamander's
skeleton shows
the typical, four-
legged plan that
evolved long ago, when
vertebrates first took up life on
land. The salamander's legs are
small and weak and splay outwards.

Large skull

JAPANESE
SALAMANDER
SKELETON

Long backbone

Small legs

*Salamander[s]
often rests wi[th]
its body on gro[und]*

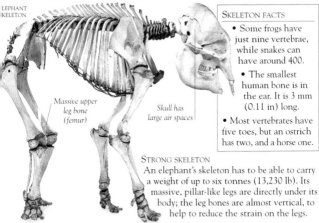

ELEPHANT
KELETON

*Massive upper
leg bone
(femur)*

*Skull has
large air spaces*

SKELETON FACTS

• Some frogs have
just nine vertebrae,
while snakes can
have around 400.

• The smallest
human bone is in
the ear. It is 3 mm
(0.11 in) long.

• Most vertebrates have
five toes, but an ostrich
has two, and a horse one.

STRONG SKELETON

An elephant's skeleton has to be able to carry
a weight of up to six tonnes (13,230 lb). Its
massive, pillar-like legs are directly under its
body; the leg bones are almost vertical, to
help to reduce the strain on the legs.

COMPARING LIMBS

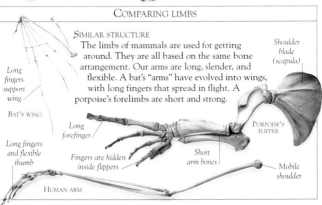

SIMILAR STRUCTURE

The limbs of mammals are used for getting
around. They are all based on the same bone
arrangement. Our arms are long, slender, and
flexible. A bat's "arms" have evolved into wings,
with long fingers that spread in flight. A
porpoise's forelimbs are short and strong.

*Long
fingers
support
wing*

BAT'S WING

*Shoulder
blade
(scapula)*

*Long
forefinger*

PORPOISE'S
FLIPPER

*Long fingers
and flexible
thumb*

*Fingers are hidden
inside flippers*

*Short
arm bones*

*Mobile
shoulder*

HUMAN ARM

MUSCLES AND MOVEMENT

THE ABILITY TO MOVE is a sign of life in the animal world. Animals move by using muscles. These contain special cells that can contract or relax, making parts of the body change their position or shape. Muscles need energy to work, and animals get this from food.

Frog is propelled forwards

Powerful muscles extend back legs

Body is streamlined in flight

JUMPING FROG
Frogs, fleas, and kangaroos move by jumping. A frog has strong muscles in its back legs that contract to produce enough leverage to push the animal through the ai

HUMAN MUSCLES

A pair of muscles raises the forearm

Triceps relaxes

RELAXED
Muscles pull but they do not push. They are often found in pairs where they work against each other. When the arm is at rest, the muscles are relaxed.

Biceps contracts

CONTRACTED
To raise the forearm, the biceps muscle contracts and the triceps relaxes. To lower the arm again, the triceps contracts and the biceps relaxes.

MOTION FACTS

• A flea can jump 100 times its own height using energy stored in pads in its leg joints. A cat flea can leap 34 cm (13.4 in).

• A sea gooseberry moves through water by beating clusters of tiny hairs called cilia.

FASTEST MAMMALS

The cheetah is the fastest animal on land over short distances.
Over long distances, the pronghorn antelope is faster.

COMMON NAME	SCIENTIFIC NAME	MAXIMUM SPEED	
		KM/H	MPH
Cheetah	*Acinonyx jubatus*	105	65
Pronghorn antelope	*Antilocapra americana*	86	53
Mongolian gazelle	*Procapra gutturosa*	80	50
Springbok	*Antidorcas marsupialis*	80	50
Grant's gazelle	*Gazella granti*	76	47
Thomson's gazelle	*Gazella thomsoni*	76	47
European hare	*Lepus capensis*	72	45

*Limpet is held
fast by its
muscular foot*

STUCK FAST
A mollusc such as a limpet
has special muscles that stay
contracted for hours and
use up very little energy.
The muscles are used to
close the mollusc's shell,
or to clamp it to a rock.

ROUGH LIMPET

SIDEWINDER MOVEMENT
Most snakes curve from
side to side as they push
against the ground. This
is known as serpentine
movement. The
sidewinder is different.
It throws itself forwards,
leaving a distinctive trail.

FOUR-LEGGED MOVEMENT
Animals with four legs
move in a coordinated way.
To walk, a cheetah moves its
front right leg and its rear left
leg forwards and then the opposite
pair. However, when it runs, its
front legs move together and then
its back legs move together.

*A cheetah can
reach 96 km/h
(60 mph) in
three seconds*

CHEETAH RUNNING

Animal movement

All animals are able to move parts of their bodies, even though
some spend all their adult lives fixed in one place. The way
animals move depends on their size and shape, and also on their
surroundings. Land animals are able to push against solid ground,
but animals that fly or swim push against moving air or water.
To do this, most of these animals use wings or fins – but a few,
such as octopuses and squid, use jet propulsion.

INSECT TAKE-OFF
A locust launches itself into the air using strong
muscles in its legs, and with its wings flat against
its body. Once in the
air, the locust opens
wide both of its
pairs of wings
and flaps them
vigorously.

*Surface area of
wings increased
by feathers*

*During
upstroke, broad
wings sweep
upwards*

*Hind legs push
out strongly*

*Bird has strong
pectoral muscles
to pull wings up*

MOVING THROUGH WATER
A dogfish, like a shark, is a cartilaginous fish.
It swims by curving its body into an S-shape.
This motion propels the fish through the water,
as its body and fins push the water aside. A bony
fish swims in a different way. It
keeps its body straight
and beats its tail to
move forwards.

*Movement
begins at the
head and follows
through body*

*Tail pushes
against water
at the end of
each wave*

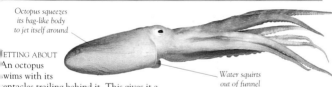

Octopus squeezes its bag-like body to jet itself around

Water squirts out of funnel

GETTING ABOUT
An octopus swims with its
tentacles trailing behind it. This gives it a
streamlined shape in the water. To propel itself forwards,
it contracts a water-filled cavity, known as the mantle,
and squirts a stream of water out of its body via a funnel.

A BIRD IN FLIGHT

MOVING THROUGH AIR
Birds, insects, and bats are the only animals capable of powered flight. They
use energy to flap their wings and push against gravity, so that they stay
airborne. A bird's wings are specially curved in a shape called an
aerofoil that helps to produce an upward lift. If the bird stops
flapping, it slows, lift decreases, and the bird starts to drop.

BLUE PIGEON

Muscles now push wings downwards

Downstroke pushes bird up and forwards

Wings move up for a new upstroke

Wing movement produces lift to counteract gravity

Dogfish body bends in S-shape

Flat fins maintain fish at same level in water

Head swings around and new curve starts

NERVOUS SYSTEM AND BRAIN

NERVE CELLS, OR NEURONS, carry signals from one part of an animal's body to another, so that it can work in a coordinated way. Together, neurons form a network called a nervous system. In many animals, this is controlled by the brain, which receives and processes information from the nerve cells.

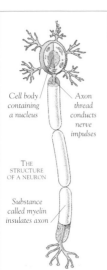

Cell body containing a nucleus

Axon thread conducts nerve impulses

THE STRUCTURE OF A NEURON

Substance called myelin insulates axon

CARRYING SIGNALS

A typical nerve cell has a cell body, with a nucleus, and an axon that carries signals. In vertebrates, the insulated axon helps signals travel quickly.

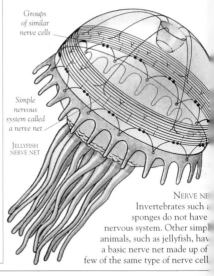

Groups of similar nerve cells

Simple nervous system called a nerve net

JELLYFISH NERVE NET

NERVE NE

Invertebrates such a sponges do not have nervous system. Other simp animals, such as jellyfish, hav a basic nerve net made up of few of the same type of nerve cell

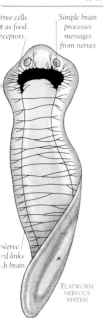

Nerve cells act as food receptors

Simple brain processes messages from nerves

Nerve cord links with brain

FLATWORM NERVOUS SYSTEM

BRAIN AND NERVE NET
A flatworm has a simple brain, which is connected to two nerve cords that run the length of its body. The nerve cords carry sensory signals to the brain. Once the brain has processed the signal, it makes the body respond.

BRAIN STRUCTURE

Cerebellum controls involuntary movements

Cerebrum

FROG BRAIN
The brains of vertebrates are divided into three main regions. The medulla controls vital processes, such as breathing. The cerebellum controls posture. The cerebrum deals with voluntary movements. A frog's cerebrum is quite small.

Medulla

Cerebrum   Cerebellum

Medulla

BIRD BRAIN
A bird's brain has a large cerebellum that enables it to control the complex movements involved in flight. Its cerebrum is larger than a frog's but it is not folded.

MAGNETIC RESONANCE IMAGE OF HUMAN BRAIN

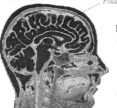

Folded cerebrum

HUMAN BRAIN
By far the biggest part of the human brain is the cerebrum. It is a large folded area of nerve cells split into right and left cerebral hemispheres. It governs memory, learning, and senses.

Medulla

SENSES

ANIMALS USE THEIR SENSES to gather information about the world around them. Many animals rely on their eyesight, but others depend on different senses. Some insects and mammals have highly developed hearing, and use sounds to build up an "image" of their surroundings.

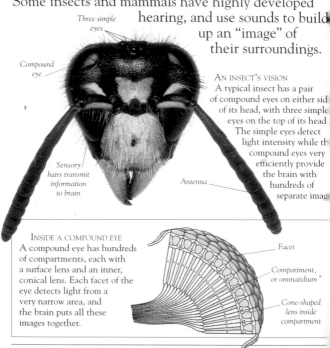

Three simple eyes

Compound eye

Sensory hairs transmit information to brain

Antenna

AN INSECT'S VISION
A typical insect has a pair of compound eyes on either side of its head, with three simple eyes on the top of its head. The simple eyes detect light intensity while the compound eyes very efficiently provide the brain with hundreds of separate images.

INSIDE A COMPOUND EYE
A compound eye has hundreds of compartments, each with a surface lens and an inner, conical lens. Each facet of the eye detects light from a very narrow area, and the brain puts all these images together.

Facet

Compartment, or ommatidium

Cone-shaped lens inside compartment

CHAMELEON

Eye is able to swivel independently

DOUBLE VISION

When a chameleon spots its prey, it can keep one eye on it and still check all around for predators. This is because it is able to move its eyes independently. The chameleon's brain receives two separate images and must make sense of them. As it nears its prey, the chameleon focuses both eyes on it and takes careful aim.

WHITEFIN DOLPHIN

Chameleon has wide field of vision

Cricket's ears are near the knee joint on its front legs

ECHO-LOCATION

Some animals send out high-frequency sounds to put together a picture of the world. Dolphins and bats emit squeaks that bounce off surrounding objects – including prey – and return to the animal as echoes. They are interpreted by the animal's brain.

SENSING SOUNDS

Insects such as crickets and grasshoppers learn about the world mostly through their ability to detect vibrations. Crickets have "ears" on their knees made from a taut membrane that is sensitive to sound vibrations.

CENTRAL AMERICAN CRICKET

HEARING RANGE OF SELECTED ANIMALS	
Sound is measured by its pitch in units called Hertz (Hz). A higher Hertz number means a higher pitch – a lower number, a lower pitch.	
SPECIES	HEARING RANGES IN Hz
Elephant	1 – 20,000 Hz
Dog	10 – 35,000 Hz
Human	20 – 20,000 Hz
Bat	100 – 100,000 Hz
Frog	100 – 2,500 Hz

More senses

In addition to using their eyes
and ears, animals have special organs
to give them extra information about
their environment. Taste and smell are
similar senses that detect chemicals
and help animals find food. In the
water and in the dark, animals need
special senses to survive.

*Gundogs have
an excellent
sense of smell*

BRAQUE DU
BOURBONNA

DOG SCENTS

A dog's most advanced sense is its sense of smell.
Moisture on a dog's nose helps to dissolve scent
particles. Inside its muzzle is a large folded
area that traps scents and passes sensory
information to the brain. A large part of a
dog's brain is concerned with interpreting scents.

TASTING THE AIR

*Snake uses Jacobson's organ
to sense the presence of food,
enemies, or a mate*

INDIAN
PYTHON

*Snake
uses its
tongue
to "sniff"
the air*

Nostril

*Jacobson's
organ*

Tongue

JACOBSON'S
ORGAN

A snake has a special sense organ in the roof of
its mouth called the Jacobson's organ. It flicks out
its tongue and collects chemical particles from the
air. These are transferred to sensory cells in the Jacobson's
organ so that the snake can taste the chemicals.

USING ANTENNAE
In a dark cave, a cave cricket relies on its very long, sensitive antennae to find its way. Antennae are sensory feelers that pick up air movements, smells, and vibrations.

NIGERIAN CAVE CRICKET

Antenna helps cricket feel its way in the dark

SENSE FACTS
• A dog's nose has 200 million scent receptors. A human nose has five million.

• A dragonfly can spot an insect moving 10 m (33 ft) away.

• Some bats can detect a tiny midge 20 m (65.5 ft) away.

LATERAL LINE
Most fish have a line of receptors on the sides of their bodies called a lateral line. This system detects changes in water pressure and signals to the fish that there is movement nearby.

MIRROR CARP

Large, shiny scales mark the lateral line

SENSING GRAVITY

Eyes can detect shadow of a passing fish

STAYING THE RIGHT WAY UP
A scallop has organs called statocysts that help it to stay upright. Each is a round chamber with a ball that is pulled down by gravity so that it rests against sensory hairs. These indicate to the scallop which way up it is.

Sensory tentacles around lip of scallop

Scallop jets along in water

Hard, stony ball pulled by gravity

Sensory hairs line chamber

DIAGRAM OF A STATOCYST

BEHAVIOUR

THE THINGS THAT AN ANIMAL DOES and the way that it does them make up its behaviour. This may include the way an animal finds food, looks after itself, protects its territory, finds a partner, or cares for its young.

A penguin must keep its feathers waterproof

CARING FOR FEATHERS

To keep its feathers in good condition, a bird must spend time each day caring for them. It pushes its beak through ruffled feathers to smooth them out and remove parasites such as feather lice. Penguins and other water birds spread oil from a special gland through their feathers to keep them waterproof.

Special gland near the tail containing oil

KING PENGUIN

Large, branched antlers are really jaws

Beetles have tough protective wing cases

FIGHTING STAG BEETLES

FIGHTING FOR TERRITORY

Some animals fight to defend their territory from competitors. Male stag beetles have powerful jaws that they use to grasp a rival and lift it out of the way.

USING TOOLS

Some animals have learned to use a tool to help them find food. Sea otters, for example, anchor themselves in a seaweed called kelp, and use a stone from the sea bed to break open shellfish. They rest the stone on their chest and smash the shellfish against it. They can then eat the contents.

BIRD MIGRATION

ARCTIC TERN
Some birds fly long distances (migrate) to avoid bad weather or find food. Arctic terns fly from the Arctic to the Antarctic.

AMERICAN GOLDEN-PLOVER
This bird makes the longest migration of any land bird. It breeds in Canada and flies south to Argentina for the winter.

SHORT-TAILED SHEARWATER
After breeding in the south of Australia, this shearwater flies around the North Pacific and back again.

GREATER WHITETHROAT
The greater whitethroat is a small warbler that breeds during spring and summer in Europe. It migrates to Africa for winter.

Communication and defence

To survive, animals have to communicate with their own kind, and defend themselves against predators. Animals communicate in many ways. Some use sounds, while others use visual signals or chemical messages. Animal defences include camouflage, armour, and poisons.

CHEMICAL COMMUNICATION
Many insects communicate using chemicals called pheromones that they release onto the ground or into the air. The female Indian moon moth makes a pheromone that attracts males from far away.

INDIAN MOON MOTH

Moths are able to respond to scents

Bee performs waggle dance in the hive

HONEYBEE DANCE
When a honeybee locates a good source of nectar, it will return to the hive and inform other bees of its find. The bee performs a waggling dance that surrounding bees are able to interpret. It tells them the location, distance, and quality of the food.

BIRDSONG
Animals such as birds and frogs communicate with sounds. A bird has a chamber called a syrinx that can produce a range of sounds to warn other birds to stay out of its territory.

ROBIN IN SONG

CAMOUFLAGED INSECT

This spiny stick insect relies on camouflage to escape attack. It hides among foliage, where its body resembles a cluster of dead leaves. This disguise makes it very difficult to find, but works only if the insect remains still.

GIANT SPINY STICK INSECT

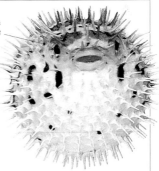

Brightly coloured frog is easily seen in the forest

POISONOUS YELLOW MANTELLA

POISON FROG

Some frogs contain poisons in their skin that protect them from predators. They have brightly coloured skin to warn predators that they are poisonous.

While stick insect stays still, it is hidden in the leaves

PORCUPINE FISH

When the fish relaxes, its spines lie flat against its body

Fish looks fearsome when spines are erect

PUFFED UP

The porcupine fish has an ingenious method of defence. When it senses danger, it fills up with water and sticks out the spines that cover its body. This makes the fish virtually impossible to eat.

REPRODUCTION

ALL LIVING THINGS REPRODUCE. Animals do this in two ways. For most species, two parents come together in a process called mating to create a fertilized egg. In a few very simple animals, one individual reproduces itself

Peacocks fan out their tail feathers in a display to the peahen

PEACOCK

COURTSHIP
Before an animal can reproduce, it must first find a partner of the opposite sex. To attract a mate, male animals put on a display and act out a ritual known as courtship. This complex behaviour forms a bond between the pair.

ROD-SHAPED BACTERIA ESCHERICHIA COLI

Offspring are identical to the parents

ASEXUAL REPRODUCTION
Many simple forms of life, such as bacteria, reproduce by splitting in two. Animals such as aphids produce new individuals from an unfertilized egg.

MALE FROG FERTILIZES EGGS

The male frog sprays the eggs with his sperm

SEXUAL REPRODUCTION
Most reproduction requires that a male and a female parent come together so that the female's sex cells are fertilized. A frog's eggs are fertilized externally but in some animals the male's sperm enters the female to reach the egg cells inside her body.

REPRODUCTION RATES

Some animals can reproduce extremely rapidly, but only a
few of their offspring survive to become adults.

SPECIES	BREEDING AGE	OFFSPRING PER YEAR
Northern gannet	5–6 years	1
Rabbit	8 months	10–30
Nile crocodile	15 years	50
Fruit fly	10–14 days	Up to 900

DOGFISH
EGG CASES

*Egg case
hung by
tendrils
from
seaweed*

BIRD'S EGG

A bird's eggs develop
outside the mother
and are encased in
a hard shell. Inside,
the embryo is
surrounded by
membrane layers
that protect it.
When a chick is
fully developed it
hatches (breaks
out of its egg).

Yolk

Shell

Inner membrane

Embryo

Air sac

EGG CASES

The female dogfish releases
rubbery egg cases, each
containing an embryo. The
embryo grows inside the
case, living on yolk that acts
as a food store. The fish
emerges after 6 to 9 months.

*Kittens born at
the same time may
look different*

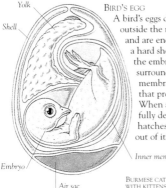

BURMESE CAT
WITH KITTENS

CARING FOR YOUNG

Mammals such as cats
give birth to live young
that are helpless for the
first few weeks. The young
rely on their mother's milk
until they are strong enough
to find their own food.

GROWTH AND DEVELOPMENT

AS LIVING THINGS GET OLDER they usually grow bigger. Parts of their bodies grow at different rates, so that their proportions gradually alter. Some animals grow all their lives; others develop rapidly when they are young, then stop when they are mature. Some animals can grow a new body part to replace a lost one.

GROWING A NEW TAIL

TREE SKINK
If a predator catches a tree skink by its tail, the tail breaks off at a fracture point, letting the skink escape. A new tail gradually grows, containing rubbery cartilage rather than bone. Eight months later, the tail has regrown to its original length.

Tail shed at fracture point

Growing new tail uses a lot of energy

1 STARTING LIFE
A hen's egg starts life as a single cell. Once it has been fertilized, the cell divides many times and these new cells form the chick's body.

Chick uses egg tooth to crack shell

2 BREAKING FREE
During hatching, the chick pecks through the shell, and kicks its way out. It now breathes fresh air for the first time.

Wet down feathers soon dry

GROWING A SHELL

Many molluscs grow hard shells by depositing crystals of calcium carbonate. As the mollusc grows, its shell grows too. Bands in the shell show each season's growth.

TRITON SHELL GROWTH

Whirls become larger and more pronounced

A fully developed shell has a thick lip

GROWING UP

Newborn cub is vulnerable

Eight-week-old cub is more independent

At 12 weeks, cub play-fights, preparing to catch its own prey

FOX CUB

A newborn fox cub is helpless for the first few weeks of life and its mother must take care of it. At eight weeks, it can walk and find its own food, though the mother still provides milk.

Chicks are able to find their own food

4 FOLLOWING THEIR MOTHER
The chicks now have dry down and can walk. They recognize their mother's call and soon recognize her by sight as well.

3 NEWBORN
The young chick has a well-developed head and feet but its wings are immature. It can run around and will peck at the ground looking for food.

METAMORPHOSIS

As ANIMALS GROW, their bodies change shape. Some animals change slightly, but the young of amphibians, fish, and insects look very different from the adults. This process of change is called metamorphosis. Insects change shape in two ways – either by complete metamorphosis (changing shape suddenly), or by incomplete metamorphosis (changing by gradual stages).

COMPLETE METAMORPHOSIS: THE LADYBIRD

Eggs laid on the underside of leaves

Soft, pale larva emerges

Adult larva feeds on aphids

1 THE EGG
A ladybird changes shape completely as it grows up. The egg takes about four days to hatch.

2 LARVA EMERGES
A soft-bodied larva hatches from the egg. Its first meal is its egg, which contains nutrients.

3 MATURE LARVA
The mature larva walks around slowly and cannot fly. Its colours warn off predators.

Larval skin is shed and pupal skin forms

Wing cases gradually change colour

Adult ladybird feeds on aphids

4 FORMING A PUPA
After eating enough aphids, the larva attaches itself to a leaf, ready to pupate.

5 YOUNG ADULT
A soft, yellow-winged ladybird hatches out of the pupa. Its wing cases start to harden.

6 MATURE LADYBIRD
The adult ladybird looks very different from its larva. It has its adult colours and is able to fly.

INCOMPLETE METAMORPHOSIS: THE DAMSELFLY

1 NYMPH
A damselfly nymph lives underwater, but carries out its final moult out of the water.

2 PULLING FREE
Blood pumped into the thorax makes it expand and burst out of its nymphal skin.

3 OLD SKIN
The adult head pulls out of the nymphal skin and leaves its mask behind.

4 SOFT WINGS
Free of its old skin, blood fills the damselfly's wings, making them longer.

5 GROWING
Thorax and abdomen are still growing. The wings are delicate.

6 ABLE TO FLY
The adult is ready to fly. Its abdomen is long and shiny and its wings are transparent.

INSECT METAMORPHOSIS

Insects have three or four stages in their life-cycles, depending on whether they undergo complete or incomplete metamorphosis. The stages are often very different in length. The first section of this chart shows the length of time needed for the four stages of complete metamorphosis.

SPECIES	EGG	LARVA	PUPA	ADULT
Bluebottle	1 day	8 days	9 days	35 days
Ladybird	4 days	18 days	15 days	9 months
Large white butterfly	14 days	1 month	6 months	2 months

INCOMPLETE METAMORPHOSIS IN INSECTS

SPECIES	EGG	NYMPH		ADULT
Periodical cicada	1 month	17 years	–	2 months
Mayfly	1 month	3 years	–	1 day
Cockroach	1 month	3 months	–	9 months

ECOSYSTEMS

LIVING THINGS DO NOT EXIST IN ISOLATION; they constantly interact with each other and with their environment. The study of these interactions is called ecology. Groups of organisms and their surroundings make up separate ecosystems. An ecosystem can be a pond, a forest, a beach, or an entire mountainside.

UNIQUE PLANET
Earth is the only planet known to support life. Its atmosphere contains the elements that are essential to sustain life and to protect us from the harmful effects of the Sun's rays.

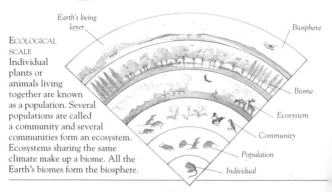

ECOLOGICAL SCALE
Individual plants or animals living together are known as a population. Several populations are called a community and several communities form an ecosystem. Ecosystems sharing the same climate make up a biome. All the Earth's biomes form the biosphere.

Earth's living layer

Biosphere

Biome

Ecosystem

Community

Population

Individual

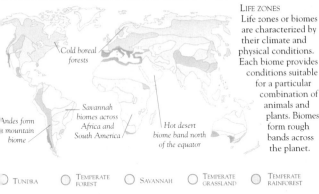

LIFE ZONES
Life zones or biomes are characterized by their climate and physical conditions. Each biome provides conditions suitable for a particular combination of animals and plants. Biomes form rough bands across the planet.

Cold boreal forests

Savannah biomes across Africa and South America

Andes form mountain biome

Hot desert biome band north of the equator

| ○ TUNDRA | ○ TEMPERATE FOREST | ○ SAVANNAH | ○ TEMPERATE GRASSLAND | ○ TEMPERATE RAINFOREST |
| ○ BOREAL FOREST | ○ DESERT | ○ TROPICAL RAINFOREST | ○ MOUNTAIN | ○ SCRUBLAND |

EXAMPLES OF BIOMES

TUNDRA
Around the Arctic region are areas of tundra. Here the soil stays frozen for most of the year and only mosses and lichens grow. The climate is very dry.

TEMPERATE FOREST
Northern Europe and North America are known as temperate – their climates are neither very hot nor very cold. Deciduous trees flourish in these areas.

NUTRIENT CYCLES

ALL LIVING THINGS need chemical nutrients. These include carbon, oxygen, nitrogen, and water, and trace elements such as copper and zinc. Chemical nutrients are constantly recycled through the Earth's biosphere – they pass between living and non-living things.

Carbon dioxide is given out by green plants during respiration

Animals breathe out carbon dioxide

Animals take in carbon from plants

Carbon dioxide absorbed by plants during photosynthesis

Bacteria break down or decompose dead matter and produce carbon dioxide

Dead plants and animals dec

NUTRIENT CYCLE FACTS

• At least 25 of the Earth's 90 elements are used by living things.

• Plants absorb one-tenth of the atmosphere's carbon every year.

• Some parts of a nutrient cycle can take seconds, while others take thousands of years.

CARBON CYCLE

Carbon is a part of all living things. It moves around the living world in a constant cycle. Plants absorb carbon dioxide from the atmosphere during photosynthesis and animals take in carbon when they eat plants. Carbon is released when plants and animals decompose

OXYGEN CYCLE
During photosynthesis, all plants release oxygen. Living things take in oxygen to break down the energy in their food.

NITROGEN CYCLE
Nitrogen is needed by living things to make proteins but it must be combined with other elements before it can be used. Some nitrogen is combined by lightning, but most is combined by bacteria that live in soil.

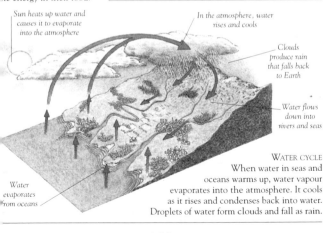

Sun heats up water and causes it to evaporate into the atmosphere

In the atmosphere, water rises and cools

Clouds produce rain that falls back to Earth

Water flows down into rivers and seas

Water evaporates from oceans

WATER CYCLE
When water in seas and oceans warms up, water vapour evaporates into the atmosphere. It cools as it rises and condenses back into water. Droplets of water form clouds and fall as rain.

FOOD WEBS AND CHAINS

IN ANY COMMUNITY, living things are linked together in food chains or webs. Energy is passed along the chain in the form of food. At the base of the chain are the primary producers, usually plants, which make their own food. When animals, or consumers, eat plants, energy is passed on, though a great deal is lost along the way. Poisons can also be passed through the chain.

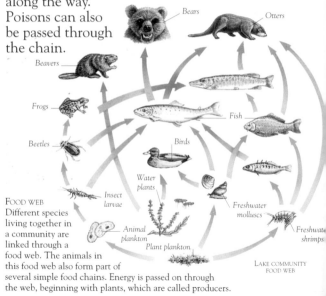

Bears

Otters

Beavers

Frogs

Fish

Beetles

Birds

Water plants

Insect larvae

Freshwater molluscs

Animal plankton

Plant plankton

Freshwater shrimps

FOOD WEB
Different species living together in a community are linked through a food web. The animals in this food web also form part of several simple food chains. Energy is passed on through the web, beginning with plants, which are called producers.

LAKE COMMUNITY FOOD WEB

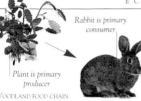

Rabbit is primary consumer

Plant is primary producer

WOODLAND FOOD CHAIN

FOOD CHAIN

A food chain contains living things that provide food for each other. The chain usually has only three or four links because energy is lost at each stage. The first stage of the chain is typically a plant.

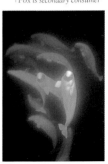

Fox is secondary consumer

TROPHIC LEVELS

Ecologists call each stage of a food chain a trophic level. There is more living material and more energy available at the first trophic level, the primary producers. Energy is used up by organisms at each successive layer of consumption so that less can be stored and passed on.

TROPHIC LEVELS PYRAMID

At this trophic level, there are fewer consumers

Less energy available at this level

Energy is used up by living things

Primary producers

BELUGAS' POISON CHAIN

Belugas in North America are part of a river food chain. Toxins pumped into the river are absorbed by plankton, then passed to fish that eat plankton, and then to whales that eat fish. The toxins have become concentrated in the whales.

CONSERVATION

HUMAN ACTIVITY has a great impact on the environment. Humans use up the Earth's resources and leave behind a great deal of waste and pollution. To protect the environment, we are learning to practise conservation and to manage our use of natural resources.

CLIMATE CHANGE
A rise of a few degrees in the Earth's temperature has a significant effect on the environment. It can cause rivers, such as this one in Spain, to dry up, threatening freshwater fish and amphibians, and other animals that depend on the river.

HABITAT CHANGE
Humans have drastically altered the natural world. Large amounts of land have been cleared to make way for the increased demand for houses and roads. As a result, the balance of the ecosystems in those areas is upset.

Trawlers locate and process huge amounts of fish

OVER-FISHING
Technological advances in fishing have led to greater yields. Huge trawlers now catch such vast amounts of fish that the fish population in some areas has been severely reduced. Fishing bans have been enforced in an effort to help fish stocks recover.

REINTRODUCTION

In the 1970s, the red kite was on the verge of extinction and a programme was set up to reintroduce the bird to Britain. In programmes such as this one, young animals are raised in captivity and then set free. They are released in special areas where their progress can be carefully monitored.

CONSERVATION FACTS

• Since 1700, 200 species or subspecies of birds have become extinct.

• Over 1,000 of the world's bird species and 500 of its mammals are currently endangered.

• Conservation has saved species such as the grey whale and Hawaiian goose.

ALLIGATORS

Wild animals sometimes need to be protected by law. Alligators used to be hunted for their skins and became endangered. The alligators of the southern US are now protected by a law that limits hunting.

NATURE RESERVES

All over the world, nature reserves have been set up. This one in Kenya protects animals, such as rhinos, from poachers. The reserves preserve the environment and the animals, and attract tourists whose money helps maintain the reserves.

CLASSIFICATION 1

BIOLOGISTS USE CLASSIFICATION to identify types of living things, and show how they are related through evolution. Classification details and species totals alter as more is discovered about the living world. This scheme is based on five kingdoms. It includes the most important categories in each group.

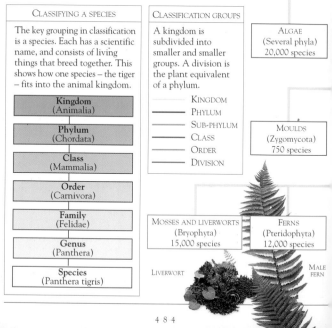

CLASSIFYING A SPECIES

The key grouping in classification is a species. Each has a scientific name, and consists of living things that breed together. This shows how one species – the tiger – fits into the animal kingdom.

Kingdom
(Animalia)

Phylum
(Chordata)

Class
(Mammalia)

Order
(Carnivora)

Family
(Felidae)

Genus
(Panthera)

Species
(Panthera tigris)

CLASSIFICATION GROUPS

A kingdom is subdivided into smaller and smaller groups. A division is the plant equivalent of a phylum.

KINGDOM
PHYLUM
SUB-PHYLUM
CLASS
ORDER
DIVISION

ALGAE
(Several phyla)
20,000 species

MOULDS
(Zygomycota)
750 species

MOSSES AND LIVERWORTS
(Bryophyta)
15,000 species

FERNS
(Pteridophyta)
12,000 species

LIVERWORT

MALE FERN

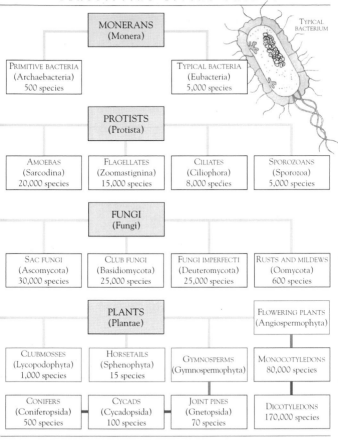

MONERANS
(Monera)

TYPICAL
BACTERIUM

PRIMITIVE BACTERIA
(Archaebacteria)
500 species

TYPICAL BACTERIA
(Eubacteria)
5,000 species

PROTISTS
(Protista)

AMOEBAS
(Sarcodina)
20,000 species

FLAGELLATES
(Zoomastignina)
15,000 species

CILIATES
(Ciliophora)
8,000 species

SPOROZOANS
(Sporozoa)
5,000 species

FUNGI
(Fungi)

SAC FUNGI
(Ascomycota)
30,000 species

CLUB FUNGI
(Basidiomycota)
25,000 species

FUNGI IMPERFECTI
(Deuteromycota)
25,000 species

RUSTS AND MILDEWS
(Oomycota)
600 species

PLANTS
(Plantae)

FLOWERING PLANTS
(Angiospermophyta)

CLUBMOSSES
(Lycopodophyta)
1,000 species

HORSETAILS
(Sphenophyta)
15 species

GYMNOSPERMS
(Gymnospermophyta)

MONOCOTYLEDONS
80,000 species

CONIFERS
(Coniferopsida)
500 species

CYCADS
(Cycadopsida)
100 species

JOINT PINES
(Gnetopsida)
70 species

DICOTYLEDONS
170,000 species

Classification 2

Animals have been studied more closely than any other forms of life. Biologists have identified and classified nearly all the species of vertebrates (animals with backbones) although it is likely that new species of fish await discovery. By contrast, the world of invertebrates is not so well documented and there may be many more species to be identified.

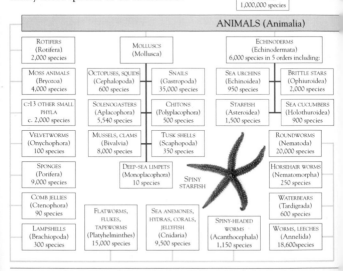

Springtails
Bristletails
Diplurans
Silverfish
Mayflies
Stoneflies
Webspinners
Dragonflies
Grasshoppers,
crickets
Stick and leaf insects
Grylloblattids
Earwigs
Cockroaches
Praying mantids
Termites

Lice
Thrips
Booklice
Zorapterans
Bugs
Beetles
Ants, bees, wasps
Lacewings and
antlions
Scorpionflies
Stylopids
Caddisflies
Butterflies and moths
Flies
Fleas

INSECTS
(Insecta)
1,000,000 species

ANIMALS (Animalia)

ROTIFERS
(Rotifera)
2,000 species

MOSS ANIMALS
(Bryozoa)
4,000 species

C:13 OTHER SMALL
PHYLA
c. 2,000 species

VELVETWORMS
(Onychophora)
100 species

SPONGES
(Porifera)
9,000 species

COMB JELLIES
(Ctenophora)
90 species

LAMPSHELLS
(Brachiopoda)
300 species

MOLLUSCS
(Mollusca)

OCTOPUSES, SQUIDS
(Cephalopoda)
600 species

SOLENOGASTERS
(Aplacophora)
5,540 species

MUSSELS, CLAMS
(Bivalvia)
8,000 species

DEEP-SEA LIMPETS
(Monoplacophora)
10 species

SNAILS
(Gastropoda)
35,000 species

CHITONS
(Polyplacophora)
500 species

TUSK SHELLS
(Scaphopoda)
350 species

SPINY
STARFISH

FLATWORMS,
FLUKES,
TAPEWORMS
(Platyhelminthes)
15,000 species

SEA ANEMONES,
HYDRAS, CORALS,
JELLYFISH
(Cnidaria)
9,500 species

SPINY-HEADED
WORMS
(Acanthocephala)
1,150 species

ECHINODERMS
(Echinodermata)
6,000 species in 5 orders including:

SEA URCHINS
(Echinoidea)
950 species

STARFISH
(Asteroidea)
1,500 species

SEA CUCUMBERS
(Holothuroidea)
900 species

BRITTLE STARS
(Ophiuroidea)
2,000 species

ROUNDWORMS
(Nematoda)
20,000 species

HORSEHAIR WORMS
(Nematomorpha)
250 species

WATERBEARS
(Tardigrada)
600 species

WORMS, LEECHES
(Annelida)
18,600 species

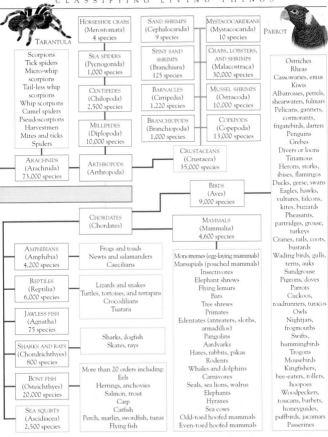

TARANTULA

PARROT

Scorpions
Tick spiders
Micro-whip scorpions
Tail-less whip scorpions
Whip scorpions
Camel spiders
Pseudoscorpions
Harvestmen
Mites and ticks
Spiders

ARACHNIDS (Arachnida) 73,000 species

HORSESHOE CRABS (Merostomata) 4 species

SEA SPIDERS (Pycnogonida) 1,000 species

CENTIPEDES (Chilopoda) 2,500 species

MILLIPEDES (Diplopoda) 10,000 species

ARTHROPODS (Arthropoda)

SAND SHRIMPS (Cephalocarida) 9 species

SPINY SAND SHRIMPS (Branchiura) 125 species

BARNACLES (Cirripedia) 1,220 species

BRANCHIOPODS (Branchiopoda) 1,000 species

MYSTACOCARIDEANS (Mystacocarida) 10 species

CRABS, LOBSTERS, AND SHRIMPS (Malacstraca) 30,000 species

MUSSEL SHRIMPS (Ostracoda) 10,000 species

COPEPODS (Copepoda) 13,000 species

CRUSTACEANS (Crustacea) 35,000 species

BIRDS (Aves) 9,000 species

CHORDATES (Chordates)

MAMMALS (Mammalia) 4,600 species

AMPHIBIANS (Amphibia) 4,200 species

Frogs and toads
Newts and salamanders
Caecilians

REPTILES (Reptilia) 6,000 species

Lizards and snakes
Turtles, tortoises, and terrapins
Crocodilians
Tuatara

JAWLESS FISH (Agnatha) 75 species

SHARKS AND RAYS (Chondrichthyes) 800 species

Sharks, dogfish
Skates, rays

BONY FISH (Osteichthyes) 20,000 species

More than 20 orders including:
Eels
Herrings, anchovies
Salmon, trout
Carp
Catfish
Perch, marlin, swordfish, tunas
Flying fish

SEA SQUIRTS (Ascidiacea) 2,500 species

Monotremes (egg-laying mammals)
Marsupials (pouched mammals)
Insectivores
Elephant shrews
Flying lemurs
Bats
Tree shrews
Primates
Edentates (anteaters, sloths, armadillos)
Pangolins
Aardvarks
Hares, rabbits, pikas
Rodents
Whales and dolphins
Carnivores
Seals, sea lions, walrus
Elephants
Hyraxes
Sea cows
Odd-toed hoofed mammals
Even-toed hoofed mammals

Ostriches
Rheas
Cassowaries, emus
Kiwis
Albatrosses, petrels, shearwaters, fulmars
Pelicans, gannets, cormorants, frigatebirds, darters
Penguins
Grebes
Divers or loons
Tinamous
Herons, storks, ibises, flamingos
Ducks, geese, swans
Eagles, hawks, vultures, falcons, kites, buzzards
Pheasants, partridges, grouse, turkeys
Cranes, rails, coots, bustards
Wading birds, gulls, terns, auks
Sandgrouse
Pigeons, doves
Parrots
Cuckoos, roadrunners, turacos
Owls
Nightjars, frogmouths
Swifts, hummingbirds
Trogons
Mousebirds
Kingfishers, bee-eaters, rollers, hoopoes
Woodpeckers, toucans, barbets, honeyguides, puffbirds, jacamars
Passerines

WEIGHTS AND MEASURES

TWO MAJOR SYSTEMS OF MEASUREMENT exist: metric and imperial. Although some countries still use the older imperial system, scientists worldwide use metric.

THE SEVEN BASE SI UNITS

SI (Système Internationale d'Unités) is the standard system of units for scientists worldwide. There are seven base units, from which the other units are derived.

Quantity	Symbol	Unit
Mass	kg	Kilogram
Length	m	Metre
Time	s	Second
Electric current	A	Ampere
Temperature	K	Kelvin
Luminous intensity	cd	Candela
Amount of substance	mol	Mole

IMPERIAL & USCS UNIT

Imperial units include the pound, mile, and gallon. With no scientific basis, it is a complex system. In the US, this system is called USCS (US Customary Systems).

STANDARD KILOGRAM

STANDARDS

Several units have precisely defined standards. This ensures that everyone means the same thing when stating measurements.

THE STANDARD SECOND

One second is defined as "the duration of 9,192,631,770 periods of the radiation corresponding to the transition between the hyperfine levels of the ground state of the cesium-133 atom."

THE STANDARD KILOGRAM

A standard kilogram is kept in carefully controlled conditions at the Bureau of Weights and measures at Sèvres, France.

THE STANDARD METRE

One metre is defined as "the length equal to the 1,650,763.73 wavelengths, in a vacuum, of the radiation corresponding to the transition between the levels 2p10 and 5d5 of the krypton-86 atom."

NUMBER TERMS GREAT AND SMALL*

Prefix	Symbol	Meaning	Prefix	Symbol	Meaning
tera	T	One million million	deci	d	One-tenth
giga	G	One thousand million	denti	c	One-hundredth
mega	M	One million	milli	m	One-thousandth
kilo	k	One thousand	micro	μ	One-millionth
hecto	h	One hundred	nano	n	One-thousand millionth

*Prefixes inserted before a unit signify multiples or fractions of that unit.

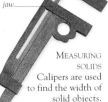

Adjustable jaw

MEASURING SOLIDS

Calipers are used to find the width of solid objects.

MASS AND WEIGHT	
METRIC	
1 gram (g)	
1 kilogram (kg)	1,000 g
1 tonne (t)	1,000 kg
IMPERIAL	
1 ounce (oz)	
1 pound (lb)	16 oz
1 stone	14 lb
1 hundredweight (cwt)	8 stones
1 ton	20 cwt

LENGTH	
METRIC	
1 millimetre (mm)	
1 centimetre (cm)	10 mm
1 metre (m)	100 cm
1 kilometre (km)	1,000 m
IMPERIAL	
1 inch (in)	
1 foot (ft)	12 in
1 yard (yd)	3 ft
1 mile	1,760 yd

LIQUID MEASURES

Measuring jugs are used to find the volumes of liquids.

MEASUREMENT FACTS

• France was the first country to adopt the metric system. King Louis XVI approved it in 1791, the day before he tried to flee the Revolution.

• China was the first country to use a decimal system. Wooden rulers divided into units of ten have been found and dated to the 6th century BC.

• In England, the length of the human top-thumb joint was a widely used measure that became the precursor of the inch.

AREA			VOLUME		
METRIC			METRIC		
1 square millimetre (mm²)			1 cubic millimetre (mm³)		
1 square centimetre (cm²)	100 mm²		1 cubic centimetre (cm³)	1,000 mm³	
1 square metre (m²)	10,000 cm²		1 cubic metre (m³)	1,000,000 cm³	
1 hectare (ha)	10,000 m²		1 litre	1,000 cm³	
1 square kilometre (km²)	1,000,000 m²		IMPERIAL		
IMPERIAL			1 cubic inch (in³)		
1 square inch (in²)			1 cubic foot (ft³)	1,728 in³	
1 square foot (ft²)	144 in²		1 cubic yard (yd³)	27 ft³	
1 square yard (yd²)	9 ft²		1 fluid ounce (fl oz)		
1 acre	4,840 yd²		1 pint (pt)	20 fl oz	
1 square mile	640 acres		1 gallon (gal)	8 pt	

CONVERSION TABLES

FOOT RULE

LENGTH CONVERSION

TO CONVERT:	INTO:	MULTIPLY BY:
IMPERIAL	METRIC	
Inches	Centimetres	2.54
Feet	Metres	0.3048
Yards	Metres	0.9144
Miles	Kilometres	1.6093
METRIC	IMPERIAL	
Centimetres	Inches	0.3937
Metres	Feet	3.2808
Metres	Yards	1.0936
Kilometres	Miles	0.6214
Metres	Furlongs	0.005
Metres	Fathoms	0.547
Kilometres	Nautical miles	0.54
Metres	Chains	0.0497

VOLUME CONVERSION

TO CONVERT:	INTO:	MULTIPLY BY:
IMPERIAL	METRIC	
Cubic inches	Cubic cm (ml)	16.3871
Cubic feet	Litres	28.3169
Cubic yards	Cubic metres	0.7646
Fluid ounces	Cubic cm (ml)	28.413
Pints	Litres	0.5683
Gallons	Litres	4.5461
METRIC	IMPERIAL	
Cubic cm	Cubic inches	0.061
(millilitres)	Fluid ounces	0.0352
Litres	Cubic feet	0.0353
Cubic metres	Cubic yards	1.308
Litres	Pints	1.7598
	Gallons	0.22

AREA CONVERSION

TO CONVERT:	INTO:	MULTIPLY BY:
IMPERIAL	METRIC	
Sq inches	Sq centimetres	6.4516
Sq feet	Sq metres	0.0929
Sq yards	Sq metres	0.8361
Acres	Hectares	0.4047
Sq miles	Sq kilometres	2.59
METRIC	IMPERIAL	
Sq centimetres	Sq inches	0.155
Sq metres	Sq feet	10.7639
Sq metres	Sq yards	1.196
Hectares	Acres	2.4711
Sq kilometres	Sq miles	0.3861

MASS AND WEIGHT CONVERSIONS

TO CONVERT:	INTO:	MULTIPLY BY:
IMPERIAL	METRIC	
Ounces	Grams	28.3495
Pounds	Kilograms	0.4536
Stones	Kilograms	6.3503
Hundredweights	Kilograms	50.802
Tons	Tonnes	0.9072
METRIC	IMPERIAL	
Grams	Ounces	0.0352
Kilograms	Pounds	2.2046
	Stones	0.1575
	Hundredweights	0.0197
Tonnes	Tons	1.1023

COOKING MEASURES

Object	Metric	Imperial
1 thimble	2.5 ml	30 drops
60 drops	5 ml	1 teaspoon
1 teaspoon	5 ml	1 dram
1 desert spoon	10 ml	2 drams
1 tablespoon	20 ml	4 drams
2 tablespoons	40 ml	1 fl oz
1 wine glass	100 ml	2 fl oz
1 tea cup	200 ml	5 fl oz (1 gill)
1 mug	400 ml	10 fl oz (1/2 pint)

2.5 ML (1/2 TEASPOON)

OVEN TEMPERATURES

Gas Mark	Electricity		Rating
	°C	°F	
1/2	120	250	Slow
1	140	275	"
2	150	300	"
3	170	325	"
4	180	350	Moderate
5	190	375	"
6	200	400	Hot
7	220	425	"
8	230	450	Very hot
9	260	500	"

FAHRENHEIT TO CELSIUS TO KELVIN

°F	°C	K	°F	°C	K	°F	°C	K
-4.0	-20	253	32.0	0	273	68.0	20	293
-2.2	-19	254	33.8	1	274	69.8	21	294
-0.4	-18	255	35.6	2	275	71.6	22	295
1.4	-17	256	37.4	3	276	73.4	23	296
3.2	-16	257	39.2	4	277	75.2	24	297
5.0	-15	258	41.0	5	278	77.0	25	298
6.8	-14	259	42.8	6	279	78.8	26	299
8.6	-13	260	44.6	7	280	80.6	27	300
10.4	-12	261	46.4	8	281	82.4	28	301
12.2	-11	262	48.2	9	282	84.2	29	302
14.0	-10	263	50.0	10	283	86.0	30	303
15.8	-9	264	51.8	11	284	87.8	31	304
17.6	-8	265	53.6	12	285	89.6	32	305
19.4	-7	266	55.4	13	286	91.4	33	306
21.2	-6	267	57.2	14	287	93.2	34	307
23.0	-5	268	59.0	15	288	95.0	35	308
24.8	-4	269	60.8	16	289	96.8	36	309
26.6	-3	270	62.6	17	290	98.6	37	310
28.4	-2	271	64.4	18	291	100.4	38	311
30.2	-1	272	66.2	19	292	102.2	39	312

TEMPERATURES

• To convert Fahrenheit (°F) into Celsius (°C), use the following formula:
$$°C = (°F - 32) ÷ 1.8$$

• To convert Celsius (°C) into Fahrenheit (°F), use the following formula:
$$°F = (°C × 1.8) + 32$$

• To convert Celsius (°C) into Kelvin (K), use the following formula:
$$K = °C + 273.16$$

Thermometers measure temperature on Celsius and Fahrenheit scales

Index

A

aa lava, 162
Aborigines, 301
absorption lines, 292, 295
abyssal plain, 219
acceleration, 71
acid rain, 55, 175
acids and acidity, 54–5
acoustics, 108, 109
activation energy, 49
activity series, 50
additive process, mixing colours, 100
adhesives, 61
aerial photographs, 148
Africa, 149
air: air masses, 252–3, 267
  atmosphere, 146–7
  composition, 47
  pressure, 74, 75, 251
  winds, 248
aircraft, 75, 105
Al-Sufi, 382
Aldrin, Buzz, 380, 388
algae, 395, 406
lichens, 404, 405
alkali metals, 44–5
alkaline-earth metals, 45
alkalis, 56–7
alligators, 483
allotropes, 34
alloys, 40–1
Alpha Centauri, 308
alpha rays, 24
Alps, 201, 203

alternators, 120
altocumulus clouds, 257
altostratus clouds, 257
aluminium, 192
amber, 191, 409
ammonia, 56
amoebas, 403
amperes, 116
amphibians, 434–5, 474
analogue signals, 127
analysis, chemical, 64–5
Andagoya, 247
Andromeda galaxy, 276
animals, 395
  amphibians, 434–5
  arthropods, 428–9
  behaviour, 466–9
  birds, 438–9
  blood and circulation, 450–1
  breathing, 448–9
  cells, 403
  classification, 484, 486–7
  communication and defence, 468–9
  conservation, 482–3
  ecology, 476–83
  fish, 432–3
  food webs and chains, 480–1
  fossils, 182–3
  growth and development, 472–3
  hearing, 107

insects, 430–1
invertebrates, 424–31
mammals, 440–1
metamorphosis, 474–5
muscles and movement, 456–9
nervous system and brain, 460–1
nutrition and digestion, 444–5
pollination, 420
primates, 442–3
reproduction, 470–1
reptiles, 436–7
senses, 462–5
skeletons, 452–5
teeth and jaws, 446–7
annual plants, 416
Antarctica, 149, 245
antennae, 465
anthracite, 194
anticyclones, 242, 254–5
apes, 400–1, 442
Apollo astronauts, 331, 378, 380, 388
aquifers, 229
arachnids, 428
Archaeopteryx, 398
Arecibo telescope, 367
Armstrong, Neil, 333, 388
"aromatic" compounds, 59
arthropods, 428–9
asexual reproduction, 470
ash, volcanoes, 161
Asia, 149

Acknowledgements

Contributors to this title include:
Editors: Tim Hetherington, Esther Labi, Scarlett O'Hara, Clint Twist.
Designers: Janet Allis, Alexandra Brown, Jacqui Burton, Susan Downing, Carlton Hibbert, Clair Watson.
PAGEOne: Chris Clark, Matthew Cook, Thomas Keenes, Neil Kelly, Sarah Watson.

Dorling Kindersley would like to thank:
Hilary Bird for the index; DK Cartography for the maps; Michael Dukes for assistance; Robert Graham for editorial assistance; Peter Griffiths and Stephen Oliver for model making; Dr. David W. Hughes of Sheffield University for professional advice; Robin Hunter for artwork; Stephen Johnson of International Computers Ltd, Manchester; Kodak; Dr. M. Matson and Dr. A. Roberts for reference material; Alison McKittrick for additional picture research; National Meteorological Office, London; Natural History Museum; Old Royal Observatory, Greenwich; Caroline Potts for picture library services; Science Museum; Scientific American; University of Archeology and Anthropology, Cambridge; and Martin Wilson and Steve Wong for design assistance.

Photographs by:
Peter Anderson, Geoff Brightling, Jane Burton, Peter Chadwick, Andy Crawford, Geoff Dann, Philip Dowell, Andreas von Einsiedel, Neil Fletcher, Frank Greenaway, Colin Keates, G. Kevin, Dave King, Cyril Laubscher, Mike Linley, Andrew McRobb, Tracy Morgan, Roger Phillips, Tim Ridley, Karl Shone, S. Shott, J. Stevenson, Clive Streeter, Harry Taylor, Kim Taylor, Jerry Young.

Illustrations by:
Zirrinia Austin, Rick Blakely, Richard Bonson, Bill Botten, Peter Bull, Kyokan G. Chen, Julia Cobbold, Richard Coombes, Luciano Corbella, Brian Delf, Bill Donohoe, Richard Draper, Mike Dunning, Angelica Elsebach, Simone End (Linden Artists), Eugene Fleury, Roy Flookes, Mark Franklin, Mike Grey, Robert Garwood, Will Giles, Mick Gillah, Jeremy Gower, Andrew Green, Mike Grey, Nick Hall, Nick Hewetson, John Hutchinson, Stanley Johnson, Norman Lacey, Richard Lewis, Kenneth Lilly, R. Lindsay, N. Loates, Chris Lyon, Andrew Macdonald, Stuart Mackay, Kevin Maddison, Janos Marfy, Sergio Momo, Richard Orr, Sandra Pond, Daniel J. Pyne, S. Quigley, Jim Robins,

363tr, 363cr, 368b, 369c, 369b, 372tr, 374tr, 375cl, 376tr, 378tr, 380tr, 380br and jacket, 381cr, 381bl, 384clb, 387cb, 388-389, 389cl, 390cr; NASA 3br, 262tr, 476cl; National Maritime Museum 2tr; Natural History Museum: 6tr, 183bc, 184cl, 185bl, Peter Chadwick 413tr, Philip Dowell 439tr, 447tr, Colin Keates 409cr, 429cl, Dave King 427cr, Karl Shone 472cl, 472cr; N.C.A.R. 265br; N.O.A.A. 253cr; Novosti: 391tl; Scarlett O'Hara 443cl, 479tl; Oxford Scientific Films/London Scientific Films 18br, 413br; Pictor International 44r; Planet Earth: J.B. Duncan 482bl, J. Fawcett 164tl, R. Hessler 165tr, Robert A. Jureit 409tc, J. Lithgoe 210tr, Mike Potts 483bl, W. M. Smithey 207bl, N. Tapp 204bl; Rex Features: A. Fernandez 161t; Royal Greenwich Observatory 367cl; John Sanford 300tr, 359br; Dr. Seth Shostak 367tl; Starland Picture Library/ESO 289tl; UPI/Bettman 386cr; Science Photo Library: D. Allan 206t, Alex Bartel 33tl, 43tr, 364tr, Dr Jeremy Burgess 382tl, 414bc, 421tl, ESA 357br, Fred Espenak 297t, Dan Farber 262br, S. Fraser 261bl, François Gohier 366tr, P. Hawtin, University of Southampton 402bl, J. Heseltine 174tl, Manfred Kage 404bl, James King-Holmes 129br, Mehau Kelyk 461br, Patrice Loiez/CERN 12–13, 23cl, David Mclean 358tr, Lawrence Migdale 129cl, NASA 35tr, 222, 360tr, NOAO 363c, David Parker 65cr, 129tr, 133br, Pekka Parviaimen 299tl, D. Pellegrini 212tr, Max Planck Institute of Radioastronomy 366bl, 386b, John Reader 401cl, Roger Ressmeyer, Royal Observatory Edinburgh/Anglo-Australian Telescope Board 268–269, 278tr, 282bl, 302tr, F. Sauze 216tr, Starlight 296tr, Simon Terrey 15c, U.S. Navy 89b; SIPA Press 168tl; Solarfilma 162tr; Frank Spooner Pictures: Barr/Liaison 160br, Garties/LN 163cl, Vitti/Gamma Liaison; Sporting Pictures (UK) Ltd 71t; Telegraph Colour Library 138–139; Tony Stone Images: 178t, 180br, 196tr, 198tr, Peter Lambreti 483br; John Lund 40tl; US Space and Rocket Center, Alabama 2cc; Tony Waltham 156cl, 158tl; Weymouth Sea Life Centre: Frank Greenaway 459br; L.White 226t; Jerry Young 433tr, 435cl, 441c, 456c; Zefa 63cl, 87cl, 170br, 202cl, 260t, 392–393. Jacket: Getty Images: spine clb; Science Photo Library: front bc; spine ca; inside front tr; Jerry Young: front cra.